SOCIAL FRANCE

AT THE TIME OF PHILIP AUGUSTUS

BY

ACHILLE LUCHAIRE

Membre de l'Institut

AUTHORIZED TRANSLATION
FROM THE SECOND EDITION OF THE FRENCH

BY

EDWARD BENJAMIN KREHBIEL, Ph.D.

Professor of European History, Leland Stanford Junior University

NEW YORK
PETER SMITH
1929

TRANSLATOR'S PREFACE

AMONG the pleasantest experiences of my first visit to Paris was my meeting with M. Luchaire. It chanced that he had taken extensive notes in the provincial archives of France upon the period of Innocent III, a field in which I was interested, and it was to consult him about these that I visited him. His knowledge of English was not much greater than my limited acquaintance with his mother-tongue, and the interview was hardly a success from any standpoint except the humorous. A subsequent conversation by means of an interpreter proved more fruitful, and I came away with what was verily M. Luchaire's treasure,—his manuscript notes, which represented years of patient and costly labor in various parts of France. The boundless kindness and confidence indicated by his intrusting these notes to me, and his subsequent interest in me and my plans, left me with an ardent desire to requite his services. It was not given to me to do so during his lifetime. If, however, I succeed in the following pages in bringing English readers who do not know French to enjoy the work of this charming Frenchman who did not know English, I shall feel that I have in some measure appropriately repaid the debt I owe him.

It is, however, not only, or even chiefly, my personal relations with this French scholar that prompted me to undertake this translation. I am a firm believer in social history, indeed in anything that will bring out the human side of the past. It is for this reason that Luchaire's work appealed to me and that it is now placed before English readers. That the book has its shortcomings I know; that it is prolix in some parts and often repetitious I am fully aware; but that, even as it is, it is worth translating I am confident.

That the translation will meet with the approval of its readers I am not so sure. It is intended to be a faithful rendering of the original, without deviation in any essential. The inequalities in the text are in some measure, no doubt, to be

attributed to the translator; in part they find their explanation in the unevenness of the original, which is accounted for
by M. Halphen's preface.

For invaluable aid I take this place to express my indebted-
ness to Miss Ella Beaver, Mr. Louis Lengfeld, Miss Belle
Rankin, and Miss Marjorie Seeley, students in Leland Stanford
Junior University.

EDWARD B. KREHBIEL.

STANFORD UNIVERSITY,
April 15, 1912.

CONTENTS

PREFACE

THIS study on French society at the time of Philip Augustus was the sole unpublished work found among the papers of M. Achille Luchaire. After having determined to write an exhaustive history of the reign of Philip Augustus, and after having for five years (1895-1900) made that reign the subject of his courses at the Sorbonne, Luchaire in 1901 turned his efforts in other directions and abandoned a project which had seemed on the point of coming to fruition.

The appearance of the first parts of Alexander Cartellieri's *Philipp II. August, König von Frankreich,* no doubt largely influenced Luchaire to take this action. The book of Cartellieri, though perhaps too minute and somewhat lacking in perspective, proved to be conscientious and accurate in every respect. If a French history of Philip Augustus was to be given to the public, was it not sensible to await the completion of this German work?

Social history, however, remained outside of the domain appropriated by Cartellieri. This was a gap worth filling. Luchaire had carefully kept the manuscript of the lectures he had delivered on this particular subject, and after having, in 1899, extracted a chapter on the University of Paris,[1] he, in 1900, entered upon a complete publication in the *Séances et travaux de l'Académie des sciences morales et politiques.* Two chapters appeared in succession in this collection entitled *L'État matériel et moral de la population* (1900), and *Paroisses et les curés* (1901)[2]; then, having claimed the field,

[1] *L'Université de Paris sous Philippe-Auguste.* Paris, Chevalier-Marescq, 1899. 59 pp. (Forms a part of the *Bibliothèque internationale de l'enseignement supérieur* published under the direction of M. F. Picavet.) Chapter III of this volume is a reproduction of this article with a new introduction.

[2] These form Chapters I and II of this volume. The part on the cult of relics also appeared with a special introduction in *La Revue de Paris,* année 1900, IV, pp. 189-198 (*Le culte des reliques*), and the part treating of the *capuchonnés* in *La Grande Revue,* année 1900, XIII, pp. 317-328 (*Un essai de révolution sociale sous Philippe-Auguste*).

Luchaire postponed the publication of the other chapters. However, in January, 1908, he published an article on marriages and divorces in the feudal world [3]; and he freely drew on his materials for the volume on the reigns of Louis VII, Philip Augustus, and Louis VIII, which he contributed to Lavisse's *Histoire de France* in 1901.[4]

In his caution to leave nothing to the accident of improvisation, Luchaire prepared his lectures with such care that the process of shaping them for the press would have been a simple matter for him: all that was required was to remove occasional prolixities, recast the lectures into a limited number of chapters, and now and then correct the form. This labor, which a sudden death prevented Luchaire from completing, was a delicate task for another to undertake. I have voluntarily restricted my alterations to such as were strictly necessary, and, when omissions appeared necessary, I have, as far as possible, adopted the method pursued by Luchaire himself in the pages which he had published. I have touched the style but slightly, and then with great caution: the author alone could retouch the work satisfactorily in this respect. Had he lived, he would undoubtedly have added several complementary chapters on the mendicant orders,[5] on the king and his court, on commerce and corporations, etc. He would, perhaps, have added bibliographical information and notes. But, such as it is, I believe that the book may be useful to historians, and that, like the six volumes on Innocent III, it will charm and instruct the public interested in the past.

LOUIS HALPHEN.

[3] *Au temps de la féodalité.   Mariages et divorces.   Revue bleue,* 1908, 1er *semestre,* pp. 39-44.   This appears in Chapter XI of this volume.

[4] Some of the pages of that work are, in consequence, repeated in this.

[5] During the academic year 1899-1900 Luchaire gave four lectures on the mendicant orders; but the manuscript of these lectures was not in a state to justify publishing them.   Besides, the substance of the lectures is incorporated in the pages devoted to this subject in Lavisse, *Histoire de France,* III, 1re *partie,* pp. 352-363.

SOCIAL FRANCE

AT THE TIME OF PHILIP AUGUSTUS

CHAPTER I

THE MATERIAL AND SPIRITUAL CONDITION OF THE PEOPLE

" THE world is ill; it grows so old that it relapses into infancy. Common report has it that Antichrist has been born at Babylon and that the day of judgment is at hand." In writing these lines, Rigord, the monk of Saint-Denis, was ignorant of the fact that other monks had expressed the same sentiment in all preceding centuries. Why this discouragement and these sinister predictions? Because the popes of his day were short-lived and succeeded each other with a strange rapidity; because Saladin had taken Jerusalem in 1188, that most fateful of all years,—" those born in it had only twenty-two, instead of thirty-two teeth "; finally, because natural calamities and scourges from heaven and earth, one after another, fell upon men and made them despair of their future.

Earthquakes, especially, dismayed them. Anjou was shaken in 1207; Normandy, in 1214; Gascony, in 1223. The tremor of March 3, 1206, was felt at the same time in Burgundy and Limousin. According to the monk of Saint-Martial, the shocks came in the middle of the night. Monks, saying their offices in the choir, took to flight, and laymen leaped from their beds; it was observed that even the birds trembled with fear and that water-courses were more boisterous than usual; and, to appease an irate Heaven, an extraordinary procession was arranged at Limoges.

Within forty-three years (1180-1223) fourteen cyclones ran riot with frightful ravages. Harvests and vineyards were destroyed, houses demolished, roofs carried away, belfries and towers beaten down, and turrets overthrown. The storm of Dun-le-Roi, in 1206, crushed a noblewoman with her two children beneath its ruins. That of 1221 lasted eight days and killed forty persons in the vicinity of Paris and Beauvais. While mass was being celebrated in the château of Pierrefonds, lightning struck it; the officiating priest and twenty-four assistants were grievously wounded; five were killed. The chalice containing the Host was reduced to powder; but, lo! the Host itself remained untouched.

One can imagine the damage done by floods. There were no means of forewarning those who dwelt by streams; reservoirs, dams, and dikes hardly existed; the bridges, overloaded with houses and crowded with shops, were not built to resist the swelling of the waters. The inundations of 1185 at Metz, of 1195 at Auxerre, of 1205 at Caen, of 1213 at Limoges left doleful traces. In 1196 the two bridges of the Seine at Paris were carried away, and Philip Augustus found himself obliged to quit the *Cité* and take refuge on Mont Sainte-Geneviève. The flood of 1219 rendered the *Petit pont* unapproachable, and many burghers returned to their homes by boat. The monk of Sainte-Geneviève, who was an eye-witness, describes the enormous rising of the Seine in 1206, the year in which all the streams simultaneously overflowed their banks:

"In the month of December, 1206, God smote the kingdom of the French. Rains fell with extreme violence, streams became torrents, the largest trees were rooted up, and in certain cities buildings were utterly destroyed. But of all places, Paris, the capital and the soul of France, was most sorely tried. The city was entirely inundated, and was affected to its very foundations; one could go about the streets and squares only by boat. Most of the houses fell, and those which remained upright were so shaken by the unending pressure of the waters that they became a menace. The stone bridge, known as the *Petit pont*, could not resist the impact of the torrent; great cracks were already visible and its collapse was momentarily expected. Thus was the precious city, the queen of them all, plunged into sorrow. Priests moaned, virgins mourned, Paris succumbed under the weight of her grief, and no one could console her."

Science has not yet found the means of compelling overflowing streams to return to their beds, but our fathers knew

one: they instituted processions in which they exhibited relics.
The citizens of Paris, in 1206, had recourse to their favorite
saint, Geneviève. A procession forms on the height on the
left bank of the river, with the relics of the saint in the lead.
It reaches the *Petit pont*. "To cross it," relates the monk,
"it is imperative to lean neither to left nor to right, but to
keep exactly in the middle. The passage over the bridge,
which threatens to crumble under the furious blows of the
water, is exceedingly dangerous,—but Geneviève with her
people crosses the raging Seine: the bridge supports her less
than she supports the bridge." At last the cortège reaches
Notre-Dame, and forthwith the waters begin to recede and
the rain ceases. From the church comes the saint, still followed by the citizens; the bridge totters, but is crossed a
second time, and the relics of Geneviève resume their place
in the sanctuary. Half an hour later, at nightfall, after
every one has returned home, the bridge falls. Three arches
are carried away by the current.

Next to water, fire was the daily terror in medieval cities,
with their narrow, winding streets lined with overcrowded,
wooden houses. A stone house was uncommon. The authorities gave a bounty to citizens who built of stone: in the little
village of Rue in Picardy, they were exempt from taxes. In
these vast collections of inflammable materials, with only the
most rudimentary means of fighting fire (we know of no
text of this epoch which makes even the slightest allusion to
the organization of a relief corps), a burning house menaced
the whole quarter; often the entire city. Repeated fires became dreadful. From 1200 to 1225, Rouen burned six times.
Not even the largest stone structures, churches, and the
enormous fortresses were spared. The keep of Gisors burned
in 1189, on the very day that Richard the Lion-Hearted made
his entrance. When the château of Pompadour, in Limousin,
burned, the keep collapsed and twenty persons perished in
the burning pile. The flames reached the houses and streets
so rapidly that it was impossible to escape. In 1223, two
hundred persons were victims of fire in the village of Verlène,
in the district of Nontron.

In years when drought prevailed, or streams, springs,
and wells dried up, fires multiplied from one end of France

to the other. In 1188, Rouen, Troyes, Beauvais, Provins, Arras, Poitiers, and Moissac were the prey of flames. Some of the details of the fire of Troyes have come down to us. The fire began at night on the fair-grounds and quickly spread to the residences. The abbey of Notre-Dame aux Nonnains, the collegiate church of Saint-Étienne which had just been rebuilt, the palace of the counts of Champagne, and the cathedral, Saint-Pierre, all burned. The flames moved so rapidly that the monks of Notre-Dame had not time to escape and were burned alive.

These scourges of fire also occurred in years of storm and lightning. In 1194, a number of towns and villages were struck by lightning. This was the year of the great fire at Chartres, which destroyed so many unfortunates and almost obliterated the ancient cathedral. Struck by the frequency of the fires, popular imagination accepted the most sinister explanations. Rigord relates that ravens were seen flying from one place to another in the burning towns; in their beaks they carried burning coals and set fire to all houses which had escaped.

To these not infrequent catastrophes were added systematic fires set by men-at-arms. It is well known that war at that time meant ravage, and, especially, the burning of towns, châteaux, and cities belonging to the enemy. Arson was a military operation, well regulated and organized; in short, an institution. Besides its foragers, who pillaged the fields, every army had its *boutefeux*, charged especially with burning barns and houses. Nearly every page of the *Chansons des Lorrains* shows them at work. The hosts of Garin are getting under way to concentrate at Douai. " The incendiaries fall upon the villages, the surprised inhabitants are burned or led captive with manacled hands. The smoke thickens, the flames grow, and the terrified peasants and shepherds flee in every direction." Further on it is the great city of Lyon which is captured and sacked. " On the morrow [after the pillage] Duke Bégon on arising, commands fire, which is prepared and set in a hundred places. No one will ever know the number of those who perished in this great conflagration. From the fields the retreating army could see the towers crumble, the monasteries burst open, and could hear the despairing cries of the women and the little folk.''

The same scenes occurred at Verdun and Bordeaux, where '' eighty citizens, not counting women and children, were reduced to ashes.'' Feudalism seemed to take a ferocious delight in seeing flames consume burghers' houses and the villeins who resided in them. One of the heroes of the *Chanson des Lorrains,* Bernard de Naisil, was among the defenders of Bordeaux. Resting his arms on the window of the château and holding in one hand the helmet he had just removed, he gazed upon the burning city. Said he to Fromont: '' There, we are rid of a great care; Bordeaux is in flames. We are much stronger than we were this morning.''

History and fiction combine their testimony on this point. It is enough to enumerate the places burned in the wars of Philip Augustus: Châtillon-sur-Seine, Dreux, le Mans, Évreux, Dieppe, Tours, Angers, Lille. The fire of Lille, ordered by the king of France to punish the defection of its citizens, '' burned everything, even to the peaty soil of the place,'' says the historian, William of Armorica. If one would know what such a campaign of arson, a regular part of all wars of the time, meant, he should read the accounts of the expedition of Louis of France, son of Philip Augustus, against Flanders in 1214, several months before the battle of Bouvines, when Nieuport, Steenvorde, Bailleul, Hazebrouck, Cassel, not to mention villages and hamlets, were systematically given over to the flames. At Bailleul the incendiaries barely escaped being victims of their own work. The chronicle of Bethune relates that the streets were so obstructed with fugitives and carts, and the night was so dark, that Louis and his knights had great difficulty in making their way to the gates.

Epidemics, another sign of divine wrath, ran an unobstructed course among the anemic and squalid people in the undrained and unpaved cities, where houses were nothing more than leaky hovels, and streets, veritable sewers. At Paris, '' the most beautiful of cities,'' the citizens buried their dead in the meadow of Champeaux, the site of the present market. The cemetery was not closed. Pedestrians crossed it and markets were held there. In rainy seasons this charnel-house became a nauseous bog. It was only in 1187 that Philip Augustus built a stone wall around it, and then out of respect for the dead, rather than for the public health.

Two years later the king and the Parisians determined to make an attempt at paving, but only on the main streets which led to the city gates. The rest remained a slough, a choice breeding-place for those contagious diseases against which the middle ages knew no preventive or curative measures. Men submitted to them as to a chastisement from on high, a divine fire, *ignis sacer, ignis infernalis*. For the sick, those who burned, *ardentes,* the remedies always remained the same: processions, public prayers, expositions [of relics] in the churches, and supplications to some healing saint, Saint Firman or Saint Antony. At Paris, persons ill of the plague were brought to Sainte-Geneviève or to Notre-Dame, without fear of aggravating the epidemic. Besides contagions, there was leprosy the perennial scourge of all France, a respecter of neither rich nor poor. And often, in addition to all these ills, as though to complete the work of war and pest, famine, most destructive of all, held sway.

It takes some effort of imagination to picture the economic condition of medieval France, especially the agricultural conditions, so different from those of to-day. The extensive forests and moors, the limited arable land, the rudimentary agricultural methods, the incessant compromising and annihilating of the peasants' efforts by war, or by the hard feudal laws of the chase, all explain why land yielded small returns, and why the necessary balance between production and population did not exist, except in years of abundance. The inadequacy of traffic increased that of production. Since each district was isolated, and currency was scarce, nobles and clerics depended very largely upon incomes in kind from their tenants; and these incomes, by way of caution, they stored in their granaries and cellars. The subjects, the agriculturists, lived on what remained after the deduction of the seigniors' portion. In good years the surplus of grain and wine might be sold, but the poor and insecure roads, and the enormous tolls and duties laid on goods by the seigniors, shackled trade. Markets were poorly provisioned; produce, half of which nowadays enters into trade, was then almost entirely consumed at home, and towns were correspondingly less populous and trade less active. And thus it came about that in normal years the absence of a demand and the infrequency of transactions depreciated prices; whereas, in years of want, the supply found itself suddenly far beneath the demand and prices rose to frightful figures. There was some improvement over the eleventh century, in which forty-eight famine years are recorded; yet, in the reign of Philip Augustus, eleven famines occurred. Men died of hunger, on an average, one year in every four. The famine of 1195, following in the wake of the hurricane which had destroyed the crops of 1194, was heartrending, because it lasted four years. Grain, wine, oil, and salt reached extraordinary prices. People ate grape-skins in place of bread and even dead animals and roots.

On Easter-day, 1195, Alix, the lady of Rumilly (a seigniory of the diocese of Troyes), was surprised to see the parochial mass very poorly attended. The curé informed her that most of the parishioners were busy hunting roots in the fields to appease their hunger. Touched by pity, Alix caused provisions to be distributed, and commanded that forever after one-third of the tithes, which belonged to her, should be remitted to the parishioners on Easter-day; and, besides, each of them was to be given a five-pound loaf of bread. But what could charity accomplish in the face of so enormous a disaster! "In 1197 a countless throng of persons died of hunger" (*innumeri fame perempti sunt*), says the chronicle of Reims. Such expressions as *multi fame perierunt, moriuntur fame millia millium,* appear again and again in the histories, and they must be taken literally.

Hunger in this period meant not only privation, misery, and suffering; it meant death. To understand to what extent it decimated whole provinces of France, one should consider what happens even nowadays in certain districts of South Africa, Australia, and Hindustan. Even the rich and powerful suffered; the chronicler of Liège states that they were reduced to eating carrion. And he adds: "As for the poor, they died of hunger (*multitudo pauperum moritur*). They fell dead in the streets. We could see them lying at our church doors at early morning, moaning, dying, and begging for the alms which were distributed at the first hour." But

the monks themselves were in want. " In that year [1197]
the wheat gave out. From Epiphany to August we had to
spend more than a hundred marks for bread. We had neither
wine nor beer. Fifteen days before harvest we were still
eating rye bread.''

The cries of the starving made themselves heard far beyond the boundaries, in Italy, and even in Rome. Pope Innocent III, in a letter to the bishop of Paris, naturally attributes
this scourge to the wrath of God, *flagellum Dei*. It is a punishment for the sin which Philip Augustus, king of France,
committed in putting aside his legitimate wife, Ingeborg of
Denmark.

It is the misfortune of the times that each of these calamities engendered others. Famine produced brigandage. " To
escape death by starvation, many persons became robbers and
were hanged,'' says the chronicler of Anchin. He misstates
the facts: the greater part of the brigands lived on their
thefts with impunity.

*

*   *

Imagine a social state in which security for property and
person does not exist; no police, and little justice, especially
outside of the larger cities; each one defends his purse and
his life as best he can.

Robbers operate in broad day and on all roads, by preference attacking sanctuaries where gold and precious objects
abound. The chronicler of Saint-Martial of Limoges, Bernard Itier, notes the frequent disappearance of silver vases,
golden chalices, and manuscripts ornamented with jewels. A
sneak-thief carried away the famous gold reliquary given
by Charlemagne to the chapter of Saint-Julien de Brioude; he
was never again seen, and the canons could do nothing but
launch a terrible litany of anathemas against him:

"May he be accursed living and dying, eating and drinking,
standing and sitting! Be he accursed in the fields, the forests, the
meadows, the pastures, the mountains, the valleys, the villages, the
cities! May his life be short, and his goods pillaged by strangers!
May an incurable palsy fall upon his eyes, his brow, his beard, his
throat, his tongue, his lips, his neck, his breast, his lungs, his ears,
his nostrils, his shoulders, his arms, etc.! May he be like a thirsty

hind, tracked by his enemies! May his children be orphaned and his wife widowed and crazed!"

A poor defence this excommunication of malefactors! As though France had not enough of her own, England sent her audacious thieves in addition. In 1218, an islander from beyond the Channel attempted to appropriate the silver vessels and candelabra of Notre-Dame in Paris. After having remained concealed for several days in the top of the nave, then filled with timber-work, he came down at night by means of a rope with loops to seize the objects he coveted. Unhappily for him, the lighted candles set fire to the silk hangings arranged for the feast of the Assumption; a blaze flared up, people gathered, and the thief was taken.

Some of the more dangerous brigands moved about in armed bands, plundering travelers and merchants, burning farmsteads, and even attacking small villages. In 1206, a group of crusaders, returning from Constantinople, were traveling toward Picardy, their native land. They had escaped the Lombards, and the Alpine mountaineers; but at Saint-Rambert, near Belley, they were assailed by a band of brigands. Their baggage was plundered; and, as they carried with them precious relics, they were eager to redeem themselves. Some leagues further on, at Ambrenay, there came another band and another ransom. And, without doubt, it was the same for a great part of the journey.

These parasites of the highway were, for the most part, mercenary soldiers, Aragonese, Navarrese, Basques, Brabanters, and Germans—desperadoes come to enter the service of kings and princes. When their pay stopped, they robbed and murdered on their own account. These *routiers* or *cottereaux* of Philip Augustus, who reappear in the "grand companies" of Charles V, and the *écorcheurs* of Charles VII, are an open sore of society, a necessary evil, an instrument of war which all the world decries, yet which no one can do without. In vain the church excommunicates these brigands and fulminates against those who employ them. They supply the lack of feudal forces, therefore are they seen in all campaigns and in all wars. Their chiefs rendered such important services that kings made them great person-

ages, well paid and provided with titles and fiefs. Three of
the bandits thus honored remain celebrated: Mercadier, the
friend and general-in-chief of Richard the Lion-Hearted;
Cadoc, the ally of Philip Augustus; and Fulc de Breauté, the
agent of John Lackland.

The ravages of these paid or unpaid hordes in hostile, and
even in friendly territory, were simply frightful. In northern France the Capetians, the Plantagenets, and certain counts
of Flanders and Champagne were able to restrain the scourge
and combat it with success,—but what could be done beyond
the Loire in Berry, Auvergne, Poitou, Gascony, Languedoc,
and Provence, regions more difficult of defense and surveillance? There the highwayman flourished; fires, murders, and
rape everywhere marked his passage; especially did he prey
on religious houses and churches; he seemed to hate the priest
and to feel an obligation to outrage everything which per-
tained to religion and to worship. This was because the
clerics had more that was worth taking, and because by excommunication they aroused the people against him. The
brigands of Berry burned churches at pleasure and took captive whole troops of priests and monks. "They called them
chantres in derision," says Rigord, "and said to them, ' Come,
chanters, intone your psalms,' and at the same instant they
showered on them blows with their fists and with rods.
Beaten thus, some died; others escaped the torment of a long
imprisonment only by paying ransom. These demons trampled the sacred Host under foot, and made garments for their
concubines out of the altar-cloths." The prior of Vigeois
tells us that a chief of one of these bands sold monks at
eighteen sous a head. Must we think that the chroniclers exaggerate? In 1204, a letter of Innocent III formally accuses
an archbishop of Bordeaux of living surrounded by brigands,
and of governing his province through terror of them; he told
his retainers what blows to strike and participated in the
profits.

Some years later the Albigensian war broke out. Naturally
leaning toward heresy, the brigands rushed to Languedoc;
without their aid the counts of Toulouse and Foix would
never have been able to resist the chevaliers of Simon de
Montfort for so long a time. Masters of the abbey at Moissac,

some brigands amused themselves the whole day by ringing
the bells.   In the cathedral of Sainte-Marie at Oloron, in
Béarn, they profaned the Host, decked themselves in priestly
fineries, and pretended to sing the mass.   These pleasantries
were accompanied by their usual misdeeds; burning churches,
and ransoming or tormenting priests.   The catholic chronicler,
Peter of Vaux-de-Cernay, is indignant at the extent of this
sacrilege.   Yet the crusaders had no right to reproach their
foes: Simon de Montfort also hired brigands, among others the
Spaniard, Martin Algais, who, to be sure, deserted him and
went over to the count of Toulouse.   The catholics having captured Algais in 1212, first dragged him at a horse's tail, and
then hanged him.   In a letter directed to the king of Aragon,
the inhabitants of Toulouse complained of the extreme severity
of the bishops:

"They excommunicate us because we use brigands; yet they
themselves employ them.   Do they not admit to their friendship
and board those who killed the abbot of Eaunes, and mutilated the
religious of Bolbonne?"

It is instructive to hear the frightened accents in which an
abbot of Sainte-Geneviève recounts to his monks the vicissitudes of a journey from Paris to Toulouse—"the length of
the way, the danger in crossing streams, the danger from
thieves, the danger from bandits, Aragonese and Basque."
He made his way across ruined and deserted plains, having
before his eyes only the signs of desolation, most mournful
sights; villages in ashes, houses in ruins, church walls half-
crumbled, everything destroyed to the very ground, and
human habitations become the lairs of wild beasts.   "I con-
jure you, my brethren," says the traveler in closing, "to pray
to God and the Blessed Virgin for me.   If They judge me capable of further service to our church, may They show me the
grace of helping me back, safe and sound, to Paris."

Beyond the Rhone, in the unhappy province of Arles,
nominally governed by the emperor of Germany, brigandage
and feudal anarchy were endemic.   Pope Celestine III enumerated for Archbishop Imbert the various categories of
malefactors whom he ought to punish:

"Deal rigorously with those who despoil the shipwrecked or annoy travelers and merchants; excommunicate those who dare to establish new tolls. I know that your province is the prey of Aragonese, Brabanters, and other bands of strangers; smite them, but smite also those who hire these brigands and receive them into their châteaux and villages."

The church exerted herself but, limited to spiritual arms, accomplished nothing. Sometimes, when the deeds of the brigands became altogether intolerable, seigniors and kings permitted a few executions. One day Richard the Lion-Hearted surrounded a band of Gascons near Aixe, in Limousin, and inflicted various kinds of punishments on them: he drowned some in the Vienne, cut the throats of others, and put out the eyes of eighty of them. The brigands of Berry, being poorly paid by Philip Augustus, revolted and devastated the country. The king induced them to come to Bourges under the pretext of giving them their pay. But, once in the city, the gates were closed, and the king's men-at-arms attacked, disarmed, and deprived them of all the money they had stolen. But generally the crimes of highwaymen went unpunished, the nobles being their accomplices, or not daring to act against them. The evil steadily grew. Bands of plunderers on the march were augmented by the addition of all disreputable and outlawed characters: vagabonds, fugitive monks, unfrocked priests, and nuns escaping from the cloister.

The terrified inhabitants of central France had long since reached the absolute limit of human endurance. About 1182 the point of saturation was reached, and from the excess of calamity and despair there emerged a popular movement, in itself something uncommon. A profound agitation occurred, a combined effort of rich and poor, of nobles and villeins, with the purpose of establishing a military force to keep order. The issue at stake was to destroy brigandage and make life tolerable for all.

As in all great crises of this character, a celestial vision gave the original impetus. The Virgin appeared to a carpenter of Puy-en-Velay, named Durand Dujardin, and showed him a picture of herself holding Christ in her arms, and bearing this inscription: *Agnus Dei, qui tollis peccata mundi, dona nobis pacem.* Then she instructed him to seek the bishop of

Puy and organize a brotherhood of all who desired the maintenance of peace. In the eleventh century the episcopacy had
organized associations of the peace of God, but, after a
time, in consequence of poor organization, most of these
leagues dissolved. This, now, was not only the peace of God,
but also the peace of Mary, the great divinity of Puy, the
patroness of the cathedral, the Virgin before whom the pilgrims defiled.

The carpenter's society grew with astonishing rapidity,
spread to neighboring regions, and soon to all the provinces
of central and southern France. Within a few months, from
the end of December, 1182, to April, 1183, an army of peace
was formed in each district. And this astonishing departure
aroused the enthusiasm of Rigord, the monk of Saint-Denis,
so that he exclaimed: " God has hearkened to the wretches
who have groaned so long in oppression and affliction. He has
sent a savior, not an emperor, not a king, not a prince of
the church, but a poor man, Durand.'' The legend, of course,
grew richer as it spread. The chronicler, Gervase of Canterbury, describes the carpenter as a sort of Christ, who preached
the word and was followed by twelve apostles, twelve citizens
of Puy.

Strange to say, a northern chronicler, a Premonstratensian
of Laon, does not accept the supernatural origin of the society
of peace, but gives a rational explanation of it. According
to him, it was a piece of fraud perpetrated by a canon of
Puy. Seeing that the brigands hindered pilgrims from coming to Notre-Dame, and that the profits of the church from
that source threatened to cease, he and a young man, one of
his friends, exploited the devout simplicity of the carpenter,
Durand. The friend, dressed like a woman, with a sparkling
crown of jewels on his head, appeared as the Virgin Mary
to the artisan, who was praying in church, and charged him
to make her pleasure known to the people; those who failed
to observe her wishes would die within a year. Notified by
the carpenter, the citizens immediately flocked into the church,
and the canon, speaking in the name of the man who saw
the vision, informed his listeners that the Virgin had obtained,
from her all-powerful Son, peace for all men, and those who
refused to swear peace and opposed the action of the society

would be stricken by sudden death. The crowd hastened to take the oath, the society was established, and soon filled town and country.

The account of Geoffrey, prior of Vigeois, in Limousin, who wrote near the scene of these events, gives the mean between the miraculous tradition and the entirely rational account of the chronicler of Laon:

"God, who exalts the weak and puts the powerful to shame, touched the spirit of a man of lowest degree, and of humble appearance, a simple and timid carpenter of Puy. He sought Peter, Bishop of Puy, and laid before him the necessity of securing peace. The bishop was much astonished at this sermon coming from lips so base, and the crowd began to jeer at him. But when Christmas came the carpenter had more than a hundred adherents who had sworn to the pact of peace. Soon he had five thousand of them; after Easter one could no longer count them."

Whether it came from God or man, the brotherhood of Puy itself is beyond all doubt. As a means of recognition, the brothers wore a uniform, a small hood of white cloth or linen; whence their name *capuchonnés, capuciati,* or "white hoods." From these hoods hung two bands of the same material—one falling over the back, the other over the breast. "It resembled the pallium of an archbishop," says the prior of Vigeois. To the front band there was attached the miraculous emblem—a pewter badge showing the Virgin and Child and the words, *Agnus Dei.* Each Pentecost the members of the association paid an assessment. They swore to observe the rules of good conduct, to go to mass, not to game, blaspheme, frequent taverns, wear foppish garments, or carry poniards. An organization to proceed against the brigands was undertaken. It was, first of all, necessary to prevent being like them; discipline and morality alone could deserve victory from God. Some of the brethren lived saintly lives; indeed, miracles were performed on the graves of certain of the "white hoods" killed by the brigands. The soldiers of this army of uplift formed an intimate free-masonry, whose members swore absolute devotion to each other. If a "white hood" had by chance killed a man, and the brother of the victim was a member of the society, he was expected to take the murderer home with him, give him the kiss of peace, and sit and drink with him. There is Christian charity carried to heroism!

The institution spread to all classes of society; it included barons, bishops, abbots, monks, simple clerics, burghers, peasants, even women. Societies similar to that of Velay were established in Auvergne, Berry, Aquitaine, Gascony, and Provence. Members of these associations called themselves "the peace-lovers," or simply "the sworn." Their number was considerable; still the chronicles exaggerate it: *numerus infinitus*. One would like to know how they accomplished their difficult task of healing society, to understand the organization of their armies, to see them on the march and in battle with the brigands. But, save for two or three episodes, all these details are lacking.

In 1183, "the sworn" of Auvergne massacred three thousand brigands, a victory which, it is said, did not cost the life of a single brother. Soon a concerted action was arranged between the associates of Berry, Limousin, and Auvergne. The brigands *en masse* took refuge in the little town of Charenton, in Bourbonnais, while the army of the allies collected at Dunle-Roi. The seignior of Charenton, Ebbe VII, was requested to expel the brigands from his territory, something easier to command than to do. Ebbe had recourse to a ruse: he strongly urged the bandits to quit Charenton and fall on their enemies. "When once you are engaged with the sworn," said he, "I shall suddenly fall upon their rear and not one will escape." The bandits agreed, and left the château, the gates of which were at once carefully closed. But, hardly were they in the field, without a place of retreat or a hope of escape, than they were surrounded. "When they saw themselves betrayed," says the chronicler of Laon, "like wild beasts which a strong hand subdues, they lost their natural ferocity; they did not resist, but allowed themselves to be slaughtered like sheep." Ten thousand brigands perished in this butchery; in their camp was found a mass of crosses, gold and silver chalices, not to mention the jewels of inestimable value worn by the five hundred women following the camp (July, 1183).

Twenty days later there was another execution in

Rouergue; the famous bandit chieftain, Courbaran, was taken prisoner near Milhau, and hanged with five hundred of his followers. His head was carried to Puy. Another brigand, Raymond the Brown, captured by the brothers of peace at Châteauneuf-sur-Cher, had his throat cut. Brigandage became dangerous in a measure; at last one could breathe, live, and move freely.

Unfortunately, this great movement drew after it political and social consequences, which had not been foreseen. Professional robbers and assassins were not the only ones threatened by the new institution; all who disturbed the public peace, the nobles, ever ready to plunder the serf and hold him for ransom, were included in its proscription. Why let the habitual brigandage of feudalism go unpunished? How close one's eyes to the intolerable abuse and exploitation of the people by their seigniors? Little by little this association, in which the bourgeois element was dominant, took on the character of an enterprise directed against seigniorial powers. This institution, arising at the initiative of an artisan, had a leveling tendency, because it assigned equal rights and powers to all members of the league, regardless of their rank. The fusion of townsmen and countrymen into one body with a common object became a double-edged weapon: some used it to destroy brigandage; others, quite naturally, thought of using it for the reform of society in favor of the lower classes. A revolution, a truly formidable menace to the privileged classes, was hatching.

It was not given the time to materialize. As soon as the prelates and the nobles perceived the danger and realized that the brothers of peace would attack the established order of things, they faced about and a strong reaction began. In the chronicles of monks and clerics, these confederates, in whose honor God had performed miracles, and who were so piously enrolled under the banner of the Virgin, now suddenly became disturbers of society, anarchists, and heretics, whose activity ought to be suppressed without delay. In 1183, Robert, monk of Saint-Marien of Auxerre, wrote a laudatory résumé of the exploits of the " hoods." In 1184, he considered them heretics, *secta capuciatorum*, and said: " As they insolently refused to obey the great, these have allied to suppress them." To the anonymous chronicler of Laon their work was the result of a mad fury, *insana rabies capuciatorum:*

" Everywhere the seigniors trembled; they dared not exact from their vassals more than the legal services; the greater the exactions, the greater the danger; they were compelled to be content with the revenues which were due them. This foolish and undisciplined folk had reached the height of madness; they dared to notify counts, viscounts, and princes that it behooved them to treat their subjects with more consideration, under pain of quickly experiencing the meaning of their indignation."

What an interest this proclamation of the brothers of peace would have had for history! But the church has not preserved it for us.

The historian of the bishops of Auxerre goes even beyond his fellows. He calls the confrères " abominable reprobates," and their attempt a " horrible and dangerous presumption."

" There was in Gaul a widespread enthusiasm which impelled people to revolt against the powerful. Though good at the outset, the movement was nothing else than the work of the devil, disguised as an angel of light. The league of the sworn of Puy was only a diabolic invention (*diabolicum et perniciosum inventum*). There was no longer fear or respect for superiors. All strove to acquire liberty, saying that it belonged to them from the time of Adam and Eve, from the very day of creation. They did not understand that serfdom is the punishment of sin! The result was that there was no longer any distinction between the great and the small, but a fatal confusion tending to ruin the institutions which rule us all, through the will of God and the agency of the powerful of this earth."

But there is something still more serious: the monk of Auxerre attributes the enervation of religious discipline and the growth of heresy to the " hoods." Were they themselves not heretics of a kind, social and political heretics?

" This formidable scourge (*pestilentia formidabilis*) began to spread in most parts of France, especially in Berry, Auxerre, and Burgundy. The adherents of the sect reached such a height of folly that they were ready to take by force the rights and liberties they claimed."

Repression was not long in coming. The details about it we know only from what happened in the diocese of Auxerre.

A bellicose noble, Hugh of Noyers (1183-1206), a firm enemy
of heretics and a resolved adversary of all rival powers,
had just become bishop. The " white hoods " were numerous
in his territory, and even on his own domain.

" With a multitude of soldiers he came to his episcopal town of
Gy, which was infected with this pest, seized all the sworn he found
there, inflicted pecuniary losses on them, and took away their hoods.
Then, in order to give all possible publicity to their punishment, and
to teach the serfs not to rise against their seigniors, he commanded
that for a whole year they should go with heads uncovered to heat
and cold and the inclemency of all seasons. In summer one could
see these unfortunates bareheaded in the fields scorching in the sun,
in winter shivering with cold. They would have passed the year
thus, had not the uncle of the bishop, Gui, the archbishop of Sens,
been moved to pity and obtained a remission of their penalty for
them. By this means the bishop rid his possessions of this fanatical
sect. The same was done in other dioceses, and thus, by the grace
of God, it entirely disappeared."

Such is the strange history of that popular movement,
which ended by having those who set out to secure social
order treated as its enemies. In their turn the hooded found
themselves tracked like bandits by the clergy and the nobility. It even seems that finally the powers let loose upon
them the very brigands whose extermination they had sworn.
The bands that had escaped the brotherhood again took the
field. One of the most ferocious brigands, the Gascon, Louvart,
in 1184 undertook to avenge the massacres of his followers.
" He surprised an army of the hooded," says the chronicle of
Laon, " in a locality called Portes de Bertes, and destroyed
it so completely that thereafter they dared show themselves no
more." Later he took the town and the abbey of Aurillac
by assault, and carried the château of Peyrat, in Limousin
Meanwhile Mercadier sacked Comborn, Pompadour, Saint-
Pardoux, massacred all the inhabitants of the faubourg
Exideuil, and shared the benefits of his raids with the nobles
of the land. This prowess he maintained for sixteen years.
This great effort of the people, supported by order-loving
men of all conditions, had turned against the people themselves. Brigandage again flourished, the bandits were again
the masters of the fields, and a considerable part of France

relaxed into a reign of terror and desolation, which, for it, was the natural condition.

*

* *

In this atmosphere of misfortune and fright the most characteristic trait of the middle ages appeared: the belief in marvels, portents, and the frequent intervention of supernatural forces. Superstition under a thousand forms is always at the bottom of individual intelligence and is the common mark of all classes of men. In this respect the middle age directly carried on the ancient world, and the Christian of the time of Philip Augustus resembled the pagan of former times. Impregnated with the supernatural, haunted by childish fancies and by visions well known to weakened constitutions, he was convinced that everything was an omen, a forewarning of punishment from on high, a good or a bad sign of the will of Heaven. To him, natural scourges were only visitations of the power of God or the saints: he must submit or seek to avert these calamities by prayer. There lay the chief utility of the church, and the first cause of her influence. The prayers of clerics and monks were the most important public services and must suffer neither interruption nor respite, for they were the safeguard of the entire people.

All the superstitious practices of antiquity were transmitted to the feudal age. Vainly did the church combat this survival of paganism. Superstition, stronger than religion, molded the idea of Christianity to its own uses. The church herself could not prevent it. Monks who wrote history shared in the belief of their contemporaries.

The prior of Vigeois, in Limousin, asserts that one could foresee the ills with which his land was afflicted through the whole year 1183: the wolves in the forest of Pompadour howled steadily throughout the day of the feast of Saint Austriclinian. The southern French, especially, had inherited from the Romans a belief in augury. In the midst of the Albigensian wars, Count Raymond VI of Toulouse refused to execute a convention because he had seen a bird, a crow, which the peasants call Saint Martin's bird, flying on his left. A robber-chief, Martin Algais, was vastly delighted at seeing a white bird of prey pass from left to right, and, boasting mightily, said to the baron who hired him, " By Saint John, Sire! Whatever happens, we shall be victors."

In 1211, a noble, Roger of Comminges, was going to do homage to Simon de Montfort. Just as the ceremony began the count sneezed. Immediately Roger, greatly troubled, took aside his escort and declared that he would not do homage, because the count had sneezed but once: everything done that day would turn out badly. But at last Roger yielded, at the instance of his companions, and from fear that Simon de Montfort would accuse him of heretical superstition. " All Gascons are very foolish," concludes the chronicler, Peter of Vaux-de-Cernay. But was this northern monk, whose writings abound in miracles, less credulous than the Gascons?

Men believed in charms and sorcery. The council of Paris, under the presidency of Bishop Eudes of Sully, about 1200, expressly advised parish priests to keep baptismal fonts under lock and key, to prevent sorcery. Divination of the future by lot, also a legacy of antiquity, was in common use. A book, the Gospels, the Psalter, or the Bible, was opened and the first lines read contained a presage. Those who went to war, or on a crusade, did not fail to consult the lots on the outcome of their enterprise. Simon de Montfort, before taking the cross, had opened a Psalter and sought to obtain a presentiment of his destiny. The church did not forbid the practice; she used it herself. On many an occasion, when a chapter confronted the question of instituting a bishop or a canon, the Gospel was consulted, and, from the verse found by chance, a prognostication (this is the sacred word, *prognosticum*) of the future of the recipient was made.

Chance! A word void of all meaning to people of the middle age! Everything is a manifestation of the divine will: this is the principle of the judicial duel and of ordeals; it is a judgment of God. How could the church condemn a consultation of lots which made use of holy books? In the *Chansons de la croisade des Albigeois*, Pope Innocent III himself, before replying to the prelates who urged him to disinherit the count of Toulouse in favor of Simon de Montfort, demanded a moment of delay. " Barons," said he, " take notice, if you please, that I consult." He opened a book and, perceiving from the lot that the destiny of the count of Toulouse was not evil, he attempted to plead his cause before the hostile assembly.

Those whom the church decried were the sorcerers, *sortilegi*, the professional prophets, the exploiters of the unsuspecting, the deceivers, who now and then sought their prognostications even in the table of Pythagoras. The middle age has left us some collections of verses, or very vague phrases, obscure prophecies which fortune-tellers use to this day. One of these documents, edited in Provençal, is in the form of a chart, from which hangs a row of silken threads, corresponding to the series of verses or prophecies. The person who seeks to know his future touches any thread he chooses, and the corresponding verse informs him vaguely of his destiny.

Astrologers' predictions had free play. They were often made public, the sinister ones in such a way that terrors caused by actually existing calamities were increased by imaginary fears created by these prophets of evil. Toward the close of 1186, one of these prophecies, in the form of a letter from Jewish, Saracen, and Christian astrologers, was circulated over France and all of western Europe. This letter prophesied frightful cataclysms for the following September, at which time the planets were going to be in the constellation Libra. A hurricane, such as no one had ever seen, was going to raise all the dust and the sand from the earth's surface and engulf towns and villages. The only means of escape would be to take refuge in tunnels and caverns. Besides the cyclone, there would be earthquakes, plagues, floods, and wars among Christians. Finally, a conqueror would come who would institute most horrible butcheries.

This lugubrious missive is mentioned or cited by a goodly number of chroniclers; all note its sad effects. " Even the savants were thoroughly frightened," says the monk of Saint-Marien in Auxerre. " As the fatal time approached," asserts an English chronicler, " clerics and laymen, rich and poor, fell into despair." The archbishop of Canterbury ordered a fast of three days. To check this panic and reassure the people it was necessary to put out a counter letter, written by a savant of Cordova to the archbishop of Toledo, in which it was stated that the prediction had no foundation. Finally September arrived—and passed like all other months. What a relief! " We have escaped," cries the annalist of Anchin, " from the danger of a great hurricane. Praised be God! No one, except Him or His ministers, can reveal the future. We,—we do not believe that any chance astrologer or Toledan necromancer can foretell His will."

Comets and eclipses were more than ever causes of fright. A certain Master Eudes, in a letter to the archbishop of Reims, predicted that all who should look upon the eclipse of the sun on May 1, 1184, would have their complexions changed to the same color. The comet of July, 1198, announced the death of Richard the Lion-Hearted. The lunar eclipse of 1204 brought a disastrous winter. The comet of 1223 was only a harbinger of the death of Philip Augustus.

The heavens were a theater of extraordinary phenomena. In 1182, the inhabitants of Limousin saw the moon change from black to red, and then resume its natural appearance. In 1185, a house of fire appeared several times in the air. In 1192, some people of Perche saw an army of chevaliers descend from the sky, fight, and then disappear. A dragon occupied the horizon in 1204, on the very evening of the death of the archbishop of Reims, William of Champagne. In 1214, there was a ball of fire; in 1222, an enormous star, a burning torch, conical in shape, which threatened to set the earth afire.

No less did terrestrial marvels strike the imagination. At Rozoy-en-Brie, at the instant of the sacrifice of the mass, the wine was actually changed to blood, the bread to flesh: visible transubstantiation! In a church of Limousin, several crosses appeared on the altar-cloth. " This miracle," says the prior of Vigeois, " was confirmed by a viscountess, an abbot, and by all the people; only, one could not well determine the color of the crosses. God alone knows what He wished to signify thereby." In a church of Tarn the blood circulated in a statue of the virgin. At Châteauroux, during the war between Philip Augustus and Henry II, a brigand, who was throwing dice before a church door, in a fit of rage hurled a stone at a statue of the Virgin holding the Child Jesus. The arm of the Child was broken off, and a great deal

of blood flowed from the wound. The precious blood, capable
of effecting marvelous cures, was kept; and John Lackland
took the arm and never parted with it.

The chronicle of Rigord alone cites three or four instances
of resurrections. Geoffrey of Vigeois knew a dame of Limoges
who had the fortune after death to interest Mary Magdalene.
The saint touched her lips and the body regained life. A king,
anointed and consecrated as was Philip Augustus, could not
fail to be an object of divine protection. Three times at
least, in his wars against feudal lords and the Plantagenets,
he was miraculously carried out of harm's way. No one
doubted that the souls of the dead returned to torment the
living. The son of Hugh of Marche, in 1185, killed a knight
named Bertrand, and the ghost of this Bertrand did not
cease to rise before the face of the murderer until the victim's
family had obtained satisfaction.

The intervention of the devil is nearly as frequent as that
of the saints. Not content with terrifying people, he sometimes took possession of their bodies. William of Armorica
bears witness that a knight of Brittany was suddenly, while
at table, entered by the devil, who spoke through his mouth.
A priest was called, and the devil cried out because the priest
brought with him a book of exorcisms; but it took some days
to make him abandon his victim. Another time a demon took
it into his head to assume the figure, arms, and steed of a
departed noble. In the field he appeared to one of the friends
of the deceased and commanded him to mount behind him
on the steed. After covering two hundred paces or so, they
suddenly found themselves confronted by a large troop of
chevaliers, who upbraided the ghost for his tardiness. " Come
along," said he, and set off with these spirits, whereupon his
friend, frightened, fell off the horse and remained unconscious on the ground for a long time. "'I saw him this morning," says the historian of Philip Augustus, " just as he was
telling the facts to the archbishop; he showed us the place
where this strange episode occurred." To keep at a distance
these diabolic apparitions and mischievous spirits, no one
ever slept without a light. A night-lamp was always lighted
above the bed.

The innumerable miracles performed at saints' tombs, by

seeing or touching relics, will be considered later. But there were also living saints whose marvelous doings the contemporaries of Philip Augustus attest. Alpaïs, a cowherd of Cudot, in the vicinity of Sens, ate nothing for ten years. She lived, constantly lying down, her body wonderful in its thinness, and her figure of angelic beauty. When there were great religious solemnities, she was seized with ecstasy and, led by an angel, walked in heavenly places. After several days she came to herself, feeling that she was reëntering darkness. She saw what was far away and predicted the future. The chronicler of Saint-Marien of Auxerre adds that he has spoken with her several times, and has come away stupefied at the knowledge and speech of this girl, brought up in the country. The anonymous chronicler of Laon mentions another person, Mathilda, through whom divine power worked in the same way.

Among the wonder-workers most celebrated in this epoch, two men have played an historic rôle: they are the two preachers of crusades—Eustache, abbot of Saint-Germer-de-Flai, and Fulc, curé of Neuilly.

The abbot of Saint-Germer had revealed a vision to the Plantagenet King Henry II, in which the premature death of his two eldest sons was predicted. Charged with preaching the fourth crusade in England, he, like Saint Bernard, scattered miracles along his path. For him to bless a fountain was enough to make it restore sight to the blind, speech to the dumb, strength and health to the weak. Reaching a village which wanted water, he gathered the people in the church, and in their presence struck a stone with a staff and, lo! water flowed forth, healing all maladies. At London he undertook to reform manners, he forbade trade on Sunday, and tried to compel the citizens to be charitable. This was very difficult. The English clergy, jealous of his success, considered him a nuisance and forced him to go back to France, crying after him, " Why dost thou come to reap the harvest of others? "

Fulc of Neuilly, the great agitator, had the gift of persuasion, the irresistible eloquence which swept thousands into the holy war; this converter of sinful men and women was, in addition, an envoy of Heaven, and he proved his mission

by miracles. French and English chroniclers try to outdo
each other in telling how he healed the blind, the deaf, the
dumb, and the palsied by prayers and by a mere laying-on
of hands. But not all believe these marvelous stories, for
Rigord declines to go into details, complaining of the unbe-
lief of men. The Englishman, Roger of Hoveden, is less
reserved. He pictures the saint at Lisieux rebuking the
clergy of the place for irregular living. Furious, the clerics
seize him, throw him into prison, and put his feet into irons.
But, by the grace of God, Fulc frees himself and preaches
at Caen, where he astonishes the crowd by his miracles. The
keepers of the castle at Caen, thinking it will please their
master, imprison him, and also throw him into chains. Again
he issues from his dungeon, and pursues his roving life. This
extraordinary man persuaded women of ill-fame to become
respectable mothers, and induced usurers and confirmed debauchees to give all their goods to the poor. '' These miracles,'' says an English chronicler, '' were no less astonishing.''

*

*   *

In this human society, excited by daily sufferings and
terrors, and living in the midst of hallucinations and visions,
everything happened, even the improbable. Some historians
have questioned the truth of one of the most unbelievable
occurrences of this epoch, the children's crusade of 1212.
They have seen in it only the stuff of which a popular legend
is made. Nevertheless, research has shown that this strange
episode is historical. The movement spread from France to
Germany like a contagion; German children, like French children, made their crusade at the same time and under the
same influence. The agreement of the chroniclers of both
countries is so striking that one must accept it as a fact.

In June, 1212, a shepherd of Cloyes, near Vendôme, a
young boy named Stephen, had a vision like the carpenter
of Puy. God, in the form of a poor pilgrim, asked him for
a piece of bread and gave him a letter, charging him to go
and reconquer the Holy Land and deliver the Holy Sepulcher.
A little later, when the shepherd was driving his sheep from
a cultivated field, to his astonishment, he saw them kneel
before him and beg for mercy. Then it was indeed a divine

mission. He traveled over the land, uttering the cry of the crusades: "Lord God, arouse Christianity! Lord God, give us the true cross!" As he worked miracles everywhere, other shepherds joined him, and soon a crowd of children, aged twelve or thirteen years at most, chose him as leader of the crusade. The chronicle of Rouen would have us believe that be had nearly thirty thousand under his orders, forming an immense procession with crosses and banners. Other children, inspired like Stephen (just as in the fifteenth century several Joans of Arc appeared), are said to have raised similar bands in various parts of France and then to have joined the command of the shepherd of Cloyes. According to a monk of Saint-Médard, in Soissons, some miracles announced this new type of crusade. Countless numbers of fish, frogs, butterflies, and birds were seen emigrating from the seaside. Likewise, a multitude of dogs assembled near a certain château of Champagne, separated into two camps, and fought a furious battle, which very few survived. Coming events cast their shadows before them.

How could this army of children form and organize in the face of the opposition of parents and local clergy? To those who asked them where they were going, the children responded, "To God." The masses favored them. They believed in the miracles of Stephen, and were convinced that God verily manifested His will through these innocent souls, and that their purity would redeem the sins of men. Wherever they passed, the inhabitants of towns and villages, far from stopping them, gave them supplies and money. Every one struggled to see the leader of the shepherds, the agent of God; and sought a hair of his head or a bit of his clothing as a relic.

Finally the state became aroused. Philip Augustus, after having sought the opinion of the prelates and masters of the university of Paris on the matter, commanded the children to return home. A part of them obeyed; the greater number did not. Even the papacy dared not heartily disapprove of the enterprise. Innocent III, so attached was he to his desire for a crusade, contented himself, it seems, with saying, " These children shame us; while we sleep, they cheerfully go forth to deliver the Holy Sepulcher."

The church was, to a great extent, responsible for this affair. To induce the French to take the cross, Rome each year sent preachers who, on crossroads, in public places, and in churches, never ceased urging the Christians to leave their homes and set out for Jerusalem. During the pontificate of Innocent III, the ardor and intensity of this propaganda fired the imagination to an inconceivable degree. Women and children, particularly, were aroused. The chronicler, Albert of Stade, reports that at Liège some hundreds of women, driven by religious enthusiasm, writhed in ecstatic convulsions. Without doubt, the same nervous contagion contributed in France to the formation of the army led by the shepherd of Cloyes.

This army did not continue to consist solely of children. Priests, merchants, peasants, and even some adventurers, bad characters who had nothing to lose and who formed the usual following of crusades, joined it. Passing town after town, these soldiers of Christ, whose number ever increased, at last approached Marseilles, which had been selected as the port of embarkation. In the lead came the wondrous child, Stephen, borne on a richly ornamented vehicle, surrounded by a bodyguard; behind him marched a multitude of pilgrims of both sexes.

The children made an arrangement with two Marseilles ship-owners, Hugh Ferri and William of Porquères, who said they were willing to transport the young crusaders to Syria " for the glory of God." They secured seven vessels, in fact, and packed the children on them. Two of the vessels ran aground near Sardinia, on the island of San Pietro, and were lost with their passengers. The others were taken to Bougie, then to Alexandria, by the ship-owners, who had evolved the plan of selling the children in the slave markets. Thus several thousand of the children found themselves transported to the court of the caliph, and among them four hundred clerics. " They were treated very kindly," says the chronicler Aubri of Trois-Fontaines, " because the caliph, under the guise of a cleric, had studied at Paris." Oriental sovereigns already sent their children to the university.

It is a satisfaction to know that the two wretches responsible for the outcome of this child's crusade, did not go unpunished. In the war which the German Emperor, Frederick II, conducted seventeen years later against the Saracens of Sicily, the two men attempted another crime. They conspired to sell the emperor to the chief Sicilian emir, but, instead, the emir was captured by the Germans and hanged. His accomplices perished on the same gallows. When, in 1229, Frederick II concluded a treaty with the Sultan Al-Kâmil he stipulated that a certain number of the unfortunate crusaders of 1212 be freed. One of them reported that not all of his companions in misfortune were released; seven hundred still remained in the service of the governor of Alexandria.

*

*   *

The true religion of the middle age, to be frank, is the worship of relics. How could men of that time raise themselves to the metaphysical and moral conceptions of Christian doctrine? To the masses religion was the veneration of the remains of saints or of objects which had been used by Jesus or the Virgin. It was believed that divine intervention in human affairs manifested itself especially through the power of relics. Therefore, hardly anything was done, whether in public or private life, without having recourse to the protection or the guarantee of these sacred objects.

Relics were brought to councils and assemblies; on them the most solemn oaths were taken, treaties between entire peoples and conventions between individuals, were sworn. They were the shield and buckler of cities. Was there need of asking God to end a long-enduring rain? A procession was held and the relics were shown. Whoever undertook a distant pilgrimage, a dangerous voyage, or a campaign of war, first went to pray to a saint, to see and touch a relic. The chevalier put some relics in the hilt of his sword; the tradesman, in a little sack suspended from his neck.

One of the most frequent penances enjoined by the church, and one of the surest means of safety, the great fountain of spiritual benefits, was a pilgrimage to the tomb of some saint. The more remote and difficult of access the shrine, the greater was the merit of the pilgrim. These saints and relics, moreover, were graded like earthly powers. Happy those who could venerate the bones of an apostle, one of those privileged beings who were in touch with Christ; happy, above all others, those who could visit Jerusalem and the Holy Sepulcher! But it was not necessary to leave one's country; the Christian found right in France well-known sanctuaries to which the believers flocked: Sainte-Geneviève at Paris; Saint-Denis; Saint-Martin at Tours; Mont Saint-Michel; Notre-Dame at Chartres; Notre-Dame at Vézelay; Saint-Martial at Limoges; Notre-Dame at Puy; Rocamadour; Saint-Foi at Conques; Saint-Sernin at Toulouse. Here the sinner put himself at peace with God and gained a quiet conscience; the sick found a cure, for saints heal more surely than medicines. The *physicus,* be he Christian or Jew, was very expensive, and was only an ignorant empiricist. The medical journals of the time were collections of miracles, *libri miraculorum,* written in the centers of pilgrimage.

The marvelous powers of relics are not only noted in writings of a special character, but they also form a considerable part of the woof of chronicles. The monks who wrote them were interested in advertising the efficacy of the relics from which their abbey drew its prosperity. At Saint-Denis, Rigord either omits or states in a few lines historical facts of the highest importance, but he writes two large pages about the procession of 1191. Philip Augustus, the king of France, was then on a crusade; his only heir, Prince Louis, fell ill of dysentery, which gave cause for serious alarm. The monks of Saint-Denis were brought to Paris, carrying the sacred relics: the crown of thorns, a nail from the cross, and an arm of Saint Simeon. The procession reached the church of Saint-Lazare; there it was met by another gigantic procession, comprising all the regular and secular clergy of Paris, with the bishop, Maurice of Sully, in the lead, and an enormous crowd of students and citizens. The procession moved to the palace in the *Cité,* where the sick child lay. A cross was traced on his abdomen with the relics, and all danger of death disappeared. Some months later it was a question of obtaining from Heaven the deliverance of the Holy Land, and the happy return of the king to his country. This time they were content with placing the bodies of the sainted martyrs—Denis, Rusticus, and Eleutherius—in view on the altar of the great abbey church. The members of the governing regency, the

queen-mother, Adèle of Champagne, the archbishop of
Reims, and many of the faithful were guests at this exposition.

All churches sought to procure some relics; this was a
vital matter, and the first care of their founders was to collect some of these precious objects. We possess a sort of
journal of the acquisitions of relics made by the priory of
Tavaux between the years 1180 and 1213. There is no more
curious document.

In 1181, the abbot of Couronne, the head of the mother-
house, gave the priory some relics of Saint Peter, Saint
Lawrence, Saint Vincent, and Saint Genesius. In the next
year a friend of the prior told him of an abandoned chapel,
where there was a very old reliquary full of anonymous relics;
they were taken to the priory. The same year a priest presented the monks of Tavaux with a piece of the garment of
the martyr, Saint Thomas, a fragment of the Holy Sepulcher,
and one of the stones with which Saint Stephen was stoned.
A little later were acquired the relics of Saint Martial, Saint
Gregory, Saint Hilary, Saint Germain of Auxerre, Saint
Ausonne, Saint Eustache, Saint Féréol, Saint Front,
Saint Vedast, and some hair of Saint Peter. A steward sent
some relics of Saint Basil and Saint Flavian. The founder
of the church, Aimeri Brun, who had made a pilgrimage to
Jerusalem, made a gift of a flask of oil which had flowed from
a statue of the Virgin. The prior, likewise, began a quest;
from the famous sanctuary of Saint-Yrieix he brought two
teeth of the Prophet Amos, some relics of Saint Martin and
Saint Leonard; and, by another series of acquisitions, several
relics of the Theban Legion, of Saint Priscus, and some bone-
lets, hair, and bits of the cloak of Saint Bernard; and, last
of all, a bit of wood from the true cross. But no one could
equal the cellarer of the priory, Gérard, as a relic-hunter and
collector. It is to him that the monks of Tavaux owe the
relics of Saint Peter, Saint John the Evangelist, Saint
Saturnin, Saint Sebastian, Saint Eustelle, and of the Patriarchs Abraham, Isaac, and Jacob. Thanks also to him, the
abbey of Saint-Yrieix sent relics of Saint Peter, Saint Paul,
of Saint Sixtus, Saint Lawrence, Saint Nicolas, and Saint
Leonard. From the monastery of Hautmont came relics of

Saint Benignus, Saint Cæsar, Saint Amand, and of the Holy Innocents.

Such are the relics of known origin; but the journal of Tavaux mentions a good many others, of the highest interest to the faithful: bits of the Virgin's cloak, hair of Saint Stephen, a fragment of the manger of Bethlehem, a part of the Virgin's shoe, a small portion of the incense which the Magi carried to Bethlehem, hair of Saint Paul, a fragment of Saint Andrew's cross and of the stone on which Christ stood when he ascended into heaven, a finger of John the Baptist, a tooth of Saint Maurice, a rib of Saint Andrew, a piece of Mary Magdalene's hair-cloth, a scrap of the jaw-bone of Sainte Radegonda, etc.

One must consider that all these objects were acquired within a very few years, and by a church of a Poitevin priory which had no especial reputation.

Contemporaries accepted them with admirable assurance; they were not critical as to their origin, and asked no questions as to their authenticity. No one wondered at the prodigious mass of relics scattered in a thousand different places, nor at the impossibility of explaining the existence in several sanctuaries of a unique object, for every one had faith. It was only in the higher places of the church that there was any disquiet at the excessive developments which this material form of religious sentiment was taking. Innocent III attempted to limit it by recommending to the French clergy that they accept only objects of indisputable authenticity.

The doubts and prudent precautions of the leaders of the church were ill-received by the masses, and those prelates who ever dared to express their skepticism ran great risks. They were regarded as evil characters and as enemies of religion.

At the end of the reign of Louis VII, in 1162, a sudden rumor spread among the citizens of Paris that the head of Sainte Genevieve had disappeared; that it was, without doubt, stolen; it was no longer in its reliquary. Great excitement! Louis VII was enraged (*immensa furoris ira exacerbatur*), and swore by the Saint of Bethlehem that, if the relic were not found, he would have all the canons of Sainte-Geneviève whipped and expelled. He sent soldiers to the abbey to guard the treasure and other relics, and commanded the archbishop

of Sens and his suffragans to proceed with an investigation.
The canons were in distress, and above all the prior, William,
who, as guardian of the shrine and the treasure of the church,
felt himself directly questioned.

On the day fixed for the investigation the king and his
court, the bishops, abbots, and a crowd of curious persons
fill the church of Sainte-Geneviève. The archbishop of Sens
and his suffragans have been officially designated to be present
at the uncovering of the body of the saint. The box is
opened, and—the head and other relics are found intact. Seeing this, Prior William cannot contain his joy, and with a
loud voice intones a Te Deum, which fills the church and
which the people chant with him. This incident had not
been foreseen in planning the ceremony. Indignant, Manasses
II of Garlande, bishop of Orléans, cries out: '' Who is the
intriguer who dares chant the Te Deum without the authorization of the archbishop and the prelates? And why this
explosion of joy? Because the head of some old woman,
(*vetulae cujusdam*), which the monks have surreptitiously
placed in the shrine, has just been found! ''

The accusation was grave, and William replied with heat:
'' If thou knowest not who I am, do not begin by slandering
me. I am not an intriguer, but a servant of Sainte Geneviève.
The head thou sawest is, without doubt, that of an old woman;
but it is well known that Sainte Geneviève lived a pure and
immaculate virgin to the age of seventy years or more. There
is no need for doubt to enter any mind; let a pyre be prepared, and I, with the head of the saint in my hands, will
pass through the fire without fear.''

Sneeringly, the bishop responded, '' For that head I would
not put my hand in a cup of hot water, and you, you would
enter a furnace! ''

Finally the archbishop of Sens saw fit to intervene. He
ordered the bishop to keep silent, and openly praised the zeal
of William in defending the sainted virgin. '' As for the
slandering bishop,'' adds the author of the life of Saint William, by way of moral, '' his crime did not remain unpunished.
Some years after, beset with accusations of all sorts, he was
driven from his episcopal see, and finished his miserable life
by a death which was no better.''

Here the historian, in his desire to make known to all the chastisement of a despiser of relics, has taken great liberty with history. The truth is that the bishop of Orléans, the skeptic, was never deprived of his functions; he remained a bishop more than twenty years after the incident of Sainte Geneviève, and died peacefully in his bed.

To meet attacks and to keep the faith of believers alive, " expositions " or even " revelations " of relics were instituted. The presence of the sacred remains in the shrines was verified, a procedure which always reassured consciences; and searches were conducted under altars and in tombs for new objects of veneration. In either case the religious solemnity demanded the assembling of all authorities of the land, and drew a large concourse of people. The church gained by it in every way.

It was imperative to guard these precious objects with the greatest care. The owners of relics had to fear warriors, like the seignior of Limousin, who, in 1182, stole the body of Saint Ancildus from Saint-Martial and concealed it in the chapel of his château, *ad tutelam castri;* and also robbers like those who in 1219 removed the remains of Saint Leocadia from the priory of Vic-sur-Aisne at night. The people could not do without the saint; they found her again at the bottom of the Aisne.

It was also necessary to contend against competitors; for often several churches claimed to possess the same relic. The inconvenience was slight when the rival establishments were remote from one another; but two well-known and neighboring churches could not long remain in competition without scandal. In 1186, there were exposed in Saint-Étienne, at Paris, thirty-two hairs of the Virgin, an arm of Saint Andrew, and the head of Saint Denis. But this head already existed in the celebrated abbey where the kings of France are buried. The monks of Saint Denis protested; in 1191, the silver box containing the whole body of Saint Denis was opened in the presence of representatives of the Capetian government. They made it a point to put the head apart in a special shrine, which was open for a whole year to the gaze of pilgrims.

This incident was the more disagreeable to them because

they had already had considerable difficulty in combating a sentiment hostile to their relic. From the time of Louis the Pious they had claimed that the Saint Denis, whose body they possessed, was Denis the Areopagite, that celebrated bishop of Corinth converted by Saint Paul. They would not admit that their saint was a Gallo-Roman bishop, an obscure martyr of later date, who had been put to death with Rusticus and Eleutherius by the pagans of Montmartre. They considered as enemies those skeptics who dared maintain that their Saint Denis could not be the Areopagite, because, according to certain documents, he had never left Greece, but had died and been buried there.

For five centuries this question had consumed floods of ink and had raised bitter discussions. Abelard was driven from Saint-Denis, where he had found refuge after his misfortune, for having indiscreetly disturbed the traditional conviction of the monks. The controversy, always bitter, still continued in the time of Philip Augustus. The doubts lived on and increased; and the chief of royal abbeys truly suffered from them.

Pope Innocent III, in 1216, found the remedy. One of his legates, Peter of Capua, had had the good fortune to discover in Greece a tomb which, it appeared, was unquestionably that of Denis the Areopagite, and had carried the body to Rome. Innocent III made a present of it to the prior of Saint Denis, who had just attended the Lateran Council, and he accompanied this gift with a letter dated January 4, 1216, a document worth reading. To send the monks the body of Saint Denis, the Areopagite, of a properly certified origin, was equal to saying that they did not already possess it. In order not to appear to take a part against a tradition dear to the great French abbey, the pope adopted a neutral position, stated that there was a difference of opinion, epitomized the history of the contention, and added, " Wishing to hurt neither the one nor the other of the convictions before us, we present to your monastery——", he did not say " the body " of Saint Denis, for that would have touched the point at issue, but he ingeniously employed a very vague word, *pignus*, that is a token, a souvenir, *sacrum beati Dionysii pignus.* " In that way," said he, " since you will have both bodies, no one can doubt that, between the two, you have that of the Areopagite.''

To problems of this kind the church could find other solutions. For a long time the monks of the abbey of Saint-Pierre-le-Vif, at Sens, and those of the abbey of Jouarre, were at rivalry over the possession of the body of Saint Potentin. In 1218, an unusually solemn exposition of the relics of Saint-Pierre-le-Vif was arranged; on the very day, by a providential chance, the bishops gathered at Sens found in the tomb of the saint written proof that the remains offered to the veneration of the faithful were, indeed, those of Saint Potentin.

A similar difference in Auvergne toward the end of the twelfth century started a quarrel between the monks of Mozac and those of Issoire. From time immemorial the Christians of Auvergne and elsewhere had been satisfied that the body of Saint Austremoine, the apostle of Auvergne, reposed at Mozac. It was considered well established that, in 764, Pepin the Short had presided at a Council of Volvic, and that the remains of the saint had then solemnly been transported to Mozac, from which place they had never been removed. But, at the beginning of the reign of Philip Augustus, a rumor spread in the district that the head of the saint was in the church at Issoire. A legend arose, according to which a seignior of Aquitaine, named Roger, who was present at the ceremony of translation in 764, had surreptitiously detached the head of Saint Austremoine and placed it in his château, Pierre-Incise. Thence it was said to have passed to the monks of Charroux, the celebrated Poitevin abbey, and finally to have found a resting-place at Issoire. The middle age has left us a whole literature of pseudo-historical writings, made of whole cloth, to explain the peregrinations of some relic or other and favor the claims of a given church. In the eyes of our fathers it was a pious act, in no wise reprehensible, to put the interests of some saint or monastery ahead of the truth. The motive was considered, and a forger was excused for his devotion.

The legend spread by the monks of Issoire had a disastrous effect on Mozac; the latter sanctuary threatened to be abandoned for the rival establishment. In 1197, the abbot of

Mozac asked the bishop of Clermont to come and institute a verification of the relics of Saint Austremoine in the legal way. The chest which held them was opened and the complete body was found, tightly wound in linen and silk, " in the same condition," says the record, " in which King Pepin had left it." The bands still bore the imprint of the royal seal. Doubt was no longer possible; the victory remained with Mozac.

To-day these matters appear to us to be of small moment in the history of France; then they were of vital interest. For medieval society there were no more important events than an exposition or translation of relics, a miracle performed at the tomb of an apostle or saint, a dispute over the possession of a sacred body. When, in 1204, the French and Venetians had taken Constantinople, the whole of France, stirred to its depths, uttered a great cry of joy. Was it at the thought that a Latin Empire would replace the Greek, or that our feudalism would establish a second France on the shores of the Bosphorus and the Ægean Sea? By no means. The cause of this boundless delight was that knights and pilgrims would return with their share of a particular booty, the fruit of a systematic pillage of Byzantine churches; that in all provinces there would be an enormous distribution of Oriental relics. The fourth crusade brought a sudden, unexpected, and unheard-of increase of Christian riches. There is the fact which mightily interested the masses; and it is precisely that which our general histories fail to mention.

CHAPTER II

PARISHES AND PRIESTS

THE preceding pages have shown that religious sentiments and religious fears were in the time of Philip Augustus still the most effective motives of individual and collective acts, the most powerful of all human levers. This lever was in the hands of the clergy.

Despite the violent attacks which were beginning to be leveled against her, the church steadily retained her exalted place in the respect of men. It was because she fulfilled, and alone could fulfil, the greater part of the social functions which have to-day devolved upon the state. Historians, like Henri Martin, who do not admit the legitimacy and necessity of this rôle of the church, have not at all grasped the middle age. Doubtless the essential function of the clergy was to pray and perform religious offices for the entire nation. But it was also the teaching staff; it preserved scientific and literary knowledge. It was charged with the care of the poor, the sick, and the pilgrims. It decided a great part of all civil and criminal cases. Armed with excommunication and interdict, it contributed to policing. It presided over all civil acts of the faithful. For feudal sovereigns it was the indispensable instrument of rule and administration. Finally, almost alone, it formed the classes which practised the liberal professions—doctors, teachers, judges, and lawyers. All the intellectual and moral interests of society, and an important part of its material affairs, were intrusted to it. In short, this international corporation of churchmen did not stop with directing the common destiny of Christendom; it was, in addition, the mainspring of all national organizations.

Landed proprietor, master of a considerable amount of territory; capitalist, unable to alienate property, but, despite

37

all canonical prohibitions, engaged in every kind of business, even that of money-lending; privileged in every way,
evading the direct tax and often also the indirect; exempt
from military service, judged by special tribunals, the clergy
of this epoch had an incomparable position. Nothing in the
France of to-day can give an idea of it.

But one must remember that the clerics of the middle ages
were like their times. Their traditions and professional rules
did not protect them sufficiently from violent habits and gross
manners, the atmosphere which they breathed with all their
contemporaries. In striving to better and pacify feudalism,
they did not escape the influence of the dominant régime, and,
in spite of themselves, yielded to the contagion of example.
Any number of the tonsured, coming as they did from the
military class and leading a noble's life, shared the sentiments, the prejudices, and the vices of their kind. Under
the cassock and the frock there were the same vivacity of
behavior, the same exuberant passions, the same taste for
battle. Failing to expend their energy and their need of
exercise in wars, they compensated themselves by revolts, conflicts as to rights and duties, and rude competition between
temporal and religious interests. In churches and cloisters
there fermented the feelings of independence and rebellion,
which are characteristic of feudal temperaments. Flesh and
blood retained their dominion over this kind of priests. A
rough and militant church was she, justifying her immense
power by the services she rendered to the people, and having
a virtue and an intelligence vastly superior to that of other
classes; she had not the submissive, servile, and pliable appearance of the modern priesthood. She lived, she moved,
and she fought like every other body of society.

*

*   *

At the base of ecclesiastical society was the parish, served
by a curé; that is, by a guardian of souls, *qui habet curam
animarum*. The greater number of curés belonged to the
secular church and depended entirely on the bishop. But,
when the parish was the property of an abbey or a chapter,
it could be intrusted to a canon regular or even to a monk

endowed with the priesthood and delegated to this service by his establishment. The combination of several parishes and their dependencies, the village altars served by chaplains, formed a group called a deanery or archpresbytery, depending on the region. The dean or archpriest, the natural intermediary between bishop or archdeacon and the cures of single parishes, exercised the right of jurisdiction and correction over the latter. Such was the lower clergy, in direct contact with the peasant, itself drawn largely from the populace, the most numerous, but at the same time the most irregular and least manageable element in the church.

The history of these rural priests is obscure. Parishes of those times left no archives. Records of episcopal visits do not exist for the epoch of Philip Augustus. As for the chroniclers, they tell only of ecclesiastical magnates, of bishops, chapters, and abbeys which rank among the seigniories. The sources are especially devoid of information respecting material and external conditions. Illuminators of manuscripts and sculptors pictured bishops, abbots, and monks; they did not dream of presenting cures. The seals of parishes and deaneries with which these priests validated the civil acts of their parishioners—such as gifts, sales, and testaments— are, unhappily, small in size and bear hardly anything else than symbolic objects: the *Agnus Dei,* the *fleur de lys,* the eagle of St. John, the chalice used at the mass. It is unusual if one of them, like that used by Renaud, archpriest of Bourges in 1209, shows a priest officiating before an altar upon which is seen a pyx. The museum of Bayeux contains a small bell of the time of Philip Augustus; it bears its date, 1202, something very unusual. It is true that some of the parochial churches where these cures officiated are still in existence. But how few can be dated with certainty! Some of them rival the sanctuaries of celebrated cathedrals or abbeys in wealth and elegance; such are those two beautiful specimens of gothic art—Saint-Pierre of Gonesse and the church of Petit-Andely.

In other parts of France, in the central and southern provinces, the parochial clergy strove less to be luxuriously installed than to be prepared to resist nobles, warriors, bandits, and pirates. Therefore, the cures constructed massive churches, provided with heavy pillars, with high walls, and with belfries like donjons. There they could give asylum to the peasants round about. Still it was to be feared that the curé would use them to tyrannize over his parishioners and to resist his bishop. The council of Avignon, in 1209, speaks of the abominations which occur in certain fortified churches "where unworthy priests transformed the house of the Lord into a den of thieves." It forbade the fortification of churches and cemeteries; bishops were to destroy everything which gave a sanctuary the appearance of a château.

The parish priests found another means of guarding against the dangers of isolation and of securing themselves against the exactions and violence of the barons. They formed brotherhoods among themselves, or even with laymen, veritable mutual assurance societies with rules, which they swore to observe, and with penalties pronounced against those who should violate them. But the church, hostile to the communes and the corporations of the bourgeoisie, had her reasons for mistrusting these brotherhoods, even though they consisted of churchmen. The council of Rouen in 1189 condemned them. "Canonical regulations detest this kind of association, *canonica detestatur scriptura*," say the bishops. And the ground they give is singular: "This is because it is difficult to observe the rules of the brotherhood, and because they are the cause of perjury for some." The truth is that the episcopacy would not tolerate an instrument of independence in the hands of the lower clergy. The brotherhoods of priests disappeared. Still it seems that the association of priests of Crépy-en-Valois (*confraria presbiterorum de Crespeio*), organized under Philip Augustus, did not alarm the authorities, for it endured throughout the middle age, and, contrary to the rule, the documents of its history have come down to us.[1]

Still the fears of the bishops were well-founded. If they wished to keep the personnel of the parishes under that direct authority which became theirs on the day they took the miter and crozier, they had to preserve in the country priests a

---

[1] Bibliothèque Nationale, Nouvelles acquisitions latines, No. 2311.

spiritual and religious character, without which they would promptly have lost their control.

*

*   *

The parish was not then, as now, a purely ecclesiastical organization. This petty seigniory with its special character belonged not only to the church represented by the bishop or his delegate, the archdeacon; it was, in certain respects, also the property of the " patron." And this patron was often a layman, the owner of the neighboring château, an ordinary knight, a notable resident of the village, and sometimes a more important personage—a count, duke, or even the king.

The lay patron possessed a church under his patronage exactly as a family property which passes from father to son. Besides the satisfactions to his vanity, the chief place in the church and the honors in the procession, he received a share of the tithes and the revenue of the parish, a share which he could sell, give away, or pledge like any other possession. Finally, he had the right of " presenting " to the living— that is, of designating the curé, reserving the confirmation and investiture to the bishop. In many parts the curé was no more than the vassal, partner, agent, or tenant of the patron. One can imagine what kind of bargains resulted from this presentation to livings by laymen who were under the necessity of converting their patronage into ready money.

Still, under the influence of religious ideals and of the growth of monastic orders, the evil diminished day by day. The consciences of certain patrons were moved and troubled by the situation of the parishes, so contrary to the order of things religious and laws ecclesiastical. Impelled by the fear of hell, they strove to rid themselves of this dangerous possession. They gave, or rather sold—for often these gifts were only concealed sales—the churches and the revenues they had to some nearby monastery, to a celebrated abbey, or to the bishopric. Thus the revenues of the church returned to the church, and churchmen became the patrons who nominated the curés, a warranty for a better selection of the parochial clergy. But, in the time of Philip Augustus, this progressive movement had not reached the same stage in all dioceses.

Many parishes, perhaps the majority, still remained under lay patronage, a grievous situation for the dignity and even the morality of the incumbent priests, and unfavorable to the exercise of episcopal rights.

The first of these rights, and one of the most important, was the control of the foundation of parochial churches and chaplaincies; for new ones were always being created, and the church did not lack the opportunity of extending her spiritual and temporal domain, and of increasing the number of clerics. As soon as the church, to satisfy the needs of the faithful, determined to divide a parish, some benefactor, in order to insure the safety of his soul, paid the expenses of the foundation. It was the episcopal authority which decided the matter.

Toward the end of the twelfth century the church of Saint-Pierre of Ribemont, a large town in the environs of Saint-Quentin, was under the patronage of the neighboring abbey of Saint-Nicolas-des-Prés, and the widely extended limits of the parish included the locality of Villers-le-Sec; but there was only one curé to serve Ribemont and Villers. The inhabitants of the latter requested the bishop of Laon to declare their chapel an independent parish, because they had a little church, Notre-Dame, in their midst where baptisms and interments had taken place for many, many years. They stated that the distance between Ribemont and Villers was too great for the one priest of Ribemont to serve both churches satisfactorily. Besides, the priest lived within the walls of the château of Ribemont; this made it difficult for him to come out, especially at night, and thus it happened that residents of Villers died without having received the Extreme Unction and without having been able to make their wills.

This question of division gave rise to a long process which reached as far as Rome. The abbot of Saint-Nicolas and the curé of Ribemont did not wish to have the parish divided. They asserted that the revenues of the church of Ribemont were not enough to support two persons. The people of Villers, on the other hand, urged on by a cleric who aspired to the leadership of the future parish, persistently demanded the separation. But they did not stop with pleading and with exhausting every degree of jurisdiction. They came to blows.

On the strength of a certain judgment the priest of Villers, imagining himself curé already, one day entered the chapel of Notre-Dame, together with all the faithful. The abbot of Saint-Nicolas hastened forward to forbid them to enter. He was put out of doors, and complained that he was even struck. The men of the abbey came up in force and surrounded the chapel, which the priest of Villers refused to leave. There he was watched by sentinels, who did not let him get out of the chapel or out of sight, and who deprived him of nourishment for four days. They proposed to reduce him by starvation. The wretch would rather have died than surrender what he considered his right had not the bishop of Laon ordered the siege to be stopped. Innocent III, on May 16, 1198, concluded to authorize the division. But the town of Villers proved too poor to sustain its new curé. The abbot of Saint-Nicolas and the curé of Ribemont showed the greatest ill-will in giving the curé of Villers any part of the revenues of the old parish. In 1204, the bishop of Laon intervened anew, at the order of the pope, to settle the difference: "Seeing," said he, "that since the division the priest of Ribemont has less to do and he of Villers lacks the necessary resources, the abbot of Saint-Nicolas shall be compelled to give the latter a measure of wheat in addition to the living furnished to the curé of Ribemont." A curious history this, which shows us the papacy as supreme authority intervening in the most minute affairs of the ecclesiastical life of the land.

When some individual founded a church, the ecclesiastical authorities accepted the gift eagerly, but they took good care to fix the conditions. They no longer permitted the founder to be, as had once been the case, the absolute master of his church and curé. In 1195, the seignior of the district of Beauvoir, in Limousin, sought from the bishop of Limoges the permission to build a parochial chapel in his town. The bishop assented, but stipulated that the curé be endowed; the whole income from the tithes should be his and, in addition, the kitchen of the seignior should furnish him the necessities of life for the balance of his days; the chaplain should be subject immediately to the bishop and should always be appointed by him. In 1202, two property-holders announced that they stood ready to pay the costs of a chaplaincy at Rennemoulin (Seine-et-Oise), provided the chapel was served by a member of the order of the Trinity. The bishop of Paris gave the authorization, but in the charter, together with a detailed statement of the revenues, he inserted a clause, by which he reserved the right of naming and dismissing the curé and of exacting an oath of obedience from him. It was not enough for a founder to give an endowment; when, in 1204, a lord of Chevreuse obtained the permission to establish a parochial church and chapel, he was compelled to give the site on which to build the church with its presbytery and cemetery, and the chapel with its garden; only during his life and that of his wife should he enjoy the advowson, which after their death should revert to the bishop. The heyday of feudal patronage had passed; the church was becoming more and more distinct from the lay world; she accepted gifts, but she chose not to be subject to those who gave them.

The bishop took these precautions even when the foundation proceeded from a churchman, either to secure his own rights or to assure the maintenance of the general condition of things. In 1204, a deacon of Saint-Cloud desired to endow a special chaplaincy in the grand chapel of the bishop of Paris at Saint-Cloud. Two conditions were imposed upon him: after the death of the founder and his brother, who were to be the first curés, the bishop should name their successors; and the chapel should never enter into competition with the parish church of Saint-Cloud in the collection of offerings and other parochial revenues. It was important to see that these new services did not operate to the detriment of the old.

This was a serious matter, like all questions in which the material interests of men are at stake; and especially serious if the founder was a monk, because then it became an eternal competition, a permanent conflict between the secular church and the congregations. The latter were interested in multiplying the creation of churches served by the monastic clergy; for these increased their influence as well as their temporal resources. In 1205, the monks of the priory of Deuil sought permission to build a chapel at Gonesse. The bishop of Paris, in sanctioning it, carefully safeguarded the interests of the curé of Gonesse and of Saint-Pierre, the parish church. The curé should as before keep the income from visits, confessions, burials, marriages, churchings, baptisms, and the offerings of the five high feast days—Christmas, Easter, Pentecost, All Saints' Day, and the Nativity of Saint Peter and of Saint Paul. To be sure, these five feasts should also be celebrated in the chapel of the monks, but these were expressly forbidden to admit any of the parishioners of Saint-Pierre to their mass on those days. Detailed as these rules were, they could not foresee all the causes of trouble, and the interested parties found means of circumventing them. At the time of Philip Augustus, contests between curés and monks on the subject of parochial rights were of daily occurrence in all provinces; the rivalry of the monastic, menaced the secular clergy more and more. A new chapter was to be added to the story when the mendicant orders appeared.

*

* *

Another difficulty lay in the recruiting of the parish clergy. When the patronage was clerical the true curé was the bishop, the dean of the chapter, or the abbot; the officiating clergyman was only a substitute, a vicar. He had all the cares without the dignity; he received only a small part of the revenues of the parish. Here was the first fault. Churchmen who held the advowson to parishes felt the necessity of avoiding too poor a choice. But lay patrons, more concerned about their own interests than the capacity of the candidates, nominated their own creatures or even sold the living to the highest bidder.

The parishes, then, were managed by unworthy or ignorant clerics, who often enough were not priests, and refused to strive to attain that rank. Many of them, either incapable or too young, did not take the trouble or had not the right to officiate personally in their churches. They did not reside there, and had services performed by more or less underpaid substitutes, who themselves had little promise. Others, husbands and fathers, arranged to transmit their benefices to their sons. Inheritance of these functions did actually exist in some parts, despite all prohibitions.

True, the bishop had the right and duty of controlling the nomination of the curés. The patron was obliged to present his candidate to him. The bishop, prompted by the archdeacon or dean, examined the candidate and was expected to refuse to invest him with the cure of souls, if he showed himself unfit or lacking the canonical qualifications of age and morality. But how could all bishops do their duty in an age which lacked means of communication and regular and effective facilities of control? Usually the bishop contented himself with approving the choice made by the patrons. The examination was a joke: the candidate declined a Latin noun, conjugated an indicative mood, named the principal parts of a verb, chanted a little, and that was all.

The law was not only misapplied; it was evaded. A candidate who feared the examination of his bishop had himself ordained by a bishop of some other diocese, of another province, or even by one of the many bishops *in partibus* (*transmarini*). All that was necessary was for him to show his diocesan an act of ordination sealed with an episcopal seal. And, if the head of the diocese was seized with scruples and refused to accept the curé presented by his patron, the rejected candidate appealed to Rome. This made an investigation and a decision by papal delegates necessary. During all this time the parochial office remained vacant, and its function suffered; or, perchance, the intruder installed himself provisionally in the living, and ended by keeping it. All these operations were condemned by a series of councils, an indication that it was impossible to stop them. The papal prohibitions were hardly more effective. Lucius III, in 1181, wrote to the archbishop of Rouen:

"Do not allow clerics to serve parishes, who are not priests and who are not disposed to enter the priesthood. Do not, hereafter, accept those who are not disposed to enter the priesthood. Do not, hereafter, accept those who are unwilling to officiate in their churches in person. When patrons make a bad choice, name an incumbent yourself, and do not let appeals to Rome stop you."

In 1185, Urban III commanded the abbot of Fécamp " not to tolerate it that, in certain churches of his patrons, the sons of curés succeeded their fathers.'' Habits and customs were stronger than law.

These cures did not regard themselves as church functionaries subject to the bishop. The bishop was far away, and his tours of inspection intermittent; he could not make his rounds complete. To be sure, the curés were compelled to come to the chief place of the diocese to attend the annual synod, where the bishop reminded them of the duties of their positions, gave them useful advice, disciplined those who had been accused by means of penance, suspension, or removal. He required their attendance at the synod all the more strictly, because it gave him a chance to collect a tax. But priests with uneasy consciences took good care not to make the journey. One of the first statutes of a synod held between 1197 and 1208 by Eudes of Sully, bishop of Paris, commanded clergymen to attend assemblies in person or, in the event of having a legitimate excuse for not coming, to be represented by a chaplain or a cleric; manifestly not all cures came. Attendance upon synods was probably quite regular in a diocese like that of Paris, where the presence of Philip Augustus assured comparative peace. But how could a bishop hope to assemble all the priests of his diocese in the provinces, where the suzerain was impotent or war was perennial? The cure withdrew into his church, where he was almost as safe as the lord of the neighboring castle.

Disobedience, even open rebellion, was not rare. In 1192, the synod of Toul threatened those excommunicated, suspended, and deposed clerics who persisted in saying the mass and in performing the duties of their offices, with deprivation for good and all of every benefice and ecclesiastical function. The council of Rouen excommunicated clerics who took forceful possession of a living against the wish of the bishop and with the aid of a layman. Preachers thundered against these rebellious priests:

" When some one undertakes to rebuke them for a fault they appeal to the supreme tribunal of the pope. They delight in bringing an action against their superiors, and insolently dare their bishops. Just as soon as any one attempts to correct them they begin to cry: ' To Rome; to Rome!' They delude the pope, they artfully fill his bosom with lies, and they slander all who are set over them."

At last the papacy itself found this crying abuse of appeal to Rome intolerable, fatal to the whole hierarchy and to all discipline, and Lucius III did not hesitate to brand it in a letter addressed to Maurice of Sully, bishop of Paris:

"We hear that certain priests of your bishopric do not blush openly to violate the law respecting concubinage and that, when you seek to reprove them, they meet you with an appeal to Rome. They think they can in this way evade the lawful penalty, and persist in their vice. But the process of appeal was not invented to facilitate the sinning of priests. By virtue of our apostolic power we grant you the following right: every priest who, informed and notified, cannot or will not submit to canonical purgation within a space of forty days, shall be suspended. You shall pronounce against him, despite any objection he may make and, notwithstanding every appeal to our court. Recalcitrants shall be punished by the loss of their benefices and livings."

A sage measure; but, as a matter of fact, the well-known phrase "notwithstanding every appeal," a platonic satisfaction for the bishops, was never seriously applied. It still behooved the diocesan authority to be prudent in the use of its right to proceed with rigor against a rebellious priest. The cleric of this age, unworthy as he was, was a sacred being, upon whom it was dangerous to lay one's hands.

A priest had been convicted before Bishop Eudes of Sully of leading a vicious life and was compelled by the authorities to leave Paris. The bishop died in 1208; immediately the condemned returned to Paris without permission, and continued his scandalous conduct. But the new head of the diocese, Peter of Nemours, had the audacious fellow arrested. He was thrown into the episcopal prison of Vitry. When he attempted to escape by digging the ground of the cell in which he was incarcerated, he was transferred to a safer prison at Saint-Cloud. There he made himself so disagreeable that one day the warden lost his patience, abused the prisoner and struck him,—a grave mistake! for it was forbidden to strike a cleric. The bishop was informed of what had happened, and commanded the prisoner to be set at liberty. The warden, knowing what consequences his act would have, abandoned his position and fled.

The affair did not end there. The dishonored and incorrigible priest, in his turn, became accuser and brought an action against his bishop. In 1209, Peter of Nemours appeared before a court of arbitration, composed of the abbot of Saint-Victor and a canon of Notre-Dame. The priest was perfectly willing to admit that the bishop was not responsible for the outrage and the violence of which he had been the victim, that the guard had acted without orders and without the knowledge of his superior, and he swore, with his hand on the Gospels, that for this reason he would never attempt to avenge himself upon the bishop or his connections. But he demanded to be restored into the favor of the bishop. At the request of the arbiters and as an evidence of reconciliation, Peter of Nemours was obliged to give him the kiss of peace.

*

*   *

Carefully reading the commands and prohibitions of councils, one soon perceives that the chief occupation of the church authorities was to put a stop to the misconduct and viciousness of the lower clergy. To the church this was a secret malady, a running sore. Southern France apparently suffered especially from it. If we may believe the catholic chroniclers, the character of the curés of Aquitaine, Languedoc, and Provence had fallen to the last stage of degradation. William of Puylaurens asserts that they were held in utter contempt:

" They were classed with the Jews. Nobles who had the patronage of parochial churches took good care not to nominate their own relatives to the livings; they gave them to the sons of their peasants, or their serfs, for whom they naturally had no respect."

The council of Avignon of 1209 states, in substance, that " priests do not differ from laymen either in appearance or in conduct," and that " they are forever plunging into the most shameful debauchery (*immunditiis et excessibus implicantur*)." One can understand the readiness with which

the southern peoples abandoned Catholicism and embraced
the teachings of the Albigenses and Waldenses.

Still, it need not be supposed that the priests of the north
were spotless. Less secularized and better controlled, they
still laid themselves open to serious charges, which the church
herself did not spare them. Conciliar decrees contain the
outlines of a description of manners which is rich in color, and
of which these are the principal features.

In the first place, without speaking of those who are curés
only in name and that only for the purpose of obtaining the
revenues of their living, the active clergymen too willingly
avoided the duty of residence. Everywhere they were seen
outside of their parishes, on the pretext of studying in the
schools, of seeking a shrine, or of visiting a colleague. Yet
they were not supposed to absent themselves without the consent of the bishop or his representative.

Their behavior was not seemly for churchmen. Not a few
let their hair grow and concealed their tonsure. After the
fashion of laymen, they wore green or red materials, open
vestments, large sleeves, trimmings of silver or some other
metal, garments scalloped at the bottom, and pointed shoes.
They carried arms and walked about with dogs and falcons.
Infractions of church laws were just as numerous as were
the liberties denied to priests on pain of losing their
benefices. Amongst other things, they were forbidden to
have more than a given number of dishes at table. If clerics
hoped to have authority over their parishioners, they must
begin by being different from them.

These curés were not content with being priests; they practised other professions. Some were lawyers, some doctors,
others were stewards or officers of a lay seignior, and still
others full-fledged business men, trading in grain and wine
and lending money at high interest. Councils stormed violently against these merchant-priests and usurers. They were
allowed to be attorneys in certain special cases only—those
in which the interests of the church, of widows, or orphans
were at stake. To be precise, they could still appear in
behalf of their parishioners, but they were forbidden to exact
fees. Their sole claim was to have their expenses paid, provided these were not padded. " We perceive from your

communication," wrote Honorius III to the bishop of Poitiers, "that certain clerics of your city and diocese, in their avidity to make money, trample under foot the dignity of the sacerdotal office. They perform the duties of attorneys to an imprudent extent, much to every one's chagrin. Others forget clerical honor to the point of engaging in trade and buy and sell merchandise. They seem traders rather than clerics. Thus they debase the high calling with which they are endowed."

Avarice drove them to acts still more reprehensible. Regarding the parochial church as their property, they rented it to some private individual; they sold or mortgaged the buildings or grounds which belonged to the benefice, without the authorization of the bishop. They gave certain persons, especially their relatives, shares of, or incomes from, the revenues of the parish. When their purses were exhausted, they pawned the sacerdotal vestments and utensils used in the services. In a word, they exploited their benefices in every possible way. The outcome was that some curés, not content with coining money out of their own charges, rented other churches and extended their operations to them. Everything had its price, even the title and the functions of the dean.

Needless to say, these business men shamelessly exploited their sacerdotal functions and the administration of the sacraments. They performed clandestine marriages for money; they demanded pay before performing the ceremony of baptism, marriage, burial, or Extreme Unction. That they accepted a compensation afterwards, but never before, may be true; yet, they should have exacted nothing before or after. "They are forbidden to leave the bodies of deceased parishioners above ground in order to extort money," decreed the council of Paris in 1208. That of 1212 condemned certain curés who compelled invalids to bequeath sums for masses to be said for one, three, or even seven years. Manifestly they could not say all these masses; they unloaded them upon hired substitutes. Finally, according to a canon of the council of Rouen of 1189, the curés scandalously abused their privileges by excluding from church and sacraments those parishioners whom they disliked, or from whom they desired to make some profit.

Still, if they had conscientiously performed the duties of their ministry! One of the most important of these was preaching. But a great many of the curés, profoundly ignorant, did not preach at all, and for a good reason. Still, as it was necessary for the parishioners to be instructed, they imported professional preachers. There were clerics, and even laymen, who made a business of itinerant preaching. Fortunately for the incompetent curés, these moved from parish to parish for a pecuniary consideration. They even gave rise to an occupation of a peculiar character: they formed " preaching companies," which contracted by the year for all the sermons of the diocese, or of a group of parishes, and furnished preachers to those who required them. There is proof that this strange organization actually operated in Normandy.

The church was alarmed; in several instances she forbade the employment of itinerant preachers. She feared, and not without reason, that these strangers would spread the seed of false doctrines amongst the people, and that heresy would steal in through the sermon. The council of Paris of 1212 forbade all sermons by strangers, unless they were authorized by the bishop of the diocese, and also forbade curés to allow mass to be said by unknown priests.

One is curious to know what could have been the nature of the teaching given to the parishioners by clerics almost absolutely illiterate, incapable even of memorizing or of reading correctly from the collections of ready-made sermons, such as that which Maurice of Sully, bishop of Paris, had prepared for the use of his diocesans. To make up for their incapacity and to impress their hearers, certain village curés in the remoter regions employed childish tactics. When they preached, they placed on the edge of the balustrade of the pulpit a wooden crucifix, within which was concealed a spring, by means of which the preacher could move the head, eyes, or tongue of Christ without any visible movement of his hands. The spring was set in motion by means of an iron rod, which extended through the whole length of the crucifix and its base, and which was worked by means of the foot. One of these fraudulent crucifixes, coming from a little church in Auvergne and dating from the end of the twelfth century, is to be seen in the Musée de Cluny (Museum number, 724).

Finally, the councils reproach the curés with letting parishioners dance in the church, in the cemeteries, in processions, and with being present themselves at these dances, as well as at the improper exhibitions given by players and buffoons. They were accused of being gamesters; dice, even chess, and frequenting taverns were forbidden them. Some of them were blamed for their repulsive slovenliness and for the poor care of their churches. With an especial vigor were branded the two vices most common in this class: intoxication and incontinence. The less reprehensible of the clerics were those who kept a concubine at the presbytery, whom the people quite naturally called the '' priestess,'' and the councils *focaria,* '' the keeper of the house '' or of '' the hearth.''

The preachers at the time of Philip Augustus justify the strictures of the councils by giving testimony quite as unfavorable to the parochial clergy. '' Our priests,'' says Geoffrey of Troyes, '' immersed in material things, disturb themselves little about those of the spirit. They differ from the laymen in dress, not at heart; in appearance, not in reality. They belie by their deeds what they preach from the pulpit. Tonsure, garb, and speech give them the superficial varnish of piety; underneath the sheep's clothing are concealed hypocrites and ravening wolves.'' When Bishop Maurice of Sully, in the preface to his preacher's manual, addresses himself to the curés of his diocese, he himself unreservedly reveals their weak points, their bad manners, their ignorance, and their repugnance to preaching. He is obliged to remind them that a blameless life, *vita sancta,* is necessary in a priest who daily approaches the altar, and that their first virtue, next to continence, should be sobriety. He also urges them to be humble, to love their neighbors, to be patient and generous; on the other hand, he desires them to have a correct knowledge, *recta scientia:* for which reason they should read and procure books from which they can learn their duties—the indispensable liturgical works, a book of sacraments, of collects, a formulary for baptisms, a calendar, a psalter, a book of homilies, and a penitential. Finally, they must preach, not only by example, but by word of mouth—an essential part of their ministry, a duty which they are forbidden to evade.

Compare the specific accusations made by the councils and preachers of this period with the conditions denounced thirty years later in the Journal of Visitation of Eudes Rigaud, archbishop of Rouen: the exact agreement of the facts leaves no doubt respecting the sad intellectual and moral condition of the lower clergy. The church herself fully confirms the evil. When one sees her judge her members so harshly, why be surprised at the attacks and the caustic satires of profane literature? The picture which we have just painted on the basis of ecclesiastical documents does not differ from the Journal of Eudes Rigaud, which might, for all the world, be an exact and living commentary on the fiction of the epoch.

According to the most competent specialists, these lays for the greater part belong to the end of the twelfth or the beginning of the thirteenth century. The historian of Philip Augustus, then, may seek in them particulars about customs and traits of real life, which form the framework within which the fancy of the narrator plays, and which, so to speak, unintentionally escape from his thought and pen.[1]

The authors of the tales particularly blame the lower clergy. To them a priest is, of necessity, a perverted and sensual creature, who delights in adventures at the expense of noble and plebeian husbands. But they do take care to distinguish between the common cleric, the student who has only the tonsure and garb and is free to marry, and the curé—properly speaking, the minister of the parish. The cleric—the lover of the stories, as M. Bedier has very aptly expressed it—is interesting, and ordinarily fortune favors him; the curé—gluttonous, covetous, formidable in every respect to his flock—

---

[1] In his excellent *Histoire de la littérature française* (1896), M. Lanson seems to attribute no historical value, or at least very little, to the *fabliaux*. According to him the authors described only imaginary social deformities or exceptional evils. They spoke of priests who lived evil lives; " but what brings mistrust, is precisely that there are too many of them." As far as the conduct of the parochial clergy of the country is concerned, it is enough to compare the conciliar texts of which we have given the substance, the Journal of Eudes Rigaud of the thirteenth century, and the contents of the archives of the district of Troyes (Inventaire sommaire, 1898) of the fifteenth century, with the *fabliaux*, to convince one's self that the romancers were not exaggerating.

is nearly always mistreated and dishonored as a villain. He is the laughing-stock and the victim. These scandalous stori-ettes generally end in his confusion and misfortune; some-times even in his death. The narrators fasten upon this char-acter with a ferocious pleasure and drag it through the mire. This malignant asperity of satire can be explained only by an accumulated malice against these unworthy priests, given to abusing their office by exploiting and dishonoring their parishioners. But in the excesses of these comical or gro-tesque narratives there abound traits of the time taken from life, and truth appears with the exact color of the past.

Nothing is more instructive than the tale entitled *Le prêtre et le chevalier*. A knight arrives at a village and, not know-ing where to spend the night, questions the first person he encounters, " By the soul of thy father, name for me the richest man of this locality." " It is our cure," responds the other, " the richest person for ten leagues round about; but at the same time perfidious and most selfish; he loves no one but himself. About his house are scoundrels . . . hor-rible as wolves or leopards. It were better to go to the home of the priest, for of two evils one should choose the lesser." " Where is the chaplain's house? " " That one yonder, with the chimney; the one so pretty and stylish." The knight rides up to the house and sees the curé stretched upon his back at the window. He requests entertainment for the night. " Sir Knight," says the cure, " leave me in peace and be on thy way. I shall lodge no one, not even the king, should he come hither. I am alone with my niece, and my· friend," (the word serves in this literature to designate the priestess). The chevalier persists, " I will give thee of my possessions what thou requirest for a handsome altar." Then the curé deigns to notice him and the bargaining begins. Before receiving the stranger, he stipulates that five sous (ten francs) shall be paid for each dish to be served. The knight agrees to the price. He enters; Dame Avinée (the symbolic name of the friend) prepares the table; the host himself assists in the kitchen: he shells the almonds. Then a sub-stantial meal is served and, after dessert, the cure presents his guest with an interminable bill, in which every article is reckoned at five sous—the meats, the wine, the salt, the table, the cloth, the pots, the oats for the horse, the hay, the stable-litter, even the bed upon which the chevalier is to sleep. Little matters the strange conceit by which the chevalier managed to pay his debt without opening his purse: the point at issue is that in this little comedy there is not a shadow of complaint at the cunning of the concubinary priest or at his irregular establishment.

The family life of the priest and the priestess became a part of the times; almost a social institution. A curé depicted in the story, *Boucher d'Abbeville*, enjoys a comfortable home, for he has many conveniences and possesses a number of animals. He, too, has a " friend," who, aided by a servant, does the honors of the presbytery. She sups with him and with his guest, the butcher of Abbeville. " They were richly served with good meat and good wine; white linens were produced to make a bed for the butcher." Betimes in the morning the priest arose. " He and his cleric went to the convent to chant and do their duty; the dame remained sleeping." This lady is portrayed for us as " very pretty and caressable." She is clothed in a green, well-pressed petticoat, with clinging folds. She proudly fingers the folds at her waist. Her eyes are bright and smiling. She is pretty and pleasant as one could wish." We are even permitted to witness a private scene in which the lady insults and strikes the servant with her stick. " Lady," says the latter, " what have I stolen from you?" " My barley and my wheat, wretch; my peas, my lard, and my fresh bread." Clearly, she is mistress of the house. What proves that this family life shocked no one is another instance in which a priest in wrath against the priestess cried, " You shall no longer be my friend." He threatened to expel her, and to do it before all the neighbors.

The curé feared only one power, the bishop; but the bishops of romance are not especially severe. One narrator tells of three persons living at the presbytery—the curé, his mother, and his friend. The mother complained to the bishop that her son did not give her the bare necessities of life, though he found nothing too beautiful to clothe the " priestess." " He gowns her well and beautifully. She has a pretty skirt and a good cloak; two good and beautiful fur-coats—one of squirrel, the other of lambskin—and a costly silver-tissue, of which many people speak.'' The bishop summoned the curé to his court together with two hundred other curés, and threatened him with suspension if he did not treat his mother with more consideration. He never thought of rebuking him for living with a friend.

Still (and this very likely partakes of historic fact) a less good-natured bishop of Bayeux commanded a curé of his diocese to dismiss his priestess, named Dame Auberée. He closed by condemning the priest to abstain from drinking wine, if he failed to obey the command. Dame Auberée, a sly creature, counseled the priest to obey: he would no longer drink wine, he would sip it. Informed of the subterfuge, the bishop forbade the offender to eat goose. '' Good! '' said the dame to the curé, '' in place of eating goose, you will eat as much gander as you like, for you have more than thirty of them.'' Again came the injunction of the bishop, who forbade the curé to sleep on his feather-bed. Dame Auberée made him a bed of pillows. It is impossible to relate in detail how these two culprits compelled the bishop to say no more.

In certain tales one sees in what a strange way the curés discharged their functions. Here a priest falsely charges a villein with having married his godmother, expels him from the church, and fixes his fine at seven livres. There, on a Good Friday the officiating clergyman, at the point of chanting the Gospels, becomes confused in the bookmarks of his missal, with which he is none too well acquainted, and, losing his head, he stammers some vague Latin words, quite out of place in the liturgy of the Passion, until he is perfectly sure that all his parishioners have had a chance to contribute to the collection. Elsewhere the curé is the victim of a trick which a penniless cleric played on his innkeeper. He promised the hotelkeeper, who demanded payment, that the curé would pay for him. The two went together to the church. There the cleric drew the curé aside: '' Sire, I have taken lodging with this good fellow, your parishioner; since last night a cruel ailment troubles him: he has had a slight attack of insanity. Here are ten pence; read a gospel over

him.'' The curé said to the tavernkeeper, '' Wait until I
have said my mass and I will attend to your affair.'' The
latter, thinking that he was going to be paid, was reassured
and patient, but in the interval the cleric made his escape.
The mass finished, the curé desired his parishioner to kneel;
but the latter stoutly declared that he wanted money, not exorcisms. What could be a better proof of his malady! Held
by the strongest swains of the parish, he protested in vain; he
was sprinkled with Holy-water, a gospel was read over him,
but of the sum owing him he obtained not a mite.

It would be easy to compare the prohibitions of councils
with the corresponding features of the tales and show how
the latter explain the former. To give a single example: the
church authorities often forbade parish priests to play at dice.
The tale, *Du prêtre et des deux ribauds*, tells of a curé who
lost his money and even his horse at playing dice with two
fiddlers whom he chanced to meet on the way. The highwaymen had cheated; their dice were loaded, and it was not
without trouble that their victim regained possession of his
mount, though not of his purse.

*

*   *

In endeavoring to understand the condition of the parochial
clergy of the time of Philip Augustus, there is no use in
looking for analogies in present France, where the greater
number of our rural priests has, as a whole, become respectable and respectful to the laws of the church. One should
look beyond the Atlantic at the inferior status of the Spanish
clergy, in Chile, or in Peru, or among the American catholics
of the South: the concubinary curés and their more than
easy manners, sanctioned by the tolerance of Creole life, carry
us back to the heart of the middle age. Still the middle
age had the excuse of the low state of surrounding civilization, the rustic locality from which the priests came and
where they were compelled to live. Besides, it is fair to
think that the parish priests as a body were not so vicious
and incapable as one might suppose from the accusations
of their superiors and from the derision of the minstrels.

We know at least one curé among the contemporaries of
Philip Augustus who was quite the opposite of an ignoramus,

for he occupies a high place in the historical literature of his time. This exception is worthy of notice.

This curé, Lambert, was attached to the church of Ardres, the principal place of a petty serjeanty, belonging to the county of Flanders. He was a married priest, or perhaps had been married before taking orders; at any rate, he himself speaks of his daughter and two sons without the least hesitation. The date of his birth is not known any more than that of his death; all that is certain is that he lived at the beginning of the thirteenth century; the last item in his chronicle belongs to the year 1203.

This chronicle portrays him constantly engaged in the performance of his duties. It was not always pleasant to do them. No more than the monks were the curés sheltered from the brutality of the feudal barons.

Baldwin II, count of Guines and seignior of Ardres, had a son, Arnoul, whom the archbishop of Reims excommunicated for an act of violence. The strict duty of the curé was to heed the decree of anathema and forbid the excommunicate to enter the church. One day it came to pass that the count of Guines notified Lambert that his son had just been absolved by an agent of the archbishop, and that he should ring his bells to announce the absolution to all the parishioners. This assertion of the father seeming insufficient, the troubled curé sought an avenue of escape and requested a delay, to secure information. Finally he decided to go to Baldwin in person. He met him on the road, accompanied by his son and an escort of soldiers. Baldwin received him with a fearful volley of reproaches and insults; that of disobedient and rebellious priest was the kindest of these. "Terrified," writes the curé, "by the thunder of his voice and the lightning of his eyes which glowed like burning coals, blasted by his invectives, I fell from my horse almost unconscious, at his feet. The soldiers helped me up and I regained my saddle as best I could. It was only after I had ridden for some time in his suite that he deigned to show me a more encouraging visage."

Some time after, about 1194, Arnoul married a lady of the neighborhood, Beatrice of Bourbourg. The nuptials were held at Ardres with great pomp. The account of Lambert

permits us to be present at one of the ceremonies in which
the priest played an important rôle—the benediction of the
marriage-bed:

" At nightfall, when groom and bride were placed in the same bed,
the count of Guines, filled with the zeal of the Holy Spirit, called
me and my two sons, Baldwin and William, and also Robert, curé of
Audruicq, and asked us to sprinkle the pair with Holy-water. We,
therefore, passed completely round the bed, swinging our censors
filled with precious spices, and called down upon them the benediction of Heaven. When we had performed our office with the greatest
possible care and devotion, the count, still filled with the grace of
the Spirit, raised his eyes and hands to Heaven and cried: ' Holy
Lord, Almighty Father, God eternal, Who hast blessed Abraham
and his seed, pour forth Thy mercy upon us. Deign to bless Thy
servants joined in the holy bonds of matrimony, that they live in
good accord in Thy divine love, and that their offspring increase
until the end of the ages.' We responded ' Amen,' and he added:
' My dear son Arnoul, who art the eldest of my children, and whom
I love above all others, if there is any virtue in a blessing which a
father gives his son, and if it is true that a tradition of our ancestors gives us this right, I bestow on thee, with clasped hands, the
same favor of benediction which God, the Father, formerly gave
to Abraham, Abraham to Isaac, and Isaac to his son Jacob.' Arnoul
bowed his head toward his father and devoutly murmured a *Pater
noster*. And the count replied, giving the greatest force and expression to his words: ' I bless thee, saving the rights of thy brothers,
that thou possess my blessing forever and ever.' We all responded
' Amen,' after which we left the nuptial chamber and each went to
his home."

Cultured and erudite, this curé of Ardres furnishes one
of the earliest examples of something nowadays quite common: the need which the parish priest experiences of studying the past of his church and of the locality where it is
situated. Lambert made himself the historian of the seigniory
of Ardres and of the county of Guines. This, he himself declares, he did in the first place to please his master, whom
the affair of the excommunication had chilled toward him, but
also for the pleasure of communicating to others the fruit of
his learned researches, to exhibit a learning rare in those
days among his kind.

An enthusiasm dominates this priest, and exuberantly displays itself: the love of his parish and of the seigniory which
surrounds it. For him, the whole world is contained in this

diminutive fief. In his eyes every part of it assumes imposing proportions. In his dithyrambic dedication to the seignior of Ardres, he celebrates the glory of Arnoul II as though he were treating of Cæsar or Alexander. And in the body of the same work, speaking of the domains of Baldwin II of Guines—vassal, like all other barons along the shore of the Channel, of both France and England,—he asserts that his fief is one of the most precious pearls of the crown of France and one of the diamonds which glitter with a bright effulgence upon the diadem of the kings of England. A little further on he compares Baldwin II to Jupiter, David, and Solomon. Elsewhere, the siege of the castle of Sangate reminds him of the siege of Troy, and he adds, "Had Troy been as well defended with soldiers as Sangate, it would have withstood the Greeks."

Very proud of his knowledge, Lambert in his preface at one point mentions Ovid, Homer, Pindar, Virgil, Priscian, Herodianus, Prosper, Bede, Eusebius, and Saint Jerome—a mixture of the sacred and profane which was characteristic of the time. He plumes himself on writing a beautiful style. The truth is that his far-fetched, involved, and obscure phrases weary the reader with their pretentiousness, as laborious as his derivations of certain names are ridiculous. Still, the writer does not altogether lack warmth and movement; several of his narratives have good color and leave a lively impression. He taxes his ingenuity from the start to vary his narrative and to reawaken the interest of his reader. He puts the second part of his story, that which concerns the origin of the seigniory of Ardres, into the mouth of an old chevalier, Gautier de Cluses, whom he imagines recalling the past in the midst of the little seignioral court.

In short, the curé of Ardres has certain qualities of the historian. First, impartiality: for, though he exalts the seigniors of Ardres, he does not conceal their weaknesses, not even their vices. Throughout one finds a most realistic and lively picture of petty feudalism. Though he lacks a critical sense in the matter of sources and indiscriminately piles up historical facts and legends, he everywhere strives for accuracy. He is cautious with the documents found in historical books and in the cartularies. He himself says that, in the absence of written sources, he has questioned old residents. In the latter part of his work he, like a conscientious witness, relates what he has seen and heard. Finally, he has the good sense not to attempt to write a universal history from the time of Adam and Eve, as did all other chroniclers. He remarks that he has broken with that custom, " to seclude himself in the annals of a very little county." It is regrettable that his example was not oftener followed!

This parish clergyman, then, somewhat raises the reputation of his class, which, as we have just shown, had great need of it.

CHAPTER III

THE STUDENT

WHEN one studies the documents which relate to the ecclesiastical society of the end of the twelfth and the beginning of the thirteenth centuries, one discovers that the names of a good many canons and bishops are preceded by the word *magister,* master. They have obtained the master's degree, the permission to teach (*licentia docendi*) in the great schools, the universities. They are graduated, a thing characteristic of their time: for a hundred years earlier the degree of master was rarely found. In the time of Philip Augustus these teaching degrees tended to become an almost necessary qualification for obtaining important benefices and the chief dignities of the church. The extent of education among the upper classes of clerics is a notable fact of the highest importance, an index of a very interesting social progress. Nearly all members of the higher clergy began as students: the schools were the nurseries of chapters and prelacies. And it is the student—or the scholar, *scolaris,* as he was then called—who is now to occupy our attention.

*
* *

Certain passionate admirers of the middle ages have gone so far as to hold that in the France of that epoch there were as many, if not more, schools than there are to-day. This is a decided exaggeration; but the truth is that, for that age of inferior civilization, schools were more numerous than one would suppose. There was one wherever there was a center of religious life, an ecclesiastical community of any importance, especially in northern France. In every diocese, besides the rural or parochial schools which already existed, but of which we know nothing at all at the time of Philip Augustus, the principal chapters and monasteries had their

schools, their clientèle of masters and pupils. Here were instructed not only choir-boys or novices destined to pass their
entire lives in a cathedral church or an abbey, but scholars
who wished to enter the clergy in order later to engage in
liberal professions or to hold benefices from the church; and
the sons of nobles and seigniors, or laics, desirous of completing the very elementary education their teachers had given
them, were also welcomed. In a word, to understand the conditions in the field of instruction of that day, one must picture
a society in which there were no other educational institutions
than these large and small seminaries, where the clergy was
molded and recruited.

Thus it was that at Paris there existed three groups of
scholastic establishments: first, the school of Notre-Dame, or
the group of schools of the bishopric or cathedral, placed under
the immediate direction of two dignitaries of the chapter—
the cantor, who supervised the elementary schools, and the
chancellor, who controlled the advanced schools; second, the
schools of the principal abbeys, notably of Sainte-Geneviève,
of Saint-Victor, and of Saint-Germain-des-Prés; third, private
schools, founded by clerics who had masterships, the license
(*licentia docendi*), and who taught without restraint, though
always under the control of the bishop or of the chancellor.
A goodly number of these schools—conducted by savants,
philosophers, or theologians of renown—were in the *Île de la
Cité;* and, after the example set by Abelard, even on the
left bank near the *Petit pont;* and above all, on the northern
slope of the height of Sainte-Geneviève. Similarly in Champagne we find three schools of the first kind, which are merely
dependencies of three cathedral chapters: the school of Reims,
which is the most celebrated; the school of Châlons-sur-
Marne, and the school of Troyes; then the monastic schools,
the appendants of the great abbeys of Montiéramey, Montier-
la-Celle, Saint-Remi of Reims, and Saint-Nicolas of Reims;
and, finally, the smaller schools of certain priories, without
mentioning the elementary schools.

In short, it was the church which gave instruction, which
created masters and conferred upon them the capacity of
teaching. Bishops, chapters, and abbots had the supreme direction and control of teaching in the whole extent of their

spiritual and feudal jurisdictions. No one could teach without their authorization.

It was a considerable power which had thus passed into the hands of ecclesiastical society, but the directors of that society took some pains to make it acceptable and justifiable. At the end of the twelfth century, they already strove to proclaim and to carry through two principles dear to modern society: the gratuity and the freedom of higher instruction.

In 1179, the third Lateran council, under the presidency of Pope Alexander III, in its eighteenth decree, took an action of extreme importance. "Every cathedral church shall maintain a master to give free instruction to clerics of the church and to needy scholars:" this meant gratuitous instruction, at least for those who could not pay. "Persons who have the duty of directing and supervising the schools—that is, chancellors and doctors—are forbidden to exact any remuneration whatsoever from candidates for granting them the license to teach:" this is the freedom of the teaching profession. "The license shall not be refused to worthy applicants:" this, at least in a certain sense, is the freedom of teaching. The eleventh decree of the fourth Lateran council, held by Innocent III in 1215, renewed the regulations. It further determined that, in every archiepiscopal or metropolitan church, a master of theology, a *theologus,* should be named to teach his subject to priests of the province and to watch over the conduct of the parochial priesthood.

These two decrees were the sign of real progress. By means of them the church, which had the monopoly and control of public instruction, attempted to justify the important power she enjoyed. The papacy, within the hands of which religious authority was concentrated, openly sought to complete, unify, and regulate this scholastic organization, which, during the eleventh and twelfth centuries, had step by step established itself in many French dioceses in the form of isolated and spontaneous creations. In respect to the crucial matter of the liberty of opening a course or a school, the middle age had thus obtained a sort of franchise from Rome. And the prescriptions of the councils did not end with being written on parchment; efforts were almost immediately made to put them into effect.

Hardly two years after these principles had been pronounced at the Lateran council of 1179, they received a striking application at Montpellier. In establishing the freedom of higher instruction through a charter of January, 1181, William VIII, seignior of Montpellier and immediate vassal of the bishop, without doubt acted in harmony with the church; for many other documents of that time prove that the school of Montpellier, like all other schools of the epoch, was strictly subordinate to the clergy. William VIII declares himself opposed to every monopoly of teaching medicine in his city and seigniory. Notwithstanding the most ardent urging and the most alluring offers of money *precio seu sollicitudine*, he will never grant any one the exclusive privilege of " reading " or of conducting schools in *materia medica* (*in facultate physice discipline*). The motive is curious and expressed with perfect lucidity: " Seeing that it would be too atrocious and too contrary to justice and religion (*contra fas et pium*), to convey to a single individual the right of teaching so excellent a science." Consequently, he authorizes all persons, whosoever they be (*omnes homines*), and whencesoever they come, who wish to conduct a school of medicine at Montpellier, to teach in his seigniorial city with full and complete freedom, regardless of any opposition; and closes by charging his successors not to depart from this line of conduct. This was as positive a declaration and application of principles as the partizans of the liberty of teaching could wish; too positive, in fact, for the lord of Montpellier made no mention of the qualifications which society has the right to require of those who constitute its medical corps. Later ecclesiastical authority found it necessary to regulate and define this concession by surrounding medical instruction with restrictions conformable to public interest.

In regulating the exercise of the right to teach with a liberalism which it would be highly unjust not to recognize, the central power of the church gave especial attention to the " great schools," or the *studia generalia,* an expression much used in contemporary writings.

Under " great schools " are to be understood those in which the national, or indeed international, youth gathered, and where the whole range of the knowledge of the time was taught: in the first place, the " liberal arts," the *trivium* and *quadrivium*, the immutable foundation of the academic edifice, the traditional curriculum still divided and organized as in the time of the Carolingians; in the second place, the special studies of a professional character—medicine (*physica*), civil law (*leges*), canon law (*decretum*), and theology (*sacra pagina*). Students of the liberal arts or " artists," medics, lawyers, decretists, theologians—all these followers of the universities who sought a sacerdotal career or what we to-day call the " liberal " professions—by preference crowded into certain cities. Paris, Orléans, and Angers in the north; Toulouse and Montpellier in the south, were, in the time of Philip Augustus, the preëminent school-centers. But some of these great centers of general studies already had specialties which attracted the Frenchman and the stranger: at Paris, dialectic and theology; at Orléans, civil law and rhetoric; at Montpellier, medicine. Before the growing prosperity of these schools, others—as Chartres and Reims, which had had their period of glory in the eleventh century—declined and were obscured. Bit by bit they fell to the rank of local seminaries.

A common trait of these schools is the cosmopolitan character not only of the students, but also of the teachers. Knowledge being then entirely ecclesiastical, and the church of the time cosmopolitan, education had the same character. Paris, like Orléans and Montpellier, furnished graduated clerics for all Europe. Not a few foreign masters were provided with benefices, canonries, or even bishoprics in France, and *vice versa*. National boundaries did not exist for the ecclesiastical power, which had its head and government at Rome. The exchange of clerics between different countries became all the more frequent because the papacy, of its own accord, began to distribute a certain number of benefices in France as well as elsewhere, and bestowed them on strangers. As illustration, it is enough to mention two literary and religious notables of the end of the twelfth century. While John of Salisbury governed the bishopric of Chartres, the Frenchman, Peter of Blois, who all his life in vain sought a benefice in his native land, particularly in Chartres, was chancellor of the archbishopric of Canterbury, and died as archdeacon of London.

This internationalism of the student population surprised no one, and the ruling powers, even at Paris, found no especial trouble with it, at least during the time of Philip Augustus. His father, Louis VII, had had to complain of the foreign students. According to a letter of John of Salisbury, dated 1168, the German students at least verbally manifested the hostility they felt toward France and the king who showed them his hospitality. "They talk magniloquently," he writes, "and swell with menaces (*minis tument*)." He adds that they made fun of Louis VII "because he lived simply among his subjects, because he did not conduct himself like a barbarian tyrant, and was not always seen surrounded by a guard like one who fears for his life (*ut qui timet capiti suo*)." The same author states that the French government about that time expelled foreign students, but he speaks of the incident as entirely exceptional in hospitable France, "the most lovable and most civilized of all nations (*omnium mitissima et civilissima nationum*)."

Nothing like this occurred under the government of the victor of Bouvines. Still, between 1180 and 1223, there began in the principal academic centers that important transformation, thanks to which these groups of masters and students became powerful corporations, capable of fighting successfully against all forces hostile to their development. *Universitas magistrorum et scolarium;* under this title appeared a new organism in ecclesiastical society. An understanding of the origin and the true nature of this "university movement" is desirable.

To begin with, it is evident that the constituent elements of universities existed some time before the formation of the organizations themselves. The "university" was not created solely by the material fact that a corporate union or mutual-aid associations were established by masters and students; the moral bond, the similarity of feeling, of ideas, and of scientific method which unified a great part of the scholarly world, must also be taken into account. Certain it is that the school of Paris became conscious of itself and of its intellectual unity from the day on which a teacher, like Abelard, managed to collect about him the youth of France and of Europe. In this sense the university of Paris existed from the second third of the twelfth century.

From another point of view the great association called " university " was itself only a collection of smaller academic associations. In the bosom of the general corporation there were lesser corporations: those which embraced the masters and scholars devoted to a special field of study, called " faculties," after the middle of the thirteenth century; and those which embraced the masters and scholars having the same native land, the " nations." The general corporation, at least at Paris, appears to have been the resultant of two minor corporations—those of the masters and the scholars. The difficult and obscure question in all this is precisely at what epoch the general corporation and the individual corporations were formed. The profound labors of certain savants have failed to dissipate the obscurities and penetrate the mystery. Father Denifle himself, the incontestable master of this field, could do no more than reach approximations. These academic institutions, like all other medieval institutions, were not created in a day by means of legislative statute, but by a series of consecutive creations and of a gradual process, the traces of which history has not preserved. Certain dated texts reveal for the first time the existence of the faculties, the nations, the universities, but there is nothing to prove that their organization was not earlier by some years than the document which mentions these.

In France, only two academic associations had been named university at the time of Philip Augustus: those of Paris and Montpellier.

As to Paris, it is in an act of 1215, issued by the cardinal, Robert of Courçon, that one encounters the first use of the words *Universitas magistrorum et scolarium;* and it is in a bull of Honorius III of 1221 that the matter of a seal, which the masters and scholars of Paris have " recently " had made for the use of their corporation, is discussed. But many previous acts show us the masters and scholars acting like an organized body. At any rate, the association of teachers appears in an act of Innocent III of 1208-1209, and that of the scholars in an episcopal act of 1207. Unquestionably,

furthermore, the general corporation already had its chief or
director (*capitale*) in 1200, the year in which it received its
first-known privilege from the king of France, for in that
famous charter Philip Augustus very evidently includes the
whole personnel of the great Parisian school, both masters
and students, under the term *scolares*. Likewise, all that one
can say of the origin of the faculties is that they begin to be
mentioned with their chiefs or " managers " after 1219. As
for the " nations," which appear for the first time in 1222,
Father Denifle believes that they were formed after the faculties and later than 1215. The opinion of such an erudite has
great weight; but it is only conjecture. Light fails here; one
must resign himself to darkness.

The actual university of Montpellier, as far as the union
of its faculties goes, was not officially named and organized
until it was done in 1289 by a bull of Nicholas IV. But
the faculty of medicine, at least, was an organized body after
1220, and already called itself " university " in a restricted
sense. The statute of Cardinal Conrad of Porto, which
organized it or sanctioned its organization, is the oldest act
creating a French faculty. In it one can clearly see of what
the original bond between the members of the association
consisted.

To begin with, it was placed under a special jurisdiction, at
least in civil matters; and the special judge was one of the
teachers named by the bishop of Maguelonne. He sat together
with three other professors (among whom was the oldest in
service), but as a court of first instance only. Appeal could
be taken from his decisions to the bishop, who, be it added,
kept entire control of criminal justice. Besides this civil
judge, " who can be called the chancellor of the university,
cancellarius universitatis scolarium," there was room for another high office, that of the oldest professor. He should
enjoy certain privileges of honor: he should have the power
of fixing the time and length of academic vacations. Here
is seen dawning the authority of the head of the faculty,
whom later texts call the " dean."

The corporation of Montpellier, then, had its officials and,
in part, its own jurisdiction. Another article of the statute
of 1220 puts its character as a mutual aid association against

outsiders beyond all doubt: " If a master is attacked directly or through one of his adherents by one who is not of the school, all other masters and scholars, summoned for the purpose, shall bring him counsel and aid." Relations of close fellowship could be expected to arise between members of the teaching staff: " If a professor is in litigation with one of his pupils about his pay, or for any other reason, no other professor shall knowingly accept the student before the latter has given or promised satisfaction to his former master." Professors are forbidden to engage in unfriendly competition: " Let no master attract the disciple of another master by means of solicitation, gift, or any other means whatsoever, for the purpose of winning him away." A final clause, in effect, proves that there was indeed a sort of fraternity: " Masters and students shall punctually attend the funerals of members of the university."

The university was a brotherhood almost entirely composed of clerics; masters and students had the tonsure; collectively, they constituted a church institution. To say that the creation of universities was one of the characteristic signs of the emancipation of the mind in the religious domain, and that the " university movement " had as its principal object the replacing of the clerical schools of chapters and abbeys by corporations imbued with the lay spirit, is a gross error. Universities were ecclesiastical associations and were organized accordingly. The first act emanating from the university of Paris (1221) is a letter addressed to the monks of the order of Saint Dominic, recently established in the city. The members of the university, as brothers of the Dominicans, desired to participate in the benefits of their spiritual works; they sought the favor of being interred in their church or cloister with the same funeral honors as were reserved for members of the congregation. To convince oneself of the religious character of these academic associations, a glance at the seal of the university of Paris is quite enough.[1] It is divided into several sections. In the niche above,

[1] The oldest specimen of this seal we possess dates from 1292 (Arch. nat., K. 964). Cf. Douet d'Arcq, *Invent. des sceaux des Arch. nat.*, No. 8015. Admitting that the original seal was not entirely similar, it must at least have had as religious a character.

which is the largest and the place of honor, appears the
Virgin, Our Lady, patron of universities and of the church
in which the great school of Paris was born.   To the left is
the bishop of Paris, bearing his crozier; to the right, a saint
encompassed by a cloud.   These are important personages.
In the lower frames, which are very small, teachers and scholars appear.   The whole is dominated by the cross.   How could
this fraternity, dedicated to the Virgin and composed of
clerics and monks, signify the lay element and independence
of thought?

Still, it is true that the university was born of an effort
for independence; but, as far as the academic associations
were concerned, the point at issue was escaping from the local
ecclesiastical power, only to submit exclusively to the domination of the central power of Christendom; that is, to the pope.
No more than the great schools of the preceding age did the
universities cease to be ecclesiastical institutions; but they
did cease to be diocesan institutions under the control of the
bishop or his chancellor.   They became an instrument of
power in the hands of Rome, which meant a weakening of the
episcopacy and the strengthening of the Holy See.   It was
the popes who created or developed these university corporations when they wished to take possession of the institutions
of higher instruction.   And it is easy to understand why they
wished to do this.   In the hands of bishops, chapters, chancellors, and doctors, the right of granting permission to teach
was regarded and practised as a source of profit.   In many a
bishopric the high and noble calling of the professorship found
itself subjected to oppressive formalities, restrictions, or even
tyrannical conditions, which paralyzed and perverted its functions.   Venality kept pace with intolerance: the permit to
teach, the "license," was sold; it was granted or refused
without any system, according to the caprice and interests of
a body of canons or a diocesan dignitary.   A reform movement arose; the papacy undertook to carry it through, naturally, for its own profit.   The work was delicate, for, though
favoring the development of the universities, the popes were
bound to treat the bishops with caution and not shake tradition too rudely.   How their diplomacy managed to gain
ground and attain its object is well known.

The history of the origin of French universities is, in this sense, nothing more than a phase of that larger evolution which from the beginning of the middle ages tended to exalt the papal monarchy above local ecclesiastical authorities. It would have been surprising had the supremacy of Rome not sought to establish itself in a domain so important as public instruction. In this field there was something worth conquering, and the conquest was brought about by a close alliance of the papacy with academic organisms. From the standpoint of the higher interests of instruction and knowledge, it was not regrettable.

*

*   *

Beginning with the reign of Philip Augustus, the university of Paris played a considerable rôle in French society and was an institution admired by the whole of Europe. In 1169, a king of England had already spoken of it as a moral power, the opinion and decision of which ought to be law. In his struggle with Archbishop Thomas à Becket, Henry II, the founder of the Plantagenet Empire, declared himself willing to accept the arbitration either of the king's court in France, of the French clergy, or of the " school of Paris." At the time when Philip Augustus succeeded his father, the abbot of Bonne-Espérance, Philip of Harvengt, wrote to felicitate several of his friends on being able to study in Paris, " the city of letters." " Happy city," he adds, " where the students are so numerous that their multitude almost surpasses that of the lay inhabitants."

In a letter which must have been written shortly before 1190, Guy of Basoches, a cleric from Champagne, wrote a dithyrambic eulogy of Paris, the royal city where he lived, of all the most attractive.

" The *Grand pont* is at the center of things; it is surrounded with merchandise, merchants, and boats. The *Petit pont* belongs to the dialecticians (*logicis*) who cross or walk upon it while debating. In the *île* (the *Cité*), alongside the palace of the kings which commands the whole city, stands the hall of philosophy, where study reigns as sole sovereign, a citadel of light and of immortality. That *île* is the eternal home of seven sisters, the liberal arts; it is there also that decrees and laws resound from a trumpet of most noble eloquence; there, finally, bubbles the fountain of religious learning, from which flow the three limpid brooks which water the prairies of intelligence (*prata mentium*), that is theology under her triple form of history, allegory, and morality."

This high-flown testimony of Guy of Basoches is important for its age alone; but also because it shows the place where the schools were located and what three classes of instruction they gave: the arts, canon and civil law, and theology. There is no mention of medical teaching, which, without doubt, was as yet restricted and unnoticed. But from the time of Philip Augustus medicine was taught. The proof of this is found in a panegyric on the university of Paris, which the historian, William of Armorica, included in a passage of his chronicle under the year 1210.

"In that time letters flourished at Paris. Never before in any time or in any part of the world, whether in Athens or in Egypt, had there been such a multitude of students. The reason for this must be sought not only in the admirable beauty of Paris, but also in the special privileges which King Philip and his father before him conferred upon the scholars. In that great city the study of the *trivium* and the *quadrivium*, of canon and civil law, as also of the science which empowers one to preserve the health of the body and cure its ills, were held in high esteem. But the crowd pressed with a special zeal about the chairs where Holy Scripture was taught, or where problems of theology were solved."

Theologians, decretists, "artists," professors, and students formed this multitude of *scolares Parisienses,* who appeared in the first ranks in all solemnities of the reign of Philip Augustus. They were seen, in 1191, taking their place in the grand procession which the Parisian clergy organized to procure from Heaven the healing of Prince Louis, the sole heir to the crown. After the battle of Bouvines, in 1214, they took a prominent part in the popular rejoicings and proved their attachment to the dynasty by feasting and dancing incessantly for seven days and seven nights.

The reputation of the university of Paris was so firmly established that in 1205 the first Latin Emperor of Constantinople, Baldwin of Flanders, prayed the pope to use all his efforts to induce some of the masters of Paris to come and reform the educational conditions of the Empire. Innocent III wrote to the university (*universis magistris et scolaribus Parisiensibus*), to make clear how important it was that this Greek church, which after a long separation had finally been reunited to the Latin Church, should have the benefit of their ardor and knowledge. Putting before them the most alluring prospects, he even invited them to migrate to the Orient *en masse* (*plerosque vestrum*). Greece, let it be known, is a true Paradise, "a land filled with silver, gold, and precious stones, where wine, grain, and oil abound." In spite of these inducements, the doctors of Paris do not appear to have left the *Petit pont* and the *Cité* in great numbers to go and "read" on the Bosphorus. Twelve years later Honorius III again addressed an invitation of the same kind to them; but this time they were to go a shorter distance, to Languedoc, there to sow sound doctrine in a soil moistened by the blood of the Albigenses.

The church was proud of this great school, an immense seminary where France and Europe supplied their needs. Nevertheless, a certain group of ecclesiastics, austere or discontented spirits, did not join in the general enthusiasm. Seeing above all else the dangers of this enormous agglomeration of clerics in one center, they denounced the abuse of knowledge and the perils which faith encountered in the midst of this cosmopolitan youth, burning to know and discuss everything. Between 1192 and 1203, Stephen of Tournai called the pope's attention to "the malady which has little by little slipped into the university body" and which will become incurable if a remedy is not quickly administered.

The first symptom of illness, according to him, is the abandonment of the old theology. Students applaud only those who bring them something new (*solis novitatibus applaudunt*), and the professors aim rather to advertise themselves by this means than to stand by the true tradition. "All their efforts tend to please, to retain, and to mislead their auditors." And the censor rises up against that pitiless dialectic which whets itself upon the dogmas and the most sacred mysteries of religion.

"Babblers of flesh and bone (*verbosa caro*) irreverently discuss spiritual things, the essence of God, the incarnation of the Word!

In the crossways one hears these subtle logicians divide the Invisible Trinity! There are as many errors as there are teachers, as many scandals as there are hearers, as many blasphemies as there are public squares."

This conservative, for the sake of his cause, appreciably overstates things, but the expressions he employs are interesting. Together with other evidence, they prove that the teachers of the time were not lodged in palaces. There were not even always university sites. The masters held their lectures in their own homes, before pupils seated on the ground, or, in the winter, upon straw. As houses were small, those who desired a large audience held their school in the open air, in their own narrow confines, in the crossways, or in the public squares.

Stephen of Tournai is especially indignant over what happens in the teaching of the liberal arts. Some of the masters are entirely too young.

"These well-primped adolescents have the impudence to occupy masters' chairs; they have no down upon their chins, yet behold them in the positions of mature men. They write manuals too, *summas*, poorly digested compilations freshened but not made tasteful by the salt of philosophy."

The conclusion of the complaint is that all these abuses must needs be corrected by the pope. This irregular and disjointed organization should be subjected to fixed rules and to a respect for tradition.

"It is not fitting that things Divine be thus demeaned and made vulgar playthings. It is not meet that almost anybody may be heard shouting at the street corner: 'Here is Christ, He dwells with me!' Let not religion be cast as food unto dogs and as pearls before swine."

Many contemporary preachers were of the same opinion. Alain of Lille compares the university men who engage in incessant refining in logic to "talking frogs." Geoffrey of Troyes treats the grammarians and their scholars as beasts of burden or asses: *jumenta sunt vel asini*. Absalon, abbot of Saint-Victor, openly attacks those who occupy themselves with other things than seeking to understand man and God.

" Our scholars, puffed up with a vain philosophy, are happy when, by force of subtlety, they have come upon some discovery! They do not accept the shape of the globe, the property of the elements, the beginning and the end of the seasons, the force of the wind, the bushes or their roots! Here is the object of their studies: they believe that they will find the reason of things. But the supreme cause, the object and the principle of everything, they only see with blear eyes if at all. O, ye, who would know, begin not with the sky, but with yourselves; see what ye are, what ye should be and what ye shall be. Of what use is it to discuss the ideas of Plato, to read and re-read Scipio's Dream? What good is there in all these inextricable arguments which are the fashion and in that craze for logical subtleties in which many have found their destruction?"

A condemnation of science is here pronounced by the abbot of Saint-Victor; happily, that monk's was a voice in the desert, and the human mind, come what might, pursued its onward march. Many clerics, without being hostile to the part taken by the scientific movement and without wishing to subject all knowledge and instruction to theology, still made some reservations, criticised certain tendencies and certain deeds as contrary to the organization, as well as to the spirit, of the church.

In the study of those liberal arts which were comprised in the *trivium,* the masters and scholars were strongly drawn to profane literature, especially to Latin poetry. They abandoned everything else to read and write Latin verse. They composed songs, tales, odes, comedies, often in a most frivolous vein, a circumstance to be explained by the general coarseness of manners and by the naïve enthusiasm of the clerics, who, in olden days, admired everything indiscriminately. Many were the lettered prelates who made their first public appearance through playful poems, modeled on Ovid or other erotic poets—sins of youth which ripe age expiated by edifying productions. The severest critics, Stephen of Tournai and Peter of Blois, in this respect had none too clean consciences. A brother of Peter of Blois, William, who was a benedictine abbot, wrote a Latin comedy, *Alda,* the conclusion of which would not bear translation. A sort of sensual idolatry of paganism is what the study of the humanities led to in the case of many clerics. As for the *quadrivium,* the sciences properly speaking, since they were less attractive in themselves and brought only a meager return, the mass of students neglected or abandoned them entirely.

The utilitarian spirit was developing among them. To obtain a prebend, a prelacy, it was enough, in a pinch, to have studied the liberal arts. After the *quadrivium,* the student left the school provided with a benefice. Either he surrendered it to study theology or returned to it after a longer or shorter absence, depending upon his inclinations, meantime escaping the burden of a canon's or curé's life. A student who was not content with his elementary course had the choice between the branches of higher instruction—medicine, canon law, civil law, or theology; but, a practical man, he picked the most lucrative. With civil law he might become a judge and administrator in the courts of the lay lords; with canon law he was fitted for the same functions under a church lord. Medicine was already becoming a paying profession. Theology it was which suffered from this new spirit; but those who controlled the clergy and wished to maintain things in their traditional condition could not allow it to be sacrificed. Theology, the science *par excellence,* the final aim of all teaching, must be protected against the utilitarians; and, indeed, every effort was made to fetter this vexatious tendency and preserve to the university of Paris its character as the international center of theological studies. At the beginning of the thirteenth century, Prévostin, a chancellor of Notre-Dame, in a sermon, severely blamed the young clerics who abandoned the Holy Scriptures to devote themselves to civil law. And we shall see the papacy prohibiting the study of that law.

The university of Paris gave an opening to its adversaries in other respects. It is evident that, in a great city like Paris, the presence of so great a number of clerics, assembled from all parts of France and Europe, introduced certain dangers to public order and morality, especially to the morality of churchmen. There were present not only young people who were working for a degree in order to obtain benefices and dignities; the university also attracted a crowd of monks, canons, and curés, who, under the pretext of completing their education with the masters in vogue, were delighted to leave their abbeys, chapters, or parishioners. Popes and councils vainly strove to stem this pressure of clerics toward the " city of letters," to bring them back to the observance of their professional duties. For the defenders of the ancient discipline it was a great scandal.

Many of these cosmopolitan students belonged to the class of poor itinerant clerics, *vagi scolares,* who to earn their bread engaged in any trade whatsoever. Debauchees, frequenters of taverns, and knaves—the " goliards," as they were then called, swelled the number of minstrels, composed Latin verses of a satiric or bacchic vein, or wrote the most licentious stories in French. A certain number of our *fabliaux* are the work of errant clerics, accustomed to live on expedients and alms. They are depicted in the story of the *Povre clerc,* the hero of which, a student without hearth or home, seeks his livelihood at the hand of public charity.

" He had studied at Paris so long that he found it expedient to leave the city because of poverty. There was nothing more to pawn, nothing more to sell. He saw perfectly well that he could stay in the *Cité* no longer: evil had been the days he spent there. As he no longer saw whither to betake himself, it seemed better to abandon his studies. He set out for his native land, for which his heart yearned: but of money he had not a bit, which much distressed him. The day on which he departed he had nothing to eat or drink. In a town upon which he came he entered the home of a peasant and found there only the landlady and a servant: ' Dame,' said he, ' I come from the school; I have journeyed far this day. Be kind to me, and lodge me without more ado.' "

And he was lodged; but, as always, it was the master of the house who bore the costs of this hospitality. Mischievous and roguish, always ready to tease the burghers and seduce the burgesses: that is the scholar-cleric of literature as well as of reality.

A contemporary of Philip Augustus, the Italian teacher, Buoncompagno, writing his as yet unpublished *Antiqua Rhetorica* about 1215, gives a description—somewhat indefinite, to be sure—of the wretched students of Bologna. The life they led must have resembled very closely that of their unfortunate Parisian companions.

" I ought to spend my time in following courses and study-

ing," writes one of these poor devils, "but want compels me
to go begging to the doors of churchmen."

"I am reduced to crying twenty times in succession: 'Charity,
my good seigniors!' and generally to hear the response: 'God be
with you.' I betake myself to the houses of laymen where I am
rudely repulsed, and if perchance some one says to me, 'Wait a moment,' I receive a bit of disgusting bread, which the dogs would not
have. Professional beggars, oftener than I, get the bad vegetables
and the skin and sinews that one cannot eat, the offal that is thrown
away, the damaged wine. At night I course about the city, stick
in one hand and wallet and flask in the other: the stick to protect
me against the dogs, the wallet to collect the leavings of fish, bread,
and vegetables, and the flask for water. Often it happens that I
fall into the mire, that mire of Bologna which smells like a corpse,
and thus all besmirched I return home to satisfy a growling stomach
with the leavings that have been thrown me."

The existence of these wretches, a menace to public security,
presently stirred up the church. Soon began that series of
councils which thundered against these loose-lived clerics,
these goliards, and prohibited them to wear the tonsure; that
is, to claim ecclesiastical privilege. But, beginning with the
reign of Philip Augustus, private charity endeavored to found
institutions of refuge to supply these poor students with food
and shelter. This is the humble origin of the "colleges,"
of those endowed establishments, with which the left bank
of the Seine was little by little to be covered. Having become
centers of instruction, they presently came to constitute the
university itself.

The beginning of these establishments was made in a charitable grant of 1180, in which a burgher of London named
Josce, returning from Jerusalem, bought a hall in the Hôtel-
Dieu of Paris and provided an income which permitted
eighteen clerical scholars to eat and sleep there. In return,
they undertook to watch over the dead of the hospital by turns
and to carry the cross and Holy-water at burials. At a later
date they were to move from the Hôtel-Dieu and to have a
house of their own. Thus was established the oldest of the
Parisian colleges, that of the *Dix-huit*. A pattern had been
given: other colleges would be established, such as that of
Saint-Honoré, founded in 1209 by the widow of Stephen

Bérot for thirteen poor scholars. Even at that time another house of refuge for students, Saint-Thomas du Louvre, was in full operation, for in 1210 its officials requested permission of Innocent III to build a chapel and to have a cemetery of their own.

In the university of Paris there was an element making for immorality and disorder that was difficult to suppress in the lay domestics (*servientes*), attached to the service of students. These, too, in a certain measure, shared the privileges of their masters. This serving class to a large extent consisted of rascals who victimized even the students. The Dominican, Stephen of Bourbon, recalling his youth, part of which he spent as a student at Paris in the later years of Philip Augustus, frankly states that the *garçons* of the scholars "were nearly all thieves." When these servants went to market or to the retailers for their masters, they managed to make "as high as seventy-five and even four hundred per cent." on their purchases.

Under these conditions the frequent appeals of the student to the paternal purse is intelligible. The greater part of students' letters preserved in the formularies of the twelfth and thirteenth centuries have this as their burden. From M. Léopold Delisle I borrow the translation of a missive sent by two students of Orléans to their family in the last years of the twelfth century. One would wager that it came from the Latin Quarter yesterday.

" To our Dear and Revered Parents, Greeting and Filial Obedience. May you be pleased to learn that, thanks to God, we continue in good health in the city of Orléans and that we devote ourselves entirely to study, bearing in mind what Cato has said: ' It is glorious to know something.' We live in a good, stylish house, separated from the schools and market by only a single building, and we can therefore attend our daily courses without wetting our feet. We also have some good friends who are well advanced and thoroughly desirable in every way. We heartily congratulate ourselves upon it, for the Psalmist has said: *cum sancto sanctus eris* ["With the pure thou wilt shew thyself pure "]. But because the lack of equipment hinders the achievement of the aims we have in view, we believed we ought to appeal to your parental love and to ask you to have the goodness to send enough money by the bearer to buy some parchment, ink, and ink-stand and such other things as we need. You will not leave us in embarrassment, and will insist that we finish our studies properly, so as to be able to return to our country with honor. The bearer will also take charge of the shoes and hose which you may have to send us. You can also send us news of yourselves by the same means." [1]

Certain persons did not always distinguish between the good students, the bad ones, and the cosmopolitan crowd of valets which exploited the youth. The preachers of the time of Philip Augustus were not gentle with the Parisian scholars. To be sure, this was especially the case with the chancellors of Notre-Dame, born enemies of the university. Peter Comestor reproaches them with being too fond of wine and good cheer:

"In eating and drinking, there are not their equals; they are *devourers* at table, but not *devout* at mass. At work they yawn; at banquet they stand in awe of no one. They abhor meditation upon the divine books, but they love to see the wine sparkling in their glasses and they gulp it down intrepidly."

In this matter the professors themselves did not always set a good example. Peter of Blois, in one of his letters, sharply lectures a master of arts who, he says, has changed "from a dialectician of the highest power to an accomplished drinker (*egregium potatorem*)," and, heaping up quotations of the Holy Scriptures, he attempts to turn him from his insobriety. Peter of Poitiers, another chancellor, insists especially on the depravity of manners:

"What a shame! Our scholars live in baseness which not one of them would even dare to mention in his home among his relatives. They waste the riches of the Crucified with courtesans. Their conduct, aside from shaming the church, is an ignominy to the masters and students, a scandal to the laity, a dishonor to the nation, and an injury to the Creator Himself."

Chancellor Prévostin of Cremona is more specific in his complaints. He described the scholars, completely armed, coursing about the streets of Paris at night, breaking in the

---

[1] L. Delisle, *Annuaire-bulletin de la Société de l'histoire de France* (1869), Vol. 7, p. 149. Cf. the numerous examples of requests for money given by Haskins, *The life of mediæval students as illustrated by their letters*, in *The American Historical Review*, Vol. III, 1898, No. 2.

doors of the bourgeoisie, and filling the courts with the bruit of their escapades. " Every day public women (*meretriculae*) come to depose against them, complaining of having been beaten, of having had their garments cut into shreds, or their hair cut off."

A turbulent and combative spirit, indeed! but such was the university. One preacher compares the professors, in their scholastic quarrels, to cocks, ever ready to fight. The students imitated their masters, save that they quickly came to blows. From an unpublished sermon, Hauréau[1] has extracted the following utterance of Philip Augustus when the fighting scholars were mentioned in his presence: " They are hardier than knights," said the king; " knights, covered with their armor, hesitate to engage in battle. These clerics, who have neither hauberk nor helmet but a tonsured head, playfully fall upon one another with daggers: decidedly foolish of them, and very dangerous."

*

*   *

The external history of the university of Paris, to all effects, begins with a battle. In 1192, the scholars fell into a quarrel with some peasants attached to the abbey of Saint-Germain-des-Prés. These occupied the vaguely defined district which stretched away to the south and west of the monastery—either the Petit Pré-aux-Clercs, now bounded by the Rues Jacob, Bonaparte, Seine, and Beaux-Arts, or more likely the Grand Pré-aux-Clercs, which began at the Rue Saint-Benoît. This large property to which the scholars went for their diversion was the source of interminable wrangling between the abbey and the university. In the fray of 1192, a student was killed. The murder of a cleric by laymen, to say nothing of their being serfs, could not go unpunished. The students entered a complaint at Rome. The abbot of Saint-Germain-des-Prés, seriously compromised, had to prove his innocence before the archbishop of Reims and the assembled university and destroy the cottages of the murderers, who had taken flight. This reparation perfectly satisfied the court of Rome. Stephen of Tournai had some difficulty in

[1] *Notices et extraits des manuscrits de la Bibl. nationale*, VI, p. 250.

proving to Cardinal Octavian, the pope's legate, that the abbot was not implicated.

This pope was Celestine III, author of the first grant possessed by the university of Paris. By a bull addressed to the bishop of Paris some time between 1191 and 1198, he provided that all clerics living in the great city should have the right of bringing their civil cases before the jurisdiction of the church. He reminds him that the clergy has its special judges and cannot be subject to ordinary legislation. The word *scolares* does not appear in the bull; it concerns only clerics. But the reason for, and the importance of, the pontifical concession are evidently to be sought in the enormous number of clerics whom the schools of Paris attracted.

In 1200, there was a second milestone in the history of the university in the form of another battle. This time it was a rupture between the students and the citizens of Paris, supported by the provost of the king; that is, by the police.

At the time there was among the students a cleric from a powerful German family who had been proposed for the bishopric of Liège. His servant, having gone to a tavern to purchase some wine, fell into a quarrel with the tradesman, was struck, and his jug was broken. Furious, the German students took the part of their compatriot. They invaded the shop and left its keeper half-dead. Great was the excitement among the Parisians; it was without doubt not the first time they had had a grievance against the scholars. Thomas, provost of Philip Augustus, followed by armed citizens, entered the quarters of the German clerics to arrest the culprits. These resisted; the police, as often happens, had a heavy hand, and five university men, of whom several were clerics, were killed. Immediately masters and students lodged a complaint with the king: they would suspend their lectures and would quit Paris unless the murderers were punished.

A professors' strike; a suspension of lectures! even to-day this would mean serious inconvenience. At the time of Philip Augustus it was considered a public calamity; indeed, almost an offense against religion. The importance of the university of Paris for the recruitment of the clergy was such that a suspension of instruction meant a brusque check of the ecclesiastical life of Europe. The king of France did everything that was required of him. The provost of Paris was thrown into prison together with all his accomplices who could be found. Some of the murderers having fled, Philip had their houses demolished and their vines grubbed up. Some time later the scholars prayed the king to set at liberty the provost and the others condemned to life imprisonment on the condition that the guilty persons be delivered to them. They were to be scourged in one of the schools, after which they would be considered free from all blame for their crime. But Philip Augustus refused, saying that it was matter of honor with him not to have king's men chastised by others than the king. The provost remained in the royal prison for a long time. Finally he attempted to escape over the wall by means of a rope, but the cord broke and he fell from such a height as to be killed.

An important object of the collegians was to secure from the lay authorities the recognition of their position as privileged clerics, subject only to the tribunals of their order and hence no longer subject to the jurisdiction of the king's police. The celebrated charter which Philip Augustus granted in 1200 completely satisfied them. The provost of Paris could lay his hands on a scholar only in case of a flagrant offense; and then he must arrest him without maltreatment, at least if the culprit offered no resistance. And he could arrest him only to turn him over immediately to ecclesiastical justice. If the judges were not accessible at the time of the arrest, the delinquent was to be kept at the house of some fellow-student until he could be surrendered. The chief or director of the university (*capitale Parisiensium scolarium*) could not be arrested on any pretext whatever by the king's agents: the judges of the church alone had the right to put him under arrest. Even the servants or the lay domestics of the scholars had their privileges! The king's men could lay hands on them only in case of an evident offense. But it was also desirable that the students be protected against the ill-will of the citizens of Paris. These should take an oath that, if they encountered a scholar mistreated by a layman, they would not hesitate to testify to that effect before the judges. If a scholar were attacked with weapons, clubs, or stones, the laics who were witnesses of the occurrence were expected to seize the assailant and deliver him to the royal police. And, finally, the provost in office and the citizens of Paris should in the presence of the university swear to observe the clauses of this act in good faith. Thereafter each provost, upon assuming office, should take the same oath.

This is the famous ordinance not improperly regarded as the charter establishing the liberties of the university. It was a considerable grant, since it withdrew the university from civil jurisdiction, declared it unassailable and inviolable by the king's agents, and subjected it to those church judges so indulgent to the clergy. It assured the independence, and consequently the prosperity, of the great international corporation for centuries; but, in guaranteeing the scholars almost complete impunity, it had as a natural consequence the innumerable students' frays of later times. However, the charter of Philip Augustus was not, as has sometimes been averred, a decree constituting the university; it contained no provision for such an organization. In it the university appears as a body already formed and even provided with a head, the *capitale*. Who is this head? Is he of the faculty of arts, the "rector," who toward the end of the thirteenth century became the representative of the whole university? There is no good reason for saying so. Let us agree, then, that, in making the masters and scholars exclusively subject to ecclesiastical tribunals, Philip Augustus was introducing no innovations. He simply sanctioned the measures taken some years previously by Pope Celestine III, the identification of all students with the clergy.

Were all students clerics? The question was considered in 1208 when Innocent III's legate, Cardinal Gualo, imposed a reform measure on the clergy of the diocese of Paris, aimed to correct their conduct. The severest penalties were fixed for clerics who did not have the tonsure and garb of their order, who sold the sacraments, went into business, or lived with women. Should one be equally rigorous with the masters and students of the university? The cardinal believed it would be difficult, for he felt himself obliged to close his decree with a paragraph intended solely for the academic group. Delinquent scholars should not, like other clerics, be liable to immediate excommunication. The professors should first warn them collectively, and threaten them with anathema. If they persisted in their fault, the university should in full assembly pronounce a new summons, this time naming each individually. In the event of a prolonged resistance, they should be denounced before the chancellor of Notre-Dame as excommunicates, and regarded as such until they had given satisfaction to the bishop or, in his absence, to the abbot of Saint-Victor.

It was the papacy which subjected the scholars to these disciplinary rules: it was acting as sovereign with this, a privileged corporation. In 1207, Innocent III, finding the number of teachers of theology too large, had on his own authority reduced it to eight. Two years later he authorized the university to reform itself. Certain young doctors of arts had freely violated the accepted usages. They were reproached with having an improper deportment, with violating the traditional procedure in lectures and discussions, and with entirely neglecting the obligatory attendance at the obsequies of their confrères. The corporation had elected eight deputies to draw up a rule applicable to all masters. A single one of these refused to submit and to take the oath. He was expelled from the corps of professors. After a time he submitted to making honorable amends, and asked for his rehabilitation. But a bull of Innocent III (1208-1209) was necessary to permit him to reënter the university faculty.

From this intervention of the papacy in the petty affairs of university life one can imagine the rôle it assumed in important matters. Rome was the constant protectress, to whom masters and students appealed at once when the moral or material interests of the corporation were imperiled.

In 1210, the university of Paris experienced a grave crisis. What mistrustful spirits and the adversaries of scientific progress had foreseen came to pass: heresy once again crept into the instruction given under the shadow of the cloister of Notre-Dame. A master of arts and theologian, Amauri of Bène, or of Chartres, openly taught that every Christian was a member of Christ, and therefore a part of divinity, and he pushed his pantheism to its extreme consequences. The other theologians, faithful to orthodoxy, were aroused. Amauri,

attacked and condemned by all his colleagues, was compelled
to make an explanation before the pope, with whom the university had registered a complaint. Innocent, after having
heard a statement of his doctrines and the opposing opinions
upheld by the delegates of the university, in his turn dis-
approved of the heretic. The latter returned to Paris and
was there compelled to abjure his theories before the whole
university constituency. Sick with chagrin and humiliation,
he died shortly afterwards, to all appearances reconciled
with the church. His opinions lived after him.

The pantheism of Amauri, propagated and even extended
by his disciples, gave birth to a new cult, that of the Holy
Spirit: the Old Testament had been supplanted by the New;
but the latter, too, had performed its service, and the reign
of the Spirit was now to begin. Each Christian being an
incarnation of Holy Spirit, a particle of God, sacraments became useless; the grace of the Spirit was enough to save
all the world. This doctrine, issuing from theological teaching, born in the university, had university men as its apostles
and martyrs. A skilful manœuver of the bishop of Paris
and of friar Guérin, chancellor of Philip Augustus, discovered the sectarians. Nearly all of them were teachers or
students of theology, deacons or priests. One of them, David
of Dinant, who had published a manual of doctrine, fled
betimes. A considerable number of others was arrested and
arraigned before the council of Paris under the presidency
of Peter of Corbeil, archbishop of Sens.

The text of the decision rendered by the council in 1210 still
exists. It was decreed that the body of Amauri, father of
the heresy, should be exhumed and cast outside of the cemetery, and his memory excommunicated in every parish of
the province. Some of the arrested sectarians were degraded
and delivered to the secular power; some ten of them suffered death by fire in the meadow of Champeaux on the
twentieth of December; the rest were condemned to perpetual
imprisonment. Only women and persons of low estate, simple
souls whose only fault lay in having yielded to the theologians, were spared. The chastisement extended to books. The
manuscripts of David of Dinant were publicly burned. Even
Aristotle suffered from the incident. His natural philosophy

and Averroës' commentary upon it were forbidden to be studied in the university, under pain of excommunication. Finally, the council declared all to be heretics in whose homes were found French translations of the *Credo* and the *Pater noster*.

This episode was something of a disaster and a rude warning to the incipient university. In the middle ages the liberty of the professoriate, so highly extolled by the popes, did not give the liberty of teaching anything whatsoever; it halted at the bounds of orthodoxy. Schools could be opened and things sacred could be discussed with a large freedom; but dogma must never be publicly treated! Intolerance in this case did not come alone from above, from ecclesiastical authority; the professors themselves avoided a colleague who was too bold, and constrained him to abandon his opinions. They denounced him, not to the bishop of Paris or his chancellor—they were too fearful of having the episcopate, the local power, meddle in their affairs,—but directly to the pope, whose sovereign judgment they invoked in matters of doctrine.

It was the pope, therefore, to whom they addressed themselves in 1212, when there occurred the first recorded incident of that long and ardent struggle, which in the thirteenth century brought the university to blows with its immediate chief, the chancellor of Notre-Dame.

This functionary was one of the chief dignitaries of the chapter, usually a theologian of renown, a writer or an esteemed preacher. His importance proceeded from his double office: on the one hand, he wrote, sealed, and despatched the correspondence of the church at Paris; on the other, he represented the bishop as superintendent of instruction in the episcopal jurisdiction, supervised the schools, and conferred the license to teach. When the university was organized, the chancellor quite naturally found himself at its head; he continued to exercise the disciplinary and judicial powers, which he had over all schools of the diocese, over the corporation of masters and students as well.

This fact alone is enough to explain the inevitable conflict. The university, like all powerful communities aspiring to govern itself, could not get along with a master having independent authority. Outside of the corporation, and not chosen by it, he nevertheless by virtue of his position undertook to direct it, control its acts, and to intervene from day to day in its private affairs. To-day state interests and necessities are grasped by all. Not so the university men of the middle ages; they understood only privilege, and were concerned solely for the interests and extension of their organization. Their manners were violent. Besides, they felt themselves backed by the head of the universal church. Everything combined to put them into a state of perpetual conspiracy against the chancellor.

In 1211, the chancellorship was held by Jean des Chandelles, the successor of the theologian, Prévostin of Cremona, but of decidedly less reputation. According to masters and students, this dignitary did them every possible wrong. He exacted an oath of fidelity and obedience from candidates for professorships; sometimes he even made them pay for the permission to begin a course. If some schoolman committed an offense, he began by imprisoning him, even when there was no reason for believing that the culprit intended to flee judgment, and when taking bail would have been adequate. As a condition of liberating these fellows, the chancellor exacted a sum which he turned to his own uses, so that he appeared to be actuated less by a love of justice than by a desire to have a good income.

Such was the complaint upon which Innocent III seized. "In my day," cried he, "when I studied at Paris, I never saw scholars treated in that fashion." He immediately ordered the chancellor to improve his conduct, and charged the head of a neighboring diocese, the bishop of Troyes, and not the bishop of Paris, with the task of inflicting ecclesiastical censure, with no heed to an appeal, upon the chancellor if he failed to put an end to his misconduct. It was not necessary to use extreme measures against Jean des Chandelles. He agreed to arbitrate, and accepted the decision of the arbiters given in August, 1213. Victory remained with the masters and the students. Never again could the chancellor exact oath or money from candidates for the license. He was forbidden to incarcerate clerics, save in cases of evident necessity. In no trial of a schoolman, where he was the judge, could he levy a fine: he could only condemn the offender to indemnify the injured party. All this was to be an absolute rule for the future; but the sentence contained temporary clauses relative to the particular chancellor in office. The granting of the license should no longer depend on his good will. He could still give the license to whom he wished, but he might not refuse it to candidates whom the majority of the professors of theology, law, and medicine had approved as fit to teach. As for the " artists," a commission of six professors, nominated by the chancellor and the faculty, and renewable each six months, was to be the sole judge of their fitness. If the chancellor took no account of this nomination of professors, the person designated was to be invested with the license by the bishop of Paris *ex officio*. The same bishop was also to decide finally whether the chancellor might or might not incarcerate delinquent scholars.

Here for the first time the right of the bishop of Paris to intervene in the organization of the university is expressly mentioned. The bishop, Peter of Nemours, sanctioned this arbitral sentence; the first battle had been lost by the chancellor. But, at bottom, the episcopal power was struck by the same blow. This the bishop well understood, and that is why in the same act in which he registered and confirmed the decision of the arbiters he took care to add this proviso: " saving in all things our jurisdiction and the authority of the church of Paris." A formula of this character in a society adhering most rigidly to legal forms permitted the revocation of the concession, if necessary. The authority of the church of Paris was singularly easy to confound with that of the chancellor of the church of Paris.

However, the last word said in this business was not the charter of Peter of Nemours. The pope had taken notice of the complaint of the university; the pope, or his agent, must close the incident. In November, 1213, Hervé, bishop of Troyes and representative of Innocent, in a letter of ratification assembled all the preceding documents: that is, the bull of the pope, the episcopal charter containing the sentence of arbitration, and the confirmation of the chancellor. This was the end of the affair. It demonstrates very forcefully that Rome was in everything, especially in university affairs, the beginning and the end, *principium et finis.*

* *

At Paris, as at Montpellier, the first statute of organization of the university was the work of a cardinal-legate, the representative of the Holy See. Cardinal Robert of Courçon had already in 1213, as president of the provincial synod of Paris, attempted a partial reform when he forbade the curés to learn the profane sciences in the schools. If with the consent of their bishop they went to Paris, they could only study theology. The prohibition was especially emphatic for monks. Too many monks sought to leave their monasteries to hear university courses in medicine and civil law, two subjects which, they said, made it possible to minister the better to their sick brethren and to work the more usefully in the temporal affairs of their congregations. But the authorities could not let this influx of the clergy into the schools go on indefinitely, and let the church fall into disorder, merely to give clerics the leisure to be students at Paris. The council declared monks excommunicated if they did not return to their cloisters within two months.

This was only a prelude to a more general rule which, by the authority of the head of the Roman church, became a law of the university in August, 1215. This new rule was not a systematic and complete constitution, an organic decree designed to settle all questions which the material, moral, and intellectual affairs of the school might raise, but a series of articles run together without any unity and, as it were, by accident. Nothing could be more disconnected or fundamentally more incomplete. The legate simply repeated those points which experience had settled by some decision or reform. Above everything else, he concerned himself with the recruiting of professors, the conditions under which the professors worked, and with the confirmation of the essential privileges of the body. But, such as it was, the act of Robert of Courçon is notable for the light which it sheds on the habits of the university and on the abuses which were already practised in it.

An age qualification was fixed for teachers of theology as

well as for teachers of the liberal arts. The doctor of theology must be at least thirty-five years old, have had at least ten years of general studies and five years of theological training. He should not receive a license unless he led a good life, had good manners, and had proven his capacity. To be a master of arts, one must be at least twenty-one years old, have been a student for at least six years, and must possess a license under the conditions fixed by the arbitral sentence of 1213. On the other hand, one was not allowed to open a course for the simple pleasure of giving a few lectures and then moving on: the teacher had to promise to teach for at least two years.

The solemn assemblies of professors and the granting of licenses to students gave the occasion for great, prolonged, and costly banquets. The university brotherhood, like all brotherhoods of the middle ages, loved to feast. The cardinal formally forbade these orgies: *nulla fiant convivia;* he permitted only the invitation of a few friends or comrades. He was not wrong, if one considers the number of letters found in the formularies showing the deep inroad upon the purses of their fathers made by students in paying the expenses connected with attaining the mastership. The professor, Buoncompagno gives the form of a letter written from Bologna to a father to tell him of the success of his son. It begins in a lyrical strain, citing Psalms:

" ' Sing unto the Lord a new song '; for your son has successfully undergone his solemn test in the presence of an immense assemblage of professors and students. He replied without mistake to all the questions asked him, he shut up the mouths of all disputants: no one could bring him to the wall. Besides, he gave a banquet which will long be remembered; both poor and rich were invited; it was a feast without precedent. Finally, he has begun his course in such a way as to empty the schools of the others, attracting around his chair the mass of the students."

Another letter, the counterpart of the preceding one, concerns the unfortunate candidate who lacked money:

" The people invited to his banquet were so poorly fed that they did not even desire to drink. He opened his course with novices and hired listeners."

The prohibition of feasts by Robert of Courçon seems to show that things at Paris were much as at Bologna, and that among the university's traditions the sumptuous feast of the licentiate was highly prized.

If the cardinal suppressed the banquets, he still permitted the distributions of clothes and other things which accompanied the licensing. " These might be increased," he said, " so that the poor especially could benefit by them." He required the student who had become a master of arts to have a decent appearance, in keeping with his ecclesiastical position: he should wear a round cope of dark material, reaching to his heels. He should fulfil another requirement of decency, one which, it appears, university men did not often observe: attend the funeral services of members of the university. Upon the death of a scholar, half of the professors of the faculty to which he belonged were to follow the train; at the next death, it was the turn of the other half. The legislator who established this rotation took care to specify that those attending should not leave before the end of the service. At the death of a professor, all his colleagues must attend the vigil, which took place in the church " until midnight or even later." On the day of the burial all courses should be suspended.

Two articles of the constitution of 1215 determined the status of the students. " Every student," said the cardinal, " must have a master to whom he attaches himself." This was directed against the innumerable quasi-students who did not attend any course of lectures. Further, " every master must have jurisdiction over his scholar (*forum sui scolaris habeat*)," an indication of the close bond then existing between the teacher and his students. He was their director, and their judge; he was responsible for their conduct, and had, therefore, the right of correction. He was both master and magistrate.

This rule, emanating from Rome, naturally contained a clause designed to protect the university against the chancellor of Notre-Dame and the church of Paris. No one should be permitted to teach who had given money to the chancellor or to any other dignitary, who had sworn an oath of fealty, or who had surrendered his liberty in any way whatever.

Masters and scholars were guaranteed the right to form associations among themselves or with others; to form sworn leagues (*constitutiones fide, vel pena, vel juramento vallatas*) under clearly specified circumstances: if a university man had been killed, wounded, or had sustained grave injury; if justice had been denied him, if a mutual burial association was contemplated, if it was imperative to impose lodging prices on the citizens of Paris, etc. This last matter was a subject of frequent disagreement. The Paris householders took advantage of the difficulty the students had in finding lodgings to raise the price above all reason; and, under all circumstances, showed but little consideration for their tenants. "I rented a commodious apartment," wrote John of Salisbury, "but, before occupying it, I had to pay about twelve livres [fifteen hundred francs in cash]; I was not allowed to establish myself in it without paying a whole year's rent."

In short, Robert of Courçon formally recognizes the right of organization within the university. The papacy gave it a means of fighting, of defense, and of attack. It was destined to be used against the police and the citizens, but especially against the church of Paris and its chancellor. Barely four years passed after the reform when the latent conflict between the bishop and the university suddenly became active.

In 1219, Peter of Nemours, bishop of Paris, and Philip of Grève, his chancellor, excommunicated all university men, who had, or who should, league themselves together by oath without episcopal permission. Any one who had seen armed scholars running about the streets at night and had not informed the officials or the chancellor was also to be excommunicated. Fundamentally, it was part of the conflict between the bishopric and the Holy See, for the bishop attacked the university because it made use of the right of confederation which a legate of the pope had granted it. Peter of Nemours did not recognize the legality of this concession; on this point he was in direct opposition to Rome. And he so fully realized the gravity of the deed that he depended on a precedent authorized by another legate to legitimatize his step. He and Philip of Grève pretended that they were simply renewing an ex-

communication laid by Eudes of Sully, former bishop
of Paris, upon the masters and students with the approbation of Cardinal Octavian, the legate of Innocent III. But
no one has ever seen the text of this first sentence of
anathema, and Peter of Nemours, if required to produce it,
would have been unable to do so. The documents of the
time of Eudes of Sully say nothing of it. Is it not, besides,
very unlikely that a legate of the pope would have sanctioned this blow struck at the university, the protégé of
Rome?

In his bull of March, 1219, Pope Honorius III seems to
accuse the bishop of Paris of having invented the undis-
coverable decree of Eudes of Sully. At any rate, he ordered
the archbishop of Rouen to annul the recent anathema, and
threatened any one who should dare to lay anathema on the
university, *without having been authorized to do so by the
Roman Church,* with all the wrath of the Holy See. The
rights of the pope and the rights of the bishop were here
clearly at variance. Who would carry the day? The bishop
refused to yield. It became necessary for Honorius to order
another representative of the Roman power, Hervé, bishop
of Troyes, to force Peter of Nemours to obey (May 11, 1219).
Thanks to this second bull, we know certain details of the
process.

After having vainly asked the bishop of Paris to produce
the sentence of Eudes of Sully, the university men went to
the heart of the matter. " What is understood by this
offense of *coalition* with which you reproach us? Does it
mean a permissible organization for a praiseworthy and legitimate end, or an unjust or illegal coalition? " " It means,"
replied the adherents of the bishop, " any kind of a coalition, legitimate or illegitimate." " Then it is an attempt
on our rights, and we appeal to the pope." The university
decided that it would plead its case at Rome. But representation at Rome was expensive, and the professors and
scholars had as yet no common funds for this purpose. They
provided for it by a subscription (*collecta*). The masters
and the clerics swore to subscribe the sum fixed by their
advocates. The money having been collected, the representatives set out. Then the chancellor declared all the teachers

and all the students who had combined or paid the subscription, excommunicated. They were no longer admitted
even to confession.

There was great commotion among the scholars; one cannot
imagine what such a prohibition meant in the middle ages.
The university begged the bishop to recall this rigorous sentence. The canons of Notre-Dame and Guérin, the minister
of Philip Augustus, added their importunities to those of
the academic body. The bishop and his chancellor remained
inflexible: they suspended some of the professors and imprisoned some of the students; and, finally, the university
answered by a general suspension of all of the courses. '' The
voice of science was silent at Paris,'' wrote Honorius III.
It is a shame (these are his own words) '' that an officer
of the bishop harms the great school of Paris and stops the
flow of the great river of knowledge which, through its many
branches, waters and nourishes the land of the universal
church.'' The decree of excommunication was again cancelled; the chancellor '' and accomplices '' were commanded
to come and justify themselves at Rome, whither the pope
also summoned the representatives of the university.

What was the outcome of this conflict of 1219? The documents do not inform us. Only a few of the records of the
process have come down to us: namely, those emanating from
the Holy See or from its delegates. Neither the justification
of the bishop of Paris nor the motives which had led him on
are ascertainable. It was, no doubt, as always, the daily or
nightly misdeeds which the students, sheltered behind their
privileges, were forever committing, and the intolerable situation into which these privileges forced the church by compelling her to close her eyes to innumerable scandals and
to let many a guilty man go unpunished. This much is clear,
that in November, 1219, Philip of Grève, the chancellor, presented himself at Rome before the apostolic tribunal, to find
that the university, his accuser, had sent no representative.
Perhaps that body itself did not have a clear conscience;
perhaps it was sufficient to have secured an annulment of
the sentence. The plaintiff defaulting, the chancellor returned to Paris and resumed his office.

It was in the last days of this year of troubles and during

the following year that the mendicant friars of the newly
founded order of Saint Dominic were being introduced into
Paris and into the quarter of the schools,—an event of great
importance in university history.

This new monastic creation furnished the papacy, on which
it entirely depended, a thoroughly devoted army. Between
the Dominicans and a university, both directed and protected by the same power, sympathy could all the more readily be established, because they had a community of interests.
If the university, forever at war with the bishop of Paris
and with the Parisian clergy, was constantly menaced with
deprivation of the sacraments and of the religious offices,
the order of the Dominicans also from the beginning found
itself at variance with the officially constituted clergy. These
mendicants had not only the right, but also the duty, to
influence Christian souls by preaching. Many of them were
priests, who had obtained from the pope the permission to
hear the confessions of the faithful and to exercise the same
functions as the curés. This new clergy, compelled by its
rule to be without possessions and to live by begging—more
exemplary and more virtuous because, without being in the
cloister, they practised its austerities,—proved to be a strong
competitor to the priests of the parishes and chapters. The
secular clergy could not patiently witness these aggressive
monks establish themselves in the villages, and dispute the
cure of souls with those who until then had had a monopoly
of this function. On the contrary, one can imagine with
what joy the university received the new comrades. Preaching friars! it meant a full-fledged university clergy.

The first Dominicans of Paris had originally been established in a little house near the Hôtel-Dieu. In 1218, at the
demand of Pope Honorius, the university gave them quarters
and a chapel. Increased and enlarged, these quarters became
the convent of the Jacobins, situated opposite the church of
Saint-Étienne-des-Grès on the ground to-day between the
Rues Cujas and Soufflot. These preachers, installed in a
building of the university, in December, 1219, obtained the
right to celebrate divine services in it, and the pope sent
the masters and scholars a bull of congratulation. But the
priests of the parish of Saint-Benoît complained to their

superiors, the canons of Notre-Dame, of the competition of the mendicant friars, and objected to having a mass read in the chapel of Saint-Jacques. Irritated by this resistance, Honorius ordered the priors of Saint-Denis and of Saint-Germain-des-Prés to take the necessary steps to suppress it. The victory remained with the Dominicans, who were very popular on the left bank of the Seine. The first charter of the university as a body had for its object, as we have said, the alliance of the scholars and the mendicants into one religious body (1221). Many of these monks studied theology, awaiting the time, which was not long in coming, to elevate themselves into the ranks of the professors and to occupy masters' chairs. Many of the university men, on the other hand, ceased to live as secular clergy and took the dress and the rule of Saint Dominic. The two bodies soon amalgamated so well that at the time of the death of Philip Augustus, the general of the order, Master Jourdain, in a letter expressed the hope that all the scholars at Paris would finally become Jacobins.

The introduction of the order of Saint Dominic into the great scholastic center was another success for the papacy and another blow aimed at the power of the church of Paris. The passions of the adherents and the opponents of this church only became the more violent; almost immediately a new conflict broke out.

In 1220, Honorius III had transferred William of Seignelay, bishop of Auxerre, to the bishopric of Paris against the wishes of Philip Augustus, who favored another candidate. William was a combative man, who in his first position had already sustained a violent struggle against the feudal barons and against the king. At Paris he continued in the same course; he had three or four quarrels with Philip Augustus. To a bishop of this temper the university problem was simple: declare war against the teachers and scholars, and unreservedly support the claims of the chancellor. Evidently Bishop William of Seignelay and Chancellor Philip of Grève were in perfect accord.

The historian, William of Armorica, asserts that the bishop made himself obnoxious to the king and to the entire university:

"He conducted himself with such rudeness, that all the doctors of theology and those of the other faculties stopped their courses for six months, which made him detested by the clergy, by the people, and by the nobility."

But the annalist of the church of Auxerre strongly supports William of Seignelay:

"There were among the Parisian scholars real bandits, who at night ran armed about the streets, and committed adultery, rape, murder, robbery, and the most heinous crimes without being punished. Not only was the university no longer secure, but the citizens themselves did not live in peace by day or by night. The bishop knew how to rid the city of these brigands. The worst were imprisoned for life, the others hunted from Paris, and order was restored."

Given these two contradictory opinions, what was the truth? The bishop of Paris represented a very respectable cause, that of good conduct. The privileges granted by Philip Augustus to the scholars were too great; but William of Seignelay had still other grievances. In a complaint sent to Pope Honorius III in April, 1221, he accused the masters and the scholars of having formed a permanent conspiracy against his authority and that of the chancellor:

"They have made a seal and dispense with that of the chancellery. They arbitrarily fix the scale of rents, in spite of the ordinance on this subject issued by the king and accepted by the university. They have set up a tribunal of their own before which they carry all their law-suits, as though the jurisdiction of the bishop and of the chancellor did not exist. In brief, they encroach in every way on the episcopal power, and enfeeble it to such a degree that, unless good order is restored, the greatest scandals may arise and the school of Paris may be dissolved."

These accusations of the bishop are specific; they show the tenacity with which the masters and the scholars tried to shake off the yoke of the local ecclesiastical powers and to make a veritable sovereignty of their corporation.

Honorius III must have given the complaints of William of Seignelay perfunctory consideration, at least. He ordered the archbishop of Canterbury, the bishops of Troyes and of Lisieux to make an inquiry and to try to reconcile the parties.

This was such a difficult task that in May, 1222, the pope himself, while awaiting the end of the process which was unraveling itself at Rome, was obliged to impose a *modus vivendi* on the belligerents. But this act was equal to a new victory for the university. He annulled the excommunication of the masters and the scholars and forbade the bishop to incarcerate or disturb the suspected university students with a demand for satisfaction. They were to be allowed to give bail: this is the *habeas corpus* act of the school of Paris. The bishop, the judge, and the chancellor were forbidden to exact an oath of obedience or of fealty of any kind whatever from the licentiates. The prison erected by the chancellor was to be demolished. Neither the bishop nor his officers were to inflict any pecuniary punishment on the teachers or the pupils, under pain of excommunication. The chancellor was to give the master's degree in any of the faculties only to candidates whose fitness had been attested by their own professor and by a jury of professors elected for the purpose. Finally, the bishop and his officers were not to prevent the masters admitted to the licentiate by the abbot of Sainte-Geneviève from beginning their teaching.

This last prohibition reveals an important fact in the development of the university corporation. A great part of the teachers who had formerly dwelt in the *Cité*, round about Notre-Dame, had crossed the *Petit pont* and had established themselves on the north slope of Mont Sainte-Geneviève. They were being smothered on the island, and they especially wanted to rid themselves of the episcopal power which persecuted them. The masters of arts, especially, installed themselves in large numbers in the Rues du Fouarre, de la Bûcherie, and de la Huchette, centers from which they spread over the whole left bank. But the abbot of Sainte-Geneviève, the seignior of this territory, had, like the chapter of Notre-Dame, his academic authority and the right to create licentiates. The university asked him to compete with the chancellor in the conferring of degrees. The exodus of the scholars from the *Cité* and the licenses of Sainte-Geneviève were the two decisive and effective steps toward independence taken by the university against its adversaries.

William of Seignelay died at the end of the year 1223,

but the conflict continued. Philip Augustus himself died before the parties had made peace. But by that time the university had attained its ends. We have seen its constituent elements gradually evolve and we have been able to note the principal steps in its formation. By the royal privilege of 1200, the master and the student escaped from the jurisdiction of the police and of the lay sovereign. By the compromises of 1213 and of 1222 and by the decree of 1215 they began to limit the power of the chancellor, and were victorious in various contests. In all the acts of internal regulation which they accepted after 1192, they were made, or voluntarily made themselves, dependent on the pope, and freed themselves more and more from the local authority. All this decisive and rapid progress occurred during the reign of Philip Augustus. But he had little to do with it, for, with the exception of the single act of 1200, everything transpired without his participation.

The pope had full power over the professors and scholars, administrative and legislative power—power of direction, of control, and of correction; absolute power over the mind and over the body, over subjects to be taught as well as over the personnel teaching them. The most extraordinary proof of this unlimited authority is the famous bull of 1219, *Super speculam,* by which Honorius III expressly forbade any course in civil law to be opened or attended in Paris or in the neighborhood of Paris, under pain of excommunication.

Now what did the papacy want? To stop the scientific movement, to substitute canon for Roman law, to announce the inferiority of secular legislation, to prevent the civil powers from organizing, and so find a successful way of securing the dominance of church over state? This thesis has been maintained with heat by scholars of the highest rank, but it does not seem to agree with the facts or even with the language of the texts. It gratuitously attributes to the Roman Church profound designs and a Machiavellian plan to destroy the civil law, something that was certainly far from its mind. Neither Honorius III nor his successor, Innocent IV, who renewed the bull *Super speculam,* was deliberately hostile to Roman law. They prohibited it for Paris only: they allowed the study of the subject in other

French universities created after the death of Philip Augustus. They had, in truth, a double purpose: first, to fortify the study of theology by giving the university of Paris a sort of monopoly of this branch of higher learning, by making this university the school of theology *par excellence,* charged with providing for the wants of the whole Christian world; second, to forbid the monks and the clerics to abandon their professional duties and to prevent them from gaining sufficient knowledge of civil law to follow lucrative careers as officers of justice, or administrators and lawyers in Paris. The decree of 1219 was directed neither against science, nor against the liberty of the professors. It was directed against the clergy who threatened to disorganize the church by abandoning the priesthood. It was an act of ecclesiastical reform, the object of which has been misunderstood. Whatever its later significance, it shows in a positive way the essential fact of the early history of the university of Paris: it was not the king of France, it was not the bishop of Paris; it was the pope who ruled over that institution.

CHAPTER IV

THE CANON

WE have seen the cleric in the parish, and in the school; we shall now see him endowed with a benefice or a prebend in a chapter. He is devoted to religious service in a cathedral church, the seat of a bishop or of an archbishop—as at Notre-Dame of Paris, Notre-Dame of Chartres, Sainte-Croix of Orléans, Saint-Étienne of Bourges,—or in a collegiate church, which is not the residence of a bishop—as Saint-Quentin, Saint-Spire of Corbeil, Saint-Martin of Tours, Saint-Hilaire of Poitiers. These churches are really served by a community or a college of priests, deacons, and subdeacons. These are the canons, *canonici,* so-called, it has been said, because their community was subjected to a collection of canons, to a rule. But in that case the term is not very well justified. It would apply much better to those properly called religious—to the monks, who were subordinated to a decidedly more rigorous rule of community life. Really, at the time which we are studying, the canons of the cathedral and of the collegiate churches lived together only at the times when they assembled to hold their chapter-meeting or to hold services. The service finished, they had their own quarters inside the cloister, or even outside the cloister, where they could take their meals and sleep, and where they lived with their families. They were more or less in contact with the faithful in the church to which they were attached, and even outside the church—for a certain number of them exercised the function of curates, having charge of the souls of the parish. They were not isolated and systematically secluded from the world like the monks. Their cloister, in spite of the name, was not the monastic cloister: it was only the space, often rather large, where their own houses were situated; a space adjoining the church, it is true, but one which was not always actually inclosed by a wall.

The communities of canons are, then, easily distinguished from the communities of monks, for the spirit which prevailed was not the same, and the rule of life was very different. Still, one must be cautious in the use of medieval terms, which are often misleading, and about the character of its institutions, which are extremely complex. There were monks living in community who were called canons, but these were really monks under a monastic rule; and there were canons regular, in distinction from those of the cathedrals and of the collegiate churches, the canons secular. Of this kind are the canons regular of the congregations of Saint-Victor and of Prémontré. But the canons of Prémontré lived cloistered in an abbey, subject to a rule at least as severe as that of the Benedictines of Cluny or of the Bernardines of Clairvaux: they only bore the names of canons; they really belonged to monastic society.

If the secular canons were not monks, they also differed from ordinary clerics in that they lived in a sort of community and formed a spiritual and temporal seigniory, owning lands, vassals, and subjects. The chapter was a collective lord, which had its rank in feudal society. Finally, canons were distinguished from other clerics by their costumes: a surplice (*superpellicium*), a loose linen dalmatic, with wide sleeves, covering the pelisson (*pellicium*), the present cassock; and on the head an amice of thick black stuff, with a flat top, terminating at each corner in a sort of horn.

Canons had a double reason for being. First, they did their religious services, the work of continuous prayer, and of the celebration of great Christian feasts. They were, so to speak, the officers of public prayer, a function of common interest which could not be interrupted or left in abeyance without menacing the security of the people. And, then, it was they who formed the council of the bishop, and, with the bishop, constituted the administrators of the diocese; for, at the period of Philip Augustus, as a rule, the bishop was elected by the chapter, and the archdeacons, his assistants, were only canons. To pray, and in the meantime to perform administrative functions, that was their double mission.

This word canon immediately brings before our minds the picture of a person with a florid complexion, large and fat, and well paid for doing nothing. Prebend has become a synonym for sinecure. One cannot speak of canons without being reminded of those whom Boileau has so well depicted, those prelates with triple chins, those subjects of Indolence who fought over a choir-stall. It is evident that, at the period of Louis XIV, the religious services, having been simplified and the needs of the faithful having greatly diminished along with popular faith, the beneficiaries of the church lived luxuriously on their benefices without much worry. Many were not in residence, causing themselves to be replaced by vicars and only having the bother of collecting their incomes. One cannot say that similar abuses were not practised in the middle ages, and that the canons of the time of Philip Augustus did not already try to get as much as possible for a minimum of trouble. But it is certain that the service of public prayer was then complicated, the faithful firmly convinced of its necessity and therefore very exacting.

To obtain a good idea of what happened in cathedral or collegiate churches, one should read the " ordinaries," " pontificals," " rituals," or even " manuals," which every bishopric and every church possessed. They contain a minute enumeration of the chants and ceremonies proper for each day of the year, for each religious ceremony. In the middle age much more importance was attached to the exact observance of the liturgy than in the modern epoch; tradition was all-powerful, ceremonial was a sacred thing; the slightest sound of the voice, the smallest step, the minutest gesture of those officiating were anticipated, and indicated in the rituals with extreme care. It is enough to glance through one of these books—for example, the ordinary of the cathedral of Laon, which was drawn up by the dean of the chapter just at the time of Philip Augustus—to be frightened at the interminable list of anthems, responses, psalms, prayers, hymns, and public ceremonies, marches, and processions to which the canons were subjected.

Every day had its office, or rather its series of offices. The least significant of days, the one the least weighted down—for example, an ordinary week day,—still had five offices, or five " canonical hours," as they were then called: the

office of matins at sunrise, the office of lauds, the office of
the mass, after noon the office of vespers, and. at sundown
the office of compline (*completorium*). Sundays the need
increased, and there were nine offices: matins, lauds, prime,
terce, high mass, sext, nones, vespers, and compline. And
this only applied to ordinary Sundays; the complication of
the services increased on days of great solemnity. To enter
a little farther into details, take at random the offices of a
week day: for example, the sixth day or Friday after
Ascension. The office of matins comprises a chant called the
invitatorium, three anthems, three psalms, and three lessons;
laud, several anthems and prayers; mass, the traditional
chants; vespers, certain anthems and chants; compline, a
hymn and some prayers. And this is a minimum; on holidays the number of chants grows to considerable proportions.
It is well known how numerous festivals were in the calendars
of the middle ages. To the regular festivals were added the
festivals of saints honored in the diocese, the festivals of the
martyr whose relics the church possessed. And, finally, the
ordinary service, full as it was, was still more complicated
by the services arising from endowments of masses for the
dead. It was necessary to celebrate the anniversaries of the
benefactors and great persons, lay and ecclesiastical, who had
for some reason merited the recognition of the chapter.
Manifestly, the religious functions of the canons of the middle ages were not a sinecure.

Add to this that the chapter was an electoral body, called
upon to choose a bishop and certain canonical dignitaries and
to name a certain number of curés; that it was also a college
of proprietors, which had a temporal seigniory to direct and
administer. In the church, as well as in the chapter, the
canons were, therefore, sufficiently occupied. It is true that,
as ministers of the ceremonies of the church, they were aided
by a certain number of priests, of chaplains, and of clerics
not members of the chapter. It is also true that, to administer their properties, they delegated certain of their number,
known as provosts, to look after the material interests of the
community. In spite of all this, there was in the chapters
a considerable amount of work to distribute among the members; the professional obligations were pressing, so pressing

that the canons—and this is merely human—sought means of divesting themselves of them, or at least of lightening their tasks. So it came that, at the time of which we write, ecclesiastical authorities were constantly forced to hinder this tendency and, by constraint or otherwise, compel the members of the chapter to fulfil the duties of their offices.

That was the chief difficulty. The canons were always ready to take the revenues of their prebends—that is to say, the part of the property of the chapter which had been assigned to each of them,—but they showed less willingness to reside and take part in the offices. Certain of them had never put foot into the church to which they were attached; they were canons *in partibus,* provided with benefices elsewhere. They only belonged to a chapter for pecuniary reasons, to receive an income. Others were always traveling outside of the town in which they should have been living, on the pretext of studying or making a pilgrimage. Finally, others absented themselves simply to go into business or to become lawyers, and they did not even take the trouble to ask for leave of absence from the head of the chapter. A letter which Pope Urban III in 1187 sent to the provost of the chapter of Maguelonne instructs us clearly on this point.

" It is not without astonishment that we hear reports of the conduct of certain of your canons. They go away without your permission, to study civil law or profane literature, or they even absent themselves for worldly affairs, so as to be able to give themselves pleasure the more easily. Some of them are even more audacious; they leave your chapter to officiate in other churches. This is absolutely wrong and contrary to the rules. If one of your canons, after having taken the oath and the cloth of his order, emancipates himself to such a degree as to go into outside occupations, we authorize you in spite of any appeal to correct and punish him."

Instead of punishing and putting down the evil which had established itself, the church judged it better to prevent it by making certain concessions to human weakness and by subjecting the chapters in the other things to a rigorous observance. At the end of the twelfth century and at the beginning of the thirteenth the chapters imposed on themselves, or received from the superior authority of the bishop or the pope, minute rules about the " stage " and residence. These rules resemble each other greatly in their essential dispositions. One need only know a few to know them all. As types, one can cite the statutes of the cathedral of Noyon of 1213 and of 1217, that of the collegiate church of Saint-Spire of Corbeil of 1203, those of the cathedral of Chartres of 1208 and 1222, and the reform of the Parisian collegiate church of Saint-Marcel of 1205. There are everywhere the same dispositions. On one side, they grant the canons the liberty of absenting themselves temporarily in certain circumstances recognized as legitimate: a sojourn at the schools or at the university, a pilgrimage, personal service to the bishop. On the other hand, the church consents not to require work of them for the entire year: sometimes they are given six months of non-residence as at Chartres, sometimes four months as at Noyon and at Paris, on the condition that for the rest of the term of service they be aided by a vicar, to whom they must give a part of their revenue, and that they be represented in the cloister by a decent establishment. To be classed as a canon " resident "—that is to say, a resident with full powers, enjoying all his prebends—a canon must first have made a " stage " in the chapter, a sort of supernumerary service for six months, and then he must meet the conditions of actual residence indicated above. Resident canons with foreign titles, *foranei*, are admitted to the chapter; but they do not receive the revenues of their prebends. One part of this revenue is taken for the vicar who replaces them, and the rest is divided among the resident canons. Every canon guilty of illegal or overlong absence is considered as a " stranger ": that is to say, he loses the enjoyment of his prebend.

These are the general rules; but the statutes about residence contain the most detailed prescriptions to prevent a canon from circumventing the law. Those of 1213 and 1217 for the cathedral of Noyon in this respect show a curious minuteness. Suppose, for example, that a resident canon asked to spend a year at the schools. It might be an indirect means of getting free from service and of leaving without any particular object, while enjoying his prebend. The case is anticipated. The student-canon is forced to actual study during his year: he is authorized to take only a three months' vacation. If he leaves the university before time, he is obliged to come back to the chapter and to be in residence as usually required. To take a long journey— for example, to make a pilgrimage to Rome—he must have the permission of the chapter, and, when he returns, he is still forced to reside for a certain time. At the same time, the canon can be delegated for service to the bishop without losing his standing of resident, but he is not allowed to leave the bishop. If he leaves him before the usual time, he must return to the chapter and do his duty for a fixed period as a compensation.

We know very well that the most severe and most minute rules were violated. In the middle ages, more than at any other period, personal privileges, individual dispensations, given by the pope or by the chapter itself, enabled one to evade the law. In the statute of Noyon of 1217 appeared significant reservations such as these: " without leave having been obtained, without special dispensation.'' It was the way for clever or moneyed people to get through the meshes of the net. To constrain the canons really to be in residence, another measure was taken. If the respect for the rule was not enough, men were influenced by money. If a canon remained in residence in order not to be deprived of his prebend, if he remained in his cloister or his city, he could still arrange to attend church irregularly. He passed whole days without appearing in the choir, avoided certain offices, especially the office of matins, or he left before the end of the services. In doing so he committed what, in the time of Philip Augustus, was called *marrantium,* fraud. Certain chapters came to provide pecuniary punishments against the irregulars. In October, 1219, that of the cathedral of Laon, among other reforms, adopted a series of penalties for each infraction of professional duty: each office missed, each chant unperformed, cost the delinquent a forfeit of a certain number of sous or deniers.

But this system was not always easy to apply; it irritated the canons, without making them much less negligent. Instead of punishing through forfeits, it was judged better to attract through the allurement of tokens of attendance, or,

as they were then called, "distributions." The distributions
of money or even in kind are one of the characteristic traits
of the profession of canon, one of the most curious sides of
the institution. A canon received not only the more or less
steady revenues which came to him from his prebend; he was
also paid every time—or as often as it was necessary—that
he appeared at the choir to do his duty. The more assiduous
he was, the more he profited. These continual distributions
of sous and deniers to the canons and the chaplains were
indeed novel spectacles, which, however, did not at all scan-
dalize the middle ages. For these distributions occurred
right in the choir of the church, often in full view of everybody. The canons immediately received the price of an office executed, of an anthem sung. More than that, the canons
did not only receive money; they received payments in kind,
wine, and even quarters of meat. Under certain circumstances a canon was even given a full meal, *pastus,* which was
served in the refectory of the chapter by the officer called the
cook, *coquus,* who was attached to the community.

Let us, for example, open the ordinary of the cathedral
of Laon, and let us take the regular order of offices for the
week which precedes Christmas. On Monday, one of the
dignitaries of the chapter begins the anthem *O clavis David,*
and he distributes two measures of wine to his colleagues.
On Tuesday, it is the turn of the grand archdeacon; after
the anthem he serves the canons with two measures of wine.
On Thursday the wine is furnished by the hospitaler, on
Friday by the chamberlain. On great festival days the
bishop takes part in the offices, but this participation is far
from being gratuitous. At the mass on Christmas, writes
the editor of the ritual, he remains standing before the altar,
surrounded by canons, priests, deacons, and subdeacons. He
says the *Confiteor,* and each of his assistants advances and
kisses him, as they kissed in the middle ages, on the lips.
Then he says the prayer, and two canons, clothed in silk
copes, chant the lauds before him. Then they approach and
the bishop gives each of them twelve deniers "of good
money." The same distribution follows to the cantor, to
the subcantor, and to the other officers of the chapter. After
the office of the sext, the bishop, with the dean and canons,

goes to the refectory. They take their places. The steward
—for the chapter, like every feudal lord, had its great officers—rings a bell and says the *Benedicite*. The chaplain
gives the benediction. Two subdeacons bring the bishop the
water and towel; the master of ceremonies, *regnarius,* or some
one else, gives a talk; the musicians sing before the bishop
during the whole meal. At the second course the stroke
of the handbell is heard; benediction is said by the chaplain, and he is given a leg of mutton, a large loaf, and
a half-pint of wine. Then another benediction is pronounced
by the hospitaler. He is given a piece of pork on a dish.
Two canons standing before the table of the bishop sing a
hymn, and the bishop gives them some money. On Maunday
Thursday, after the same ritual, when the ceremony of washing the altars has been terminated, the bishop gives them a
measure of wine, which the canons drink in the chapter-
room. On Easter day, as at Christmas, the bishop gives a
distribution of deniers, and it is the same at all the great
feasts.

In the cathedral of Paris, at Notre-Dame, anthems were
sung, which, one might say, had a money value: those who
sang them had a right to a distribution. The expense which
they entailed was paid partly by the bishop, partly by the
dean or head of the chapter, partly by the canons who fulfilled
the functions of provosts. Eighteen of these anthems, bringing money or food, were sung in the week preceding Christmas. One of them was followed by a distribution of seventy
rolls and seventy measures of wine to the clergy of the
cathedral.

There was a distribution at the time of the installation
of a new canon, of course at his expense. There was also
a distribution at the time of each of the administrative acts
performed by the chapter, at the time of the emancipation
of serfs, the sale of lands, unexpected changes in the personnel of the officers charged with administering the capitular
goods. But it must not be supposed that the canons were
remunerated only on these uncertain occasions and on great
feast days. They were remunerated daily, even for ordinary
services, but especially when they were present at matins.
The deniers of the morning (*denarii matutinales*) were a fund

of special importance, for attendance of the clergy at matins was difficult to attain and, the ordinary resources of the chapter not sufficing, many individuals, to assure the safety of their souls, made foundations or left legacies specially designed for the distribution of money to the participants at matins. On this point documents are not lacking; among the foundations contemporary with Philip Augustus, it is enough to mention that of the sons of Ascelin, dean of Saint-Marcel, who in memory of their father, who died in 1180, gave to Notre-Dame twenty sous of income *ad denarios matutinorum;* that of 1189, likewise designed to recompense the clergy, whether canons or not, who came to the choir at daybreak; finally, the foundation of Bishop Maurice of Sully, who left an important sum, one hundred livres (fifteen thousand francs) for poor clerics who celebrated the office of matins, *ad denarios matutinales pauperibus clericis.* This seems to show that the titled canons, those who were provided with a good prebend, did not voluntarily appear at this office; they left the proceeds of it to clerics outside of the chapters, to the auxiliary priests, with whom the cathedral was filled.

The endowments of anniversaries for the repose of the souls of certain persons, for the benefactors, both male and female, of the chapter, were extremely numerous; it was a new source and a very bountiful one, upon which they drew to establish new distributions. Here the facts are more abundant. It almost suffices to open the cartulary of Notre-Dame of Paris at hazard: in 1200, on the anniversary of Hugh of Chelles, a distribution of six deniers to all those who assist in the office; in 1204, on the anniversary of Simon of Moncy, canon of Paris, forty sous to be distributed; in 1205, on the anniversary of a canon of Dun-le-Roi, sixty sous (six hundred francs), to be distributed as follows: on the day of the anniversary the members of the chapter are to receive fifteen sous at mass, fifteen sous at vespers, and the remaining thirty sous on the day that the anniversary of Thibaud, bishop of Paris, is celebrated. In 1208, another bishop of Paris, Eudes of Sully, left the chapter the necessary sum to found several distributions of deniers and sous— one on Saint Stephen's day, another on the Circumcision, one on the anniversary of the death of the donor, another on Saint Bernard's day to the clergy who should be at matins; finally, another for Good Friday, on the occasion of the " washing of feet ": that is to say, of the ceremony which consisted of washing the feet of the poor. In 1211, Peter of Nemours, bishop of Paris, insured services on his anniversary; each of the canons was to receive twelve deniers at vigils and as much at mass; the assistant clergy, three deniers at vigils and three at mass. In 1219, the dean of the chapter, Hugh Clement, left Notre-Dame a still more important legacy. Every day of Lent, excepting Sunday, the feet of thirteen poor people were to be washed in the refectory of the chapter; there was to be a distribution of money to these same poor people, and to the clerics who performed the ceremony. There were to be further distributions on the anniversary of the birth of the donor: all the members of the chapter should receive six deniers at the vigil and six at the mass. This was the regular rate for the ministrant.

These facts suffice to give an idea of the number of special ceremonies and the quantity of money to be divided which came from the foundation of anniversaries or of masses for the dead. And yet we are far from knowing the number of these legacies; in the cartularies only those which serve to recall the memory of dignitaries of the chapter or of persons of note are indicated.

But the people did not leave money only; devout people, or those who wished that their souls should not suffer too long in the other world, left endowments for distributions of food. They instituted what were called " pasts " or " stations ": that is, distributions of bread, of wine, and of meat to the canons and to the clerics of the choir. In the *Cartulaire de Notre-Dame de Paris* there is a rule of 1230, only seven years after the death of Philip Augustus, which exhibits the arrangements made by the canons of Notre-Dame in matters of this kind under his reign, and, without much doubt, much earlier. Besides the stations founded by individual donations, there were public and traditional stations, which occurred on certain fixed days at the expense of the bishop and of certain dignitaries of the chapter, or of certain Parisian churches. A distribution of this kind generally cost

ten livres, that is about fifteen hundred francs. For example, at Easter and at Christmas the clerics of the choir
received one hundred half-pints of wine and one hundred
large loaves; at Pentecost the station of pork consisted of
one hundred and thirty-seven portions of meat, or *frustra,*
which the canons or clerics divided, the highest in dignity,
as always, receiving a double portion. On the feast days
of Saints Gervais and Protais nine rams were distributed;
each ram was cut into fifteen pieces, which the clerics assisting at the office carried home. The cook of the
chapter had a right to all the skins, and his three under-
cooks, *minores servientes de coquina,* took the feet and the
heads. At the stations or distributions of pork, the chamberlain and the cook of the chapter had for their part the blood
and the bowels.

Everything was regulated with this minuteness. But it
must be acknowledged that these details give us a singular
idea of what continually happened inside of collegiate
churches. We find it hard to associate religious services
with the distribution of money and food; to harmonize the
uninterrupted sound of chanting with the clinking of money;
to conceive of chapters which are counting-houses and restau-
rants, where the canon need only appear and sing to be paid
and fed.

It is true that, at the time when the rule of 1230 was
drawn up, the inconveniences of distributions in kind were
being felt and were gradually being replaced by a distribution of an equivalent amount of money. This was then
a general tendency; in the feudal world, thanks to economic
progress, pecuniary contributions were being substituted for
fines in kind, for the corvée, for personal services. Therefore, the collecting became much easier. In the churches
the services could only gain in calm and dignity by it. Nevertheless, the use of stations and even of real meals, or
banquets, continued a long time.

Thus, in 1177, a count of Champagne had founded a
memorial service for himself in a collegiate church of Notre-
Dame of Oulchy, consisting of two dinners, which should
follow the funeral service. At the first dinner, all the clergy
who should present themselves were to be served, and the

menu was fixed by the donor: the first course a dish of cold pork, the second course a dish of goose, third course chicken fricassee, "garnished," says the deed of foundation, "with good sauce thickened with the yellow of eggs." It is to be noted that everything was anticipated. The second meal resembled the first, except that beef was served in place of the cold pork. Each guest had the right to a half-pint of wine, and the quality of this wine was determined: it was to be a good drinkable wine, halfway between the most delicate and the cheapest.

The memory of these banquets lasted for twenty years in the chapter of Oulchy. It was in 1203 that Blanche, countess of Champagne, proposed to transform the two meals into monetary distributions. Each of them cost about thirty sous, that is, six hundred francs to-day. The clergy who appeared received money. One cannot say that the change pleased them greatly. These love-feasts were the joy of our fathers. It was sweet to eat and drink in the holy place before the eye of the Lord.

*

*   *

When the canons took the trouble to be in residence, their lives were spent in the choir of their churches and in the cloisters which were next to them. Every cathedral and collegiate church consisted of two entirely distinct parts: the space open to the faithful, to the people, and that which was reserved for the canons.

On the altars of the lateral nave, of the transept, of the apsis, and in general in all the chapels of the periphery, masses and the anniversary services were celebrated by clergy who were not a part of the chapter; these were the chaplains. In great cathedrals, such as Notre-Dame of Paris, this auxiliary clergy was often numerous, for the faithful had the right to found chaplaincies on the condition of furnishing the income necessary to maintain the curé and the worship in his chapel. It was thus that, in 1217, a citizen of Paris and his wife instituted a chaplain in the church of Notre-Dame solely for the purpose of saying daily masses for the repose of their souls. All rich and devout people being able to give themselves this luxury of founding a perpetual or a temporary mass, the number of clergy who, without being canons, lived from the altars in collegiate churches was considerable and in a way unlimited. Among these clergymen or these chaplains some had the privilege of serving in the choir at the high altar, with the dignitaries and members of the chapter. And the chief of these clerics was an important person; he was called the " grand chaplain " or simply " chaplain." The ministration of this priest was necessary to the canons, many of whom had not received the priesthood; he had a conspicuous place in all solemn ceremonies and received a part of the distributions.

The church of a chapter was, therefore, filled with clerics, who sometimes officiated in the chapels, sometimes in the choir. But the choir was primarily the domain of the canons; it belonged to them as their own; it was there that they had their places, their stalls, radiating from the sanctuary, according to the character of their titles and of their seniority. The choir was that reserved part to which the faithful had no access.

It is well known that, at the end of the middle ages, all the choirs of capitular churches were more or less inclosed, at first by a partition which served as a support to the back of the stalls and ran around the high altar, and also by a loft in front of the stalls, such as that we still see at Saint-Étienne-du-Mont. The choir, under these conditions, was a little church within a church; it was generally raised several steps above the rest of the building, so that the people could hardly see the officials, save through the grilles of the doors or when the latter mounted the gallery of the loft, there to read the epistle or gospel.

Were the choirs already inclosed at the time of Philip Augustus, at the time when the great gothic churches were everywhere being built? On this point Viollet-le-Duc advances a theory which most archeologists have accepted and repeated without much reflection. According to him, when the bishops constructed cathedrals—that is, at the close of the twelfth and the beginning of the thirteenth centuries— they did it in opposition to the monastic spirit; they wanted the church to be really the home of the people, open even to popular assemblies, and wished the faithful to be in continuous touch with the clergy; therefore, no inclosures, no lofts. These could only have been put in later on, in the second half of the thirteenth century or in the fourteenth century, after long dissension between the bishops and their canons, the latter seeking for independence and wanting to be entirely shut off from the worshipers.

Viollet-le-Duc is a very learned architect and a designer much above the average, but as an historian he must be taken cautiously. His theories must be tested; this one seems untenable! At all times canons of cathedral churches have considered these edifices, and especially the choir, as their exclusive domain, and one must remand the theory of the democratic tendencies of the bishops who built our cathedrals to the realm of fiction. If it is true that the chapters did not build the inclosures and the lofts of stone before the end of the thirteenth century, there is nothing against believing that before that time the canons surrounded themselves with inclosures of wood or of tapestries and draperies, which screened them from the sight of the people. In the sources of the time of Philip Augustus, there is frequent mention of the *dorsalia,* or of the cloths suspended in the choir behind the seats of the canons. Everything leads one to think that, from the very time that the construction of the cathedrals began, the canons had the idea that the choir was a sacred place, reserved to the officials and forbidden to the laity, an idea which the permanent partitions of stone later expressed and materialized in a most significant way.

They also wished to be in their own quarters outside of the church, in the cloister. When one speaks of the chapters of cathedrals and of collegiate churches, the word cloister has two meanings. It indicates either a building adjoining a church, a gallery of arcades, square or rectangular in form, analogous to the cloisters of the abbeys and like them serving as a promenade for the canons—such, for example, as the still existing cloisters of the cathedrals of Rouen, Laon, Noyon, and Saint Lizier; or (and this is the most common meaning in the sources of the twelfth and thirteenth centuries) it simply designates an inclosure, real or imaginary, within which are the private houses of the canons. These inclosures contained varying amounts of land, sometimes an entire quarter of a city. None but canons' houses were allowed within them, though not all canons' houses were situated there. There were some which were outside the cloister proper, though enjoying the same rights. Under Philip Augustus, as under his predecessors and successors, all the canons of Paris were required to have their lodgings in the cloister situated north and east of Notre-Dame; in the beginning of the fourteenth century, the cloister of the *Cité* contained only thirty-seven canons' houses, although the canons were almost sixty in number.

What characterized the cloisters of chapters is that they had the privilege of immunity. This immunity was clearly defined in a bull of Innocent III given to the canons of Laon in 1206, which in turn is merely a confirmation of a bull of Pope Calixtus II of 1123. Neither the power of the king nor that of the bishop could be exercised in the limits of the cloister, where the houses of the brotherhood were found. No one save the dean of the chapter, and he only after a consultation with the canons and in accordance with their decision, had the right to enter it and arrest any one. In 1200, Philip Augustus solemnly confirmed the liberty and immunity of the cloister of Paris and threatened any one who should violate it with the direst penalties. Naturally, the canons everywhere reached out to appropriate the buildings embraced within the inclosure, and ecclesiastical authority at least tried to exclude from the cloister the kind of inhabitants that tended to compromise its religious character. In 1203, the chapter of Saint-Spire of Corbeil decided that the cloister could not be inhabited by a Jew. A bull of Pope Lucius III, of 1183, informs us that the cloister of Saint-Pierre, at Troyes, counted among its proprietors some laymen who rented their houses to minstrels, actors, innkeepers, and even to lewd women. The pope ordered the proprietors to occupy their houses themselves or to rent them to members of the clergy. Presently, the greatest possible precautions were taken to prevent even the houses of laity in the vicinity of the cloister from being a cause of scandal to the canons within the inclosure.

In 1223, a citizen, Étienne Bérout, wanted to build a house in Paris fronting upon a cloister of Notre-Dame. The bishop intervened and imposed the following conditions on him: He must not, without the express authorization of the chapter, erect a building more than six feet above the cloister's inclosure; he must take good care to put no window or opening in the wall which overlooked the cloister, save a dormer window, closed, barred, and high enough so that one could not from it look down into the cloister. The lateral walls of the new structure should get light through the same kind of window. In return for the graciousness which the canons showed him by letting him carry his building six feet above the wall, he agreed to give the chapter a sum of one hundred Parisian sous (twelve hundred francs). The charter which tells of this arrangement proves that the cloister of the chapter of Paris was, under Philip Augustus, already inclosed by a wall. But this was not the case everywhere at that time; the cloister of the canons of Chartres, for example, was not walled until the middle of the thirteenth century. The custom of surrounding the space reserved for canons' houses by a continuous wall had many reasons, especially the necessity of defending this place of refuge against the lay powers, and even against the bishop, and also the need of defining the precise extent of the territory under the immediate jurisdiction of the chapter.

A peculiarly rare document gives us a glimpse of the interior of a canon's house. In 1220, the dean and the chapter of Saint-Pierre-en-Pont at Orléans, in consideration of a rental of fifteen Parisian sous (about one hundred and eighty francs), rented a furnished house situated in the cloister to a nephew of one of the canons. The enumeration of these furnishings is instructive. There are: linens—two table-cloths, two towels, six sheets; furniture—six coffers or chests, four beds with four blankets and five pillows, three chairs, two tables; utensils—three copper cauldrons, one bronze cauldron, one bronze plate, one iron plate, three drinking glasses, one trivet, one fireiron with nippers, two mortars with three pestles, a series of receptacles for measuring grains and liquids, and finally a pail with a cord. If that is all the furniture of a canon, it must be said that, at least in a small provincial chapter, there was not much luxury.

*

* *

The canon is, however, a person of high position in the social world, and the chapter of which he is a member forms a real collective seigniory. It has a chief, who is elected by all the canons, and who usually has the title of dean (*decanus*); sometimes, however,—as at Soissons, Reims, Maguelonne,—that of provost. A dean or provost of a chapter is a very potent person, capable of coping with a bishop. He personifies the judicial power of a chapter, and can, like the bishop, have his tribunal, his sphere of power. His election sometimes gives rise to incidents which anger the chapter and which carry their reverberation far beyond the cathedral church. We shall mention only one case.

In 1218, the cardinal legate, Robert of Courçon, came to Amiens, visited the chapter, and found at its head a dean named Simon, who was uneducated and unworthy in other respects. He deposed Simon and, greatly irritated at the canons for making such a choice, he deprived them of the right of naming a successor. This right he reserved to the pope. Hardly had he left Amiens before the canons, little caring to obey, came together to elect. But, as it often happened, they were divided: the majority voted for a canon of the seigniorial house of Roye; the minority for a well-known teacher and preacher, the learned Jean Halgrin of Abbeville. Out of this came quarrels and lawsuits. The majority, which had on its side the common law, carried its cause before the archbishop of Reims, the judge regular; the minority, which believed it had made the better choice, addressed itself to Pope Honorius III.

The papacy, which was sustaining the universities against the bishops, also had reasons for interfering in the affairs of the chapters, and thus extending its authority over them at the expense of that of the bishops and of the metropolitans. Honorius III first delegated the bishop of Arras to settle the differences; then he decided on a more radical measure: he cancelled the election by the majority of the canons of Amiens and, by virtue of his office, he invested

Jean Halgrin with the deanship, ordering the abbot of Saint-Victor to install him. There was a furious outcry of the canons, one of them, a provost of the chapter, directing the resistance. When the abbot of Saint-Victor arrived at Amiens, the provost received him with the most vigorous protests and claimed that the bull of the pope had been secured, and even influenced in its form, by the lies of intriguers; he appealed to a pope better informed. But the delegate of Honorius did not consider this appeal of any account, and, seeing that the recalcitrants would not give ear to anything, he even excommunicated the canon who was the author of the protest. Excommunicate an appellant! this was a serious step, out of which came a new suit. The adversaries of Halgrin filed a complaint at Rome against the abbot of Saint-Victor, and another suit grew out of the first. The question was whether the provost and his partizans were excommunicated before or after the time of his appeal. The pope was obliged to ask the dean of the church of Soissons to make a careful inquiry into this special point before giving his final decision of the main question.

Meanwhile, the candidate of the minority of Amiens, Jean Halgrin, impatient to see things terminated and to enjoy his deanship, arrived at Rome. He came before the pope and pleaded his own cause with the skill of a man accustomed as preacher to impose his own opinion on his hearers; he would either resign the deanship or the papacy must energetically support him against his enemies and, without taking account of any appeal and without any other inquiry or suit and despite any opposition and all dilatory tactics, must maintain the choice it had made of him. Brought to the wall, Honorius III refused to accept the resignation of a doctor so universally renowned for his eloquence, his knowledge, and his virtue. An attempt to prove that the Holy See was deceived by a lie is an insult to its dignity. And on November 22, 1218, by an energetic act which was not characteristic of him, Honorius wrote to the abbot of Sainte-Geneviève, the principal archdeacon of Paris, and to Doctor Peter of Capua, quashing all pending cases, revoking the order he had given to start new ones, and resolutely maintained Jean Halgrin of Abbeville in the deanship of Amiens.

The episode is instructive; it proves two things: first, that the place of dean of a chapter stirred up many ambitions; and, second, that the court of Rome made itself sole and supreme judge of the differences between canons. The authority of a bishop would previously have sufficed to decide them. Here is another manifestation of the new law.

The dignity of dean was as lucrative as honorable, for, in prebends as well as in distributions, he had always a right to a double share. This dignity was in itself so considerable that certain chapters considered it dangerous; they took precautions against the chief they had chosen. At Noyon, according to a statute of 1208, the dean, before receiving the obedience of the canons, must take a solemn oath. He swears to conform to a whole series of precise prescriptions and prohibitions which are imposed on him. He will continuously be in residence, he will not accept any functions detrimental to the community, he will not hold two positions in the chapter, he will not oppose the execution of the statutes which control the partition of the prebends; at harvest time, he will not go into the barns of the chapter and obtain procurations—that is to say, take meals at the expense of the local officers of the inhabitants; he will not suspend a canon and seize his prebend without having consulted the chapter; he will not receive clerics into the choir without the permission of the chapter. In brief, the canons do not wish their dean to become a sort of absolute ruler. He must always act with the approbation of his colleagues and he must not consider the goods of the chapter as his private property. But, on the other hand, they recognize these his rights: he is the natural judge of the other canons and he exercises the cure of their souls. He is at once the magistrate and the priest of the community.

Under the dean, in the second rank, was the cantor, charged with the important service of choral exercises, of policing the church, and of supervising the clergy outside of the chapter. He carried a baton as a mark of his dignity.

A third dignitary was especially charged with the equipment and the maintenance of the establishment; he was the treasurer, called the chamberlain in certain chapters. He was the manager of the chapter, the minister of the finances of the seigniory. He had charge of the capitular treasure, not only the funds, but also the objects of value and the archives.

At the end of the twelfth century, the treasurers or chamberlains of many collegiate churches found their task greatly lightened by the creation of the new offices of church-wardens, *matricularii*, or of keepers, *custodes*. These, with their assistants, were charged with the repairing, mending, presenting of objects used in the ceremonies in the choir, with lighting the candles, ringing the bells, and guarding the church. They were both sacristans and beadles. The institution of churchwardens at the time of Philip Augustus is revealed especially by two documents: an instrument of Eudes of Sully, bishop of Paris in 1204, and a decree of 1221 by the chapter of Laon. The clerical churchwardens, much superior in dignity to the lay churchwardens, participated in the honorary and pecuniary privileges of the canons. They officiated in the choir and took part in the distributions; but all these guardians were obliged to sleep by turns in the church and were responsible for anything that disappeared.

Finally, the *écolâtre*, or chancellor, was charged with the double duty of sealing the charters of the chapter and of superintending the school of the cloister and, in general, all the schools of the diocese. In the church this dignitary was responsible for the lessons, as the cantor was for the chants. He was the librarian, was charged with keeping the books, correcting and repairing them if necessary. He was responsible for lessons which had been omitted by day or night, and was forced to read them. He examined the clergy charged with reading. He named and superintended the teachers charged with instruction. His strict duty was to be continually in residence, and to become a priest within the year in which he undertook his duties. This, at least, is what was exacted from the chancellor of the cathedral of Noyon at the opening of the thirteenth century, according to a document which carefully enumerates all his duties.

*

*   *

Ordinarily, the seals of chancellors picture them in the customary way, holding a book. But Manasses, the chancellor of Amiens, sealing a charter of 1207, did not hesitate to have himself represented in the attitude and occupation which, without doubt, pleased him best; he appeared in hunting costume, on horseback, with a bird on his wrist and a dog following him. This chancellor, like so many other canons and dignitaries of a chapter, was evidently a noble, who had the tastes of his class and led a noble's life. With this characteristic seal, we can compare that of the chapter of Roye in Picardy, which gives no indication whatever of ecclesiastical life; quite the contrary. These canons, manifestly warlike like all Picards, in 1211 wished to be pictured as knights at a gallop, with halberts, round casques, bucklers, and proudly waving banners.

Here we are far removed from the choir-stall and the altar. It is because, at the end of the twelfth century, the tendency of representatives of the large seigniorial houses to enter the churches of the canons was an accomplished fact. The chapters then recruited themselves in aristocratic circles, not only because the lay lords brought influence to bear on the nominations of canons through the bishop or dean, but also because they directly controlled a number of prebends in all parts of France. There were canonships which, through a more or less dissembled hereditary right, devolved upon the clerical members of high baronial families. At Paris, to take one example only, the collation of the prebend of the chapter of Saint-Thomas-du-Louvre—that is to say, the nomination of canons—was in 1209 regulated as follows: until his death, the bishop of Beauvais, Philip of Dreux, cousin of Philip Augustus, was to have the right of bestowing prebends; after him this right was to be exercised alternately by the bishop of Paris and by Robert, Count of Dreux. The sons of noble families were not content with filling the chapters; they shamelessly accumulated the capitular dignities. One of the first ministers of Philip Augustus, William of Champagne, nicknamed '' of the white hands,'' who died as archbishop of Reims and cardinal, had commenced as a youth by holding livings in many chapters at once; he was simultaneously canon of Cambrai and Meaux, provost of the cathedrals of Soissons and of Troyes and of the collegiate chapter of Saint-Quiriace of Provins. This accumulation was formally prohibited by the canons, but law did not exist for the powerful house of Champagne. When the great feudal houses set such an example, the small nobles in the lost corners of remote provinces did not hesitate to practise the same abuses to their own profit.

It was not only the feudal spirit which reigned in these chapters; even feudal practices came to prevail in them. In certain respects, the relations of the dignitaries among themselves, and especially to the bishops, were relations of vassals to a suzerain. A curious document, which was written between 1197 and 1208, gives the official status of the vassals of Paris at the time of Philip Augustus. There we read as follows:

" The dean of the church of Paris is the liegeman of the bishop save for the fealty due the chapter. The cantor of Paris is the liegeman of the bishop, and promises him fealty. The chancellor of Paris is the liegeman of the bishop and also promises him fealty. All the archdeacons of the church of Paris are the liegemen of the bishop and are sworn to him. The chaplain of the bishop is also his liegeman. The dean of the chapter of Saint-Marcel is the liegeman of the bishop for his deanery. It is the same in the case of the deans of Saint-Germain-l'Auxerrois and Saint-Cloud."

So all these persons in the church were bound to the bishop by a feudal tie, by liege homage, and, as a result, they swore to the bishop with the ceremonial used for the investiture of vassals. One might call it a hierarchy of barons.

Was not this a violation of the spirit and the institutions of the church and of ecclesiastical laws? Without doubt. The church could not properly allow the chaplains and the deans of chapters to be vassals of the bishops, as is proven at Noyon, for example, by the statute of May, 1208, in which the dean was expressly prohibited from doing homage to the bishop or from accepting any fief from him. But the customs of the time and the influence of the environment were stronger than all prohibitions. The canons were petty lords, many of whom lived as lords in spite of the laws, and the chapters seemed impregnated with the habits and ideas of feudalism. That is why the preachers and the councils of the time of Philip Augustus denounced the worldly behavior of certain of these bodies and the scandalous lives of their members.

*

* *

None the less, public opinion considered the canon charged with a duty, the social usefulness of which was of the highest order. The piety of the faithful continued to manifest itself by gifts of land or money to chapters, or even by the foundation of new collegiate churches or new communities of canons. Rich and devout individuals did not content themselves with founding chaplaincies or enlarging the funds for distributions of celebrated churches; they created chapters designed to pray for the safety of their souls. That is what, for example, Gautier, a bishop of Nevers, did in 1201 when he made Saint-Léger of Tannay, which before had been a simple parish church, a collegiate church. The act of this foundation has come down to us, and it is interesting as it shows how they proceeded in the time of Philip Augustus to change a parish church into a chapter and curés into canons.

People did not confine themselves to enriching chapters already in existence or to establishing new ones. As it was of general interest that the office of public prayer in the larger churches be accomplished with care and by persons worthy of this high mission, it was considered important that the canons should lead an edifying life conformable to the law of their institution. Therefore, public opinion obliged ecclesiastical authority to make frequent reforms in the organization of chapters.

These decrees of reform emanating from the pope, from the bishops, or from the chapters themselves, began appearing in great numbers in the ecclesiastical cartularies at the end of the twelfth and the beginning of the thirteenth centuries. Some had only a restricted bearing; they only imposed partial reforms. Others, on the contrary, aimed at a general reorganization of a community. At Paris, the chapter of Notre-Dame saw its ancient constitution more or less modified by reforms of 1204, of 1208, of 1211, of 1213, and of 1216, and the movement for reform extended to the chapters dependent on the cathedral—at Saint-Germain l'Auxerrois in 1209, at Saint-Cloud in 1204, at Saint-Marcel in 1205, at Saint-Martin of Champeaux in Brie in 1205, at Saint-Thomas-du-Louvre in 1209, at Saint-Merry in 1219. Outside of Paris, and from one end of France to the other, we see the same effort to regularize the lives of canons and put the constitutions of chapters into harmony with the needs of the church and with the requirements of the faithful. For the cathedral of Noyon, statutes came almost without interruption each year, from 1183 to 1218. At Chartres, there were rules in 1208 and in 1222. At Saint-Spire of Corbeil, there were those of 1191, 1203, and 1208; at Bayonne, that of 1188; at Laon, those of 1201 and of 1219; at Saint-Salvi of Albi, the reform was in 1212; at the chapter of Saint-Corentin at Quimper, in 1223, at Saint-Pierre of Troyes in Champagne, in 1183, etc. This enumeration of dates and of localities, taken at random from the whole range of territory, is of interest in itself, as it shows how seriously the age of Philip Augustus sought to secure order, peace, and regularity of conduct in the chapters, and how widespread this movement was.

All these statutes resemble each other; as is natural, because the spirit of reform everywhere attacked the same abuses and tried to introduce the same reforms. There were measures to force the canons to be in residence, to do their duties, to distribute the prebends more equitably, to regulate the rights of the dignitaries and the relations of the canons to the bishop, to create new offices, to organize the administration of the domains of the chapter on a better basis, and to define accurately the method of electing officials, especially the dean. It is by the study of these documents that one can discover the defects of the capitular régime and the more or less well-founded criticism to which it gave rise. But it was useless to multiply the rules and prohibitions, for customs and habits were stronger than the law. All that public opinion rebuked in the canons, all the vices of the institution arose from the fact that a chapter was at the same time a sacred body and a temporal seigniory, a college of priests, charged with celebrating religious offices, and an association of proprietors, interested in making their capital and lands yield good returns. The increasing recruiting of the chapters from aristocratic circles and the influence of the environment too often made these sons of nobles, tonsured and provided with a prebend, forget the religious character of their positions and to see only the financial and feudal side.

Bishops, popes, and councils strove to bring the over-worldly canons back to the observance of their religious duties, to remind them that they were members of the clergy and that they should have the appearance and habits of such. At the beginning of the thirteenth century, Stephen, Bishop of Mende, wrote a curious letter to Rome in which he strongly complained of the irregular life of his canons. "They are the reason," he said, "why the church has become an object of derision for the entire population of my diocese, and your Holiness must finally reform this state of affairs." The deans of the chapters were themselves obliged to point out the evil and to demand that it be remedied. In 1183, the dean of the cathedral of Troyes denounced the canons of his church, who refused ordination, to the bishop and to Pope Lucius III: they failed to do their duties and persisted in using the priests outside of the chapter as substitutes. The pope ordered the bishop of Troyes to excommunicate the canons who refused to become priests, and they decided that in the future no stranger would be received at the high altar to celebrate mass.

The council of Paris, of 1212, and that of Montpellier, held in 1214, have left several rules relating especially to the canons, and the accusations against them are instructive. First, the clergy lived and dressed too luxuriously—they wore red or green clothes, slippers, and short, flowing cloaks; on horseback they used golden bits and spurs; they had hawks in their houses and they carried falcons on their arms; in short, externally, they were like laymen. All these abuses must cease. In the cloister, where the houses of the canons were located, meetings for games and debauchery were held. This practice was formally prohibited. The canons were forbidden, under pain of excommunication, to hold several benefices and were ordered to rid themselves of the extra ones they possessed within two months. Certain chapters had ignorant or incapable persons over them, because they insisted on taking the dean and other dignitaries from amongst themselves; if men who were capable of filling these offices were not found in the community, they must choose outsiders as officers. And the election must be honestly conducted; care must be taken to publish the day on which it was to be held, and to warn the absent canons, so that they could come and vote. Finally, members of chapters were absolutely prohibited from going into any kind of trade, from lending on security, and from practising usury.

This last prohibition was not purposeless. Many documents prove that rich chapters lent their capital at high interest and practised certain banking operations with profit. The chapter of Notre-Dame of Paris seems to have been particularly rich. In 1216, it paid three hundred and sixty Parisian livres (almost forty thousand francs) for a golden vase ornamented with precious stones that an archbishop of Cologne had put on sale. From an act of 1204, it is clear that the canons lent money to the citizens of Paris. One of these, owing one hundred and thirty livres, having died, his widow paid thirty livres down; for the rest of the debt the chapter took the booth of a money-changer on the *Grand pont,* which she owned, as security. The same canons added the profits of agricultural enterprise to their financial ventures; they undertook large operations in the clearing of lands in the diocese of Paris, which brought them into trouble with the foresters of the king after 1185. The history of the chapter of Arras, under the administration of Raoul of Neuville, between 1203 and 1221, also puts beyond doubt the fact that, under the pretext of sales and the levying of tithes, the canons made loans at interest and realized considerable profits, which, after the death of the bishop who encouraged these operations, caused a number of lawsuits. The chapters clung to money, but they also clung to land; they did not neglect any means of enlarging their domains; they paid a good figure for land which was not given to them, and, when an important acquisition was at stake, all methods were fair in their eyes. In 1216, the canons of Saint-Martin of Tours, proprietors of the seigniory of Chablis and of its vineyards, found a chance to annex the lands of a certain Guy of Montréal; but the purchase price was considerable—

two thousand livres (two hundred and fifty thousand francs)
—and the chapter did not have the necessary funds on hand;
it did not hesitate to sell a part of the gold which covered
the table of the high altar of Saint-Martin for seven hundred
livres; a sad extremity, no doubt, but they thought that the
piety of the faithful would make up for it.

Chapters were like individuals; there were some which
understood how to manage their fortunes and who were
prosperous; others, on the contrary, who could not make both
ends meet. They were debtors instead of creditors and sometimes even found themselves bankrupt. Such was the situation of the chapter of Maguelonne in 1197. We know this
from a letter of Pope Celestine III, which enumerated the
causes of the failure: bad harvests of grain and wine, frequent private wars, and incessant quarrels between the factions among the canons. To help the chapter out of this bad
situation, the pope allowed its dean, the provost of Maguelonne, to take charge of all the churches which were subject
to the community: that is, to confiscate their revenues, gradually to cancel the debt, '' so heavy,'' says the pontifical bull, ''
'' that the canons could not support its weight any longer.''

It is easy to see that money played a predominant part
in the documents relating to the canons. A very instructive
study could be made of the division of prebends among the
members of chapters. Ecclesiastical authority was constantly
obliged to take measures to prevent the canons from considering their prebends as their own property, which they could
dispose of to related clerics. It became necessary to force
holders of prebends to participate in the expenses of the
community, for they found it convenient to take their revenues, and evade the expenses which the services and the
administration of the domain entailed. Chapters had, at the
end of a certain number of years, to be forced to make a new
distribution of prebends; for the value of these parcels of
land and revenues diminished or increased considerably in
the course of time and equality of the holders of prebends
no longer prevailed. It was even necessary, from time to
time, to force the chapters to increase the number of their
members and to divide their prebends; for, the capitular domain growing or increasing in value, those who enjoyed it

had a very natural tendency to keep the numbers small in order to get a larger prebend. This was why, in 1205, the church of Notre-Dame of Paris decided that the prebends of the vassal chapter of Saint-Martin of Champeaux, in Brie, should be cut in two. The value of each prebend had become over fifty livres: that is, a canon of Saint-Martin had over seven thousand five hundred francs of income. It was found that, in comparison with this revenue, there was too small a number of canons. Naturally, those who were in possession objected; they were calmed by the concession that the doubling of the prebends should not take place until the death or retirement of the incumbents. This proves that, even in the middle ages, administrative reforms were effected without brutality.

Really pious souls, austere consciences, were indignant at seeing communities of canons so much absorbed in temporal interests, in the form of lands and money. The preachers of the time of Philip Augustus stigmatized the eagerness with which canonships were pursued. This race for prebends angered them. " The candidates," said one of them, " fall into a delirium when there is a vacancy, as mad dogs do when the course of the moon wanes." Preachers thundered against the cupidity of the clerics who held several prebends in spite of the prohibitions of the councils. Prévostin of Cremona, chancellor of the church of Paris, and himself a canon, made this confession:

"We clerics, we want everything, spiritual treasures and temporal treasures. But the idol, Dagon, falls and the law remains firm. Time passes and eternity remains. We seek to raise up Dagon and make the temporal equal to, and even put it above the spiritual. . . . What can one say upon seeing the mass sung for money in the house of God?"

Another contemporary of Philip Augustus, Élinand, the converted trouvère, who had become a monk of Cîteaux, probably alluded to the worldly canons when he indignantly wrote of priests who appeared in public dressed like women, " with their hair curled and well parted, their faces freshly shaven, their skins polished with pumice-stone, bareheaded, bare-shouldered, tattooed, with shod hands and gloved feet."

[Sic.] Other preachers denounced the bad spirit, the spirit of insubordination among the canons:

> "If their bishop decides to rebuke them, they immediately say that the right to correct them belongs only to the dean of the chapter. If the dean wishes to reprimand them, they reply that they are under the jurisdiction of the entire chapter and not under that of the dean."

And in this instance the preachers, who had the habit of striking heavily and of enlarging on the truth in order to make an impression, did not exaggerate. The canons of the middle ages were not strongly addicted to obedience and peace; one must admit that cloisters and even churches did not seem like sanctuaries of peace and of peaceful seclusion. Men quarreled in them as much as elsewhere, and often even came to blows. Most of the clerics, sons of nobles as we have said, having come out of military surroundings, had the disposition of their class and were very bellicose.

We shall not speak here of the wars which chapters in the cities or in the country had to wage against great and petty barons, who constantly tried to invade their domains, or against the citizens, who sought freedom from ecclesiastical seigniory. These will be considered later. It is enough, for the moment, to note that the necessity of defense against the attacks of the castellans and the barons gave a peculiar character to certain communities of canons. Especially in the rugged and mountainous country, or in provinces lacking a high suzerain strong enough to police the district, chapters were constantly exposed to pillage by the seigniors, were drawn into war by a stronger force, and were therefore organized accordingly. These canons had nothing ecclesiastical about them but the tonsure; they were veritable soldiers. Ordinarily of a rich and noble family, they were ever ready to call together their kinsmen and repulse their enemies. In reality, they were chiefs of bands which were not content to be on the defensive, but avenged unexpected insults and in their turn attacked the castellans of the neighborhood. At the time of Philip Augustus, the most notable example of such chapters was that of Saint-Julien of Brioude; there were several of the same kind in Auvergne, the land of

feudal anarchy *par excellence*. The canons of Brioude were
notorious and their conduct and military life caused great
scandal. Philip of Harvengt, the abbot of Bonne-Espérance,
in his book, *De continentia clericorum,* mentioned them as
the strangest class of the warrior-priest. He described them
as coming out of the choir, where they had just sung psalms
and hymns, and running to put on helmets and breastplates
to battle on the highways. " This abnormal situation," he
said, " was well known to bishops and popes, but it had to
be tolerated; the canons were compelled to defend themselves
or the rapacity of the laity would have reduced the church
to nothing."

Exclude these exceptional communities, and consider only
the chapters under usual conditions and the relations of
canons to other members of ecclesiastical society! It must
still be admitted that quarrels were frequent and interminable; indeed, that the state of war was practically permanent.
It is not to be wondered at that churches sometimes had the
appearance of strong castles.

*

*   *

One would never finish if he undertook to write the history of all the conflicts which occurred in cathedral and
collegiate churches at the end of the twelfth and the beginning of the thirteenth centuries. It was not, however, a
condition peculiar to this period of the history of France.
Many of these quarrels had commenced long before the reign
of Philip Augustus and ended a long time after. There
were some that lasted almost as long as the medieval period
itself; generations of canons transmitted them like an inheritance. These clerics quarreled for centuries because, in
spite of all the pronouncements of justice and of all the
compromises, they never, at the bottom of their hearts, renounced the exercise of what they considered a right. In
cities where several chapters existed there were conflicts
between the various communities of canons. Often it was a
cathedral which sought to have its preëminence recognized
by the ordinary collegiate churches, which themselves desired
independence: it was the hostility of the sovereign and his

vassal. It suffices to see what happened in Troyes, in Champagne, in 1189. The canons of the cathedral Saint-Pierre were
fighting with the canons of Saint-Loup. The latter finally recognized their dependence and signed a treaty of peace. They
would assist at the high mass of Saint-Pierre on the four
great feast days of the year as a sign of their dependence;
but in return, by way of indemnification, the chamberlain of
Saint-Pierre would pay five sous after each assistance to
the cellarer of Saint-Loup. At Châlons-sur-Marne the canons
of Notre-Dame paid a quit-rent to the cathedral chapter of
Saint-Étienne, in accordance with an arrangement concluded
in 1187. They were also constrained to assist in the processions of the cathedral and to attend the services which were
celebrated there on certain great feast days. In return, the
canons of Saint-Étienne would come to Notre-Dame on the
four feasts of the Virgin. In 1206, these same canons of the
cathedral of Châlons made a strange use of their priority;
they ordered the demolition of the church of the vassal chapter of Saint-Nicolas, on the ground that it was too near the
cathedral. The canons of Saint-Nicolas sent the pope a vigorous complaint, and Rome ordered the chapter of Saint-
Étienne to rebuild the church on the same place as the old
building. It was imperative to keep order among these
clerics and to see that the small were not oppressed or absorbed by the great. At Étampes, where there was no
cathedral, the fight between the chapter of Notre-Dame and
of Sainte-Croix lasted through the whole reign of Philip
Augustus and far beyond it; popes, kings, and archbishops
exhausted themselves in vain efforts to restore peace. However, an agreement was reached in 1210, in the terms of which
Sainte-Croix saw its defeat. Money matters had antagonized
the two communities; they quarreled over the revenues of
the parish. The agreement stipulated that the priests of
Sainte-Croix should never ring bells for matins; that they
should never accept gifts from the parishioners of Notre-
Dame, that they should not make Holy-bread, that they should
not visit the sick, that the cantor of Notre-Dame should have
a good prebend at Sainte-Croix, and that the parish rights
of the new town of Étampes should belong exclusively to
Notre-Dame. It was Notre-Dame of Étampes which was the

chief chapter, the sovereign power; to her must come the honor—and also the money.

Let us now enter a cathedral church; we shall find many kinds of disputes between members of the same community. We already know that the religious services were confided to two distinct personnels; side by side with the body of canons lived a college of priests or chaplains, charged with saying the innumerable masses founded by individuals, and even permitted to officiate at the high altar. But the canons did not agree with the chaplains; the priests of the choir were rivals of those of the chapels or the altar, who, having on the whole the heaviest burden to carry, tried to exempt themselves from the jurisdiction of the chapter and to monopolize certain revenues. There were collegiate churches, like that of Saint-Spire of Corbeil, where the canons and the chaplains were always in a state of hostility; and decrees like those of 1191 and 1209, and the oath required of the chaplains of Saint-Spire before they assumed their offices did not succeed in establishing harmony.

But in the very bosom of the chapter, among the seigniors who held prebends, passions were strong and brutal and conflicts were numerous.

Election contests were a first cause of trouble. In the election of high dignitaries the canons were almost always divided; the minority would not yield to the majority, because in the middle ages votes were not only counted, they were weighed. Besides the *major pars,* majority, there was the *sanior pars,* the wiser party, and each party claimed to represent the wisest opinion. Thus there came the interminable suit in the court of Rome and, while awaiting judgment, an internal quarrel in the church itself, which often went as far as brawls. We have already noticed the events caused by the election of a dean in the chapter of Amiens. The animated incidents that were caused by the election of a mere sacristan in 1186, as related by the cartulary of Maguelonne, are worth reading. One party of the canons of Maguelonne had irregularly elected a certain Guy as sacristan. The bishop and other canons were opposed to his installation. They excommunicated the intruder and his electors. Guy persisted in keeping the sacristy and doing

his duty. At the request of the bishop, the archbishop of
Narbonne came to Maguelonne to reëstablish order. But the
sacristan, firmly clinging to his office, called to his aid the
son of the count of Toulouse and the lord of Montpellier
himself. These laymen forced their way into the hall of
the chapter, insulted and menaced the bishop and his adherents. Pope Urban III was obliged to interfere and send
special agents to terminate the quarrel.

Outside of the electoral period, peace was no better
assured, for there were disputes between canons about
prebends and parochial rights and opposition of the plain
prebendaries to the dignitaries, who were accused of overstepping their powers and taking revenues which ought to
have been given to the entire community. This was why, in
1215, the chapter of Notre-Dame of Paris was at strife with
the chancellor, who was accused of having taken more than
the right amount of the income from the seal of the chancellor. The most numerous and violent conflicts were those
between the chapters and those of their number who, under
the name of provosts, were charged with the temporal administration of the capitular domains. The tendency which
in the feudal world caused all the officers and proxies of the
lords to appropriate their offices, together with the territory
on which the office rested, and to change their positions as
agents and administrators into proprietorships, had also had
its effect in these small ecclesiastical societies. The canons
invested with provostships came to consider these their own
property and to turn the rights and revenues, which belonged
to the whole community, to their own profit. The community,
having to fear complete spoliation, was obliged to counteract
this unfortunate manifestation of the feudal spirit. It was
compelled to reduce the provosts to their real positions, as
agents, and to take from the recalcitrants the domains which
they tried to appropriate. In consequence, there was serious
strife during the whole of the twelfth century between the
canons and their colleagues, the provosts (at Chartres, at
the time of the celebrated Ivo of Chartres, it went as far as
bloodshed). At the end of the twelfth century most of the
chapters had succeeded in reclaiming their domains from the
provosts and in confiding their administration directly to the

prebendaries themselves, either by suppressing the office of provosts and making the provosts simple lay agents, or by leaving the provosts simply a nominal authority. But at the time of Philip Augustus certain chapters still fought: for example, at Bordeaux, where the canons of the cathedral of Saint-André, in 1210, obtained from one of their provosts the recognition of their rights of hunting, fishing, and justice on the land of the provost; and even at Paris, where, in 1216, the chapter of Notre-Dame regulated the position of the provost and reorganized the whole administration of the domain. As the stewardships became vacant, they were to be restored to the community, which would control them; and the living provosts were to have their hands tied in such a manner that it would be impossible to trade in the lands which had been intrusted to them.

But the great subject of discord in the bosom of the churches, the most abundant source of conflicts, and the permanent cause of disorder in cathedrals was the ambiguous position of the bishop, who was at once the colleague and the superior of the canon. The cathedral belonged to the bishop and to the chapter; it was the undivided and limited territory which these two powers were obliged to share. Realizing the litigious and bellicose spirit of the men of the middle ages, one well understands that it was often the scene of strife.

Formerly, the head of the diocese had full and complete power over the priests of the cathedral, as over those of the diocese; the properties of the church were common to all of them; the episcopal power, spiritually as well as temporally, remained complete and absolute. But when the donations of the faithful had greatly increased the domain of the cathedral; when, by the general law of the differentiation of organisms, the chapter had been separated from the bishop and capitular property from episcopal property, the bishop and canons gradually entered into competition. The chapter tried to make itself independent of the bishop first in temporal things, then even in spiritual things, and presently succeeded with the aid of the popes, who, as we know, had an interest in diminishing the powers of the episcopacy. On many points the bishop and his chapter found themselves in the position of two brothers who are enemies; and the bitterness of family hatreds is well known. Their rivalry arose from a thousand different causes, and it appeared in a thousand different forms. They disputed over everything: the church itself, its treasure, the jurisdiction over the parishes, the right to elect certain officials of the diocese especially the archdeacons, the right to designate the holders of prebends, the right to lay excommunications, etc. And in all French provinces the same antagonism produced the same result. One could at hazard take the most dissimilar regions, as remote as possible from each other; in the time of Philip Augustus their condition in this respect never differed. At Bayonne, in 1198, Pope Celestine III was obliged to intervene to regulate the division of the revenues of the church between the bishop and the chapter. At Quimper, in 1220, the strife between Bishop Renaud and the canons was still in an acute state, still more violent here because the two powers were closely associated, the bishop of Quimper being a real canon who took part in the daily distributions. Here, as almost everywhere, it was the chapter which carried the day. Renaud abandoned his claims to policing the choir and nominating the prior of the hospital, ánd he restored to the canons various objects he had appropriated. At Beauvais, Bishop Philip of Dreux, in 1212, admitted that he had not the right to excommunicate subjects of the chapter. His successor, Miles of Nanteuil, in 1219, gave the canons the power of laying excommunications, of having them published in the parishes of the diocese, and assuring the execution of them. But the officers of the bishop and the curés did not easily submit to the anathemas of the canons of Beauvais, and between 1219 and 1221 there resulted a curious incident. The cathedral chapter of Saint-Pierre had excommunicated Peter of Bury, a provost of the bishop, guilty of having imprisoned a sergeant of the canons. The curés of the different churches of Beauvais refused to publish the excommunication. The dean of the chapter several times commanded them to heed it; finally, he summoned them to his presence and declared them suspended from their offices. "Take off your albs," he said to them; "you shall not take part in the procession." Most of them then decided to obey, but two of them protested and appealed to the archbishop of Reims. The document which gives us these details is interesting, because it shows how far the independence and claims of chapters could go in certain dioceses.

We can continue our tour of France. At Orléans, in 1217, the bishop, in conflict with Philip Augustus, laid an interdict on his city and on his diocese. This time he was in agreement with his chapter, that of Sainte-Croix; but the canons of the collegiate church of Saint-Aignan refused to observe the interdict, and continued to ring their bells and to open their church. The bishop suspended the dean of Saint-Aignan. A complicated suit in the court of Rome resulted. At Tours the archbishop was, in 1211, at strife with his metropolitan chapter over the ownership of a parish, and also with the powerful chapter of Saint-Martin, about the jurisdiction over the abbey of Beaulieu. This last conflict was permanent; in 1208, it gave rise to three lawsuits—decided at Orléans, Bourges, and Chartres. At Rouen, the archbishop and his chapter were at outs over certain revenues of the town of Dieppe. The canons laid an interdict on the cathedral; the matter was submitted to arbitrators, and the dean of the chapter ended the matter by making an apology. At Verdun, there was a veritable war between the dean and Bishop Robert: the canons did not want him as their bishop; they regarded him as ignorant and unworthy. They threatened him with a suit at Rome and made him so miserable that, in 1217, they forced him to resign his position. At Bordeaux, there were frequent struggles between the archbishop and his canons; the latter, in 1181, obtained from the pope the right of electing their dean, and, in 1195, they consented to a new transaction with the archbishop. In 1188, the cathedral chapter of Saint-Pierre of Troyes accused the bishop of having taken a part of the treasure of the church, especially a golden chalice and a silver table. Bishop Manasses had to restore what he had taken. Even at Paris, where the two powers seemed to live in fair harmony, the chapter of Notre-Dame, in 1219, obtained from Honorius III the right to excommunicate their aggressors in case the bishop of Paris refused to punish them. But, to witness fierce and continuous strife and sometimes actual war between a bishop and his canons, one should go to Maguelonne. There the provost of the chapter and the head of the diocese were at outs, one may say, the whole of the twelfth and thirteenth centuries. In 1186, one of the bishops of Maguelonne, John of Montlaur, a veritable tyrant, imprisoned the canons and beat them. Things went so far that they almost all deserted the cathedral, and the popes had difficulty in inducing them to return.

We know enough of this to conclude. The elements of ecclesiastical society were in a state of war, like those of the lay world. Chapters, far from living in peace in the cathedral, too often made it a field of battle. The bishop was not master there: he was forced to divide his power with the collective seigniory of the canons, his brothers; he saw them grow at his expense and, little by little, appropriate his wealth, his jurisdiction, and his independence.

CHAPTER V

THE BISHOP

AFTER a cleric had studied and become a master of arts and had obtained the prebend of a canon or of some capitular dignity, his chief ambition was to mount a step higher and become a bishop. However, in the time of Philip Augustus the episcopate was no longer what it had been in the earlier centuries of feudalism. The bishops had, in great number, lost both their spiritual and temporal preëminence. In the diocese they were no longer absolute masters of all that constituted ecclesiastical society and of every form of religious life, as formerly they had been. The independent monasteries escaped them and obeyed only the head of the order or the pope; chapters, as we have seen, tended to become independent, even disputed the cathedral with the bishops; the archdeacons, their chief auxiliaries, sought to take from them a part of the power which they had over the parish and its curé. Again, outside the diocese the bishops had to reckon with two powers, the king and the pope, who, although far away, governed them with an ever heavier hand. The pope seemed to have gained spiritually all that the bishops had lost in this regard. Every day the papacy interfered more actively in the elections, in the nominations to benefices, the government of the bishopric, and even in the smallest details of local ecclesiastical life. As episcopal jurisdiction was rendered almost useless by the development of the appeal to Rome, the Roman treasury began to exploit the bishoprics until the bishops complained bitterly. The interference of the king in the affairs of the diocese was much less frequent and galling. But Philip Augustus did not deprive himself of the satisfaction of exacting military service with great rigor from the bishops, and especially of subjecting them in pecuniary things to a system of forced requisitions, which caused them to cry out against the persecution. Finally, the bishops had always to struggle against their constant enemies:

the bourgeoisie of the free towns, the feudal laity, the castellan, and the baron—all of whom, especially in the country which royalty was not able to police, continually overran and pillaged the lands of the church and appropriated its domains, its revenues, and its episcopal rights. Thus the bishop had to be constantly on the defensive, watching, as it were, at the breach. To sum up, it was a hard calling, and one which at the end of the twelfth century, it would seem, gave less power and brought less profit than in times past.

But the importance and brilliance of the office obscured the unpleasant side so completely that it was still sought with the same avidity. Even though the authority of the bishop was weakened, the number of candidates did not diminish. The preachers of the period had not enough violent expressions with which to condemn the pursuit for a prelacy and the intrigues of the candidates. In the time of Philip Augustus and Innocent III money no longer played the same rôle as formerly in episcopal elections. Open, indecent simony was no longer possible, except in certain remote provinces, but the favor, influence, and recommendation of the king, of an important baron, of a great seigniorial family continued to show their effects. In spite of the demands of well-understood opinion, in spite of the efforts and surveillance of the popes, the episcopal personnel—although superior, taken as a whole, in its moral and intellectual worth to that of the preceding centuries—was far from attaining to the Christian ideal. The good and bad were strangely allied. In the lists of the French episcopate there was a curious diversity of types: the educated, pious theologian; the prelate or man of letters, who was a politician and a courtier; the turbulent prelate, who passed his life in a struggle; the highwayman, who treated his diocese like a conquered province; the rapacious usurer, ingenious in oppressing the members of his diocese; the rascal, whose crimes would have dishonored the episcopate and the church if it were not profoundly wrong to judge all one class of men by these exceptions.

*

* *

The bishop of the time of Philip Augustus appears to us as the head of a diocese and as a great lord, holding a high position in the hierarchy of the nobility. Like every feudal prince, he ruled the territory of which he was proprietor and suzerain, while the revenues accruing from this right and which came to be called " episcopal income " were truly seigniorial revenues.

As proprietor, the bishop possessed directly in his domain parish churches, abbeys, lands, forests, houses, and serfs: that is to say, everything that the other barons possessed. These properties, like those of the king and other lords of the laity, were administered by officers, called provosts, mayors, deans, and sergeants, having the double character of public agents or special intendants, and at the same time that of bailiffs, tax-collectors, judges, and police agents. The domain possessed by a bishop in an episcopal city was sometimes considerable. To get a clear idea of this fact we must realize that the bishop of Paris was almost as great a proprietor as the king. The bishop of Paris under Philip Augustus possessed in the *Cité* the episcopal palace and its dependencies, the whole *Île Saint-Louis,* the land of the Culture, and of the Ville-l'Évêque, which corresponded to the land lying between Saint-Roch on one side and Saint-Philippe-du-Roule and Saint-Augustin on the other; the Champeaux, comprising the land between Rue Saint-Honoré and the Pointe Saint-Eustache; the Bourg Saint-Germain, which is a long ribbon of land reaching from Saint-Germain-l'Auxerrois almost to the height of Montmartre; and on the left bank the field of Bruneau, a plot of ground near the Rue des Noyers and the Rue des Carmes. An act of Philip Augustus, issued in 1222, shows that the bishops of Paris divided the taxes and jurisdiction of this city with the king, and that his was by no means the lesser share.

As feudal lord, the bishop also possessed fiefs and drew from them the revenues which every suzerain enjoyed. His vassals paid him homage and owed him both military and court service, thus forming his seigniorial tribunal. Certain ones among them had besides the special duty of carrying him upon his throne, the *sedia gestatoria,* when just after his election he made his solemn entry, traversing the city and arriving at the cathedral for his installation. In order to find an account of the great number of fiefs which were attached to an episcopal suzerainty, one may, for example, observe the state of vassalage of the bishop of Paris as it was fixed in a cartulary of Notre-Dame drawn up between 1197 and 1208.

The feudal status of the bishop differed from that of the lay barons especially in two ways. First, as concerns the highest suzerain—that is to say, the king—the bishop since the ecclesiastical reform of the eleventh century no longer paid homage, but limited himself to taking the oath of fealty, which, however, did not exempt him from being forced to military or court service. Then, he was himself a suzerain of a special kind of vassal: he had fiefs "incorporeal"—that is, he required homage of cathedral functionaries for their ecclesiastical benefices. He received the liege-homage of the dean, the cantor, the chancellor, the head chaplain, the churchwardens, etc.

The bishop resembled the baron all the more, as his house, his private establishment—that is, all the arrangements for the maintenance of his person and his entourage,—was the same as that of counts, dukes, and of the king. He was served by the same high and petty officers. He had his seneschal or steward, his cupbearer, his marshal, his chamberlain or treasurer, his equerry, his master of the pantry, secretaries, chaplains, without counting lesser offices—porters, builders, drivers, etc. All these functionaries, supported by him and lodged in the houses connected with the episcopal palace, served him day in, day out. But, like the high suzerains and the king, he had high honorary officers—that is, certain vassals of the diocese,—who, by virtue of their fiefs, had the right of serving him at table, at the formal feasts, during special solemnities, and throughout the day of his installation.

Such, then, was the status, as shown by its principal characteristics and taken from the temporal point of view, of a bishop seen in the normal condition of his office, who, though being a great proprietor, was yet neither count nor duke. There existed prelates—like the archbishops of Reims, Vienne, or Arles; like the bishops of Puy, Mende, Lodève, Viviers, or Langres—who were the only suzerains of their cities. They accumulated pecuniary with episcopal power, and they had, consequently, even more than their confrères, the bearing, authority, and resources of a great baron who is king in his province. There was seldom question here over the episcopate, such as presented itself in a very great majority of dioceses where the authority of the bishop was in competition with or dependent on that of a layman. And it would be interesting to see how these bishops actually lived, with what order, how they ordained their financial affairs, how their budget was regulated; in a word, to what amount the receipts of a bishopric could raise an episcopal fortune.

The documents of the period of Philip Augustus are far from satisfying our curiosity in this regard. It has been attempted to fix approximately the annual income in revenue, grain, money, forest, and river produce which a bishop of Chartres received when incumbent of his extensive diocese in the thirteenth century, and the amount, in terms of actual money, was found to be five hundred thousand francs; which is certainly a minimum, for one must add the revenues accruing from feudal rights and indirect taxes. Unquestionably, this sum of half a million is not too large in any case. One must think of the pace of the life which the bishops of that time were obliged to lead, of the frequence of journeys which their duties toward the king and pope imposed upon them, of the pecuniary demands of these two powers, and of the established traditions with regard to hospitality and charity. The duties of the episcopate were numerous, and, at the time of which we speak, the bishop did not, like his chapter, have sources of self-enrichment from the gifts and endowments of the faithful. The land and capital of the canons increased daily, while the fortune of the bishop remained practically stationary. He could only augment the revenues of the diocese by an administration at the same time energetic and clever, a thing in which not all prelates were gifted. In general, nevertheless, bishops did not die poor. Almost all—this is seen from the tenor of their wills and information from their obituaries—found means of making gifts to their churches, to monks, and to indigent persons. They enriched the treasure of their cathedrals more or less, leaving books, objects of great price, priestly vestments, and costly vases. The will of Peter of Nemours, bishop of Paris, dated June,

1218, contains a curious enumeration of objects left by him to Notre-Dame, Saint-Victor, and Saint-Martin of Tours: Spanish tapestries, coffers from Limoges, beautiful manuscripts, etc. In 1181, there died at Auxerre, Bishop William of Toucy, whose bequests to all the chapters and to all the abbeys of the diocese have been enumerated at great length by his biographer. He left to his cathedral a silver chalice and basins, valuable stuffs, and a portion of his library. Another bishop of Auxerre, William of Seignelay, the successor to Hugh of Noyers, when he quitted his bishopric for that of Paris in 1220, gave to his chapter rich pontifical vestments, a gold miter set with pearls, two silver basins goldplated, some cushions of beautiful work, a gold cross containing a relic, nine gold marks to secure a cross and chalice, houses, vineyards, and incomes. Moreover, adds the chronicle of Auxerre, his successor found all the episcopal abodes furnished and provided with an abundance of grain and wines. In 1180, John of Salisbury, bishop of Chartres, had bequeathed to his cathedral precious stuffs, a cope of great value, his episcopal ring, and all his library. Details of this kind abound in church obituaries. But one need not conclude that the possession of a bishopric was necessarily a guarantee of wealth. These generosities before and at the time of death are often to be reconciled with a poor financial condition. The history of the bishopric of Auxerre gives us a proof in the person of Hugh of Noyers, that great builder of fortresses. He had borrowed money from the treasury of the cathedral and would have restored it with usury, says the chronicler, if death had only left him time. As a matter of fact, he bequeathed this debt to his successor.

But there were others who knew how to enrich themselves. Such was the case of Maurice of Sully. Son of a poor peasant of the seigniory of Sully in Orléanais, he had studied at the university of Paris. There he led the life of a poor student. It was even said that he begged his bread and acted as servant to rich students. Master of theology, he became canon and then archdeacon of Notre-Dame. His reputation as teacher and preacher pointed him out for higher positions. Elected bishop of Paris in 1160, he had so good a talent for managing episcopal finances that he was able to get the money necessary for the reconstruction of his cathedral, and, on his death, to give a considerable amount of gifts to Notre-Dame: a house near the cloister, road-rights in the outskirts of Paris, religious ornaments, a sum of money for the decoration of the high altar, one hundred livres for roofing the cathedral, a hundred livres for poor clerics, a hundred livres for the canons diligent at matins, a hundred and ninety silver marks to buy land and vineyards, the usufruct of which his grandnephew was to have; to the abbey of Saint-Victor, nine hundred livres (more than one hundred and fifty thousand francs); to Saint-Germain-l'Auxerrois, forty livres, etc. Nor were the poor forgotten, but benefited by special bequests, the value of which is not known. Maurice of Sully, a type of the pious bishop having succeeded by his own merit, certainly possessed nothing before entering the church of Paris, showing that the functions of archdeacon and bishop enriched even those who exercised them honestly.

＊

＊　　＊

As religious head, the bishop did not only preside over the cathedral services, but had charge of supervising and con-trolling the conduct of priests in all the churches and in all the parishes of the diocese.

It was he who named the curé of the parishes directly subordinate to the bishopric, or simply conferred the charge of souls upon the curé supported by patronage. He alone had power to ordain clerics and it was his duty to induce them to accept the priesthood. Then, having ordained and installed the priests, he had finally that very hard obligation of holding them in the narrow path: that is to say, of watch-ing to see that they were well taught and well behaved. And we can see how painful and difficult the uncouthness of the lower clergy rendered this part of the episcopal task. In order to carry it on at all, it was necessary for the bishop to keep himself as much as possible in contact with the min-isters of the parishes. Behold him, then, riding to all parts of his diocese in order to make his visits—that is, his tours of inspection of rural churches: he assembles the deans or the archpriests, conducts summary inquests, hears accusations against priests, suspends, corrects, and threatens the suspected and guilty. But this work of inspector and itinerant judge did not suffice; the bishop could not always be off on long journeys, and then it was that the parish priests left their parishes to come to him. Every year he held a synod—that is, a general assembly of clerics of the diocese in the great hall of his palace or in the choir of the cathedral; and there again he preached, gave his instructions, reprimanded, and punished in a way to insure the maintenance of discipline and to reform customs.

These were both things difficult to attain, for the clerics of this period, by nature violent and unmanageable, would not accept correction easily. They resisted, especially when they were forbidden to keep concubines publicly; they appealed to Rome to suspend the punishment, and even openly revolted. The kindest and most virtuous of the bishops of this time, Maurice of Sully, bishop of Paris, was himself in struggle against his clergy. And, as if the bishop did not have enough anxiety over keeping the parish priests in hand, he was obliged to struggle for this very control against certain dignitaries who usurped his authority. These dignitaries were the archdeacons. Delegated by the bishop to help him in his task and to administer a part of the diocese in his name, the archdeacons had little by little forgotten that they were nothing but representatives of the episcopal power. They were inclined to keep the proceeds of the revenues of the diocese for themselves; they appointed, judged, and excommunicated curés at their pleasure, as if the archdeaconry were a small-sized bishopric. This was a curious example of the phenomenon of feudal appropriation carried over into ecclesiastical society. Certain it is that the bishop, threatened with being deprived of his power throughout the diocese, had to struggle to defend himself. In many dioceses there was war, secret or declared, between the prelate and his archdeacons. In all cases there was toil and constant effort on the part of the bishop to keep the rights and money belonging to him, so that at the end of the twelfth century a certain number of prelates had taken a decisive measure. Instead of delegating their authority to the archdeacon, now become their enemy, they confided it to special clerics called "clerics of the bishop," chosen and removable by them. These confidential agents traveled with them constantly, forming their permanent council, carrying their messages, aiding them in giving judgments, and collecting their revenues. These clerics of the bishop gave rise to "official" and "high vicars," two institutions dating from the time of Philip Augustus. It is thanks to them that the bishop was able to combat victoriously the usurping tendencies of the archdeacons and to maintain his disputed authority over the parish and the curé.

But in the diocese there were other organs of religious life than the parish; there were chapters and orders. There were then two classes of establishments which were another cause of labor and another source of difficulty and conflict for the bishop. Not all the canons were, like those of the cathedral, in competition with the bishop, but it was not less necessary to watch them, to oblige them to carry out their duties, and to give them regulations. As to the monks, either they were entirely exempt—that is, completely independent of the bishop—or else they were under his authority. In the first case, when the independent abbeys possessed a certain amount of wealth and fame, they were a decidedly serious obstacle in the exercise of episcopal power. Not only did they repel all interference of the bishop in their affairs to the point of not even admitting him to set foot in their churches, but they quarreled with him over jurisdiction, priories, and domains. There was constant struggle between the secular and regular clergy; certain abbots furnished opposition to the bishop even in the matter of dress, by obtaining from the pope the right to wear the episcopal insignia, sandals, miter, and crozier. The presence of exempt abbeys in the bishopric was a perpetual cause of uneasiness and irritation for the head of the diocese, but the subordinate abbeys in their turn bothered the bishop more than he wished; he had to inspect them like the parishes and correct abuses, protect them against plundering and do good in every way, particularly by means of gifts. Religious opinion required the bishops to be the benefactors of their abbeys, and even to found new ones in order to multiply the homes of learning in their dioceses.

Monks, canons, archdeacons, and curés gave enough worry

and trouble and occasions for strife to the bishop for one
to suppose that his relations with the clergy of the diocese
amply filled his time and that he had so much to do at home
that no time remained to pay attention to his colleagues and
equals, the suffragan bishops of the same province. And yet,
since he was subordinate to an archbishop, he was obliged
to fulfil certain obligations toward his superior. He had to
leave his diocese in order to assist at archiepiscopal synods
or to witness the consecration of the other bishops of the
province. Moreover, the archbishop had the right to make
use of him,—to delegate him as judge in certain lawsuits,—
so that, while supporting all alone the exceedingly heavy
weight of the diocese, the bishop was obliged, in a certain
measure, to work in the affairs of the province. But here,
too, there could be, and often was, cause for difficulties and
contentions. Relations with the archbishop were not always
peaceful; the archbishop was often tempted to encroach on
the episcopal right of judging subjects of the bishop in the
first instance, and the latter had to struggle to resist this
claim. The conflict sometimes became violent, going to the
point of open war. Thus, in 1196, we see Bishop William
of Lisieux in open war against the archbishop of Rouen,
Walter of Coutances. The latter excommunicated the unmanageable bishop and in a letter, which is extant, accuses
him with vehemence, " of having raised his heel against his
mother, the church of Rouen, impelled by a spirit of pride
and by every pestilential breath of Erebus." The misfortune
was that conflicts of this nature were not solved at home, but
that the superior and the subordinate, the archbishop and
bishop, were obliged to go beyond the Alps to seek the solution of their strife at the hands of the pope and his judges.

The pope himself was a superior in another way as redoubtable and exacting toward the bishops as were the archbishops. In the time of Philip Augustus, centralization of the
church under the hand of the papacy and the cardinals was an
accomplished thing, and the episcopate was the first victim of
this state of affairs. Thanks to the appeal to Rome, the
majority of lawsuits of ecclesiastical society were now carried before the pontifical court. But, happily, not all cases
went to Rome, for it was the habit of the pope to employ

bishops as delegates of the Holy See for conflicts of
little importance. They had charge of inquests, of hearing
parties and testimonies, and of pronouncing the final sentence in the pope's name. As if the bishop did not have enough
to do with deciding all matters of his diocese and sometimes
even those of his province, he was overwhelmed by the pope
with extraordinary duties and special missions. Maurice of
Sully, bishop of Paris, who was in office thirty-six years,
was delegated at least twenty times as judge by the popes;
which is evidently the minimum, though it would be necessary
to have all the contemporaneous documents to learn the total
number of times he was commissioned by the Roman church.

Still the bishop might think himself fortunate if the
papacy simply obliged him to perform some duty in his
country. In cases of particular gravity, when he was himself the accused or the complainant, it was necessary for him
to appear at Rome in person. Moreover, he also had to go
there when the pope assembled all Christendom in a general
council. The journey to Italy was a dreadful one for the
contemporaries of Philip Augustus, entailing great fatigue,
dangers of every kind, and considerable waste of time and
money. But the obligation was imperative, and the pope did
not allow them to escape it easily. He threatened the recalcitrants, urged the tardy, and punished those who stayed away
without valid excuse. In this connection it is interesting to
read the correspondence of Alexander III and Bartholomew,
archbishop of Tours. The archbishop had not appeared at
the third Lateran council in 1179, although his presence at
Rome was necessary to regulate many affairs of great importance. The pope wrote to him several weeks after, re-
proaching him for his absence. He bade him repair his
fault by coming to Rome by the fourth Sunday in Lent or,
at the latest, the second Sunday after Easter. The archbishop was not anxious to make the journey to Italy, and,
instead of replying himself, he wrote to Alexander by one
of his friends, Stephen of Tournai, abbot of Sainte-
Geneviève, a man on good terms with Rome. Stephen excused the archbishop of Tours as well as he could, testifying
that at the time of the council Bartholomew was sick, that
he could not have gone to Rome without danger, and that

besides it was necessary for him to go to Paris to confer
with the king. Next came another letter from the pope to
the archbishop of Tours, but this time couched in almost
threatening terms; Alexander trusted that, of course, the
prelate would come to Rome on one of the days which he
had set; he should have been punished for being absent
from the council; he had been spared only at the request
of Louis VII and his son, Philip Augustus. As for the final
delay, he would give him until next Saint Martin's day; then,
in case of non-appearance, the pope would be severe.

Bishops had to invoke legal excuses and have recourse to
every kind of legal subterfuge. The pope demanded the
journey to Italy, under pain of excommunication, and his
command often cost them their lives. The journey was not
without danger for those who undertook it; indeed, examples
of French bishops who ended their lives in Italy are not rare.
Aubri, archbishop of Reims, died at Pavia in 1218. Gérald
of Cros, archbishop of Bourges, also died in the same year,
a short time after leaving Rome. Henry of Dreux, bishop
of Orléans, having come to Rome in 1197 to ask for the freedom of his brother, the bishop of Beauvais, who had been
imprisoned by Richard the Lion-Hearted, fell sick at Siena
and never recovered. Hugh of Noyers, bishop of Auxerre,
died ten days after his arrival. The occurrence became so
frequent in the thirteenth century that the popes ended by
taking a profit from it. They decided that, whenever the
episcopal sees became vacant *in curia*—that is, during the
bishop's sojourn at the Roman curia,—the papacy should
have the right to nominate a successor to the office. If we
possessed more documents for the reign of Philip Augustus,
it is very probable that the number of French bishops whose
presence was noticed in Rome would be greatly increased.
One might mention Arnaud-Amauri, archbishop of Narbonne,
pleading before the pope in 1217 against Simon de Montfort; Walter of Coutances, archbishop of Rouen, pleading
against his suzerain, Richard the Lion-Hearted; Walter
Cornu, bishop-elect of Paris, in 1220 defending himself at
Rome against the chancellor of his church; Matthew, bishop
of Toul, a rascal of whom we shall speak again, coming to
plead his own cause in 1210 before Innocent III; and many

other examples of the same kind which would be easy to gather.

Thus we see how business, lawsuits, fatiguing moves, and more or less perilous journeys,—the normal relation between the head of a diocese and the members of ecclesiastical society, whether his subordinates or his superiors,—were carried on. To carry out this much required a well tempered mind and body. But all is not finished: we have said nothing about the outside conditions which fastened even harder obligations on the bishops. The period of the reign of Philip Augustus was marked by four great crusades, without counting a certain number of expeditions to the Holy Land of less importance. Bishops could not possibly keep out of this movement, but were forced by their position to participate in it; indeed, public opinion demanded that they should set the people a good example. They were obliged to leave their country and go with kings, great lords, and knights. And the fact is that they did not fail in this respect. A great many of them departed to fight the infidel or heretic in Spain, Languedoc, the Holy Land or Egypt, and a certain number of these pilgrim bishops never again saw their dioceses or native land.

Below is a simple enumeration of facts and dates which is eloquent enough in itself in giving an exact idea of the extraordinarily active life of the bishops of France.

Aubri of Humbert, archbishop of Reims, took part in the crusade against the Albigenses from 1209 to 1212; in 1215, he went to Rome to the Lateran council; in 1218, he departed for Syria, remaining there several months; he then embarked at Alexandria and was surprised by the Saracens at Lisbon. Freed by the knights of Calatrava, he passed through Italy again and, as we have seen, died at Pavia. In 1212, Arnaud-Amauri, archbishop of Narbonne, and William Amanieu, archbishop of Bordeaux, fought the Saracens of Spain with King Alfonso of Castile. In 1190 and 1191, Bernard, bishop of Bayonne, Girard, archbishop of Auch, John, bishop of Évreux, Manasses, bishop of Langres, Philip of Dreux, bishop of Beauvais, and Peter, bishop of Toul, took part in the third crusade, remaining in Sicily and assisting at the siege of Saint-Jean-d'Acre. In 1202 to 1205,

Nivelon of Chérisy, bishop of Soissons, and Garnier of Trainel, bishop of Troyes,—two heroes of the fourth crusade, —fought in the Greek Empire, taking Constantinople, playing an important rôle in the election of the first Latin Emperor, and then returning to their dioceses laden with glory, money, and relics. From 1209 to 1219, there was a continual coming and going of bishops who left their dioceses in order to perform their forty days' military service in the war against the Albigenses. Besides the archbishop of Reims, there appeared in Languedoc, simultaneously or successively, the archbishops of Rouen and Bourges; the bishops of Autun, Châlons, Cambrai, Limoges, Lisieux, Orléans, Paris, Chartres, Bayeux, Laon, Puy, and Saintes. After 1218, the period of the crusade of Damietta, the archbishops of Reims and Bordeaux, the bishops of Autun, Limoges, Lisieux, Beauvais, and Paris departed for Egypt and the Orient.

The fatigue and danger that a perilous and costly undertaking, a pilgrimage to a far country, or a crusade to the Holy Land, represented in the middle ages need not be emphasized. One might for this period mention a long list of bishops who died during their journeys abroad: Aubri of Humbert, archbishop of Reims, in 1218; Eudes of Vaudémont, bishop of Toul, in 1196; John of Béthune, bishop of Cambrai, in 1219; John of Vérac, bishop of Limoges, in 1218; Jourdain, bishop of Lisieux, in 1218. In 1192, Manasses, bishop of Langres, died in France, but of a sickness contracted during the third crusade; Nivelon of Chérisy, bishop of Soissons, in 1207; Peter of Nemours, bishop of Paris, in 1219; Peter, bishop of Toul, in 1191, etc. It would be interesting to compile a complete obituary; then one might see how many victims the crusades had in the episcopal personnel and how lightly these bishops considered the risks of an expedition across the sea or an absence not only of many months but of many years. Motives for going varied, no doubt, among individuals. Some took the cross from scruples of conscience, from professional necessity, from deference to the demands of the age; others, for love of adventure and in the hope of enriching their church with relics from the Orient; or simply for devotion, to reap the benefits of a campaign against the enemies of the faith. But whatever the motive, whether willingly or not, they none the less went in the face of certain peril, and this again is proof of how much activity, moral energy, and physical strength the episcopacy demanded.

The same conclusion is reached, if one considers the episcopal calling from its temporal side and studies the relations of the bishop with the lay surroundings in which he was called to live. Though proprietor and lord, he was exposed to the attacks and pillages of which church property was always the victim on the part of nobles, both great and small. Without doubt, there were certain dioceses—that of Paris, for example—where resolute government, like that of Philip Augustus, had brought about a relative amount of order. Wherever there lived a high suzerain, strong and respected, the bishop had less trouble in defending his properties and revenues from the castellans, brigands, or persecuting barons. But there were many bishoprics where the head of the diocese, ceaselessly harassed by pillages, had no other resource than to intrench himself within the episcopal house, which was transformed into a strong château, and hold himself ever in readiness to engage in battle. Let one, for example, read the entertaining history of the bishops of Auxerre in the time of Hugh of Noyers and William of Seignelay; it is nothing but a series of conflicts with all the lay powers of the diocese, a perpetual and often dangerous strife, in which the bishop defended himself, not only by acts of anathema, but with ready arms, with men-at-arms, and retainers. He found enemies everywhere: in the country the troublesome and surly petty nobility; in the cities the count with whom he shared authority, and the bourgeoisie, often organized into a commune that did not love the church lord and strove to impair his power. Among the cases of this kind which resounded loudest in the period of Philip Augustus it is sufficient to note the struggle of Bishop Stephen of Tournai with the inhabitants of his episcopal town; of Philip of Dreux and Miles of Nanteuil, bishops of Beauvais, with the bourgeoisie of Beauvais; of Hugh of Noyers, bishop of Auxerre, with the count of Auxerre, Peter of Courtenay; of Robert of Meung, bishop of Puy, with the bourgeoisie and nobility of his town; of the bishops of Ver-

dun and Cambrai with the bourgeoisie and knights of their
two cities, etc. There were dioceses where the conflict with
the laity became a real war, with sieges, massacres, and battles, and sometimes it was the blood of the bishop which
flowed. In 1220, the bishop of Puy was assassinated by a
nobleman whom he had excommunicated; in 1208, the bishop
of Verdun was slain in a riot by a lance-thrust, while already,
in 1181, another bishop of Verdun had met his death while
besieging the château of Sainte-Menehould.

These several facts suffice to show all the painful necessities, the suffering, and daily peril which the career of a
bishop comprised. To finish this demonstration there remain
to be seen the consequences which the rôle of vassal and of
high functionary to royalty entailed upon the bishop. For
—let us not deceive ourselves—the bishop, in regard to the
lay sovereign, was not merely in a position of a feudatory
who had no more contact with the suzerain once he had fulfilled his feudal obligations. The bishop was in the king's
dependence, a dependence close and intimate, and the king as
the protector of the churches exploited his bishopric in every
way. From his bishops he demanded contributions, their
presence in the royal army, and political services of every
nature. He disposed of their money, their men-at-arms, and
time without scruple; in brief, he considered them and used
them as servants and agents, of whom he could demand anything. And, if the bishops resented this manner of doing,
if they resisted demands which they found excessive, there
was conflict, there was war with all its consequences: interdict placed on the land, excommunication of persons, occupation of the land with armed force, confiscation of episcopal
incomes, proscription of the bishop, who was driven from
his see and perhaps from the kingdom.

It will suffice here to recall the more severe conflicts, nearly
all of which ended in the defeat of episcopal power: a conflict with the archbishop of Sens, in 1181, over a question
of jurisdiction; with the archbishop of Rouen, in 1196, over
a question of property; with the bishop of Paris and many
other bishops of the north of France, in 1200, apropos of
the affair of Ingeborg; with the bishop of Auxerre, in 1206,
on the subject of the royal prerogative; with the bishops of

Orléans and Auxerre, in 1210, over military services; with the bishop of Paris, in 1221, over the question of jurisdiction and property, etc. And the same quarrels which agitated Capetian France also troubled Plantagenet France. We see Richard the Lion-Hearted, in quarrels with the archbishop of Rouen in 1197, with the archbishop of Poitiers in 1180; John Lackland, in a struggle with the bishop of Limoges in 1204. On all sides things were the same: the bishop who, in his relations with the clergy and nobility of his diocese, found so many difficulties to conquer, so many adversaries to subdue, was obliged to cope with the sovereign and to strive against an oppressive royalty, a terrible superaddition of trouble, care, and danger.

By dint of concessions and docility, it was possible to avoid conflict and remain at peace with the king, but it was a peace singularly agitated and troubled by continual demands for money and services. The mere obligation of assisting at political and judicial assemblies and great gatherings of the royal army, was a source of great fatigue and considerable expense for the French prelates. The bishops sought to escape it as much as possible, but still it was harder not to attend the king's convocations than to escape those of the pope. The king was always near and held material power. In 1193, Stephen, bishop of Tournai, a peaceful man of letters, who dreaded traveling, sent the archbishop of Reims a tearful letter. The king had summoned him to appear with his men-at-arms at Mantes on the vigil of Ascension and the vigil of Pentecost. "What is to be done?" demanded the bishop.

"I know nothing of military affairs. I am vowed to religion, which is not to lead the life of the camps. Yet here I am called, who have never taken part in battle, and am ordered to arm myself, I who have never been able to bear arms. Since the time of Chilperic the kings of France have never demanded anything from the bishops of Tournai except the oath of fealty and attendance at court. It is indeed hard for me to enter into a quarrel with my lord the king, but it is certainly impossible for me to do what he wishes. I find myself between the anvil and the hammer, where I shall have to offend the king or do a service which I am unwilling to do."

A letter from this same bishop three years later shows him again overcome by the summons of Lent of 1196. He was summoned by the archbishop of Reims to come and assist at the consecration of the bishop of Châlons on March 24; was summoned by the king to be present between the Vaudreuil and Gaillon in Normandy, where there was to be an interview between the sovereigns of France and England, on March 31; was summoned finally to Paris on April 7, to be present at the lawsuit of the bishop of Paris and the abbey of Chelles. He excused himself to the archbishop of Reims:

"My Father; I am sixty-eight years old, and I feel death near. Spare thy servant; my spirit is prompt to obey thee but my flesh is weak. I cannot without great danger to my body undertake and endure such journeys. If I should start out on the roads, I would never arrive at my destination."

The bishops did not always find it convenient to allege old age and infirmities; such excuses often found the king skeptical, and, instead of accepting them, he summoned the defaulters to justice for failure in feudal duty. Then they came to the king's court or his camp, no matter how painful the journey. But it did not suffice simply to be present. At every turn the king charged his bishops with business missions and with embassies abroad. The episcopal personnel furnished him with agents, diplomats, and administrators, who cost him nothing. Thus many bishops, willy-nilly, took an active part in politics, being obliged to add to the daily business with which they were burdened the extraordinary services which were demanded of them. Without speaking of William of Champagne, archbishop of Reims, and Walter of Coutances, archbishop of Rouen,—who were veritable prime ministers, the one to Philip Augustus and the other to the king of England,—one may mention William of Chemilly, bishop of Avranches, charged in 1198 with an embassy to Germany by Richard the Lion-Hearted; William, bishop of Lisieux, sent in 1200 by John Lackland to Portugal to negotiate a suit for marriage; Hélie, bishop of Bordeaux, on whom devolved the mission of conducting Blanche of Castile from Spain to Normandy in 1200; John, bishop of Évreux, charged with several missions by Henry II and Richard the Lion-Hearted; John of Vérac, bishop of Limoges, principal agent of Philip Augustus in western France; Maurice of

Sully, bishop of Paris, charged with many diplomatic or administrative missions by the king of France. The list of these commissioned bishops would stretch out indefinitely. They were even employed to command military forces, like the bishop of Bayonne and the archbishop of Auch, who in 1190 took the office of admiral at the instance of Richard the Lion-Hearted; and the archbishop of Bourges, Simon of Sully, who in 1221 conducted a corps of the army in Languedoc which was sent against the Albigenses by Philip Augustus. Some of them made a specialty of war, as did Philip of Dreux, bishop of Beauvais, and Guérin, bishop of Senlis, strategist of Bouvines. Much did Philip Augustus owe them.

*

* *

But such labors did not yet suffice to cover all the activities of the bishop. At this time when gothic art appeared,—if not in its richest, at least in its purest and most soberly elegant form,—the majority of bishops were great builders. Contemporaries themselves were impressed by this fact. In this regard the chronicle of Auxerre contains a very appropriate passage:

" In those times men were again fired with a passion for building new churches. Our bishop [William of Seignelay] seeing that his church of Auxerre, built in the taste of former times, was badly preserved and falling from age while in all the neighboring dioceses new churches were raising their splendid apses to the skies resolved to rebuild his own according to the dictates of modern art and to intrust its decoration to more expert architects. He did not wish his church to be inferior, either in beauty of ensemble or in care of detail, to those of other bishops. Therefore he caused the ancient edifice to be pulled down commencing with the apse, so that, deprived of its antique appearance, the cathedral of Auxerre might reappear brilliant in youth and elegance and in all the magnificence of its renovation."

Note this well-marked tendency of bishops to vie with each other in the grandeur and expense of the reconstruction of their cathedrals. It was a fad, a contagious passion; each one of them, at least in northern France, wished a church built in the new style, and the old Roman churches were everywhere torn down. It was not even necessary for them to be old. At Paris, in order to rebuild his cathedral, Maurice of Sully demolished the church of Notre-Dame, which had been carefully rebuilt seventy years before under Louis the Fat. At Laon, Bishop Walter of Mortagne, in 1170, built his gothic church in place of a Roman cathedral dating from 1114. Roman was not the style of the day; something new was wanted, and that style which architects called gothic excited an admiration the expression of which has come down to us. Robert of Torigny, abbot of Mont-Saint-Michel, contemporary of Louis VII and Philip Augustus, said of Notre-Dame in Paris when he saw it under construction, " When this church is finished there will be no work this side the mountains which can be compared to it."

The construction of a cathedral was to a bishop the culminating deed of his episcopacy, preëminently his *magnum opus*. The architect to whom he confided the chief technical direction of the enterprise was the master-builder (*magister operis*), but unfortunately the names of the creators of these marvels have not come down to us. Under the orders of the architect, the workmen (*operarii*) labored: that is, the members of the corps of different trades employed in the construction and decoration of the building. It was by these aids that the bishop, seconded by his chapter, accomplished the erection of a monument which was his best title to remembrance and to recognition by the people.

And there were few episcopal cities, especially in northern France, which, during the forty years of the reign of Philip Augustus, did not at least see their monument begun; very few regions which remained aloof from this great artistic movement. A remarkable thing, noticed by others long since, is that the towns and communes where the bourgeoisie was so restless, often so hostile to the bishop and the church, were not those which built the least gorgeous cathedrals, which certainly proves that, despite the theories of Viollet-le-Duc on the lay character of the corporations which built them, the work was religious and episcopal before everything else. It was the bishop with his corps of canons who always appeared as the inspirer, supervisor, and financial backer of the enterprise. The church was his work, and not that of the bourgeoisie, whatever the participation of the faithful in the expense. To satisfy ourselves of this, let us make a tour of France; we shall see just what the contemporaries of Philip Augustus said.

First, in the region north of the Loire, especially in Capetian France, which is the cradle of the new architecture, the workshops are on all sides in full activity. At Amiens, there is Bishop Evrard of Fouilloy, who in 1220 begins to build the most complete of all our cathedrals with the plans of the architect, Robert of Luzarches. At Auxerre, Bishop William of Seignelay lays the first stone of the choir of his church in 1215, for it is the choir which was generally begun first; it is important in the first degree for the canons to be able to officiate; the nave, the portals, the towers, and the transept come after, and will be the work of one or many centuries. The work goes on so quickly at Auxerre that at the end of a year the high partition of the choir is almost finished. The chronicle does not name the architect, the *magister operis*, but it relates that, by his imprudence, he was the cause of a catastrophe. He thought that by props and transverse beams he had sufficiently strengthened the two towers of the old church which were situated on each side of the ancient choir. But it was perceived that fissures began to appear. The canons asked him whether they could continue celebrating their offices without danger. "Never fear," answered the architect. But one of his employees declared that he was not of the same opinion; that he thought it would not be safe an hour hence. The architect replied that it was useless to frighten the chapter, since the props were firm. "But," returned the canons, "are you able to assure us that there is no risk?" "I cannot guarantee anything absolutely; I do not read the future." This reply decided the canons to transfer to the chapel annex; and well for them that they did, for hardly had the bells rung in the south tower, than it fell with a crash like thunder upon the north tower. And then those miraculous acts were seen to occur which could not fail to accompany a work so pleasing to Heaven as the building of a cathedral. Two young men who were watching the masons work and who were on the tower at the moment it fell, by a real miracle had time to save themselves; while certain objects of worship were recovered from the rubbish, intact. A little later, when the workmen were laboring at the rubbish, a piece of wall which remained on the tower all at once threatened to give way. They all saved themselves, but one of them perceived that he had left his coat in a dangerous place, where the wall was tottering; he ran there and was thought to be lost; but happily God watched over him and just in time arrested the collapse of the wall, which would certainly have crushed him.

God was with those who built to do Him honor. At Châlons-sur-Marne on the 29th of August, 1183, the nave and transept of Notre-Dame, rebuilt according to the rules of the new architecture, were consecrated. Here, though an exception, they had not begun with the choir. The choir itself was not built until the first years of the thirteenth century and consecrated in 1322. At Évreux, the cathedral, also dedicated to Our Lady, had been almost destroyed in 1194 by a fire in the course of the war between Philip Augustus and Richard the Lion-Hearted. In 1202, Bishop Robert of Roye undertook to rebuild the great nave and constructed the triforium of a subdued elegance. At Lisieux, Saint-Pierre had been commenced in 1141 by Bishop Arnoul, but left unfinished by him in 1183. In 1215, it was enlarged; the choir was lengthened and was surrounded by an ambulatory and several apsis chapels. At Rouen, after 1207, they worked at the cathedral Notre-Dame. At Meaux, the gifts of Countess Marie of Champagne permitted the bishops to continue the work begun in 1170. Toward 1210 the rafters and galleries were built, and about 1220 the greater part of the choir was rebuilt. At Noyon, the cathedral begun in 1152 was practically finished in the first year of the thirteenth century. Ten years later, in 1211, Aubri of Humbert, archbishop of Reims, laid the first stone of the choir of his marvelous cathedral, but the work did not go on quickly here, the choir not being finished until 1241. But at least we know the name of the man who built it— Jean of Orbais, to whom belongs the honor, wrongly paid to Robert of Coucy, of being the first architect of the cathedral of Reims. Work was also done at Troyes, where Bishop Hervé, before dying in 1223, finished the sanctuary of Saint-Pierre and the chapels surrounding it. At Laon, Notre-Dame, so imposing with its four towers and its enormous symbolic animals hanging over the town, had been commenced at the end of the reign of Louis VII by Bishop Walter of Mortagne at about 1170. It was building all during the reign of Philip Augustus. The choir, which is the oldest part of the building, was finished in 1225, and the façade dates from the time of the battle of Bouvines.

The cathedral of Soissons was the work of one of the heroes of the fourth crusade, Bishop Nivelon of Chérisy, one of the most ardent hunters of Byzantine relics. It was to lodge them more sumptuously that he enlarged or rather rebuilt the sanctuary of his church. We are more fortunate in the cathedral of Soissons, for we know exactly at what time the choir was finished. It has its date carved in a stone in the wall and the inscription reads thus, " On May 13, 1212. the community of canons began to enter this choir."

In the valley of the Loire and its confines the buildings are less numerous, but some are among the most beautiful. At Chartres, the Roman church had been burned in 1194. Bishop Renaul of Mouçon began immediately to build an immense cathedral; about 1220 the great rose window was placed and the arches were for the most part finished. The historian, William of Armorica, compares the roof of the church to an immense tortoise shell: " See it," he writes, " as it arises anew, dazzling with sculpture. It is a work of art which has no equal in the entire world. It can withstand fire even to judgment day." At Mans, in 1217, the bishop had the choir of Saint-Julien rebuilt. At Poitiers, the high altar of Saint-Pierre was dedicated in 1199, and between 1204 and 1214 there were set up the beautiful windows of the crucifixion. Finally, at Bourges, the cathedral Saint-Étienne was begun in 1192.

This movement spread even into the most distant provinces. The primatial church of Lyon was built under the direction of Archbishop Guichard about 1175, and the cathedral Saint-Étienne of Toulouse (1211) rose in the midst of the war against the Albigenses. At Bayonne, Bishop William of Donzac laid the first stone of Sainte-Mårie in 1213. In Brittany, those of Quimper and Saint-Pol-de-Léon were

completed. In the Alps, the cathedral of Embrun was commenced. But, in the opinion of the Christian world, all these
marvels were surpassed by the great royal church at Paris,
the work of Maurice of Sully.

Notre-Dame was the thought and occupation of his whole
lifetime. It is said that Pope Alexander III, on passing
through Paris in 1163, laid the first stone of the new church.
This fact has not been directly vouched for by a contemporary, but this much is certain: that the choir was almost
entirely finished in 1177, three years before the accession of
Philip Augustus, for Robert of Torigny, abbot of Mont-
Saint-Michel, saw it at this time and speaks of it with admiration in his chronicle. "Maurice, bishop of Paris," he
says, "has been working for a long time to build the cathedral of this city. The apse is about finished, except for the
great roof." It is equally certain that in 1182, on the nine-
teenth of May, the high altar of Notre-Dame was consecrated
by a papal legate. At the time of the bishop's death, in 1196,
the roof was finished, but neither were the towers built nor
the portals of the façade complete; these were the work of
the immediate successors of Maurice, notably of Eudes of
Sully, and in all probability were not finished until 1220 or
1225. It was necessary, to prepare the site of the new cathedral, to demolish the old Roman church of Notre-Dame and
the little church of Saint-Étienne-le-Vieux, to buy and tear
down many houses, to break through the Rue Neuve-Notre-
Dame, which opened upon the vestibule and permitted a
direct approach to the two bridges.

Confronted with the great labor spent in preparation, as
well as the construction of new buildings, one wonders how
the bishops could defray such enormous expenses. Who paid
the expense of building? Whence came the money? The
question is interesting and demands a careful answer. To
begin with, there is no doubt that the bishop consecrated a
large part of his seigniorial revenues—his private fortune—
to the great enterprise. This was what Bishop Walter of
Mortagne did at Laon; this also was what Maurice of Sully
did at Paris. A contemporary expressly says, "He built
the edifice at his own expense, much more than by outside
gifts." And it is known from his will that Maurice left to

his church the sum of one hundred livres, in order to build
the leaden roof. At Soissons, Bishop Nivelon gave the site
and renounced his rights to the revenues of vacant prebends.
At Auxerre, Bishop William of Seignelay spent seven hundred livres from his own purse in the first year, without
counting the abandonment of revenues accruing from his
rights of justice; and in the following years he, each week,
gave the sum of ten livres, which amounts to about one thousand five hundred francs to-day. To the funds furnished by
the bishop from the episcopal income were added contributions from the members of the chapters, who ordinarily appropriated certain revenues for this work. Money accruing from
the regular offerings of the faithful, whether on the occasion of mass or other offices, or at the time of the exposition
of relics, was also consecrated to it. It is known that in
the middle ages the proceeds from offerings given at the
altar or for relics formed an important and perfectly sure
income. It was only the occasional man who never committed
a fault. So far as concerns Notre-Dame of Paris, Cardinal
Eudes of Châteauroux said in the middle of the thirteenth
century, "It was with the offerings of women that the cathedral of Paris was in great measure built," which was true,
though exaggerated, for the funds from gifts only partially
supported the work.

In order to excite the generosity of the faithful, there was
recourse to another means: individuals giving money were
granted remission of their penance, or were guaranteed a
shortening of their time in purgatory by means of indulgences. A contemporary of Philip Augustus, the monk Cæsar
of Heisterbach of Cîteaux, states that Maurice of Sully had
recourse to these measures. A usurer having come to consult him for means to save his soul, the bishop induced him
to consecrate to the building of Notre-Dame the money acquired by his business. The cantor of Notre-Dame, the famous Peter Cantor, when he was consulted, replied that he
ought rather to give back the money to those from whom
he had taken it. But the cantor was opposed to luxurious
churches and he did not have the cathedral to build. It was
necessary, however, to procure funds in order to raise to
God a temple worthy of Him; from the religious point of

view, the end justified the means. For this object popes willingly gave bulls of indulgence—as for example, Innocent III in 1202, to aid in the reconstruction of the cathedral of Évreux.

There was another method which many bishops used, and which was employed, for example, in the case of the cathedral of Auxerre. The priests of the bishopric or of the chapter took their most venerated relics and carried them about through the diocese, through neighboring dioceses, and sometimes even to the borders of the country and into foreign parts. On all the highways they took up collections, which went to increase the funds for the work.

Finally, to sums furnished and collected by episcopal authority, there were added voluntary gifts of private individuals. To contribute toward the erection of a cathedral was one of the many means of achieving salvation. William of Armorica, the historian,—who, as we have seen, so much admired the cathedral of Chartres when it was rebuilt after the fire of 1194,—remarks, with something of a play on words, that the fire which had consumed the old church saved many souls, the souls of those who by their money helped to build the new church. We know at least one of them, a certain Manasses Mauvoisin, who in 1195 made a gift to the church of Notre-Dame of Chartres of an income of sixty sous, which was expressly to be used in the reconstruction of the church (*ad opus ecclesie*), " and when the work already begun," says the charter of donation, " is finished by the grace of God, the aforesaid income shall none the less permanently be at the disposal of the church." In return, the donor simply demanded that the canons pray for him in this same church on the anniversary of the day of his death. At Paris, King Louis VII gave two hundred livres; the Knight William of Barres, fifty livres; a nephew of Pope Alexander III, two silver marks. At Auxerre, five years after laying the first stone of the cathedral, a " building association " was formed, composed of a group of the faithful who, desirous of gaining the indulgences attached to the enterprise, without doubt furnished funds for its achievement. It is probable that this institution spread into many other localities.

In order to participate in the spiritual benefits of the work, it was enough to give a piece of land, to furnish some materials, to undertake the expense of a stained-glass window, or of any object used in worship. And gifts of this kind abound in the archives of new cathedrals. It was a field in which the piety of individuals and corporations competed. At Soissons, Adelaide, countess of Vermandois, in order to help the reconstruction of the cathedral, caused the timber necessary to cover the apse of the church to be taken from her forests in Valois; she furnished the oak all cut and carved to make the choir-stalls, and finally she paid the expense of a great stained-glass window. Another person of the same country put in two other windows at his own expense. At Troyes, in 1218, a certain man gave to the building the right to take loose stones from his quarry. At Chartres, in 1210, the chancellor of the chapter, Robert of Bérou, made a gift of one of the choir windows. This window still exists: it represents two groups of pilgrims and the donor himself kneeling before an altar, with this inscription, " *Robertus de Berou, Carnotensis cancellarius.*" At Paris, the Cantor Albert gave twenty livres for the completion of the stalls of Notre-Dame; and the dean of the chapter, Barbedor, made a gift of a window worth fifteen livres. All these generosities, and many others which might be cited from the cartularies and obituaries, were indeed well invested, for they repaid their authors with consideration in this world and with hope of salvation in the next. Every Christian and every Christian corporation had the right thus to contribute to enrich and embellish the work of their bishop; and a theologian of the time of Philip Augustus [1] gravely propounds this question apropos of a case which is said to have presented itself under the episcopacy of Maurice of Sully: " The syndicate of the demimondaine of Paris offers to give the bishop either a stained-glass window or chalice. Can the bishop receive the gift? Yes, provided he does it without publicity." Maurice of Sully, who had a broad' mind, thought that the money of a courtesan was worth as much as that of a usurer. The excellence of the intention purified it all.

[1] Cited by Hauréau in his "Notices et extraits de quelques manuscrits latins de la Bibliothèque Nationale," II, p. 10.

To have a new church large enough to satisfy all the needs of worship, high enough to symbolize the Christian ideal, and appealing to the eye by its carving and color was what the bishop wanted for his clerics and people, while recognition and general admiration sufficed for the present to pay him for his trouble until his recompense in the world to come. This highly edifying work brought pleasure to all, both poor and powerful. Nevertheless, it displeased some. There were men so full of the spirit of monastic authority that they would not even admit of Christian luxury nor of silver lavished in the service of God. In all periods of the middle ages there were perceptible two opposing currents of Christian ideals: the antagonism of those who thought that prayer ought to be especially a testimony of the spirit, an act of faith simply expressed in an austere form without ceremonies appealing to the senses; and those who, on the contrary, believed that everything beautiful and precious among earthly objects ought to be consecrated to the divine service. Sixty years before the thirteenth century, Saint Bernard indignantly denounced " the great pride of the churches, their extraordinary length, their rich marbles and paintings." He saw in them the vanity of vanities; he declared that, " instead of adorning itself with gilding, the church ought rather to cover the nakedness of her poor, and that the money spent upon the temples had been stolen from the unfortunate." What would he have said had he witnessed the sumptuous display of gothic art, the general movement toward the construction of great churches? Peter Cantor, a moralist of his school, who found fault with the bishops for building themselves palaces, no more approved when he saw them erecting their cathedrals:

" Why build churches, as is done at the present time? The apses of these churches ought not to be so high as even the body of the edifice, for they symbolize a mystical idea: Christ, who is the head of humanity, is more humble than his church. To-day they strive to raise the choirs of churches more and more. This love for building is a fever, an epidemic." And he adds, " What are the consequences of this malady? This luxury and sumptuousness on the walls of the building has the effect of cooling piety and of lessening charitable distributions to the poor. But the churches have been constructed with the usury of avarice and by the artifice of lies."

And he branded the abuse of offerings so useful to bishops. Offerings were unnecessary, excepting in the great solemnities. There were too many churches, too many altars. " Behold," he says finally, " what was the case in Israel; it had but one temple, one tabernacle, one offertory."

Peter Cantor might have been right from the point of view of Christian asceticism, and even this argument is debatable. But, from the point of view of art, he was wrong. Had he been listened to, Notre-Dame and all the cathedrals which arose from the earth in so many places in the France of the time of Philip Augustus would not be before our eyes to-day. For one must not forget that it is by the masterpieces of Roman and gothic art, and not by literature, that the spirit of the middle ages shows its power and originality.

*

*   *

Besides their religious mission, bishops rendered other indisputable services to society, for they protected their subjects in town and country at the same time that they were defending themselves against the brigandage of the lay lords, and were the king's aids in his work of concentrating the national forces for the sake of order. This life of continual activity and of incessant strife, which was the life of the majority of them, could not help but gain sympathy and popular recognition. In reality they were often nothing but soldiers, who lacked what we to-day call episcopal virtue, but they lived and died, enjoying the respect and affection of a great majority of their diocesans. And when the historian of the bishops of Auxerre—speaking, for example, of the death of William, bishop of Toucy, in 1181, and of the universal regret it created—asserts " that it would be impossible to tell how great was the mourning throughout the entire city, and with what groanings and lamentations sorrow was shown by all who were present at the obsequies," we believe that it is not a ready-made, stereotyped phrase forming a part of an official ceremony. These men of the middle ages loved their bishop sincerely; they had need of his zeal, and we have seen that he spent himself as much for their benefit as for that of the monarchy.

The nobles, feudal lords, barons, and castellans were less

favorable to the episcopacy, and for a different reason: in the eyes of a lay lord the bishop was often an obstacle and an enemy. We shall presently discuss the perpetual antagonism which everywhere in France brought on quarrels between bishop and baron. Nobles did not write history, and as a result we do not know historically what they thought and said of the head of their diocese. We can only guess it at the best from the fact that they often made desperate war against him, braving his anathemas for a long time. But, for want of history as such, we must direct ourselves to those works of imagination thoroughly saturated with the spirit of feudalism and nobility and especially composed for listeners in châteaux. These are the *chansons de geste,* heroic poems—a literature which attained its height in the time of Philip Augustus. It must be remembered that, primarily, the *chansons de geste,* in a more or less hyperbolic form, give us the opinions which prevailed in feudal society and in military circles. But in reading these poems, written particularly to amuse or flatter men of arms, one perceives from the start that the bishops do not play—so to speak—any rôle; if they appear at all, it is as shadowy figures, as personages in the background. They are not noticed in time of peace, and it is with reluctance that they are mentioned in armies or battles. The same thing is noticed of other clerics in general, both secular and regular members of the church. The authors of the epics—such as *Garin le Lorrain* or *Girart de Roussillon*—always present the clergy in an absolutely subordinate and inferior position. If we believed them, clerics were useful only to serve as secretaries to illiterate nobles, to collect the dead on the field of battle, to place ointments on wounds, and say masses for those who paid for them. They speak of clerics only casually, in a line, and then with visible disdain.

We have no need of remarking that this indifference, this easy and contemptuous way of sacrificing episcopacy and church, is decidedly in opposition to historical fact. It is known, on the contrary, what a considerable place bishops held, not only in religious, but also in civil society; what a frequent part they took in the military expeditions, legal and political councils of kings and high feudal suzerains.

History shows them to us intervening and acting on all sides
and under all circumstances. This, then, is evidently a noteworthy example of the liberty with which the authors of
chansons de geste treated contemporary truth, and shows,
therefore, that one must be prudent when trying to draw
useful historical conclusions from these fantastic composi-
tions. It is clear that here we meet firmly fixed prejudice.
The author who wrote for the diversion of the nobles shared
all the prejudices of the nobility whom, above all, he attempted to picture; he is only an echo, an instrument of
the malice of the military caste. They had too much strife
with the bishops to recognize their superiority, to render them
justice, or even to permit having them mentioned in the
songs composed for their own distraction.

For the minstrels usually said little or nothing of these
mitered and croziered powers; when they spoke of them, it
was to present them in a most unfavorable light. For example, the author of the poem, *Garin le Lorrain:* in a sort
of introduction he spoke of the episcopacy as an egotistical,
avaricious corporation, which refused to contribute to the
expenses which the defense of the realm necessitated. When
the archbishop of Reims, the highest ecclesiastical personage
of France, was asked to give pecuniary aid to the Emperor
Charles Martel and his knights, who were ready to fight the
pagans, he replied:

" ' We are clergy; it is our duty to serve God. We gladly pray
that you may gain the victory, and may be defended from death.
As for you, knights, God has commanded you to come to the aid
of the clergy and to protect Holy Church. But why so many words?
I swear by the great Saint Denis, you shall not have an Angevin
sou from me.' ' Sire archbishop,' responded the abbot of Cluny,
' you are wrong in not guarding the memory of our benefactors.
If we are rich (for which the Lord be praised), it is from the good
lands which their ancestors bequeathed us. Let each one of us
to-day contribute something of his own; it would be foolish, by
refusing entirely, to expose ourselves to greater losses.' ' Do as you
wish,' replied the angry archbishop; ' but I would let myself be
tied to the tails of their horses before I would give two Angevin
farthings.' "

In this passage there is evidently an allusion to the
pecuniary requisitions of which the bishops were the victims

on the part of the kings of France and the popes in the middle of the twelfth century; or perhaps even an allusion to some particular episode, like that of the Saladin tithe exacted by Philip Augustus in 1188. The truth is that the church and her subjects supported this heavy tax almost entirely alone. Without doubt, some bishops murmured and let their contributions wait, and others did not yield without pressure. But, on the whole, the high clergy paid. They are seen pawning even the altar cloths and holy vessels for the aid of king or pope. The feudal poet has in this instance perpetrated an intended exaggeration, almost an historical lie.

The class of players who at this same time created and developed another kind of profane literature, the *fabliaux*, as we have seen, especially attacked the clergy and the parish curés. The bishops did not often appear in these tales, but, when they did play some rôle, it was not always just to their advantage. According to their narrator, they led scandalous lives, which, considering the example set by their superiors, explains the loose manners of the average curés. Here again the spontaneousness of the satirists, which is more than blunt, abused certain all too true facts by attributing to the episcopal personnel as a whole the faults of some of its members.

But, after all, it must be admitted that, in this respect, vernacular literature was only turning to its own uses what a certain class of religious literature said concerning the episcopacy. In the middle ages, members of the clergy were never more mistreated verbally than by the clergy itself. The nobles and the bourgeoisie, the enemies of the church, were never harder or more unjust to the episcopacy than were certain preachers, who believed themselves obliged to strike heavily in order to move and correct the more surely. Besides, many of the authors of these sermons were monks or clerics, imbued with the monastic spirit—a spirit, as we know, profoundly opposed to the official and worldly prelates of the church. One of these, Geoffrey of Troyes, leaves us the following picture of the episcopacy:

" The bishops are past masters, as wolves and foxes. They flatter and bribe in order to extort. They are devoured by avarice, burning with a desire to possess. Instead of being the friends and protectors of the church, they are its ravishers. They despoil it, selling its vestments, and violating justice. Their only rule is their own wish. See them walk; they have a proud bearing, a cruel air, sullen eyes, a harsh word. Everything in their personality breathes pride. Their conduct is the reverse of good manners; theirs is even a life of wickedness. They wish to be an object of terror to their flocks, forgetting that they are physicians, not sovereigns."

Adam of Perseigne compares the life of the clergy with that of Christ:

"He suffered, and they live in luxury; He wore hair-cloth, and they silken vestments. It is with the patrimony of the Crucified that they maintain their luxury and their pride. They care not for souls but for their hunting birds. They care not for the poor but for their dogs. They play at dice, instead of administering sacraments. The churches instead of being holy places, have become market-places and haunts for brigands."

Peter of Blois especially attacked the judges and administrators of the bishops, the " officials " who took the place of the prelate and his tribunal and relieved him in part from the worry of affairs. Lately instituted and revocable at will, these agents represented in the diocese that unity, direction, and authority so singularly compromised by the encroachments of the archdeacons, though they also abused their power:

"They have but one thought, to oppress, to fleece, to flay the members of their diocese. They are the blood-suckers of the bishop, or the sponges which he squeezes from time to time. All the money which they extort from the poor goes for the pleasures and daintinesses of episcopal life. These wranglers, hairsplitters, ready to ensnare the unfortunate litigant in their nets, interpret the law in their own way and handle justice like despots. They break contracts, nourish hatred, break up marriages, protect the adulterer, penetrate into the interior of homes under the pretext of being inquisitors, slander the innocent, and absolve the guilty. In a word, these sons of avarice, live wholly for money. They have sold themselves to the devil."

Some official documents attest how very many bishops led a life which was hardly exemplary. The decrees of two councils—the one held in Paris in 1212, and the other at

Montpellier in 1214—contain orders and prohibitions, showing us indirectly the customs of the episcopacy. Bishops were ordered to wear the tonsure and vestment of their order; they were forbidden to wear luxurious furs, to use decorated saddles or golden bits, to play games of chance, to go on the chase, to swear or to suffer one among them to swear, to introduce players or musicians to their table, to hear matins while still in bed, to talk of frivolous things during an office, or to excommunicate at random. They were not to quit their residence, were to convene a synod at least once a year, and, on their visits in the diocese, they were not to take a numerous suite with them, it being too heavy a charge to those who entertained them. They were prohibited from receiving money for conferring orders, from tolerating the concubinage of priests, from dispensing with the marriage bans, and from failing to excommunicate the guilty. Finally, they were not permitted to celebrate illegal marriages, to annul lawful wills, to allow dancing in holy places, or the celebration of fools' holiday in the cathedral, or to allow any one to proceed with legal combat and judgments of God in their presence.

One need not believe the authors of these sermons word for word, since they aim to show up the bad rather than the good, nor to conclude from the orders of the councils that the general customs of the church were deplorable. Nevertheless, it is certain that, in spite of the great reforms of the previous age, the episcopacy in great measure remained feudal. A great many of the prelates, indeed, belonged to the noble class and lived like castellans.

Hugh of Noyers, bishop of Auxerre, is the type of fighting bishop who contended against the nobles, coped even with the king, and worked eagerly to increase his territory and the revenues of his church. He built houses which were really fortresses, " surrounded by great moats, to which the water was directed from afar at great expense; protected by great palisades, surmounted by a donjon; equipped with turreted ramparts, gates, and drawbridges." One day Thibaud, count of Champagne, exercising his right of suzerain, razed to the ground the walls and towers of one of these formidable manors, leaving nothing standing except the dwelling-house. "The bishop of Auxerre spent too much," adds the chronicler of the bishop.

"He loved the society of men-at-arms and knights, and took as active a part in their exercises and sports as the dignity of the priesthood permitted. He was well lettered, reading books, and willingly remaining at study when he had time. Very active in his own interests, he cared little for those of others, and was harsh toward his subjects, whom he crushed with intolerable exactions."

At Narbonne, Archbishop Bérenger II (1192-1211), was among those who, according to the expression of Innocent III, "served no other god but money, and had a purse in place of a heart." Everything had to be paid for, even the consecration of bishops. When a church came to be vacant, he refrained from naming an incumbent, in order to profit from its revenues. He reduced the number of canons at Narbonne by one-half, in order to appropriate their prebends, and likewise retained the vacant archdeaconries. The pope writes in 1204 that one might in his diocese see "monks and canons regular laying aside the frock, taking wives, living by usury, becoming lawyers, players, or doctors." Six years later, Bérenger had not reformed; Innocent III, therefore, begged his legates to use the ecclesiastical censures against him and against his colleague, the archbishop of Auch, who it seems was no better than he.

Hélie I, archbishop of Bordeaux (1187-1206), brother of a Gascon highwayman employed by Henry II and Richard, lived surrounded by men-at-arms and subjected his diocese to regular plunder. We saw above [1] how the pope accused him of sharing the profits of his raids. Once Hélie installed himself in the abbey of Saint-Yrieix with his highwaymen, his horses, his hunting-dogs, and his courtesans, and led such a life at the expense of the inhabitants and the monks that after his departure some of them, despoiled of everything, died of starvation. In a letter of 1205, Innocent III compared him to "a bare and rotten tree, which delights in its rottenness as a beast of burden in its filth."

The most extraordinary bishop of this period was Matthew

[1] Chapter I.

of Lorraine, bishop of Toul (1198-1210). He belonged to the ducal family. Provost of the church of Saint-Dié before his election, he was already living as a magnificent and dissolute lord, squandering the revenues of his charge and forcing his colleagues, the dean and canons, to quit the place. When he became bishop, he exploited his diocese with such shamelessness that the chapter of Toul asked the pope to depose him. Innocent III ordered an investigation of his conduct, but, on the eve of the day on which Matthew was to appear, the dean of Toul was seized by some men-at-arms, placed on an ass, his feet tied together under the belly of the animal, and was taken to the bishop, who had him chained and thrown into prison. A legate of the pope excommunicated Matthew, but it was eight years (1202-1210) before his deposition became effective and the faithful of Toul could choose another bishop. During the interminable lawsuit, Matthew had built a château on the elevation overlooking Saint-Dié, from which he plundered all the country. His relative, the duke of Lorraine, was himself obliged to demolish it. Expelled finally from his domain, Matthew retired to a little hermitage in the midst of a forest, where he lived by hunting and brigandage, only waiting for an opportunity to avenge himself on his successor. In 1217, he found it. The new bishop, Renaud, was stabbed in a pass of Étival, and Matthew fled into the mountains, taking the episcopal luggage, the chasubles, the vases, and the holy chrism. It became necessary for Thibaud, duke of Lorraine, to free the church and with his own hand kill this bishop who was both brigand and assassin (May 16, 1217).

In contrast to this type of prelate, a survivor of primitive and savage feudalism, others are found—like Stephen of Tournai, William of Champagne, and Peter of Corbeil—who were theologians, politicians, men of letters, and courtiers. Even Paris, in the time of Louis VII and Philip Augustus, had a model bishop, Maurice of Sully.

Elected bishop of Paris in 1160, he did not seek to play a political rôle, although he enjoyed the confidence of both king and pope. He excelled in the moral and administrative management of his diocese, which he governed for thirty-six years. He is almost considered as a saint, and a monk of the abbey of Anchin, who saw him in 1182, has left us this enthusiastic picture of him.

" Maurice, bishop of Paris, vessel of affluence, fertile olive tree in the house of the Lord, flourished among the other bishops of Gaul. Without speaking of those inner qualities, which God alone knows, he shone without by his knowledge, his preaching, his many alms, and his good deeds. It was he who constructed the church of the most Holy Virgin, in his episcopal residence, and in this work, at the same time so beautiful and sumptuous, he employed the resources of others less than his own revenues. His presence at the cathedral was frequent, or rather continual. I have seen him at a feast which was not a solemnity, at the hour when vespers were chanted. He was not seated in his episcopal chair, but sat in the choir, intoning the psalms like the others and surrounded by a hundred clerics."

CHAPTER VI

THE MONASTIC SPIRIT

It does not seem that there was ever a time in the middle ages when the monk fully and rigorously conformed to the rule of his institution, which required him to flee all contact with the world and to live in perpetual seclusion, absorbed in study, prayer, and manual labor. The monk was an agent of enlightenment and a spiritual influence; but he was also for this very reason a social power. How could society help using for other ends the influence and prestige which monks enjoyed among the people? The greatest monk of the middle ages was Saint Bernard, but there is no monk who lived oftener and for longer periods of time outside of his abbey. He passed his life on horseback in France, Germany, and Italy. Blamed for it, he often grieved over it and scruples of conscience troubled him. He found " monstrous "—the word is his—the life to which the church condemned him. " I am," said he, " I know not what fantastic animal, neither cleric nor layman, wearing the robe of a monk and not practising its observances."

Fifty years after the death of Saint Bernard, at the end of the twelfth century, monks no longer felt these scruples. It is said that, shortly after the death of the founder of the order of Grandmont, Stephen of Muret, the tomb of this holy man, where numerous miracles were performed, attracted such a multitude of pilgrims and visitors that it angered the monks of Grandmont, whose solitude was destroyed. They objected to the saint performing miracles and threatened, if he continued it, to throw his body into a cesspool. I do not know whether this story is well founded, but, in any case, this fervor did not last. In the time of Philip Augustus, the monks not only found it very convenient and exceedingly profitable to allow laymen to come to the church in multitudes, but they themselves voluntarily left their cloister and went out into the profane world. In spite of canonical prohibitions and the severity of the rules, they were to be seen everywhere, upon every road. Philip of Harvengt, abbot of Bonne-Espérance and a contemporary of Philip Augustus, indignantly complains of it:

" Where is the road, the village, where is the crowded thoroughfare, in which one does not see the monk on horseback? Who is now able to leave his house without stumbling upon a monk? Is there a feast, a fair, or a market-place where monks do not appear? They are to be seen in all assemblies, in all battles, in all tourneys. Monks swarm everywhere that knights assemble for battle. What do they in the midst of the shock of bucklers and the crash of furious lances, and wherefore are they authorized to go out thus and ride about? "

The people of the middle ages were almost as superstitious as the ancients. But, if it was an ill omen to meet a hare, a disheveled woman, a blind person, or a cripple, it was scarcely less lucky to meet a monk. A letter of Peter of Blois contains a characteristic 'anecdote on this point. A cleric, who had his degree, Master William le Beau, was leaving an inn when he met a monk and, what is more, this monk earnestly appealed to him to reënter the inn, assuring him that he was threatened with a great disaster if he risked traveling that day. Master le Beau, adds Peter of Blois, regarding everything that did not rest on faith as foolishness, mounted his horse to join the retinue of the archbishop, whom he accompanied. "But he had gone only a few steps when, with his horse, he fell into a deep pond, from which he was rescued with difficulty." And Peter of Blois moralizes on this incident, "My opinion is that Master le Beau would have fallen into the pond even if no monk had spoken to him." Educated people, like him, no longer accepted such beliefs; but, as far as meeting monks was concerned, there was no great virtue in this attitude, as monks were at that time to be found everywhere, and he was obliged to habituate himself to meeting them.

The assertion of Philip of Harvengt is not exaggerated; it is enough to open a chronicle and read the correspondence of the time to see how the monks were employed in politics and business and how princes and kings little hesitated to take them from their cloisters and intrust them with the most diverse missions. They were discreet, clever men, understanding how to do things. The respect which their robes inspired permitted them, more than any others, to go about without fear. As negotiators and as messengers to the court and to the armies, one frequently sees them taking their places in the entourage of the Capetians and the Plantagenets.

In 1202, when John Lackland triumphed over his nephew, Arthur, at Mirabeau, a victory unhoped for but complete, he hastened to communicate his success to the body of his English councillors, who were then in Normandy—notably William Marshal, earl of Pembroke. And to whom did he intrust the message? A monk. Observe the passage which we find on this subject in the versified chronicle of the biographer of William Marshal:

"A monk set out and, traveling day and night, made his way to Marshal. He courteously delivered his message, announcing the capture of Arthur, of Geoffrey of Lusignan, of the count of Marche, of Savari of Mauléon, and of other great personages who supported Arthur. Marshal rejoiced greatly and said to the monk: 'You shall carry this news to the host of France, to the count of Eu at Arques, to give him joy.'[1] 'Sire,' said the monk to William Marshal, 'I beg your mercy. If I go there the count will be so angry that he will surely kill me. Send another than I.' 'Monk,' said Marshal, 'do not make excuses; you are the one to go. It is not the custom in this country to kill messengers. Go at once; you will find him with the army.' The monk went with a large retinue to Arques and communicated the news of Poitou to the count of Eu. The count, who had expected very different news, changed color and remained silent. He lay down in his tent, much depressed, not knowing what to do, for he did not wish to repeat to any one what he had just heard."

Philip Augustus, like his English rivals, gladly employed monks. He always kept one of them, Brother Bernard of Coudray, a Grandmontain, near him and intrusted him with the most delicate negotiations. It was William, a monk of the abbey of Sainte-Geneviève, whom he sent to Denmark to

[1] One should note that the count of Eu, brother of the count of Marche, whom John Lackland had just made prisoner, was an ally of Philip Augustus, and one of the most rabid enemies of the English king.

handle the matter of his marriage with Ingeborg, and who
brought the young fiancée back to France: the marriage
turned out badly, as is well known, but that was not the fault
of the negotiator, an excellent cleric, whom the church
canonized. An abbot of Sainte-Geneviève, the scholar and
philosopher, Stephen of Tournai, was also for many years
the man of affairs and ambassador, appointed by Philip
Augustus. We have not spoken of Brother Guérin, the
hospitaler, who was a valuable clerk of universal competence
to the king of France during the last twenty years of his
reign, for he exercised at one time the functions of chancellor, minister of foreign affairs, and chief of the army.
We know the important part which he took in the victory of
Bouvines. Monks were good for everything, and sovereigns
imposed upon them. It was not always of their own free
will that the monks left the monastery to journey afar in a
time when long journeys were as uncomfortable as perilous.
One need only to read the terrified letters in the correspondence of Stephen of Tournai, in which he speaks of his mission to Toulouse and of the countless dangers which he had
encountered; especially a note in the year 1183, in which
he thanked Heaven and man for having escaped a journey
to Rome, the king having changed his mind. One would say
that a criminal condemned to death had just received pardon.

It is not only the historical documents, properly so called,
which show us the monk taken from his convent by the rulers
and traveling the roads and busying himself with temporal
affairs, even with matrimonial negotiations. The testimony
of the *chansons de geste,* which were written in the time of
Philip Augustus, agrees exactly with that of the chronicles.
Open, for example, the poem *Garin le Lorrain,* one of those
which most certainly date from this period. Duke Hervis of
Metz entered his estate and happened to take shelter at the
convent of Gorze. He said to the abbot, in whom he had
great confidence, " Go and find me a maiden, for I want a
wife." The abbot answered that he would willingly do so,
but that he wished to know where he was to find her. " By
God who created me," said Hervis, " I want Aélis, the sister
of Gaudin. Under heaven there is not another more beautiful. Likewise, in this century there is not a better knight

than her brother." The abbot made ready immediately upon receiving the order. He left with fifteen monks and a number of knights. He was rich and traveled " very luxuriously." The roads were covered with mules, packhorses, and palfreys. A month sufficed for the mission, and he returned to Metz with the young girl. Hervis le Lorrain went to meet them. " Welcome," he said to the abbot, and, taking the girl by the hand, said to her: " Beautiful maiden, by the God who does not lie, thou art beautiful of face and form; I will make thee a very rich woman." " Sire," responded Aélis, " I give thee many thanks."

Further on the author of the poem shows us Liétri, the abbot of Saint-Amand in Pevèle, intrusted with carrying the body of his brother Bégon, whom assassins had surprised by treachery in a forest, to the mighty Duke Garin. He left with fifteen monks and twenty-six knights, and, his errand accomplished, he returned to his abbey after a fifteen days' journey. " Scarcely seated in his cloister, his monks crowded about him, asking him why he had been sent and what he had done." He satisfied their curiosity and ended by saying, " Go, pray that peace be made among these powerful barons."

Evidently the profession of messenger and negotiator was almost a specialty of the monk; a wearisome profession and one at times fraught with dangers of a grave character. The poem *Garin,* in another scene, tells of two monks whom the archbishop of Reims sent to the court of France to bear false testimony. He wished to prove an imaginary relationship between the Princess Blanchefleur and Duke Garin in such a way as to hinder their marriage. For King Pepin himself wished to marry the intended bride of the duke, his vassal. At the moment when the archbishop solemnly announced the marriage of Blanchefleur and Garin, one of the monks, whom he had stationed together with the king, advanced and stated that the father of the baron was a near relative of the father of the fiancée.

" These words threw Bégon, brother of Garin, into a fit of anger. He leaped upon the monk, knocking him down, and trampling him with his feet, and cried: ' Where have you gotten what you tell us?' He would have killed the unlucky wretch if some one had not hastened to the rescue. ' Sire vassal,' said the king angrily, ' it seems

you hold me in great contempt to beat this monk thus before me.'
'He, a monk! Sire, he is not, he is a traitor, a renegade; he has
been paid, by whom I do not know, to talk as he has. I swear
by Saint Denis, if I lay hands on him a second time he is a dead
man.' 'Enough,' answered the king, 'I shall send for the saints, and
the monks shall swear on the relics to the truth of what they have
said.' The relics came, and the two monks took the oath required
of them.''

The feudal spirit predominates in the poem *Garin*, and it
is not all well-disposed toward churchmen. Without pretending that there were many monks capable of accepting a
task as that above, it is certain that great numbers and all
kinds of them were to be seen in the assemblies and in the
court, and that they were used in all professions. They even
followed the armies, a circumstance which moved Philip of
Harvengt to wrath and to demand why they were seen in
battles and tournaments. Why? It is surprising that the
abbot of Bonne-Espérance should ask this question. He, like
all contemporaries of Philip Augustus, must have known that,
wherever there was an army, there was found a whole troop
of clerics and monks of every kind—'' men of peace,'' who
had a double mission: first, they intervened between belligerents in order to induce them, in the name of the church and
of the crusade, to conclude, if not a definitive peace, at least
a truce, an armistice. On every page of the chronicles there
is talk of the efforts of the '' religious men '' to prevent the
knights from joining battle. Then if, in spite of attempts
at peacemaking, the battle began, these clerics and monks
served to care for the wounded. They carried the wounded
to the physicians, the *mires*, and many of these physicians
were themselves monks, who had studied at Montpellier or
Salerno.

It was the monks also who performed the service of inter-
ring the dead, for the noble knight desired to be bestowed in an
abbey and was happy if, before he died, he could assume the
monastic habit. The chronicles and charters give us a thousand examples of this; the *chansons de geste* are here only
an echo of the truth. Garin said to the abbot of Saint-
Vincent of Laon: '' Let the bodies of my good friends, who
have just been killed, be collected, enshrouded, and buried.

I shall raise funds so that God may show them mercy.''
Likewise, Hervis of Metz sent for the abbot of Saint-Seurin
of Bordeaux, who came, accompanied by ten monks.
'' Seignior abbot,'' said Hervis, '' I have sent for you to bury
two varlets before the high altar of Saint-Seurin. If you
consent, I will give you a large part of my treasure.'' '' As
you wish,'' answered the abbot. Immediately bathing the
corpses, he took them to the monastery of Saint-Seurin, to
the place the duke had named. It was a windfall for the
monastery. One is, then, not astonished that the monk played
his part in the military life of the knight and that wherever
the nobles did battle and killed each other, whether in war or
in the tournaments, so frequent in the time of Philip Augustus, one finds the monks nursing the wounded, blessing and
burying the dead.

The wandering foot (*acedia*), that incurable spleen, that
mystical conception which all preachers condemned, is only
a passionate desire to leave the monastic prison to live at
large and at liberty among people who act and talk. One
of the most celebrated contemporaries of Philip Augustus,
the philosopher and theologian, Alain of Lille, spoke of it
in no uncertain terms:

" The *acedia* makes one rebel against the severity of the rule in
the cloister. They wish to eat more delicately, to sleep on softer
beds, to lessen the watching, to observe the rule of silence less, or
even break it entirely. It is this which nourishes vice, and takes
the monk away from his abbey."

Thus one sees the church taking more severe and minute
precautions to hold the monk and prevent him from quitting
his frock. In all the acts of the councils, in all the statutes
of the diocesan synods, there is on this point a prohibitory
article. '' The monk who leaves his frock shall be excommunicated,'' says the council of Paris in 1213. A canon of
the same council orders the walling up of the little doors
of the monastery, in order to take away all occasion and all
temptation to misconduct. The synodal statute of Eudes,
bishop of Toul, which dates from 1192, excommunicates fugitive monks. The reform rule of Cluny, promulgated by the
abbot Hugh V in 1203, contains a whole chapter relative

to the monks who went outside the doors of the abbey without permission.

"For it often happens that our monks go about among the houses in the villages and in the woods saying and doing that which they should not say and do, from which it results that we are blamed and the people are scandalized; therefore every monk going outside the monastery must have a letter from his abbot, a permit in good and correct form to leave."

And the reform of the abbey of Saint-Victor of Marseilles, published in 1195 by Pope Celestine III, added the now well-known precaution, " The monk who goes into the town shall never go alone: the abbot or the prior shall send with him an honest companion."

But what could rules, prohibitions, and anathemas do against the irresistible force which drew the monk from his cloister? Any pretext for leaving seemed good to him, and he used them freely.

Here, according to a sermon of Peter Comestor is a monk who is sick, or who says he is sick, and who, in order to recuperate, asks to return for a little while to his own country:

"Under the pretext of ill health he goes to his relatives; he returns to his native soil, to breathe for a few days the purer air, the air of his childhood; and when he returns he pays close attention to the time of his entrance; he never returns at mealtime or at prayers, for he dislikes a dish of cooked ribs, of the vegetables prepared without gravy, the watered wine, and the silence and mortification of the cloister."

There are other monks, and they are numerous, who leave the abbey to study in the schools, especially in Paris, where the student life, as we have seen, was not without its charms. These latter gave excellent reasons to justify their absence and their travels: they needed to study medicine, to heal their sick brethren, and law, to conduct the lawsuits of the community with good results. But the monk-scholars soon became legion: so that ecclesiastical authorities became worried, and finally took measures to keep the cloisters from being further deserted. Already the council of Tours, in 1163, had pronounced with severity against them. It prohibited the study of law and medicine, especially to those who had made profession of monastic life. Orders were given them to repair to their abbeys in two months, under pain of excommunication, and those who returned should have the last place among the monks in the choir, in the chapter, in the refectory, and should lose all hope of promotion to any dignity unless the mercy of the Holy See disposed otherwise. This prohibition was renewed in 1213 at the council of Paris. And in his famous bull *Super speculam*, 1219, which prohibited the study of law in the university of Paris, Pope Honorius III had a very harsh word for those monks who became students: " They no longer endure," said he, " the monastic silence. They repulse the law of God which converts souls, that law which they should love more than gold or precious stones." And why this flood of monks in the great schools? It is because they liked to mingle with the crowd, to reap the applause of the vulgar, and to amuse the ladies'-maids, " *ad pedisequas amplectandas.*" It is a pope who says this. To the monks who vainly multiplied objections and gave plausible reasons to justify their absence in the schools, Pope Honorius wished to have the penalty, decreed by the council of Tours, rigorously applied: excommunication without heed of an appeal to Rome.

There was a whole category of monks and nuns whom it was very difficult to retain in the cloister, and these were the noble lords and great ladies who entered the cloister because of weariness, remorse, or lack of quiet and repose. After some time they perceived that the monastic rule was harsh; they were homesick for the world, its liberties and its joys, and they doffed the cowl and returned to château life. What abbot could stop them? But the example was bad for the ordinary monks from the common people, and they utilized all opportunities which presented themselves for leaving the cloister and having provisional liberty with alacrity.

The bands which plagued all central France at the beginning of Philip Augustus' reign collected a great number of exiles and fugitives from all provinces: men and women with lost reputations, monks, canons, nuns—a medley of adventurers and adventuresses who had abandoned ecclesiastical robes and now gave themselves over to every excess.

There is on this subject an amusing tale of the year 1183, which is recorded in a biography of William Marshal in French verse. William was one day riding in Brie with his squire, Eustache of Bertrimont:

"He wished to sleep so he threw himself down by the side of the road, while the squire loosened the bridles of the horses and let them graze. While Marshal slept there passed a man and a woman both of fine appearance and mounted upon large, swift horses. The two travelers had considerable baggage packed on their mounts and were traveling rapidly. Just at the moment when they passed near Marshal the woman said in a low voice: 'O God, how tired I am.' Marshal awoke, and asked who it was: 'Sire,' answered Eustache, 'it is a man and a woman, traveling at a great rate; they have a rich equipage.' 'Put on the bridles,' said Marshal, 'for I want to know whence they come, whither they are going, and who they are.' He mounted at once but in his haste forgot to take his sword. Having overtaken the travelers he plucked the man by the sleeve of his riding-coat and demanded who he was. 'Sire,' answered the other, whom this question visibly annoyed, 'I am a man.' 'By my head,' said Marshal, 'I know right well that you are no animal.' The other disengaged himself and put his hand on his sword. 'You are looking for a quarrel?' said Marshal. 'You shall have it. Eustache, bring my sword.' The stranger hastily dismounted, but Marshal followed, and seizing him by the riding-hood pulled it so rudely that it came off; and then he saw that it was the handsomest monk one could find on this side of Cologne. 'Ha!' said Marshal, 'I have found you out. Who are you and who is this woman?'

"Much ashamed, the monk confessed that the woman was his mistress, that he was taking her from her country, and that at present they were going to a foreign land. 'Tell me, young woman, who are you and of what family?' 'Sire,' answered the young woman, weeping, 'I am of Flanders, sister of Raoul of Lens.' 'Girl, you are foolish. If you will promise to give up this folly, I will reconcile you with your brother, whom I know very well.' 'Sire, I will never be seen in the country where I am known.' 'Well, at least,' said Marshal, 'that being the case, have you money with which to live?' The monk raised the skirt of his riding coat, and took off a large belt. 'Certainly,' said he, 'here is our money. Here are forty-eight livres!' 'And what are you going to do with them, my friend? How do you plan to live with this money?' 'I'll tell you; I have no intention of investing these deniers, but I shall deposit them in some foreign village and we will live on the income.' 'A usurer,' said Marshal, 'by the sword of God that shall never be! Take the money, Eustache! Since you refuse to return, go, and the devil be with you!'

"Marshal went to his inn. There he found Seignior Baldwin and Hugh of Hamelincourt, who had arrived before him, and who laughed at him, saying, 'Marshal, you are late. You are making us fast.' 'Seigniors, do not regret it. I have made a winning of which you shall have your share. Eustache, the money!' Eustache threw the money before them. Marshal said to them: 'Take enough to pay your pledges.'[1] 'Marshal,' they asked, 'where did this money come from?' 'Have patience and I shall tell you presently.' They ate joyously, and counted the money which really amounted to forty-eight livres. Then Marshal told them in detail how he had gotten the money. 'By God's lips,' exclaimed Master Hugh, 'you were too good to leave them their horses and baggage. Here, my horse! For, by my faith, I want them to have an affair with me.' But Marshal restrained him."

Thus, one after another, the regular clergy left the cloister and lived in contact with the profane world. Monks of the court, of the army, fugitive and unfrocked monks, appeared in greater numbers than ever before. It was one of the signs of the new time.

*

*   *

However, in the great majority of convents, though the monk had become more unsettled, he had, in his method of thought and feeling, remained what he was in the past century.

His state of mind must be guessed at, for it cannot be positively ascertained. Men of the middle ages generally had no conception of autobiography: they did not analyze themselves for the satisfaction of being talked of, or preserve themselves for the curiosity of a future generation. Consequently, we can only get at their psychology indirectly, taking them unawares, as it were. We extract it from their writings.

But the writers of monastic society belong to three categories: monks who composed treatises on theology, some philosophic works, or sermons; monks who wrote chronicles, biographies, or history; and, finally, literary monks, men of wit, poets, especially satirists, troubadours clad in the robe, and, therefore, one must add, very irregular monks.

What do the theologians, the philosophers, or the authors of sermons tell of themselves? Practically nothing. In their works of tiresome scholasticism, stuffed with verses and cita-

[1] That is, to redeem objects pawned in order to pay debts.

tions from sacred books, there is not the least personal note. Not one gives the life, habits, or surroundings of the author. All that is evident from the confused mass is that the minds which compiled it were endowed with a remarkable capacity for abstraction and a curious passion for the most bizarre subtilities. It was a time when they strove to find an allegorical and mystical meaning in every word of the Holy Scriptures—the golden age of subtile paraphrase, of Byzantine commentary. The monk employed in this work treasures of ingenuity and patience. He did not always subtilize in solitude on parchment, for his own pleasure alone. When he was a preacher, as he frequently was toward the end of the twelfth century, he shared with the faithful his refinement of ideas, and the auditor, whether he comprehended or not, went into ecstasies.

Among the innumerable commentaries on the Canticles which the middle ages have bequeathed to us, that of a Cistercian monk, named Thomas, is one of the chief works of allegorical interpretation. This monk already employed symbolism, and the most skilled symbolists of after times doubtless had some difficulty in rising to his level. Each of the expressions of living tenderness, of which the Canticles are full, gives the occasion for a dissertation, according to rule, where the abstractive and analytical mania rages without limit and without check. The nature of the subject and the candor with which the author undertakes the grossest explanations makes citation difficult. One example will suffice.

In the first verse of the Canticle, the wife says to her husband, *Osculetur me osculo oris sui* [Let him kiss me with the kisses of his mouth], and this passionate appeal Thomas the Cistercian explains thus:

"It is the cry of the Jewish nation, which knows that Christ must come into the world, as it has been told by the angels, and by the prophets. This is why, desirous of seeing Him, she cries *Osculetur me,* that is to say, she longs for Christ to come, instruct, and save her. He must not send His angels, patriarchs, or prophets; He must come Himself in person. And what is this kiss which she desires, *osculum ejus?* It is the knowledge which issues from His own lips. Let Him come then, that I may learn from Him what I ought to know."

There follows a very long disquisition on the kiss, of which the author distinguishes four species. Then he even analyzes the kiss, learnedly decomposing it into its physiological elements; finally, comes a study of the diverse ways in which it is given—all defined, subdivided, rigorously classified, and symbolically interpreted. By this one can judge the rest. The allegorical commentary on the tenth verse is also very interesting, but it defies translation.

It will suffice to glance over the sermons of the preachers then most in vogue—the abbot of Sainte-Geneviève, Stephen of Tournai, Absalon, the abbot of Saint-Victor, the Abbot Adam of Perseigne, and Alain of Lille, who has been called the " Universal Doctor,"—to discover the current allegories and the popular symbolisms. They handed them on from pulpit to pulpit, and the audience heard them over and over, always with pleasure. We give only two of them: *Le Char spirituel* and *Le Verbe qui se conjugue.*

The " spiritual chariot " is that which conveys the soul of the just. It has four wheels: the two front wheels are the love of God and fellowman; the two rear wheels are the incorruptibility of the body and the integrity of the soul. In the first wheel the hub is the knowledge of the Lord, the spokes which radiate from it are meditation, and the tire of the wheel is devotion. And thus with the other wheels. The axle which joins the back wheels represents the peace of God, and that joining the front wheels represents the uprightness of intention. The bullocks which draw the chariot are the angels yoked to the beam by the bonds of the love of man. In order that the chariot may not jostle on the stones of the road, it must have before it the thought of the presence of God, behind it the scorn of the world, to the left strength of mind in adversity, to the right good use of prosperity. And whither goes this allegorical chariot? To the celestial Jerusalem.

The conjugable Word (*verbe*) is the application of grammar to religion. It concerns the Holy Word: that is to say, the second person of the Trinity. But this Word belongs to four conjugations: to the first conjugation in the bosom of the Virgin, to the second in the baptismal font, to the third on the table of the altar, to the fourth in the soul of the just. We shall state only why it is of the first conjugation in the bosom of the Virgin; because it unites itself to human nature only through love of us, and because the word which represents the act of loving, *amare,* is the model of the first conjugation. Moreover, the Word is at the same time active, passive, neuter, and deponent: active, because Christ was active in His preaching; passive, because Christ suffered the passion in the pretorium and on the cross; neuter, because, after having given up the ghost, Christ was wrapped in a shroud and put in a tomb; deponent, because, having descended into hell, Christ deposed the mighty—that is, the devils, from their thrones. Finally, the Word manifests itself also in a series of modes: indicative, by the incarnation and preaching; imperative, by the passion and the cross; optative, by the resurrection and the ascension; infinitive, by glory and eternity.

Scholastic education left an ineffaceable trace on the monk. Instilling into him from infancy the love for playing on words, of antitheses, of metaphors, of bad taste, and extravagant allegory, it gave him an intellectual malady which the long reflections in the leisure moments of monastic life brought to an acute state.

The monastic historian, who collects contemporary facts and sets them down in the form of dry chronological annals or of more devout narratives, does not escape the contagion. Witness Rigord, that monk of Saint-Denis, a physician by profession, who made himself the historian of Philip Augustus. He is a student who knows the sacred and profane authors and practises subtle exposition. His chronicles are strewn with quotations from the Old and New Testaments, and in his dedicatory epistle he finds means of slipping in some verses from Horace and Virgil. He has a very keen taste for etymology. Why does he give the surname Augustus to his hero, King Philip? Because this king, like the Cæsars of Rome, had considerably increased the territory of France, (Augustus, from the verb *augeo, auges,* he says), and also because he was born in the month of August, *augusto mense.* Rigord does not give his choice between these etymologies; he takes both into account. And he does not fail to tell us apropos of the paving of the streets of

Paris, undertaken by Philip Augustus, that the ancient name of Paris was *Lutetia,* the muddy, from *lutum,* the mud. But the word Paris itself he derived from Paris, son of Priam, whence an enormous digression devoted to the genealogy of the descendants of Priam, and to the history of the Trojan origin of France. The monk of Saint-Denis accepts with entire confidence all the genealogical fables which he did not himself invent, and he exhibits quite a scholarly precision: it was in the year 895 B.C. that twenty-three thousand Trojans, coming from Sicambria, established themselves at Lutetia and, in memory of the son of Priam, gave themselves the name of *Parisii.* Here, however, a scruple of conscience obliges him to repeat that the name *Parisii* had been explained in another way: that it had come from the Greek word *parisia,* which means audacious, bold. The Parisians are the audacious ones, Franks preëminently. And he continues his digression by a long résumé of the history of the Merovingian, Carolingian, and Capetian kings.

Among the monks the refinement of pedantic subtility was allied with an infantile credulity. Rigord believed in astrology. He makes note of all prodigies which he has heard spoken of and gives a large place to miracles in his history. He not only repeats the extraordinary cures which have been performed in his time at the abbey of Saint-Denis by contact with the relics of saints—infants brought to life, the blind and paralytic healed, etc.,—but he even introduces miracles into the life of Philip Augustus, into the wars against the feudal lords and the Plantagenets. The Capetian kings are to him providential and almost superhuman beings, the objects of divine manifestations and protection. To give an idea of the state of mind of this monk of Saint-Denis, it will be enough to quote a page of his history devoted to the year 1187:

" This same year at the feast of Saint Luke, in the month of October, Pope Urban III died: he had reigned one year and a half. His successor was Gregory VIII, who held the see a month and a half. The latter was replaced the same year by Pope Clement III, a Roman by birth."

It was a lamentable fact, these changes of popes, who became popes only to die in the chair of Saint Peter:

" It is the result of faults committed by the popes themselves, and also of the disobedience of men, their subjects, who refuse to return to righteousness by the grace of God, for no one can come out from Babylon—that is the confusion of disorder and transgression— by his own strength or his own knowledge: for that it is necessary that God grant us His grace. The world is growing old; everything grows old here below, and becomes decrepit, or rather falls again into infancy.*

But here is what especially terrified the historian and led him to see everything on the dark side. It is that '' all the infants, who were born in the year that Jerusalem was taken by Saladin, had only twenty or twenty-two, instead of the usual thirty or thirty-two teeth.''

Let us not judge Rigord by this bizarre observation. One cannot say that he merits no confidence as a historian or that he was completely lacking in critical judgment. He expresses himself thus in his preface: '' I have related those facts which I have seen with my own eyes, and others upon which I have informed myself with care. Those which I had no means of testing, I have omitted.'' Truly, Rigord's history transgresses much more by its omissions than by its lack of exactitude; at least, in the things touching contemporary events. He has even a certain concern for truth and justice, a good feature in a semi-official historian who relates the facts and actions of an all-powerful king. In the first part of the chronicle he makes Philip Augustus a hero, endowed with all virtues, but in the second he reproaches him frankly for his conduct toward Ingeborg of Denmark and the readiness with which he extorted money from his clergy. He exhibits a supreme candor in telling how he came to undertake his work and through what trials he had to pass to finish it. The first difficulty was the lack of resources and of time and the necessity of working to live, *acquisitio victualium:* medicine in the middle ages did not always support man. It was only when he had become a monk at Saint-Denis that Rigord had the food and assured protection and could go seriously to work. Another difficulty was the lack of experience. His pen was not practised in beautiful language; it wrote things with too much simplicity. Finally, the last obstacle was the difficulty of ascertaining the truth in the midst of passionate judgments and contrary meanings which obscured it. " It is astonishing," says he, " how human kind, from its origin, is rather inclined to condemn than to be indulgent, and with what facility we take things in bad part. Everything is deceit and falsehood here below. Ill is spoken of those who are good, those who are bad are justified; how can one tell where he is? " And this scruple tormented the historian so much that he was one day on the point of destroying his book, the fruit of ten years' labor; but his abbot (happily for Philip Augustus and the history of France) dissuaded him. Despite his impartiality and a certain straightforwardness, one must note in him one very strong passion—the hatred of the Jews. He reproaches them, in the first place, with possessing half of Paris and of demanding, as pitiless creditors, what was due them; and he further accuses them of killing Christian children and of desecrating the sacred vessels which their creditors confided to them as security. It was the popular prejudice. Rigord breaks into lyrical expression when, toward the beginning of his reign, Philip Augustus, with as much brutality as cynicism, plundered the perfidious Jews (*perfidi Judei*). He was not less happy when, ten years later, the same king of France, at Brie-Comte-Robert, burned eighty Jews, accused of having hanged a Christian. Rigord is in this also of his age, an age the passing of which is not to be regretted.

Another monastic historian is Bernard Itier, who was librarian and chronicler of the abbey of Saint-Martial of Limoges. He had been a monk for forty-eight years of his life, from 1177-1225: that is, during all the reign of Philip Augustus and even a little more. He passed regularly through all the grades of his profession to the dignity of precentor. His chronicle, which is essentially local, is above all devoted to acquainting us with what happened at Limoges and in the region thereabouts. Bernard Itier from time to time, by some few brief words, calls to mind the great events of the political history of the time, the salient facts about the Plantagenet kings and Philip Augustus, the Albigensian crusade, the third crusade, and always in a very scant way; he seems absolutely to ignore the battle of Bouvines. However, this monk did not remain confined without stirring from his abbey; he also, like all other monks of his time, felt the need of travel and the change of atmosphere. One sees him now at Poitou, where he himself says he remained more than three years; then at Grandmont, at Cluny, at Clermont, at Puy-en-Velay, at La Chaise-Dieu, at Saint-Martin of Tours. Pilgrimages nearly always: a pilgrimage was a very convenient thing for monks who could not accommodate themselves to seclusion.

Open-minded, Itier did not occupy himself solely with guarding manuscripts, putting beautiful bindings on them, and covering the margins with historical notes. He did a little of everything: philosophy, ethics, natural history, music, and Latin verse. But in all this there is nothing personal or original: simply reminiscences of authors of antiquity and the early middle ages, a patchwork of quotations put end to end, résumés of the knowledge of others. He wrote a kind of manual of philosophy, in the form of a catechism, with questions and answers. "What is philosophy? The love of wisdom, for the Greeks called *philo* love, and *sophia* wisdom. How is philosophy defined? It is the knowledge of things human and divine. Into how many parts is philosophy divided? Into three parts: physics, ethics or morals, and logic. Into how many parts is physics divided? Four parts: arithmetic, geometry, astronomy, and music. Into how many parts is ethics divided? Into four parts: prudence, justice, courage, and temperance." And so it goes on. There is here an evident effort to state the definitions precisely and in a concise form. Here is his definition of man, "Man is an animal who laughs, who has reason, who is subject to death, and capable of good and evil." This monk of the twelfth century localizes in the brain certain faculties of intelligence. The ability to comprehend, the *ingenium*, has its seat in the front part of the head. How does he prove this? It is because the physicians, he says, have stated that a man, well endowed with this faculty, loses it when he receives a wound in that part of the head. Likewise, there exists in the back part of the head a cell of the brain, *quaedam cellula cerebri*, where the memory resides; when this place is wounded, the memory disappears. In speaking thus, it is true Bernard Itier invented nothing; he read it, and admits it, in an ancient author.

He also cultivated allegory and symbolism. In matters of subtility he is not exceeded by that monk who was spoken of above. For him pride is a tree the trunk of which produces seven principal branches, which are the seven capital sins, from which come in the form of lesser branches all the vices of mankind. In order to overcome these capital sins and vices, one must turn to God, and this is the object of the seven petitions of the Lord's Prayer. Thanks to these seven petitions, one obtains the seven gifts of the Holy Ghost, with the gifts of the Holy Ghost are obtained the seven virtues, and finally one is given the seven beatitudes. The number seven is sacred; it is a perfect number. It is found every-where: the seven words of Jesus on the cross, the seven peni-tential psalms, the seven canonical letters, the seven damna-tions, the seven stars shining in the north, the seven rules of discourse, the seven tables of ancient law, the seven degrees for attaining the contemplation of the Lord, the seven mountains of gold which the Greeks said were sisters, etc. Some lines lower, the monk of Limoges also celebrates the number twelve.

He exhibits the same abuse of scholasticism as others, the same naïveté which sees prodigies everywhere, and the same tendency to carefully collect the various facts about mon-strosities, miracles, and horoscopes. Bernard Itier was con-vinced that those who were born upon Christmas day would die a violent death, and he mentions examples. If the walls of the Château of Limoges crumbled one day in the year 1203, it was because the day before some excommunicated priests had chanted near that part of the ramparts. In the résumé of universal history which precedes his own recital of contemporary events, the reign of the Emperor Theodosius is summarized by this single fact: in the village of Emmaus, in Palestine, a child was born, who was double above the navel—he had two breasts and two heads, and the two parts of the human trunk had a separate life; while one ate and drank the other took nothing for nourishment; while one slept the other was awake. Sometimes, however, the chron-icler adds, these two children played together and wept together. They lived two years. And, under the year 1203, he writes:[1] "One day, in the abbey of Souterraine, the monks were singing at matins the anthem *Spiritus sanctus in te descendet, Maria,* when suddenly the church was entirely illuminated by an intense light, to the great stupefaction of those present." In 1198, there died William, bishop of Poitiers, by whom Bernard Itier had been in former times ordained deacon. A great number of miracles were worked at his tomb. Bernard was a little astonished, and asked what virtue had been worth this honor. He discovered that the prelate had been a very charitable and patient man; "however," said he, "as he seemed to have led a life of sloth, there have been some people who found that the worship of his relics was not absolutely justified."

After all, Itier was not a fanatical admirer of everything connected with religion and the church. He was sometimes outspoken. Under the year 1209 he says, apropos of a legate of the pope, the Cardinal Gualo, and the exactions of which the clergy of France were then the victims, "Gualo, the legate, exasperated many people, *multos exasperavit.*" The word is striking. It explains the severity with which other monks discuss the cardinal Rome had sent to France.

The monk of Saint-Martial of Limoges possessed certain virtues for his profession of historian: he was generally exact, and he was fairly impartial. He searched for the truth with care, as is proved by the passage in his history which he himself corrected when he found that he had been deceived by false information, or he tells us of his uncertainty of what has been said. He does not take in everything without criticism. Like Rigord, he is credulous; he gives proof of a certain method in his choice of historical facts, at least for the time in which he lived. He has his preferences, his passions, but one scarcely sees them, for he almost always contents himself with setting down the facts without giving a personal appreciation. Can one reproach him for believing that Saint Martial, the patron of his abbey, had been an

---

[1] The original reads: *"Et voilà pour le règne de Théodose!"* This is clearly a mistake, as appears from the allusion to Emperor Theodosius a few lines above, and a comparison with the original. Hence the change in the translation.—*Translator.*

apostle and lived in the circle about Christ? All the people of Limousin were convinced of this: to have doubts on this point was a crime of high treason against one's birthplace. No more should one be astonished that he interests himself in the success of the crusaders, in the war against the Albigenses. He even voluntarily exaggerates it. He speaks of thirty thousand heretics killed at Béziers, of twenty thousand at Lavaur, which is a gross exaggeration. But all these massacres make for the greater glory of the Lord, and this monk, in his fashion, exterminated as many heretics as he could.

He has no more love for the infidel and their chief, Mohammed—'' a false prophet,'' he says, '' who taught that every man who killed his enemy, or was killed by his enemy, entered Paradise.'' And what a Paradise! A carnal Paradise, where ran rivers of wine, honey, and milk; where only the basest pleasures and all sorts of things full of luxury and foolishness, *quaedam luxuria et stulticia,* are known; in short, a Paradise where there are too many women; and, according to Bernard, woman is the greatest enemy of man, the cause of all evil and of all the vices of humanity.

We here recognize one of the axioms of ecclesiastical education which furnished so many of the virile tirades to preachers and passionate satires to moralists of the tonsure. One monk composed a special treatise, where he brought together a whole series of historical examples of women who had drawn men into grave faults or dangerous errors, and he also drew up a list of celebrated persons who had been persecuted by women. Woman is merely the image of Antichrist. What is the most enormous of all crimes? Adultery. Those guilty of it are not to be pitied. This infraction of the divine law, Bernard Itier assures us, will not be pardoned in this world or in the next.

Whatever they do with theology and history, these monks are, in the last analysis, merely grown-up children, molded by prejudice. They put a naïve ardor into the search for historical truth or the analysis of philosophical ideas and morals. But, above all, they amuse themselves with the exercises of scholastic philosophy. It is thus that Bernard Itier, the historian and philosopher, turns some Latin verses, and composes some acrostics and enigmas. The day when he took it into his head to write in the manuscript of his history words exclusively composed of consonants or with the vowels replaced by dots, he must have been well pleased with himself: he had found a new game.

* *

Besides the monks who are philosophers, historians, and theologians, there are the poets. Without doubt, the strangest of them all is Guyot of Provins, a monk of Champagne. We know little of his life: only what he himself tells us in his *Bible*, written between 1203 and 1208; and that is practically nothing. We do not even know where he was a monk. It comes out in his verses that he wore the black robe, that his abbey depended on Cluny, and that he had been a monk for a dozen years when he wrote his work. He seems, however, to have passed four months at Clairvaux among the Cistercians, the White monks, but he does not appear to have adopted their habit, or to have followed their rule. His satirical humor strikes with the same spirit at the Black and White monks, as we shall presently see. He seems to have been of burgher stock and without means. Before entering his cloister, he had led the life of many of the trouvères of humble condition, strolling with his verses and his music from château to château, and from court to court. For, if we believe him, he must have known personally almost all the kings and great barons of northern France and of Burgundy at the end of the twelfth century. He had even traveled abroad, for he is said to have seen the king of Aragon, Alfonso II, and a king of Jerusalem, Amauri, and to have been present at the famous court held at Mainz by the Emperor Frederic Barbarossa in 1184. He was a poet-errant, who probably traveled in the retinue of some great lord at his expense. The proverb, " a rolling stone gathers no moss," could well be applied to him, for it is certain that, at the approach of old age, he was obliged to become a monk, to secure a living and shelter. Many men of letters of the time did this. Guyot, to be sure, had a decidedly feeble stock of religious devotion: this is brought out by the way in which he expresses himself con-

cerning his fellow-monks and all the dignitaries of the
church in general, and also in all the passages of the *Bible*
where he discloses his personal sentiments on the obligations
of monastic life. He was not made for the cloister with
its mortifications.

This should not surprise us. To-day, one is a monk because he chooses to be; but it was not so in the middle ages.
In the time of Philip Augustus, the number of people who
were cloistered in spite of their wishes, the number who were
monks or nuns in spite of themselves, was considerable. One
must not suppose that the personnel of the monasteries was
entirely composed of devotees or reformed sinners. Faith
and penitence alone would not have peopled the abbeys and
innumerable priories which then covered the soil of France.
Recall that in each noble family—and these families were
then numerous—there were sons and daughters whom parents
from the cradle destined for the monastic life; remember
that younger sons left without fortunes, and daughters on
the unattached list, voluntarily imprisoned themselves in the
cloister; in exchange for a little land or income, they there
found a fairly sure shelter and bread for each day. The
weak in this way evaded the struggle of life. Recall, also,
that some entered the cloister out of pure ambition, knowing
that the cloister led to the bishopric and to the highest positions of the church. Recall, finally, that abbeys even served
as houses of discipline and that more or less repentant crimi-
nals were shut up there; the religious life was for them an
expiation, and the monastery a prison.

This was not the case with Guyot of Provins. But he,
like many others, does not appear to love his profession.
This monk absolutely lacks enthusiasm, and he allows it to
be seen in a most naïve fashion. He tells of the austerities
which they practised in the order of Chartreux, and he enumerates them with a kind of dismay:

"For nothing in the world would I be a Carthusian; their rule
is too harsh. Each monk is obliged to do his own cooking, to eat
alone, and to sleep in a solitary cell. When I see them blowing
and kindling their fires it seems to me that this is not the duty
of honest men. I do not know what the dear Lord thinks of it,
but as for me, I do not wish to live isolated even in Paradise. The

place where I had no companions would be no paradise for me. It
is not good to be alone; solitude is a bad life which often engenders
sadness and anger."

There was still another thing which Guyot did not like
among the Carthusians: that is, they did not eat meat, and
did not even give it to the sick. The harshness of this rule
grates upon him:

" These men are murderers of the sick. I would not allow a poor
man to die before me rather than give him meat. Do they forget
what the disciples of Jesus Christ ate, and what He Himself said
to them: Eat such things as are set before you, and whatever meats
the good God sends you, do not ask from whence your food and
drink cometh."

Guyot does not concede that this abstinence from meat is
necessary to the virtue of the monks. On the contrary, he has
heard it said by wise people that a diet composed exclusively
of milk, butter, and cheese is very dangerous. One should,
then, give meat to the sick, if they desire it. " Decidedly,"
he concludes, " I do not like this order. If I had entered
it, I should leave the very first day; and, if my superior did
not wish to give me leave, I should know where to find a
corner of the wall to jump over."

Here is a disposition that is quite unbecoming in a monk;
for, upon searching, it appears that there is no religious congregation in which Guyot of Provins would care to live. He
would like, however, to be a Templar. He would prefer the
Temple of Cluny, he says. But the order of Templars has
one great drawback, which is that the brothers are obliged
to fight, and our monk is nothing less than he is a fighter.

" The Templars are much honored in Syria. The Turks fear
them terribly. They defend the châteaus and the ramparts, and
in battle they never flee. But there is exactly what worries me.
If I belonged to that order I know very well that I should flee. I
should not tarry for blows, for I do not dote on them. They fight
too bravely. I do not care to be killed. I would rather pass for
a coward and live, than to be the most glorious of earth dead. I
would sing for hours for them; that would not inconvenience me
in the least. I would be very exact in the service, but not at the
hour of battle. There I should completely fail."

It would be hard to be more candid. This monk of Cluny does not even find that at Cluny all goes for the best. One cannot talk in the refectory; all night the brethren bray (it is his expression) in the church. During the day they work without rest. It is only in the refectory that one can sometimes rest. But there are other drawbacks:

"They give us bad eggs and unshelled beans. What often arouses my wrath is that the wine is too thin; they have put in too much of what the oxen drink. No, I will never get drunk on convent wine. At Cluny it is better to die than to live."

And Guyot ends by sighing for the rule of canons of Saint Augustine. "Blessed be Saint Augustine. His canons have good meat and good wine in abundance."

We now know with what kind of a monk we have to deal. This naïve simplicity has a great charm, and one plainly sees that Guyot is just the opposite of an ascetic and a fanatic. Under it all he has high sentiments. His idea, which he expresses in very clear terms, is that the work of the religious life has no value, if it is not accompanied by piety and charity:

"A congregation is builded in charity and of charity it should be full. A monk can indeed be at great pains to read, to sing, to work, and to fast, but if he has not charity in his soul it avails him nothing to my mind. He is like an empty house in which the spiders spin and wind their webs, and then immediately destroy what they have spun. Singing and fasting are not what save the soul, but charity and faith."

Observe this declaration of principle. By it Guyot of Provins appears to place himself ahead of his time, a time when religion was almost wholly in the works, when general belief attributed an absolute efficacy to the external practices of worship, and especially to the cult of the saints and of relics. One is not astonished that, permeated by such a principle, our monk, in reviewing the various congregations, including his own, found occasion to use his satirical humor, which is not malicious, for he declared at the beginning of his poem that he would tell the whole truth without attacking individuals, and he kept his word. He wisely adhered to generalities. With this reservation, we must admit that Guyot was not gentle with the monks of any color, his brothers, and that no order found grace in his eyes. What he says of each of them, making allowances for the exaggeration of the satire, is of very great interest for our study. He commences with the Black monks, those of Cluny, and reproaches the abbots of that order with being poor administrators, who ruin the priory by exploitation and who have installed in the cloister three ugly, foul, and cruel old women: treachery, hypocrisy, and simony. Then he passes to the White order, that of Clairvaux or Cîteaux, an order in which the life is hard and where one finds the least of fraternity. The Cistercians have no pity for each other. They think only of acquiring land and money; they covet everything they see, and frighten the poor people, whom they despoil of their lands and reduce to begging. At home the plain monks are miserable, but the heads of the monasteries, the abbots and the cellarers, treat themselves well. They have the money, the meats, and the big fish. They have a twofold weakness: they drink the clear wine and send the cloudy to the refectory. "It is fraternity inverted. I would rather be in Persia than in a wretched cloister where there is no pity."

We already know that our monk reproaches the Carthusians with an excessive austerity and harshness in the treatment of the sick. This is for some reason all the bad he says of them. The order of Grandmont pleases him better, for he has heard that they mortify themselves less than others. The monks talk in the dormitory, the church, and in the cloister. They like good fish and hot, well-spiced sauces. At night, upon going to bed, they bathe and carefully comb their beards; "they even cover them and divide them into three braids, in order that they may be beautiful and glossy on the day they shall be seen by outsiders." But what is bad at Grandmont and makes Guyot thankful he is not there, is that there are lay brothers, half-laymen, who govern the monks and priests, and who strike the true monks when they resist: it is a case of cart before the horse. This strife and disorder arouses the indignation of the author. His allusion to the intestine wars which revolutionized the order of Grandmont at the time of Philip

Augustus, and which then resounded throughout the Christian world, is noteworthy and confirms what the historical documents proper tell us concerning it. We shall come back to it.

Then come the White canons of Prémontré. For Guyot this is an entirely decadent order. They disagreed, the monks fought their abbots, they had great estates which they were in danger of losing, were head over ears in debt, did nothing but sell and mortgage. "What I say of them," adds the poet, "could not make them bad. They have done more than any one to destroy themselves." The Templars, with their white mantles and shining crosses, are the valiant knights, who guard their houses well and render justice; but they have two vices for which they are severely blamed—covetousness and pride. With regard to the Hospitalers, Guyot has seen them in Jerusalem, but they have forgotten their name; although very rich, they are not hospitable and know nothing of charity. Another kind of Hospitaler, the lay brothers of the order of Saint Anthony, found no grace before our author, who considers them vagabonds and charlatans. He depicts them, with bells hanging from the necks of their mounts, soliciting everywhere from Scotland to Antioch for their hospitals and giving not one sou of all they gather to the church. In each hospital there were fifty lay brothers, fat and sodden—some having five hundred, others one thousand, marks. They carried on business and even usury. They had wives and children. "The whole country is peopled with them," says Guyot, and they marry their daughters well. As for Saint Anthony, they do not care two straws about him. Finally, even the carpenter Durand, the promoter of the brotherhood of White Hoods, or *Encapuchonnés* of Puy-en-Velay,—of whom we have already read the half-legendary history,—is a victim of this pitiless critic. Guyot makes him out a vagabond and a trickster, who plainly had made his fortune by selling the insignia of the brotherhood to a multitude of credulous people. "He well knew how to deceive his world, and he deceived two hundred thousand."

This is bold, indeed, in a Benedictine! He spares others no more than the secular clergy. Curés, canons, bishops, archbishops are all put through the mill. He accuses the prelates of seeking money and honor before everything else, of selling the things belonging to the church, of being proud and covetous. His satire becomes particularly violent and spiteful when the cardinals and the papacy are attacked. In this connection he shows us how intolerable the exactions of the court of Rome and its agents already appeared to the clergy of France, and to what degree of exasperation the venality of the Holy See and of its representatives had, little by little, led them. It recalls the words of the historian, whom we quoted above, apropos of Cardinal Gualo, the envoy of Innocent III: *Gualo legatus multos exasperavit.* Guyot of Provins seems to be merely paraphrasing the monk of Limoges when he speaks of Rome and the Romans:

"O Rome, Rome! When wilt thou cease to kill mankind? Thou killest us every day. Christianity is marching backwards. All was lost and confounded from the day that thy cardinals were sent. They came blazing and on fire with covetousness; they came full of simony; they came void of reason, without faith, and without religion. They sell God and His Mother; they trample everything with their feet and devour all. What do they with the gold and silver they take beyond the mountains? If only they made roads, hospitals, and bridges with it!"

Guyot hardly dared to accuse the pope himself of taking his part in the plundering of the Christian world, but he reproaches him with closing his eyes and allowing it to be done. He advises dukes, princes, and kings not to allow themselves to be subjected by Rome—advice which Philip Augustus and his nobles were not slow to follow, if they had not already done it; for it was in 1205 that the king and the great barons of France, in a sealed letter, protested against the exactions and the abuse of power by the Holy See. Finally, the poet ends with this imprecation:

"Rome sucks us up and devours us. Rome destroys and kills everything. Rome is the source of the mischief from which spring all evil vices. It is a fishpond full of vermin. Why did not the world throw itself on Rome instead of attacking the Greeks?"

This monk proceeds with no tender hand. In the time of Luther, men said no worse things of Rome and the papacy.

Guyot of Provins is bitter when he speaks of politics; he is simply good-natured and spiteful when he attacks the shortcomings common to certain social classes and diverse professions. An old trouvère, he is full of respect for kings and great barons. He enumerates with pride all those he has known during his travels, and the list is long; but he declares that those of the present are very inferior to those who lived in his youth. They no longer hold a brilliant court, as formerly, and they no longer know how to be generous. This is a commonplace in the mouths of all trouvères. And then they have the great fault of protecting the Jews and keeping them in their lands. Guyot detested Jews, like all his fellows, but he especially blamed those princes who employed these usurers and benefited by their operations, instead of putting them out of the country. This is probably an allusion to the conduct of Philip Augustus and of several feudal lords, notably the count of Champagne.

Curiously enough, monk though he is, Guyot of Provins is not too hard on woman. He says, to be sure, that she is false at times, that she is lighter than the wind, that she often changes her mind, that she in one day forgets what she has loved for many years. But all this is pardonable. Woman to him is an enigma that frightens him, and an enigma that need not be fathomed.

" The wisest are led astray when they wish to judge or correct a woman. She has never found her master, and who can flatter himself that he knows her? When her eyes weep her heart laughs; she little considers what she says. I remember Solomon, Constantine, and Samson, whom women deceived, and truly I come to the conclusion that I have more hope of understanding the sun and the moon, those two marvels, than of understanding what woman is. There are men who teach astronomy, necromancy, geometry, law, medicine, theology, and music; but I have never known a person, at least who was not a fool, to take woman for a subject of study."

Guyot compensates himself at the end of his poem by attacking the theologians—the " divines," as he calls them. He eulogizes theology as " the art which crowns the soul, the art honored of all," but he depreciates those who practise it. They are very adept in language, but they think only of making an income. They show others the right road, but they do not preach by example. Regarding the professors of jurisprudence, or lawyers, they think only of teaching chicanery and trickery, pleading the bad as well as the good, and doing anything whatsoever in order to obtain good benefices. Finally, comes the turn of the *fisiciens*—that is, the doctors,—against whom our monk seems to have had a special grievance, for he heaps on them pleasantries which later became proverbial. "They kill numbers of sick, and exhaust themselves to find maladies in everybody. They have had me in their hands, but I do not like their company when I am well. Woe to him who falls into their power." He makes fun of their medicines. "I prefer a fat capon to all their mixtures." And he finds that those who come from Montpellier sell their syrups much too dearly. He, however, admits that, if there are some bad doctors, there are also some very good ones, who know how to strengthen the sick. "When a man is afraid of death, he is in great need of comfort, and it is by the confidence which they inspire, rather than by their medicines, that the cure is effected. When I am sick," concludes Guyot, and it is with this that his book ends, "I want some one to bring them to me. Their presence does me good. But, when the sickness leaves me, I wish that a galley would take them straight to Salonika, them and all their physic, so far that one may never see them again."

This monk is interesting, both for what he tells us of himself and of others. He is an intensely practical spirit; he has the good sense to jeer at the bourgeoisie in whose eyes the slightest excess is a sin, and to relieve the ennui of the cloister by raillery.

In this Guyot little resembles his contemporary, the monk of Auvergne, known in Provençal literature as the monk of Montaudon. We must call him this because we do not know his family name. Montaudon is the priory of which he was the head. He was a singular monk!—the type of those who passed their lives outside the cloister and reëntered it to rest from the fatigue of the world. He was, moreover, a noble of the family of the lords of Vic-sur-Cère in Auvergne. His father had at an early age shut him up in the neighboring abbey of Saint-Géraud of Aurillac. The abbot intrusted him with the priory of Montaudon. But this monk was a writer with an original and sarcastic vein. The lords of the region wrangled with him, and his fame was not long in spreading beyond Auvergne. He led the life of a trouba-dour, while wearing the robes of a monk, and traveled from château to château in all the regions of the south. According to his statements, he had seen the Périgord, Limousin, Querci, Rouergue, Gévaudan, Provence, Toulousain, Gascony, Poitou, Angoumois, Forez, and even Spain, taking his part in all the knightly fêtes, as judge awarding the prize of a sparrow-hawk at the solemn concourse at Puy-en-Velay. How did the abbot of Aurillac tolerate so unmonastic a life in his subordi-nate? He dared say little or nothing, because the monk of Montaudon, from time to time returned to his priory, whither he brought all gifts with which he had been loaded. At last he obtained the priory of Villafranca, in Roussillon, on the property of his friend, Alfonso II, king of Aragon; and the latter, adds the Provençale biographer, '' ordered the monk of Montaudon to eat of meat, entertain the ladies, and to sing and make verses.''

Here is all we know of the life of the monk of Montaudon, and it is apparent that the monk is anything but exemplary. This is seen especially in his poetry, certain couplets of which are absolutely not to be translated. It is not only in Latin that words can brave propriety; they can do it in Provençal, and the monk of Montaudon is one of the troubadours who defied propriety most brazenly.

Like all his contemporaries, he wrote love songs addressed to the woman of his fancy. But these are not the ones which here chiefly interest us. This monk is, above everything else, a satirist, and his talent displays itself particularly in the *sirvente*. He wrote one in which he said something bad of every troubadour of the time, including himself. He speaks of himself in the third person and calls himself '' the false monk of Montaudon ''—the expression is extremely appropri-ate—a monk who had quarreled with every one, who had left God and the convent for the pleasures of the table, whose poetry and songs are fit only to be thrown to the winds. He seems, however, to have had some scruples of conscience, for, in one of his poems, he tries to justify himself for being

such an irregular monk, and to prove that God Himself
authorized his conduct:

"The other day I was in Paradise, because I am gay and happy,
and deeply love the dear God Whom all obey, earth, sea, valleys, and
mountains. And God said to me: 'Monk, why did you come here,
and how do you fare at Montaudon, where you have numerous
companions?' 'Lord, I remained in the cloister one or two years,
which was enough to lose the barons' friendship; but Thou art the
only One Whom I wish to love and serve.' 'Monk,' answered God,
'do not think that you give Me pleasure in shutting yourself up
in the abbey. Why let war songs and love-plaints cease? I would
rather see you sing and laugh. The princes are more generous for
it, and the priory of Montaudon can only gain by it."

Thus the monk of Montaudon excuses himself for his infractions of the rule.

The works of our monk reveal much less of the sentiments
and ideals of their author than the *Bible* of Guyot of
Provins does of its composer, for there is not much of them,
and the extreme conciseness of the style renders the thought
obscure. He devotes several poems to ridiculing women who
use paints; and, by way of a jest, which is a little far-
fetched, he fancies that the saints instituted a suit because
women had so monopolized the red, black, and white colors,
to paint themselves, that none was left to color the images
and statues in the churches. Another series of poems belongs to
a class of which the productions of the monk of Montaudon are
almost the only examples in Provençal literature, the class of
" ennui " (*enueg*). It consists of enumerating all the things
that the poet dislikes or which bore him. This would throw
some light on, at least, the negative tastes and prejudices
of the monk of Montaudon, if one could find any ethics or
interesting psychological observations in them. But this is
not the case, as one can judge from this fragmentary
translation:

"What tires me is a good talker who performs his duty badly,
a man who always seeks to kill his neighbor, a horse with a hard
mouth, a noble who wears too haughtily a shield which has received
no blows, a bearded priest or monk, a reckless slanderer. I cannot
endure a tiresome woman who is at the same time poor and proud,
a man too much in love with his wife, knights who make trouble

outside of their country and at home powder pepper in a mortar. What provokes me is a poor falcon, a small helping when there is plenty in the kitchen, too much water in a glass of wine, meeting a lame person or a blind man on the road; I despise dry, poorly cooked meat, a preacher who lies and perjures himself, an old woman with bad manners. It annoys me to ride horseback on icy roads, or to eat without fire when it is cold."

And so on. This enumeration of unpleasant things is, on the whole, commonplace enough, and tells us little of the intimate and personal sentiments of the author. Another selection, which serves as the companion-piece of this, is just the opposite, for the monk composes a litany of things which he likes:

" Jests and gaiety please me greatly, as also fine deeds, liberality, prowess, a courageous and courteous woman who understands repartee. It pleases me greatly to see a rich and generous man, to sleep when it storms and thunders, to have a plump salmon for my meal. I also enjoy being near a fountain or a brook in summer, when the meadows are fresh and green, and when the birds are singing. I am delighted at having a good companion, to feel again the caresses of my sweetheart, and to see my enemies unhappy."

All this we must admit was not very monastic. The prior of Montaudon had not risen in his tastes above the almost vulgar mediocrity of the great majority of the nobles of his country and his time. He, at least, represents well enough the type of involuntary monk, the large class of monks who, at the wish of their fathers, had been condemned to the ecclesiastical life, and subjected themselves as little as possible to a profession they had not themselves chosen.

CHAPTER VII

MONASTIC LIFE

The epoch of Philip Augustus was not one of those periods of the middle ages which were marked by the founding of a large number of abbeys. Beginning with the middle of the twelfth century, the ardor of individuals and of the feudal princes for these endowments had considerably decreased. The large foundations of the various Benedictine brotherhoods had been made. Long before the time of Philip Augustus, France was covered with the establishments of monks and nuns: in other words, the old monastic movement which, through the voice of powerful reformers of the time of the investiture struggle, as though by magic called into being the hermitages, rural priories, and the monasteries of the towns and cities—that movement had ceased and that feudal period was closed. On the other hand, the new monachism of the mendicant orders—by which the France of Louis VIII, of Saint Louis, and of Philip the Fair was endowed with so many Dominican or Franciscan convents and churches—had scarcely begun to spread in the latter years of the reign of Philip Augustus. His period was then, one may say, an intermediate or a neutral period between two grand epochs of religious effervescence, marked by the activity and the extraordinary fervor of the builders of the abbeys.

It must not be said that, between 1180 and 1220, no monastic foundations were created. Although less active than in the eleventh and twelfth centuries, faith continued to have an influence, and the faithful, still convinced of the efficacy of material works, did not leave off establishing religious houses and insuring their duration by gifts. Let us take any province: Maine, for example. During the reign of Philip Augustus, we find in that region alone four foundations, of which three are important. In 1188, a seignior of Assé founded the abbey of Champagne, where he established the White Monks, the Cistercians; in 1189, Bernard, seignior of Ferté, founded the abbey of Pelice, with the Black Monks; in 1204, arose the abbey of Fontaine-Daniel of the order of Cîteaux, thanks to the donations of a high noble, Juhel III, a seignior of Maine; in 1218, finally, a certain Ralph of Beaumont founded a new abbey, dependent on the abbey of Couture at Mans, the priory of Loué.

Let us betake ourselves a short distance from Paris into the French Vexin, along the road which leads from Chaumont to Trie, in the neighborhood of Gisors and its feudal fortress. There, in a very pleasant dale, one still sees a vast structure, the ruins of a nunnery, which was rebuilt under Louis XIII and Louis XIV; it is the abbey of Gomerfontaine, in which the seigniors of Chaumont-en-Vexin had of old chosen interment. The Cistercian abbey of Gomerfontaine was founded in 1207 by Hugh of Chaumont, the most powerful lord of the vicinity, and the act of foundation has come down to us. Here are its essential clauses:

"I, Hugh of Chaumont, with the consent of my wife, Petronille, of my sons John and James, and of my other sons, for the salvation of my soul, of the soul of my wife, the soul of my father Galon, and of my mother Mathilda, for the salvation of the souls of all my predecessors and of all my heirs, I make and concede in pure and perpetual alms the following donation . . ."

These first lines give us the religious motives of the founder. This lord thought not only of himself and of his own welfare in the future world, but of that of all his relatives and even of all his predecessors. He sought to assure Paradise to all. And to whom does he make this gift? "To God," he says, "and to the nuns of the order of Cîteaux." He gave them his land of Gomerfontaine, with the orchard which was hard by, in order that they might serve God in that place, in an abbey dedicated at once to God and to the Holy Virgin, to Saint John the Baptist, Saint James, Saint John the Evangelist, Saint Eustache, and to all the saints. Thus, Hugh of Chaumont was not content with a single patron for his foundation, as was usual in similar circumstances; the protection of many saints, designated by name, was a much better guarantee. He invoked the protection of all the saints *en masse* (*omnium sanctorum*). There follow the provisions intended to complete the donation:

"I give to said nuns the whole tithe of my eels in the fish-ponds of Gomerfontaine and Latinville; a hundred sous each year for six years, to enable them to construct their monastery, and a perpetual rent of three measures of wheat to be taken from my mill of Gomerfontaine."

There, then, the future of the nuns was assured; but they took care to have inserted in the charter some provisional clauses:

"If the aforesaid mill should be destroyed, burned, or suspend operation, we pledge ourselves, I and my heirs, to furnish the three measures of wheat, securing them elsewhere."

Such is the substance of the charter of foundation of the abbey of Gomerfontaine, signed by the founder in 1207 in the presence of a canon of Rouen, an abbot of the vicinity, and of many other witnesses.

But one must conclude that this first gift was not considered sufficient, for two years afterward Hugh of Chaumont did a second act of charity. Besides the house and garden of Gomerfontaine, he gave it two neighboring gardens, a wood, the right of fishing one day a year, twenty sous of rent from his income from Chaumont, a vineyard, and the tithe from a specified locality. Then, from the family of Chaumont or from other families of the vicinity, came additional alms: in 1210, the gifts of two peasants and two innkeepers; in 1212, twenty-two perches of land; in 1213, an estate and ten Parisian sous in rent; in 1218, the tithe of a forest; in 1219, three perches of land; in 1220, a rent of two measures of wheat; in 1223, a house at Gomerfontaine. We witness thus the steps in the formation of an abbey's domains. Donations continued to accumulate during the whole thirteenth century, but they did not consist solely of estates, forests, and revenues in grain or in money. In 1252, a countess of Boulogne made a gift to the nuns of Gomerfontaine of five hundred herring, for their fish-days. These, then, are the reasons and conditions under which abbeys were founded during the time of Philip Augustus. In this instance it concerns a little community of nuns, a humble dependency of a powerful abbey of Cîteaux, the domain and authority of which extend only a very short distance round about its buildings and the abbey church. But, whether the religious establishment was large or small, the sentiments animating the founders and the benefactors, and the processes employed in founding the monastery and increasing its domain, were exactly the same.

Not only did the faithful found new houses, but they continued to enrich those which were already in existence; though, it is true, with less zeal than before. From 1164 to 1201, Clairvaux, the abbey of Saint Bernard, received nine hundred and sixty-four donations, being an average of a little more than twenty-five per year. From 1201 to 1242, the number began to decrease: it was five hundred and twenty-two, which still gave an average of thirteen. At Vauluisant, one of the ancient abbeys of the order of Cîteaux, founded in 1127, out of the one hundred and fourteen charters comprised in the cartulary for the years 1180 and 1213, there are sixty which mention gifts made to the monks; which proves that the Christian fervor, if it had diminished in intensity, was not extinct. In it we also see the domain of the monks increasing and their treasure growing year by year. They received all kinds of properties and revenues: lands, woods, meadows, vineyards, incomes, or rents in money; rents in kind of wine, wheat, barley, oats, flocks, even of iron and coal; rights to pasture; mills and coal mines and judicial rights. In brief, the monks were enriched and were provided with every necessity of life.

What motives animated the donors? They were always the same. Here is a woman who enriched Vauluisant "for the salvation of her soul, for that of her husband, of her children, and of her ancestors." Some made donations "for the expiation of their sins"; others because they were leaving for the crusade. In 1216, a noble, "on the point of setting out against the Albigenses," following the counsel of his friends, made his will before the priest who had the cure of his soul; and the priest made him give the abbey six pieces of land and three *setiers* of wheat from the revenue of a certain locality. It must be added that many of the donations were only to become effective posthumously: they were to be valid " after the death of the donor," valid *post mortem*. But the monk was patient, he knew how to wait, and some day or other he would come into possession.

There is a proverb: Who has land has trouble. During the reign of Philip Augustus, the abbey of Vauluisant had to undergo not less than forty lawsuits: lawsuits against neighboring religious establishments, against rival churches, and lawsuits against individuals, especially those who had had the sorrow of discovering the bequest of a parent and had refused to give up the heritage.

One of these contests of the date of 1209 is especially curious. The abbey of Vauluisant had been attacked in the courts of justice by the abbey of Paraclet. The two communities were in strife over the estate of a priest named Girard. This priest had been the almoner of the abbess and nuns of Paraclet, but he had been buried in the cemetery of Vauluisant. There was no reason for the monks considering themselves authorized to take all the objects belonging to the deceased, even to his clothes, an annotated psalter, and a sum of thirty sous in the coin of Provins. The abbess of Paraclet claimed them. The decision of the case was confided by superior authority to two arbitrators, and the monks of Vauluisant had to return what they had taken. Suits which they began against other religious communities did not always end in their favor, but, when monasteries had a case against ordinary individuals, they nearly always won their cause; often they did not even have to go into court. Men thought twice, in the middle ages, before pleading against an abbey: was it not pleading against the saint whose relics the convent possessed, and consequently against God Himself? The Christian, anxious for the safety of his soul, nearly always chose to abandon his claim or, by means of a slight pecuniary sacrifice, the monks obtained his desistence.

There was one other source of wealth of the abbeys: it was the possession of the abbey churches. In 1185, Manasses, bishop of Troyes, enumerating in detail the parochial revenues which the abbey Montier-en-Der (Haute-Marne) possessed in his bishopric, wrote to the monks:

"You have at Rosnay the right to name the curé. Each Sunday the curé shall receive a denier from the offering, but the proceeds from the other public masses are yours. In the ceremonies for women who come to be churched, that which is placed on the candlesticks is for the curé and all the rest is yours. Three days of the week, on Monday, Thursday, and Saturday, if the curé says the mass for individuals, the money which is offered is his. He also receives the proceeds of the confession and the offering at marriages. But he has no right to the tithes, they are yours. Of the money accruing from alms, the curé shall receive twelve deniers. If the alms exceed twelve deniers the surplus shall be divided equally between the curé and you."

The same details are given for each of the twenty other churches which the monks of Montier-en-Der possessed in the diocese of Troyes. Besides the proceeds from religious ceremonies, which they shared with the curé, they sometimes took the whole tithe, and sometimes the largest part of the tithe, which formed the most important parochial revenue. It was money easily earned, since the curé did all the work, and the abbey had only the trouble of collecting it. This lasted throughout the middle ages and the whole of the old régime.

It would be interesting to know whether the monks to whom so many gifts and alms, in money and real estate, were made accepted them without disturbing themselves about their source, without inquiring to what extent the donor had rightfully or wrongfully acquired the properties which he was giving up. The truth is that this scruple did not worry the monks of that time very much, for the very simple reason that, at bottom, the great mass of the faithful was convinced that giving to a saint or to God was a pious deed, which in itself justified everything. It mattered little whether the source of the gift was pure or impure; from the moment that the church was enriched, even with possessions wrongfully acquired, the sin was expiated and the wrong repaired.

A letter which a certain Simon of Namur, in the first years of the thirteenth century, addressed to Henry of Villiers in response to an inquiry on that delicate subject, reveals the sentiments and ethics of monks of that time. Simon commences, as usual, by referring to the authority of a church father, to Saint Jerome, who said: "We must guard against receiving anything from the hand of those who have enriched themselves by making the poor weep, for we should not be the associates of thieves, and it is imperative that no one may say of us, 'When thou sawest a thief, thou consentedst with him' (*Si videbas furem, currebas cum eo*)." Therefore, concludes Saint Simon, what shall one say of monks if they receive indiscriminately from all hands? There are four kinds of property which should not be given as alms: that which is acquired by simony, by usury, by robbery, or by depredation. Suppose that a usurer should wish to make a gift to a monastery. One should first warn him to return that which he has wrongly acquired. That is what Tobit said to Anna when some one brought him a kid: "From whence is this kid? Is it stolen?" But, if the usurer or robber responds, "I do not know whence it comes or to whom I should return it," what should be said? Simon of Namur does not hesitate: "In that case he ought to promise to give it to the church, and the monks, with the authorization of the bishop, may accept it." This applies to the case where the donor possessed only wrongfully acquired property. But it is possible that his possessions be of a mixed nature (*mixta bona*), that part of it was gained honestly and the rest dishonestly. It is then that the subtilities of the casuistic scholars find their employment. In a case of mixed possession, says Simon, the monks may always accept: they go on the hypothesis that the thing given was honestly acquired, since it is impossible for them to show the contrary.

Another recommendation made to the monks was not to buy an estate or any property when rumor says that the seller holds it improperly: for instance, when it is claimed by the heirs, or when it is known that they might claim it, with good grounds. And here the casuist continues to prove his ingenuity. Suppose, he says, that a usurer is in possession of an estate unjustly acquired by usury. May the monks buy it, granting that the usurer does not know to whom he should return it? On this point there are two opinions. One holds that a monastery is permitted to receive the estate as alms, if the usurer consents to make a gift of it, but that it may not be bought of him. Why this distinction? It is because the usurer restores it to the church by the gift; it is not restored by the sale. The other claims that the monks can buy even in that case; but, adds Simon, "that does not seem permissible to me." Here his letter ends abruptly; unhappily, the end of the document is lacking. We would like to see how far the resources of this special casuistry go on a question so important and complex as that of the legality of monastic acquisitions.

When one studies the cartularies of the abbeys of that time, filled with deeds of donations and purchases, it seems very improbable that the monks took the trouble to make inquiries about each of their acquisitions and heroically rejected gifts of a doubtful sort. One constantly sees them in suits against the heirs; they defend the case; they win or they compromise; and, finally, they nearly always remain in possession of the objects of litigation. However, in order to be charitable, it must be remarked that, in the epoch of Philip Augustus, the ecclesiastical authorities began to be stirred by certain scandals. A statute of the general chapter of the order of Cîteaux, in 1183, forbade the monks to receive gifts coming from a person excommunicated by name. Another statute of the same chapter, in 1201, forbade the receiving of alms from the hands of those who practised their usury notoriously. It remained a question to what extent these orders were heeded.

The supreme generosity in the faithful of that time consisted of giving oneself to a monastery, or in giving a member of the family with a part or all of the inheritance. Gifts of that kind, very frequent in the primitive age of feudalism, and until the tenth and eleventh centuries, were becoming very much less common in the epoch of Philip Augustus. Faith was no more so simple. Men less readily than formerly consented to bestow their property and personal independence upon the church or upon the saint who was its patron. They continued to do it, because they still found it to their religious or material advantage. Some agreed to be monks and to live the spiritual life, that they might be assured eternal happiness; others gave themselves to an abbey, though remaining laymen, in order to enjoy the relative security attached to possessions of the church and to have their living and shelter assured under the immediate protection of the monks.

Thus it is that, in the first years of the thirteenth century, one sees an entire family—composed of a father, his daughter, and grandmother—make a gift to the abbey of Saint-Vincent of Mans of their own persons and of a third of their patrimony. The other two-thirds they sold to the same religious establishment for the sum of twenty-two livres in the money of Mans. But this was not a gift made purely and simply out of good will. The family which gave itself, in return, required of the abbey: first, an annual rental and annuity of twenty sous; second, a rental in kind of fifteen *setiers* of grain, consisting of seven of rye and eight of barley; third, the possession of an arpent of vineyard in good condition, of an estate, and of a woodland solely for their personal use. At the death of the father, the monks were to pay one-half of the rental of twenty sous and resume half of the vineyard, the estate, and the woods. At the death of the daughter and of the grandmother, they were to reacquire the other two quarters and pay nothing more. In fact, the donors were sellers. They contracted a sort of insurance against war and famine. They placed themselves and their goods at interest. It was a financial deal, advantageous both to individuals whom the insecurity of society prevented from living independently and to the religious community which, in the final reckoning, found itself possessed of one more domain in perpetuity.

More often it happened that, when a man or woman gave himself to a monastery, it was in order to assume the monastic habit and to practise the religious life. This was expected when the head of a family gave the monks a son, a daughter, or a brother, thus singularly simplifying the family duty. On this point documents abound. Here is a noble, Hugh of Thiébauménil, who gives the abbey of Haute-Seille his son Ulrich. But every monk had to bring his dowry with him; one could not enter the cloister empty-handed: Hugh ceded a part of his freehold of Laschère. Some time after he became a monk himself and transferred another part of his freehold. Finally, after some years, his wife in her turn embraced the religious life and gave the church what remained of their common patrimony. There was a whole family cloistered and an estate forever lost to civil society. This happened in the first years of the reign of Philip Augustus. In 1194, at the other end of France, a lesser noble of the region of the Pyrenees, Raymond Bernard of Esparros, gave the abbey of Escale-Dieu his son Bernard, " in order that he may serve there as a monk," says the deed, and with him all that he possessed in the church of Mazerolles. The same thing happened in all other parts of the country. In 1193, a proprietor of Vexin gave the monks of Meulan two vineyards and two arpents of land, in order that his younger brother might enter the abbey. The donor himself appeared in the church of the abbey with the child. He placed a candlestick, which is the symbol of a gift, on the altar of Saint Nicaise. The prior of the community, with the consent of his brethren, conferred " fraternity " on the donor: that is, association in the spiritual benefits of the monks. He, in return, promised the monks that in his old age or even before, if he should so desire, he would enter their house " with his property."

We do not know whether the promise was kept in this particular case, but there is no doubt that, up to the epoch of Philip Augustus, many individuals, when they felt themselves attacked by some serious disease and felt their end approaching, took the habit, became monks, and at the same time enriched an abbey. It was the surest way for a human conscience to settle its accounts with God.

The burden of a large family in an epoch when the families of France counted a large number of children; the difficulty of giving land to sons and daughters in a way which would permit them to maintain an honorable rank; the pressure of sentiment, which urged into the cloister believers eager for peace and mortifications and repentant sinners or the faithful trembling before death and the prospect of a hell in which all the world believed—these should suffice to explain how the innumerable monasteries and priories of the France of Philip Augustus so easily recruited their personnel. But another motive must be taken into account: namely, the pressure to escape the struggle for life in a time when there was security neither for property nor for individuals and when the nobles themselves were not always sure of their next day's bread. There is a very curious page on this subject in the *Dialogues* of the Cistercian monk, Cæsar of Heisterbach, who wrote in 1221. The author presents a dialogue between a monk and a novice.

"The Monk: We often see, every day we see rich and distinguished persons, knights, for example, and citizens, come into our order for the purpose of escaping misery, preferring rather to serve by necessity a rich God, than to bear the shame of poverty in the midst of their kinsmen and acquaintances. A man who had occupied an honorable position in the world told me how he had come to enter a monastery: 'Certainly,' he added, 'if I had succeeded in my affairs I should never have entered into the order.' I have known some who did not wish to follow their fathers and brothers when these entered the monastery. They wasted the property which had been left them, and it was then only that they came and with the mantle of devotion covered the misery which brought them.

"Novice: It is not necessary to give many examples, for we see many men, especially lay brothers, enter the order for the same reason. But blessed be they who have had riches and have despised them for the love of Jesus Christ."

Finally, one must add to this diverse category of voluntary and involuntary monks all the disinherited of the world, whom infirmities or defective physique did not permit to lead a normal life. When a father had crippled children he made them clerics or monks, so that the church was obliged to take steps to avoid becoming merely a vast association of defectives. She required of her priests, canons, and especially of her bishops certain qualifications in the way of health and esthetic appearance, and opposed the admission of persons who had weak constitutions or were subject to ridicule into the sacerdotal body. In a time when bodily strength was so honored and physical beauty so appreciated among the nobles, it was important that the ministers of God should not have a grotesque or repulsive appearance. On principle, then, rules were established on this point, which were, however, often violated: it could not be otherwise. The church was always less particular about the monks, because in theory they would have but little contact with the world, and because infirmities hidden in the depth of the cloister were not likely to arouse laughter or scandal. The monasteries were also the natural refuge of a number of men who, for physical reasons, were not able to lead the hardy existence of a knight and of a number of non-marriageable women. It was a necessity which certain abbots found hard to accept. One of them, Peter Mirmet, a contemporary of Philip Augustus, became abbot in 1161 and was charged with the management of the abbey of Andres, near Boulogne-sur-Mer. "On entering the monastery," says a chronicler of the time, "he drew back in horror before the deformity of the band which he was called to lead. Some monks were lame, others were one-eyed or cross-eyed or blind, and others one-armed." A reaction was necessary. During the thirty-two years in which he was abbot, Peter Mirmet refused admittance into his monastery to all persons having any bodily defect. That was, perhaps, going to the other extreme.

*

*   *

Thanks to the liberality of the faithful for gifts of land and money, the monks were rich; and the first use they made of those riches was to make their house worthy of the saint whose relics they possessed and who had brought them so many alms. This meant the enrichment of the sanctuary with precious objects and the erection of beautiful edifices in the style of the day. It is thus, at least, that one finds things in the ancient Benedictine congregations, notably in the vast monastic empire of Cluny.

The principles of the Cistercians were different. Saint Bernard, the founder of Clairvaux, with extreme rigor banished everything from the churches of his order which appealed to the eyes or the senses, everything which could distract the monk from contemplation and prayer: no ornamented pavements, no mosaics, no stained-glass windows. Only the cross was allowed, and that was not to be large, gilded, or silver-plated. Ornaments of silk were prohibited, even in the great ceremonies. On the outside there was the same simplicity. Towers of stone were forbidden. They had to be built of wood and be of limited proportions. Small bells only were allowed, etc. We recall the celebrated decla-

ration of Saint Bernard, where he condemned the zeal of
the Cluniacs, in adorning their churches and in consecrating
art to the service of God and the saints.

" The church is resplendent with its high walls, and lacks everything for its poor. She gilds her stones, and leaves her children
naked. With the money of the wretched the gaze of the rich is
charmed. Of what good are the symbolic pictures, colored and
sculptured objects? All this stifles devotion and recalls Jewish
ceremonies. Works of art are idols which lead away from God, and
are good at most to excite the piety of feeble souls. and of the
worldly."

One could speak thus in the twelfth century, when there
was a fervor of religious reform and a rivalry between the
orders for mortifications and asceticism. But, in the time
of Philip Augustus, the fashion of beautiful structures and
of luxury in the ceremonies of the cult was so far developed
that the Cistercians themselves began to yield to the contagion. In 1192, the chapter-general of Cîteaux was obliged
to recall the abbots to the observation of the rule and to prohibit the construction of oversumptuous churches. In 1182,
it had ordered the destruction, within two years, of all the
stained-glass windows erected in violation of the precepts
of the founder. In 1213, it became necessary to prohibit
all pictures other than those of Christ. A statute, in 1183,
forbade the abbots and monks to wear chasubles of silk. But,
in spite of all prohibitions, the rule gradually ceased to be
observed, even among the Cistercians, and the Cluniac conception, that nothing was too beautiful or too rich for the
service of God, finally prevailed.

The good abbot, the model abbot, the one whom the chroniclers mention with praise, and of whom they speak most,
is he who devoted the most time, effort, and money to increasing the properties of the abbey and repairing or constructing its buildings. For the most part, the heads of abbeys
had at that time a passion for building, and it is as adept
builders. that they are presented to posterity Open, for
example, the *Histoire de Saint-Florent de Saumur*. Here
is a funeral eulogy of the sixteenth abbot, Mainier, who died
in 1203. Some few lines are devoted to his moral qualities,
and then come the essentials.

"He acquired very much property. He built many edifices, the entry to the church, the refectory, the hospital, and the reception room. It was he who began carefully and finished manfully (*viriliter*) the high wall which encloses our vineyard. May the Son of the Most High absolve this venerable abbot."

But the successor of this Mainier, the seventeenth abbot, Michel of Saumur, was a still more remarkable man.

"In temporal things God gave him such grace that there was not his equal as a constructor of buildings. It is to him that we owe our new grand hall, the greater part of our houses, and the mills which he built against the will of all the inhabitants of Saumur. It was he who enriched our church with mantles, stoles, copes, dalmatics, and tunics of silk, to the value of five hundred livres. At the end of his life he built the abbatial chamber, a masterpiece of elegance, with its beautiful bay-windows. Finally it was he who obtained the magnificent bells of the tower from Chartres at great expense."

All the eulogies resemble each other, because the tendencies were everywhere the same, and because the abbots generally took especial care of the material interests of their community. Read, for example, the passage from the chronicle of Saint-Martial of Limoges, which relates to a monk, a contemporary of Philip Augustus, the twentieth abbot, Isembert.

"He was a very gentle and peaceful man, who knew how to please the powerful. In his youth he governed first of all the priory of Ruffec. There he built the church, cloister, the houses, all the workshops, and the entire wall from its foundations. It was he also who furnished the priory and built the altar, and the gilded shrine of Saint Alpinien. Finally he increased the revenue in such a way that seven monks could live there, where before two had had trouble to find their maintenance. At Saint-Martial, itself, he rebuilt the infirmary with such magnificence that one would have said it was the palace of the king. Thanks to his acquisitions the provostship of Verneuil annually brings us four hundred sous. From that sum he set apart ten livres to increase the fund intended for clothing the monks. He built a mill at Aigueperse, and he assigned sixty sous for an additional meal to be given the brothers on the Monday which follows the second Sunday after Easter. The chapel of the cemetery was built and dedicated through his efforts, and it was he finally who built the cellar near the chapel of the Virgin. Thanks to the revenues with which he enriched the abbey two hundred poor received a meal at the almonry, three hundred at the bakery, and the brothers at the refectory."

To manage to obtain money and to spend freely for the service of God, for the poor, and for the convenience of the monks, was to the abbot of the middle ages the surest way of living in the memory of men and of insuring his salvation. The most important event in the administration of an abbot, and one which formed an epoch in the annals of the monastery, was the construction of a church. The abbatial church is the large shrine which covers the small one containing the relics of the patron of the abbey. The higher and loftier it is and the more the saint is honored, the greater is the veneration which the sanctuary excites; and, consequently, the greater the offerings and money of pilgrims. The monks had an interest in having their church of the greatest grandeur. The money devoted to a building was well invested, temporally as well as spiritually. This explains why the contemporaries of Philip Augustus saw the churches of abbeys arising in all parts of France, as sumptuous as the cathedrals.

To the south of the Loire, the Roman style produced two beautiful abbatial churches—Saint-Julien of Brioude and Sainte-Croix of Bordeaux; but those in the north—the abbey of Val, the church of Longpont (Aisne), the choir of Montier-en-Der, the church of Saint-Yved of Braisne, that of Saint-Pierre-le-Vif of Sens, the abbey of Ourscamp, the church of the abbey of Saint-Mathieu-du-Finistère, and the " Merveille " of Mont Saint-Michel—are mostly in the gothic style.

The last structure, the work of four abbots,—Robert of Torigny, Jourdain, Raoul of Isles, and Thomas of Chambres, contemporaries of Philip Augustus and Louis VIII,—is a masterpiece of monastic art. It is composed of two separate buildings, of many stories. On the west is the cellar (1204-1212), which is surmounted by the splendid chapter-room, called " Chevaliers " (1215-1220), with its four naves, its pointed arches, and sculptured keystones, its columns finished with rich capitals, and its two fireplaces with mantels in the form of pyramids; and above, the cloister, finished at the end of the reign of Saint Louis, one of the jewels of gothic art, where everything is made to charm: the elegance of the arch-work, and of the small columns, which run in two rows, and the infinitely varied richness of the sculpture which runs throughout the length of the gallery. To the east lie the almonry (1204-1212), and the refectory (finished in 1218), so imposing with its double nave, with its two large windows, and its high arches resting on slender, soberly decorated columns. This group of buildings is placed on the summit of an inaccessible rock, resting on a wall of singular roughness, sixty-six meters long and from forty to fifty high. This abbey is a fortress, which testifies to the ruggedness of the monk and the turbulence of the time.

It is the same with the church of the Black Monks of Saint-Victor of Marseilles, rebuilt in 1200. With its two towers resembling keeps, its porch and walls built of enormous uncemented blocks of Pelasgian appearance, its four thick buttresses supporting the polygonal apse, and its few high windows, it was made to sustain sieges. The history of the monks of Saint-Victor is, in fact, filled with wars and combats, with the suzerains of the city and with the counts and lords of the region.

*

*   *

Similar cases were not at all rare in that epoch. In all provinces where there was no powerful and commanding baron capable of acting as police, anarchy was permanent, and the monk, like all others, was attacked and obliged to defend himself, if he did not wish to be ruined.

The chronicler, Geoffrey, prior of Vigeois, a dependency of Saint-Martial of Limoges, relates the events of which he was eyewitness during a single year and a half, in 1182 and 1183. Here are the depredations and exactions which the monasteries of Limousin had to suffer during that very short period. We may believe him: he does not exaggerate, is not even particularly indignant; it seems that he was accustomed to these scenes of war and disorder. In November, 1182, the cloister of the priory of Chalais was destroyed by a relative of the viscount of Castillon. The monks were scattered, and the soldiers seized the relics of Saint Ancilde and carried them to the castle of their captain, in order to protect it. In February, 1183, the citizens of Limoges took advantage of the war between Henry II, king of England, and his eldest son, Henry the Young, to satisfy their grudges against the monks of Saint-Martial. They devastated the magnificent gardens of the abbey, demolished five or six small churches which belonged to it, burnt the belfries of Saint-Martin-lès-Limoges, another of their dependencies; destroyed the belfry, walls, workshops, and the church itself. A few days later, a band of mercenaries seized two monks of the abbey of Pierre-Buffière and dragged them along, half-naked, till they bought themselves off. An adventurer in the pay of the English, says the chronicler, made a specialty of seizing monks and of offering them for sale at eighteen sous apiece. In March, 1183, the son of the king of England, Henry the Young, invaded the abbey of Saint-Martial and drove out all the monks, even the novices and the school children. Such dignitaries as the dean, the precentor, the subcantor, and the provost of the abbey had to pass the night out of doors. " Who would believe it," adds Geoffrey of Vigeois, " if these facts had not had a number of witnesses? " The following day, Henry the Young compelled them to surrender all the treasure of the sanctuary, the altars, the golden statues, the chalices, the cross, and the shrines. It was only a loan: he gave them a receipt sealed with his seal. But all these riches were put on sale or given as security to pay his soldiers, and were seen no more. In May, the same prince carried away the treasury of Grandmont and that of the abbey Couronne; he stripped also the monasteries of Dalon and of Obazine. In October, 1183, the priory of Vigeois was menaced by a band of soldiers, and the monks carried away the most precious objects, in order to store them in a safe spot. A few days later another priory of Saint-Martial, Saint-Pardoux of Arnet, was ransomed in its turn: the monks were obliged to buy back their property for six hundred and fifty sous; the men of the priory were taken captive and were held until the prior had paid the sum required for their ransom. At Saint-Géraud of Aurillac, the chief of the band taxed the monastery fifteen thousand sous. We may stop here. The enumeration is sufficiently instructive, for it covers a period of only twelve months, and we can conclude that, at that time, it was not good to live in the monasteries of central France.

We may assume that the same things happened in all the regions which were the scene of a war between kings or barons; and war often broke out, to the misfortune of the peasants and monks, who were its principal victims. The monasteries irresistibly attracted the soldiers, because of their riches. The religious devotion of the time did not prevent their being pillaged or even burned: a sacrilege, no doubt, but one which could easily be atoned for by a gift or a pilgrimage. This is a matter on which we could speak at length: we shall return to it later. Let us note for the moment simply that, in feudal atmosphere with its incessant wars, abbeys, though fortified, were not a very safe shelter, and that it was necessary to struggle for life and property there as elsewhere.

But many other reasons prevented monastic life, composed of prayer and labor, from being carried on peacefully and regularly as it ought. The hastiest glance over the documents is enough to reveal the principal disorders from which the regular clergy then suffered in all parts of France and in all congregations. In temporal affairs the communities of monks and nuns were badly managed, and they got into debt, until almost completely ruined. Internal divisions disturbed them and weakened them considerably. Finally, the rule was no longer observed: scandals of every sort occurred, and the ecclesiastical authorities found themselves obliged to intervene constantly in order to subject the monks to the obligations of their positions; to impose reforms on them, with or against their will. In the material, as well as in the moral, conditions of monasteries signs of decadence were not lacking, and precisely this decadence of the orders of the ancient Benedictine system is one of the characteristics of the history of the French church and of France during the epoch of Philip Augustus.

To communities as well as to individuals the financial question, the question of the budget, has at all times been a vital question. The history of the middle ages furnishes plenty proof of this. In the thirteenth century, to give only two examples, the disappearance of the French communes, those strong republics of northern France, was due in large part to the bad financial organization, to their inability to provide for their expenses, or to meet their liabilities. Many of them ended in bankruptcy, by which the royal power benefited. The question of money dominated all the internal and external policy of the monarchy during the reign of Philip the Fair and of his first successor, after having held a place in the affairs of Philip Augustus not sufficiently noted by historians. But it was not only the kings and common people who suffered from the evil of money: we see, when we study the feudal laity, that many of the noble families were terribly indebted, ruined by usurers, were obliged to mortgage or sell a patrimony, which thus went to pieces, in order to fulfil their obligations and keep their rank. The church itself did not escape the general calamity, and the monasteries especially suffered from it. The German monk, Cæsar of Heisterbach, relates a curious anecdote on this subject in his *Dialogues,* written in 1221:

" One day a usurer deposited a sum of money in trust with the cellarer of our order. He put it in a safe place with the money of the monastery. Later the usurer demanded his deposit. The cellarer opened the coffer and found there neither the money of the usurer nor the money of the monastery. The locks were intact, the seals of the sacks had not been broken; there was no reason to suspect a theft. It was clear that the money of the usurer had devoured that of the monastery."

The allegory is clear, and is amply justified by the facts. Thus, in 1196, the abbey of Saint-Bénigne of Dijon borrowed the sum of seventeen hundred livres from a Jew named Valin at the rate of sixty-five per cent. The abbey went eleven years without being able to pay anything, so that, at the end of the eleven years, the debt of seventeen hundred livres had increased to nine thousand eight hundred and twenty-five livres. In 1207, Blanche, countess of Champagne, was obliged to take over the debt of the monks of Saint-Bénigne, and, in 1222, Alix, duchess of Burgundy, had to reimburse a Jew named Salamine, who was also a creditor of the abbey of Saint-Bénigne and of the abbey of Saint-Seine. In order to indemnify its creditors and bondsmen, its moneylenders, Saint-Bénigne was compelled to sell considerable property which it possessed in Burgundy. Similarly, in 1220, we see

the abbey of Saint-Loup of Troyes admitting that it owed
four hundred and fifty livres of Provins to a Jew of Dampierre; it gave as security the whole village of Molins in
Aube, on which it had already granted him a life annuity.
At Verdun, shortly after the year 1197, the abbey of Saint-
Vanne found itself loaded with debt, and a chronicler relates
the following story on the subject. The monastery had an
abbot to elect; on the demand of Agnes, countess of Bar, a
monk of Cluny, named Stephen, was chosen to direct Saint-
Vanne. One day, when the new abbot found himself in the
presence of the countess, she demanded of him how he intended to root out the inextricable thicket of thorns, which
was the cause of the abbey's bad financial condition, and in
which it had been entangled for a long time. " Our debts? "
replied the abbot; " they will be paid with the red tunic of
Saint-Vanne; I have full confidence in it." He meant to say
that the abbey would pay the debt with the relics of the
saint to whom it was dedicated. This was, in fact, one of
the means which indebted monasteries employed to free themselves. The chronicler was indignant at what he considered
a cynical response of the abbot, and added:

" Such irreverence was punished on the spot. There before the
eyes of the ladies and the barons who were present the abbot suddenly fell, touched by a stroke of paralysis. He began to foam
at the mouth and to tear himself with his nails, and he never
recovered the use of his speech from that day. At sight of these
things the countess gave the order for him to be lifted and carried
away to a couch."

Here was a chronicler who took such matters seriously.
There were other regions of France where they were not
shocked to see the monks coin money from the relics of their
patron saint.

Let us, in imagination, betake ourselves to Saint-Martial
of Limoges. Here, also, the monastery and priories sank under the weight of their debt. In 1213, the sacristan owed a
thousand sous, and the abbey twenty thousand more. In
1214, the debts of Saint-Martial increased to more than forty
thousand sous. " In such a situation," says the chronicler
Bernard Itier, " the church is truly in danger." In 1216,

the abbot personally owed twenty thousand sous. "For twenty years," adds the chronicler, "the usurers have extorted incalculable sums from our abbots, and they boast of continuing it." In 1220, the abbey was so loaded with debt and so impoverished that the abbot, Raimond Gaucelin, was on the point of resigning. Fortunately, however, the report of miracles performed on the grave of Saint Martial commenced to spread, and money flowed into the monastery to such an amount that the abbot was able to rid the monks of a large share of their creditors. Here the miracle occurred very opportunely, indeed.

At the other end of France, in Provence, the abbey of Saint-Victor of Marseilles, in 1185, found itself in an even more critical condition. It owed eighty thousand sous to the Jews of Marseilles, and was compelled to give them a certain amount of its property, which comprised villages and churches. Churches to the Jews! The bishop of Antibes, in order to avoid this scandal, felt compelled to buy off the creditors himself, giving them half of the sum in cash; and, in a cartulary of Saint-Victor, we have the charter by which the abbot surrendered to him a castle and all the revenues of the sacristy as a compensation for his expenditures.

The scene is everywhere the same. In the Cluniac priory of Charité-sur-Loire, in 1209, the prior Geoffrey, crushed with debt and interest, was obliged to sell the important seigniory of Laigneville, near Senlis, to the Templars for ten thousand livres of Tours. In 1200, Raoul, abbot of Saint-Germain of Auxerre, was compelled to sell the gold and jewels which decorated the shrine of Saint-Germain. The saints themselves were plundered by those who had charge of serving them, and there was not a year when monks did not give the gold and silver paraments of the altar—chalices, crosses, and even sacerdotal vestments—as security to usurers, who were then nearly always Jews. Knowing the sentiments of the middle ages in regard to the Jews, one can comprehend the enormity of the scandal without considering that the accumulated debts often led to actual bankruptcy of the monasteries. The monks finally scattered, and the abbey, deprived of a means of existence since it had lost everything, disappeared. It cannot be doubted that a large number of monastic establishments, which are not found later than the end of the middle ages, ceased to exist for this reason, succumbing under financial embarrassment.

In the Cistercian order, the founders took the greatest precautions to avoid such catastrophes. It appears, however, that their successors did not succeed any better in preventing the Cistercian abbeys from getting into debt than in making them observe the rules, which forbade the acquisition of real estate, for, at the end of the twelfth century, the chapter-general of Cîteaux almost every year uttered a cry of alarm. In 1181, it said in its seventh statute, "It is truly a matter for shame that one sees certain of our brothers running their house into debt in order to buy wine." And, in 1182: "The debts increase in enormous proportions. They threaten the ruin of many of our communities. Every house which has more than fifty marks of debt is prohibited from buying any land or constructing any new buildings." The statute of 1184 permits abbots to sell movable property and even real estate in cases of absolute necessity, where the debts are overwhelming and must be paid. In 1188 there was a new prohibition against buying land and against building. But the prohibitions remained ineffectual, and two years after the death of Philip Augustus the abbey of Cîteaux itself, the head of the order, which should have been an example, was in such a desperate situation that the whole congregation was obliged to come to its aid and to vote it a subsidy.

How did the monks use their money? Without doubt, their greatest expenditures were in the purchases of land, and especially of buildings. But it must be noted that they had other heavy expenses. They were first of all obliged to give many alms and shelter travelers, pilgrims, and beggars. One of their strictest duties was to feed the poor, clothe them, and even give them temporary shelter. In every notable abbey there were two important offices: that of the almonry and the hostelry; and two special dignitaries had charge of the offices. In the Cistercian order the almoner was called the "porter" (*portarius*). He must always have in his cell, situated near the entrance to the monastery, loaves of bread ready to be given to the passersby who might need them. Cæsar of Heisterbach states that, in 1217, fifteen thousand poor received alms at the gate of his abbey in one day. Every day on which meat might be eaten, until harvest time, a beef was killed and cooked with vegetables, and the whole distributed to the poor. On fish-days the meat was left out and only vegetables were given. The alms of bread were so large that the abbot feared his granaries would be emptied before the harvest and suggested to the baker that he make the loaves smaller. " But," said the baker to him, " I put them into the oven small and they come out large." It was a permanent miracle, and Cæsar adds, " The grain was seen to increase in the sacks."

Another very burdensome obligation devolved upon all monks, whether vassals of the king or of the lord of the province, or subordinates of the prelates and of the pope: to meet the pressing needs of the church or simply to fill the voids in the royal treasury, monks had to pay taxes, under the pretext of aiding a crusade; and these were rigorously collected. We recall what certain monks, like Bernard Itier and Guyot of Provins, said of the rapacity of the Romans, that is, of the papacy, its cardinals, and its agents. This abuse, the Roman exaction, had, by the end of the twelfth century, taken on such proportions that the chapter-general of Cîteaux could not refrain from complaining publicly and from taking measures to have it cease. In the statutes of the year 1193, the seventh article ends thus: " It is necessary to write to the pope to inform him that Gregory, cardinal of the title of Saint Angelo, exacts new taxes from the abbots of our order, of which there has been no instance up to this time." And the chapter-general punished the abbots who had given the legate money by a day of penance on bread and water.

As regards the demands of the royal treasury, it is enough to see how Philip Augustus dealt with the abbey of Saint-Denis in 1186, as related by Rigord. William of Gap was then its abbot. That year the king called upon the monks of Saint-Denis to deposit with him a thousand marks in money. It was a very large sum, and the abbot was not able to comply. " One day," says Rigord, " the king, passing by Saint-Denis on the business of the realm, entered the abbey as though it were his own room. But the abbot, informed of the coming of the king, in great fright hastened to call his brothers into chapter-meeting, and tendered his resignation.'' These few lines tell volumes: he had to abdicate or pay.

The abbot, then, was not always responsible for the bad financial condition of his community: he had constantly to struggle against more or less unjust and unreasonable demands from without, and often to struggle unsuccessfully. But when, to make things worse, the head of the monastery was a bad administrator, a negligent person, or a prodigal, everything went from bad to worse, and complete ruin came at last. The greatest objection to the rule of Saint Benedict was that it gave the abbot an almost absolute temporal power over the monastery. He was entitled to passive obedience; he had all the rights. He was the sovereign of the establishment: he was called *dominus*. It is true that, to counterbalance this almost autocratic power, the rule required him to consult the assemblage of his brothers, the chapter. In theory he was bound to take their advice, but in fact he very often enjoyed an authority without limit and without control. He administered the property of the community as he pleased, without rendering an account of his administration to delegates of the monks who were under him. When this sort of absolute monarchy fell into the hands of an honest and systematic man, affairs of the community could not suffer; they might even prosper. But when the abbot was feeble, without personal worth, or disposed only to satisfy the passion of greediness, the debts of the house increased and all was lost. That is why, in the councils of that epoch, urgent recommendations to abbots were always being adopted. What they were forbidden to do, for example, in the canons of the council of Paris in 1243, reveals what they did. The following enumeration speaks for itself:

" 1. The abbots shall not exercise the functions of advocates and judges.

" 2. They shall not be followed by a large escort, and shall not have too many young domestics around them.

" 3. They shall not give the goods of the monastery to their relatives.

" 4. They shall not allow young women to enter the monastery.

"5. They shall not take the priories from those in whom they are vested in order to transfer them to persons of their family.

"6. They shall, twice a year, receive the accounts of the officers of the abbey and of the priories.

"7. They shall not handle important affairs, and borrow large sums without the advice of the seven oldest monks, chosen by the chapter for that purpose."

There is here a very clear attempt to limit the abbot's power over the temporal affairs and to substitute constitutional for absolute monarchy.

"8. They shall not sell the priories.

"9. Finally the abbots and priors are expressly forbidden to menace and maltreat monks who shall propose to the chapter measures tending to reform the house."

In 1216, at the council of Sens, it was necessary for ecclesiastical authority to direct abbots and priors to render an annual account to the chapter of the amount of their expenditures and of the state of the finances of the community. And the same council forbade them to borrow beyond a certain amount, especially of the Jews. These regulations were renewed nearly every year at all the meetings of the bishops which occurred during the thirteenth century, a proof that they were but little observed. When, in the time of Saint Louis, an archbishop of Rouen wrote a journal of his pastoral visit and pointed out the misdeeds committed in the religious establishments under his inspection, on each page of the journal appear the words *non computat:* this abbot does not render an account to his chapter. Often the abbots themselves did not know what the debts of their community amounted to. It seems incredible, but these administrators neither kept accounts nor drew up a budget.

When the councils and bishops failed, the popes intervened and imposed reforms on the monasteries threatened with failure. That, for example, is what Pope Celestine III did in 1195 to save the abbey of Saint-Victor of Marseilles from ruin. The pontifical decree gave the abbot full authority to dismiss bad priors. He exacted a collective tax from all the priories of the abbey to aid the abbey itself and to diminish its debt. The pope also commanded the priors to pay the tax which each owed the abbot regularly at the usual times; for the system of subject-houses was one of the most frequent causes of the bad financial condition of the abbeys, inasmuch as the priors refused to contribute toward the expenses of the mother house or to make the annual payment of a part of their receipts to the chief place. Strict injunctions were given the priors against parting with their real estate and against contracting debts larger than a hundred sous without the consent of the abbot. They were ordered to come every year and give an accounting to the chapter-general. Cumulative expenses of the priories must be limited, and the abbot or grand-prior must not practise exactions on the priories. Finally, the abbot himself had not the right to borrow more than a thousand sous without the consent of his chapter; and, in general, he was forbidden to transact any important business or the more serious matters of the monastery without having first taken the advice of the chapter or of a majority of the chapter. By this decree of reform one can judge the others; they all resemble each other, and their number and frequent repetition prove that the evil was great and that it was very difficult to root out the abuse. Making new rules was relatively unimportant; putting them into execution was decidedly more to the point.

In spite of councils and of popes, the monastic world was too often exposed to real catastrophes. Abbeys, completely ruined, closed their doors and disappeared. In order to prevent such scandals, it was not rare to have the church punish abbots who were unruly or deceitful by suspending or even deposing them. In 1205, Robert, abbot of Couture, the great monastery of Mans, was dismissed for having wasted the revenues of his house in a scandalous manner. Two years before the pope had proceeded in the same way to depose Arnold, abbot of the monastery of Saint-Michel of Cuxa in Roussillon. He can be taken as the type of the bad abbot. Not content with neglecting the domains of his monastery and with allowing the conventual buildings to fall into ruins, he had given away, mortgaged, or sold the largest part of the lands and revenues of his community, so that the abbey had fallen into the last degree of misery. The lay sovereign of Roussillon, Peter II of Aragon, had to intervene, and rendered a decision, by virtue of which the sales effected by the Abbot Arnold were declared null and void and redeemable at a price which arbitrators chosen by himself should fix. The measure may appear somewhat despotic to us today, but in that time when the interests of the church and of its domain—that is, property of God and the saints, hence sacred and inalienable—were at stake, private agreements and the rights of individuals did not count.

Let us, to conclude, cite a letter of Stephen of Tournai, written to the archbishop of Reims and relating to a monastery in insolvency, the monastery of Bredeene. It brings us to the heart of things, and the incident which it reveals to us, far from being isolated, then occurred frequently enough everywhere. The large abbeys were not permitted to die, but the small ones, not being helped, went to pieces themselves without creating comment:

" We proceeded to the monastery of Bredeene, to hold our synod there. But what was our astonishment! and what a sad spectacle for the church, what a scandal for strangers! We had been told that the abbey consisted of twelve regularly established monks, that the offices were there celebrated punctually, that the poor were fed, the unfortunate comforted, and pilgrims harbored. We arrived, and what did we behold? Buildings in ruins, no sound of religious services, everywhere silence and desolation, not a monk to serve the holy place. We found ourselves facing a desert; one would call it a miserable hovel in a vineyard or a field of gourds. And yet, the abbey had possessed large estates with rich tithes; but nearly everything had been mortgaged or sold. That unfortunate church had no one to care for it except a solitary priest. The parishioners lamented and complained deeply. They stated that the church had been founded and enriched by the donations of their ancestors, and they persistently claimed what had disappeared."

And what did the bishop do in this case? He placed the interdict on that deplorable (*lacrymabilem*) church, forbade the celebration of divine offices there, and prohibited the parishioners from paying tithes or from making any offering whatever as long as the monks and the prior, to the last man, had not returned. We do not know the effect of this measure, for the correspondence of Stephen does not say anything about it, but we may assume that the disaster was absolute and that the abbey of Bredeene only went to swell the list of ruined and dissolved monasteries.

*

*   *

Another evil of the monastic world was discord. Disobedience, open rebellion, and internal struggles raged in the house of peace and prayer.

In 1212, the abbot of Cluny commanded a member of his order, Geoffrey of Donzy, prior of La Charité,—who lived scandalously,—to come to the chapter-general. Geoffrey refused, and sent a monk to the abbot, who declared that his prior appealed to the pope. The abbot himself went to La Charité to compel the monks to return to their duty. Scarcely had he crossed the threshold of the priory with his suite when he was greeted by a shower of stones, hurled from the bell-tower. His horse was badly wounded and he himself, half-killed, " trembling in all his members, and livid," says the letter of Innocent III which relates the incident, had to seek refuge in the home of a citizen. Soldiers, hired by the prior, occupied all the high places of the buildings of the priory, organized a patrol, and closed the gates of the town. It became necessary to parley with the rebels.

An interview took place at one of the gates between the representatives of the chapter-general and Geoffrey of Donzy, who appeared surrounded by monks carrying enormous cudgels. The prior declared that he had no concern about the chapter and its corrections. " He was responsible in spiritual matters to the pope alone, and in temporal matters to the count of Nevers, under whose care his priory was placed. He would not accept any proposal for peace or any agreement until the abbot should leave the town." The chapter excommunicated him with all his accomplices, removed him from his office, and put a monk of Cluny in his place. But to execute these measures required the help of Philip Augustus, who obliged the count of Nevers to force an entrance into the priory.

In the statutes of the chapter-general of Cîteaux there often appear conspiracies formed by the monks against their abbot. The chapter, in 1183, compared the conspirators to thieves and incendiaries and declared them liable to excommunication. That of 1191 decided that the leaders should be expelled from the abbey and transferred to another establishment of the order, where they should each week receive the discipline and should for a whole day be put on bread and water. The head of the congregation of Saint-Victor of Marseilles also had the greatest difficulty in retaining under his dominion the dependent abbeys or the priories which were always disposed to free themselves. The rebellions were so frequent that, in 1218, every monk charged with the administration of a priory was obliged to take the following oath:

"I swear by the Holy Gospels of God in your hands, Seignior Abbot, that from to-day henceforth I will be obedient to you and to your successors, the abbots of Saint-Victor, and that I will, with all faithfulness, fulfil the office which I receive from you. Any time that it shall please you, on the advice of the elders of the monastery, to relieve me of my post, I swear not to protest anything, and to place in your hands without protest or resistance, the priory with all that is dependent on it."

Even tragedies were not lacking. In 1186, the abbot of Trois-Fontaines of the order of Cîteaux was assassinated by a monk. In 1210, the canons of Salles, near Rochechouart, murdered their prior at the moment when he arose to sing matins. In the same year, the abbot of Fontgombault was poisoned. In 1216, a monk of the abbey of Déols was killed by one of his brothers. The history of the abbots of Saint-Vanne at Verdun, at the end of the twelfth century, is nothing more than a series of revolts and enforced abdications. That of the abbey of Sénones, crushed with debt, is scarcely more edifying. At Tulle, in 1210, the monks were divided into two factions, each of which elected its abbot; the consequent conflict brought about the destruction of the monastery. Very nearly the same catastrophe happened at Saint-Martial of Limoges, where, in 1216, three abbots disputed over the crozier.

What envenomed these conflicts was that the monks, in the struggles among themselves or in their revolts against the abbot, appealed to the support of outsiders. They appealed from their abbot to higher ecclesiastical authorities, to the bishop, the archbishop, the pope, or even at times to the laity, against the laws of the church. The correspondence of Stephen of Tournai puts this beyond all question. For example, the regular canons of Saint-Jean-des-Vignes of Soissons entered into an open struggle against their abbot, Hugh. The canons, who were delegated to direct what was called a priory-cure, lived like parish curés, which was hardly in keeping with the rules of their order. The abbot of Saint-Jean-des-Vignes sought to preserve his authority over these canon-curés: he sought to reserve the right of transferring them, dismissing them, or recalling them to the abbey at any time he judged suitable. But this did not take the canons into account, and they invoked the support of the bishop of Soissons, who defended them against their superior. Out of this came a lawsuit in the court of Rome. The abbot and the bishop went to Rome to plead their causes, but, as always, the process dragged itself out eternally. Tired of the delay, they submitted their case to arbitrators, who decided in favor of the abbot. Stephen of Tournai wrote a very fiery letter on the subject to the pope, in which he formally accused the canon-curés of having acquired money, which their rule forbade, and of using it to corrupt the bishop and influence him to work in their favor.

In the abbey of Saint-Amand of Tournai, the monks complained of their abbot to the archbishop of Reims and refused him obedience. The archbishop ordered Stephen of Tournai to make an inquiry, and he reported on his commission in these terms:

" At your order, O my father, I went to Saint-Amand where I found the monks far from amiable.[1] The rebels continue in sedition and will perhaps die impenitent. They have nothing with which to reproach their abbot; he is a learned man, pure, sober, and peaceful, and an honest man. Of what do they complain? That he is more inclined to economy than to extravagance, and that he is not familiar enough with the sign language,[2] and that he does not know how to say the words bean, cheese, and egg with his fingers."

Pretexts, all of them! Stephen of Tournai adds that he attempted to punish the leaders of the conspiracy by trans-

---

[1] *Non amandos.* Stephen of Tournai was fond of puns.
[2] Language similar to that of our deaf and dumb, which the cloistered monks used when the rule of Saint Benedict forbade their speaking.

ferring them temporarily to another monastery and prohibiting them from leaving, under threat of excommunication. But the rebels did not obey their bishop any more
than their abbot, and they found the means of being absolved by the vidame of the archbishop of Reims, of which
the bishop of Tournai then complained with indignation.

He also addressed a strong protest to the bishop of Bourges,
who protected the monks of Saint-Satur, a monastery of
Berry, against their abbot. They appealed to the archbishop
as soon as the abbot gave evidence of seeking to bring the
order to the observance of the rule, and the latter allowed
himself to be so influenced by their lies, says Stephen, that
he commanded the abbot not to proceed against any of his
monks as long as the suit begun by them in the archiepiscopal
court was undecided. But Stephen of Tournai remarked
very properly to the archbishop that such an injunction was
a disaster for the monastic clergy. No discipline was longer
possible in the abbeys; there was disorder, dissoluteness, confusion in everything. He entreated the archbishop to give
the abbot of Saint-Satur the right, consecrated by the rule of
Saint Benedict and by the canons of the councils, of regularly correcting the faults of the monks; the right of ap-
pointing, changing, and dismissing the officers placed under
his orders.

It is in the letters of Stephen of Tournai that the story
of the monk Nicolas of Saint-Martin of Tournai is found—
who, eternally in struggle with his abbot, one fine day, after
having stolen the seal of the community, fled from the abbey,
forged false letters intended to ruin his accuser, and, equipped
with these documents, went to Rome to lodge his complaint.
Stephen of Tournai was obliged to write to the pope, to warn
him against the allegations of the fugitive monk, and it was
on this occasion that, at the beginning of the letter, he gave
vent to the following opinion on the inveterate evil from
which the monastic world suffered:

"It is a very common and usual fact that there are sons of contradiction and disobedience in our holy communities who love lawsuits and disputes, who sow hatred among the brethren, who delight
in producing scandals, and in preparing civil wars which ruin us
and make us an object of scorn for the stranger."

When the abbot was a dishonest man or a spendthrift, he usually sided with the younger monks, stirred them up against the older ones, who were thus reduced to impotence, and thus, sustained by the vigorous and turbulent faction of the community, he wasted the property of the abbey as he pleased. Instances of this kind are not rare, and we are informed among others, again by Stephen of Tournai, of an abbot of Saint-Martin of Tournai, named John, who used such methods until he provoked the most intolerable scandal. The archbishop of Reims and the bishop were obliged to take rigorous measures. The abbot, John, threatened by excommunication, submitted to confessing his faults and to signing a document, making the following promises on the Gospel:

" I promise to preserve perpetual chastity, to assist regularly in the offices, to eat in the refectory with the brethren, to sleep with them in the dormitory, not to entertain any but respectable guests in my chamber, to take with me, when it is necessary to leave the monastery on business, old and discreet brethren about whom there can be no unpleasant gossip, not to allow any monk to go out unless he is accompanied and for no reason except that of urgent necessity, and especially not to allow young monks to leave the abbey to go to plays, processions, or places of worldly amusement. Finally never to make a decision without having previously consulted a council of six monks whom the bishop shall designate from among the older brethren."

This is a series of promises which fully enlightens us concerning the conduct of the heads of certain abbeys.

The facts disclosed in the letters of Stephen of Tournai will suffice to bring to light the internal vice which disorganized and broke up the ancient Benedictine order: the tendency of the monastic personnel to thrust aside the authority of its natural head, the abbot, and to rely on outside powers to resist him. But what shows best how deep the evil was, is the civil war which broke out in the order of Grandmont and lasted nearly seventy years.

The order of Grandmont in Limousin, founded in 1073 by Stephen of Muret, at the outset received a very strict rule. Like the Cistercians and the Carthusians, the Grandmontains, in the beginning, went to the extreme of asceticism and mortification. One of the characteristic traits of their rule was

the absolute isolation of the monk, his anxiety to avoid
all contact with the worldly element and to spare himself
every occupation and every thought of a temporal nature,
in order to devote himself exclusively to prayer and to tasks
of moral perfection. The founder of the order also desired
the care of the material interests, to be confided exclusively
to a company of lay brothers, who should be instructed to
look after the subsistence and support of the monks, who
were the true religious; the latter, absorbed in monastic services, were to live a purely spiritual life, without any cares
of a profane sort. The intention was excellent, and all went
well during the first years of the foundation. But when, in
the course of the twelfth century, the order,—heaped with the
gifts of kings, high barons, and the faithful of both France
and England,—had great possessions, both in land and
money, it was necessary to increase the number of lay brothers charged with the administration, in the same proportion,
because the monks of Grandmont were not permitted to aid
in any way and did not even have the right to write letters
or pass acts. Thus the order of Grandmont, at the accession of Philip Augustus, presented the curious phenomenon
of a religious congregation which was composed of a small
number of monks who were governed in temporal affairs by
a body of lay administrators twenty times as large. The
monks could do nothing and knew nothing of the material
and financial status of their monasteries. The lay brothers,
on the contrary,—who only belonged to the monastery externally,—had all the money, all the property, and all the
authority in their hands. The latter, having the numbers
and the material power, naturally came to believe that they
represented the order itself and that the real management of
the congregation,—that is to say, the office of the prior-
general, the head of the mother house of Grandmont, and
the positions of the individual priors in the branch houses,
the obediences,—should belong to them. This was the re-
versal of the natural order of things, as the contemporary
writers, especially Guyot of Provins, said. A religious congregation, dominated and directed by laymen, was, to use a
metaphor which was frequently applied to the condition,
putting the plow before the oxen.

War was inevitable between the clerical and lay elements of the order of Grandmont: it broke out in 1185 on the occasion of the election of a prior-general, the monks having one candidate and the lay brothers another. The schism lasted three years, and the destruction which was the consequence affected every house of the order. In all the convents of the Grandmontains the lay brothers deposed the monks, shut them in their cells, gave them scarcely anything to live on, oppressed them with bad treatment, and did not even hesitate to expel them. It was a terrible scandal! Bishops, kings, and popes intervened to stop it and to reestablish peace between the hostile brothers, but scarcely had the mediators ceased their efforts than the struggle broke out more violently, and everything began anew.

In 1188, after serious efforts on the part of the papacy and of the government of Philip Augustus, peace was believed to be definitive. Pope Clement III annulled the election of the two priors-general, about which the chapter was wrangling; caused a third to be elected, to whom a large majority of the Grandmontains swore obedience; renewed the privileges of the congregation, and confirmed the rule. On his side, the king of France sanctioned the unexpected agreement with his approval; and the heads of the two factions appeared before him and gave each other the kiss of peace. But, two years later, war raged anew within the order: everywhere the same scenes of violence were repeated; the same expulsions of monks by the lay brothers took place. The monks appealed to Rome, where their suit was conducted with traditional slowness. But the papacy, which should have ended the debate by stringent measures, hesitated, did not act, and for a very simple reason, which Stephen of Tournai gives, without any beating round the bush, in a letter addressed to the pope. It was not the monks, but the lay brothers of Grandmont who had the money, and these boasted of using it to render all the claims of their adversaries useless.

"They did not rely on justice; they placed their hopes, as they themselves said so that any one could hear it, in their pecuniary gifts, and in the corruption which they freely practised."

However, the disorders took on such proportions that the Capetian government found itself obliged to intervene for the second time. In 1190, Philip Augustus, before leaving for the crusade, summoned the monks and lay brothers of Grandmont to Saint-Denis and used threats and prayers to persuade them to keep the peace. But scarcely had he left than the quarrels were revived, while the representatives of the two factions continued to plead before an irresolute, powerless pope at Rome. It was then that Stephen of Tournai, in concert with the abbots of Saint-Denis, Saint-Germain-des-Pres, and Saint-Victor, wrote that letter of 1191 to the pope, in which he denounced the abuses committed by the lay brothers and the deplorable situation of the oppressed monks, and threatened the Holy See with the indignation of the king of France.

Nothing was done. The papacy, even that of Innocent III, did not dare to settle this inextricable affair. In 1214, they were still struggling within the order of Grandmont, and the pope received a distressing letter from the monks.

"What is going to become of us, wretches that we are, fallen under the hard bondage of the laity, and the object of scorn and derision to all who know us? We continually cry out and complain but no one hears our cry; we have thoroughly exposed our sufferings, but no one comes to our aid. There are no more prophets in Israel! Moses is no more, and his successor does not imitate his works. Joshua is not faithful to his people; he has made an alliance with the stranger; he has become corrupt, and he now pleads against us. We do not see in all the people a leader called of God to deliver us from the lay brothers. They oppress us in an incredible way, . . . destroy the houses of our order, violate the rules of religion, waste the goods of the community, and distribute them to the lay members of their families, or to their friends. They lay violent hands on us, threaten to break our heads if we attempt to resist their caprice in any way whatever, and in order to punish us they put foul things into our food. They claim all our temporal goods, and then pretend to teach us in spiritual matters. . . . One would never finish if he attempted to complete the list of outrages, calumnies, threats, and deeds of which we are the victims on the part of those false brothers, especially this year. O Holy Father, we are sending to you, as bearers of this letter, our true brothers, men faithful and religious and of good repute. You can learn from them in full confidence what would take too long to set forth in writing. They have been eye witnesses of the things they will reveal to you. We throw ourselves at the feet of Your Holiness; we devoutly pray and beseech you, if you have any sentiment of pity, to grant the request which our brethren shall present on behalf of our whole group. You are our hope; since your promotion to the see of Saint Peter you have been our only refuge. Save us, Seignior, from the dominion of the barbarians, from the servitude to the laity to which we have been subject for so long a time, as a punishment perhaps for our sins. If your support fails us who will aid us? We do not see any one besides you to whom we could have recourse. Make an end of our suit, which no one has yet settled conclusively. Our letter is already too long and risks fatiguing you. We close now, your humble though unworthy servants, tried beyond all limits and profoundly anxious. Seignior, have mercy on us."

The popes of the middle ages were often broader-minded and more accessible to sentiments of humanity and justice than those who represented them. They were better than their cardinals and legates: as was true, for instance, of Gregory VII, who was much less uncompromising and harsh than those who acted in his name; and this also applies to Innocent III, who was often betrayed by his agents. What brought on the crisis of Grandmont was the singular attitude of the cardinals sent to France, and especially of the legate, Robert of Courçon. He showed such partiality in favor of the lay brothers that they availed themselves of it to renew their excesses. Beaten, wounded, expelled from their convents, the monks appealed to the legate of the pope. Robert of Courçon replied by suspending their prior-general and declaring their appeal null and void. Thereupon Innocent III reproved his agent in very strong terms:

" Truly we are astonished at you, on being informed of your incredible conduct. A man possessed of reason would not have dared to act in that way. By what right are you constituted judge of appeals to us? What wise and prudent man would permit himself to declare the prior of Grandmont suspended from office after his appeal legally lodged at Rome? How are you on your own authority able to absolve these lay brothers, and to exempt them from obedience to their superiors? "

And the pope ended by annulling the act of his legate, by confiding to the archbishop of Bourges the task of executing the decisions justly made by the prior of Grandmont.

This letter of Innocent III was dated in the month of March, 1214, but a proof that it did not produce any great effect is the fact that two years later, in 1216, the order of Grandmont being still the prey of civil dissension, the same pope wrote to the archbishops of Bourges, Sens, and Tours, ordering them to punish those who were in insurrection against the prior-general and against the rules of the congregation. The troubles continued until the middle of the thirteenth century.

CHAPTER VIII

THE NOBLE AT WAR

CONSIDERING feudalism as a whole, with the exception of an élite class of which we shall speak later on, the habits and customs of the nobles had not changed since the eleventh century. Almost everywhere the castellan remained a brutal and pillaging soldier, making war, fighting in tournaments, hunting in times of peace, ruining himself in excesses, oppressing his own peasants, levying contributions on those of his neighbors, and sacking the lands of the church.

At the beginning of the thirteenth century, the monks of the abbey of Saint-Martin-du-Canigou drew up an interminable list of misdeeds committed by Pons of Vernet, a castellan of Roussillon. This noble was a veritable brigand.

"He broke down our fence, and seized eleven cows. One night he entered our property at Vernet and cut down our fruit trees. The next day, he seized and bound two of our servants in the woods and took three sous and six deniers away from them. The same day, he took the tunic, stockings, and shoes of Bernard of Mosset on our farm at Egat. Another time he killed two cows and wounded four others on the farm of Col-de-Jou and he carried away all the cheeses that he found there. Another day, he forced the men of Rial to ransom themselves for fifteen sous, and their fear was so great that they put themselves under the protection of Peter Dumolait, in consideration of fifteen sous down, and an annual rental of a pound of wax. At Églies, he took one hundred and fifty sheep, a donkey, and three children whom he would not give up without a ransom of one hundred sous, some capes, some tunics, and cheeses. Another time, he took a tunic from Peter of Rial, a leather-strap and a knife from Bonfils, two capes, a fur, and a table-cloth from Pierre Amat. . . . And, after he and his father, R. du Vernet, had sworn in the church of Sainte-Marie of Vernet that he would leave the abbey in peace, he stole eight sous and seven hens from our men of Avidan, and he forced us to buy over again the boundary-line of Odilon which his father had sold to us. . . . He stole from us our herd of Vernet, consisting of more than five hundred sheep, and he seized four men, who, happily, succeeded in escaping. He then seized two men of Odilon whom he ransomed for fifteen sous, and one of whom is still in captivity."

This Pons of Vernet was not the only tyrant of the canton; in the same mountainous region other barons of higher rank acted similarly: the only difference was that their field of operations was wider and their profits were larger. The will of Guinard, count of Roussillon, written in 1172,—that is, a few years before the time of Philip Augustus,—is a most instructive document. It was feudalism itself at the point of death, admitting its robberies, and trying to expiate them by indemnifying its victims. Almost all the articles of this testament were modeled on the same formula; here are the most expressive:

" To the church and the inhabitants of Palestres, because of the harm which I have done them, I return two thousand Melgueil sous.
" To the men of Céret, because of the misdeeds from which they suffered, one thousand Melgueil sous.
" To the men of Candeill, from whom I stole their herd, I give one hundred Melgueil sous.
" To Peter Martin, a merchant of Perpignan, for the harm which a robber caused him, I give one hundred and fifty Melgueil sous."

This Count Guinard had evidently had his share in the robbery.

" To the men of Villemolaque, one thousand sous; to the men of Canomals, three hundred sous; to the men of Moreillas, five hundred sous; to the men of Boulon, five hundred sous; to the men of Domanova, one thousand sous; to the men of Begis, one hundred sous . . ."

This is not the end of the list. There follows a formal unambiguous confession:

" On account of the share of the pillage of Pons of Navaga, which I received (*pro parte atrocini Pontii de Navaga quam ego habui*), I give one thousand Melgueil sous, and I direct that one hundred new tunics be given to the poor out of this sum."

It would be impossible to show more clearly that Guinard, count of Roussillon, was participating in the profits of a band of robbers.

It is not probable that these two lords of Roussillon, about whom chance has given us information, were exceptions. They acted we will not say like all the nobles of their country,—for in all times and in every country there are honest men,—but like many men of their caste. If we betake ourselves to other parts of France, we see the same spectacle. In Berry, in 1209, the lord of Déols and, in 1219, the lord of Sully were declared guilty of having plundered merchants; and Philip Augustus was obliged to interfere and treat them with rigor. And the great barons, the feudal sovereigns, stole like the ordinary castellans. Gui V, viscount of Limoges, found it convenient to send his soldiers to seize goods in the markets, and he imprisoned those who resisted them. Hugh III, the duke of Burgundy, always at the end of his resources, was really a robber on the great highways: he plundered the French and Flemish merchants who crossed his lands; and this was one of the reasons for Philip Augustus' expedition into Burgundy in 1186.

The famous Renaud of Dammartin, count of Boulogne, one of the greatest lords of this time, the special enemy of the king of France and the man who worked hardest to organize the coalition vanquished at Bouvines, was in other respects only a common brigand. One of his recent biographers, M. Henri Malo, has tried to ennoble this man by representing him as the incarnation of feudal hatred for monarchical centralization. He has shown that this baron, in fighting against royalty, was merely true to his principles and fought for the independence of his possessions, as a man who wanted to remain master at home. That is all very well, but, as a matter of fact, we know that the count of Boulogne received money from the English and the Germans to resist Philip Augustus and to raise enemies against him on all sides. The idea of a nationality or of a country to which one must be loyal barely existed among the great lords of the time of Louis XIV and Condé; the more reason why one should not search for such a spirit in a baron of Philip Augustus. But M. Malo was, at any rate, obliged to recognize that his " good-looking, brave and strong, intelligent and learned " hero did not content himself with the rewards of his political rôle; he was, besides, a robber with an armed band, and a vulgar pillager of peasants, merchants, and citizens.

" From the beginning of the government of Renaud of Boulogne," admits M. Malo, " his reputation of loving money and of securing it by somewhat sharp practices was already well established: it is true that, if he loved it, it was only to spend it; the nobility of this motive, however, could not convince the people whom he despoiled of the righteousness of his procedure. Every one tried his best to escape him, and whole communities found it prudent to put their wealth out of his reach: the inhabitants of Calais, for instance, confided all their wealth to the monks of Andres in 1191." And M. Malo himself tells us a few of these " somewhat sharp practices " which Renaud of Boulogne employed to fill his purse. He pictures him stealing the flocks of the monks of the neighborhood, seizing the grain which they had stored in their barns, and appropriating what suited him from their woods, their lands, and their meadows. He tells us another exploit of his which caused a great stir in 1190. William, bishop of Longchamps, an old chancellor of Richard the Lion-Hearted, exiled from England, came to seek a place of refuge on the soil of France. He landed on the shores of Boulonnais. But hardly had he entered the country before Renaud fell on him with his troop and took from him his horses, his baggage, the sacred vases of his chapel, even his episcopal cope, and then allowed him to continue on his way. The episode created a scandal. The archbishop of Reims reprimanded the young count of Boulogne severely, demanded the return of the stolen goods, and excommunicated the robber. Nothing came of it. " Renaud," says M. Malo, " listened to the remonstrances, but returned nothing, not even the cope of the bishop." This was the man whom his biographer calls " the type of the great French lord of the end of the twelfth and the beginning of the thirteenth century." And when M. Malo, a little later, adds, " At this period, the pettiest owner of a coat of mail or of a tower believed he had a right to pillage and assault anybody passing within reach of his sword," and justifies this phrase by examples taken from the counties of Guines and of Boulogne, where the ravages of

the feudal lords were frightful, he states a fact, a truth,
which could be applied to almost all France.

The men of the time recognized this themselves. Giraud
of Borneil, a troubadour who wrote at the beginning of the
thirteenth century, deplored these habits of pillage, unworthy
of men of the sword:

> "I used to see the barons, in beautiful armor, giving and follow-
> ing tournaments, and I heard those who had delivered the best
> blows spoken of for many a day. Now, honor lies in stealing
> cattle, sheep, and lambs. Oh, fie upon the knight who drives off
> flocks of bleating sheep, or pillages churches and travelers, and then
> appears before a lady!"

Another contemporary, also a Provençal troubadour, Bertran of Lamanon, composed what was called a *tençon*, a
satiric dialogue, in which he ridiculed Gui, a former brigand,
who had become a bard:

> "Friend Gui, I am indeed charmed with your good sense, for
> you propose to try every occupation. I hear it said that you, who
> for so long infested the highways, have now advanced so far that
> you represent law and order. After having stolen cattle, goats,
> lambs, and sheep, you have become a minstrel and recite verses
> and songs. You have raised yourself to a higher honor."

Giraud of Borneil, whom we have just quoted, was the
better fitted to complain of the ravages of the lords, because
he himself had been their victim. These men had, no respect
for poets. One day Giraud was returning from the court
of Castile, where he had been received with enthusiasm and
overwhelmed with gifts; as he was passing through the
mountains of Navarre, he was despoiled by the officers of
Sancho the Strong, king of Navarre.

Feudalism lived on booty: it stole by robbing merchants
and travelers; it also stole by levying illegal taxes on the
peasants and the citizens of the fief; and this exploitation
was universal. To brigandage by force was added brigandage
by seigniorial agents, which consisted of arbitrary taxes and
corvées. It had, no doubt, decreased in many respects within
the century, for a certain number of cities, towns, and even
villages had obtained guarantees in the form of charters or

contracts. The seignior finally began to comprehend that the way to get a return from his fief was not to exhaust it by exaction and turn it into a desert. But, one must admit that the nobility did not everywhere show this elementary intelligence; and, if there were many localities which were guaranteed against arbitrary exploitation by a duly executed charter, much more numerous were those which had no franchises and which the seignior could fleece at will. The cities found a means of defence; but what resistance was possible in the country? The property and the life of the peasant were hardly safer in peace than in war.

On this subject one should read the bold utterances against feudal excesses contained in one of the sermons expressly addressed by the famous preacher, Jacques of Vitry, to the princes and the knights, *ad proceres et milites:*[1]

"All that the peasant amasses in a year by stubborn work, the knight, the noble, devours in an hour. . . . Not content with his pay as soldier, not content with his revenues and with the annual tax levied on his subjects, he further despoils them by illicit taxes and heavy exactions. The poor are exhausted, the fruit of their years of pain and sorrow is extorted from them."

Especially does the preacher attack the odious right of mortmain. He thunders against the nobles who steal the inheritance of the dead, the goods of the widow and the orphan:

"The father dies, and the seignior takes from the unfortunate children the cow which should have nourished them. Those who take advantage of the right of mortmain are murderers, because they condemn the orphan to death by hunger: they are like the vermin which feasts on corpses."

Elsewhere he compares the nobles to wolves, and their agents and officers to crows:

"As wolves and jackals devour a carrion, while the crows croak overhead awaiting their share in the feast, so, when the barons and the knights pillage their subjects, the provosts, the preceptors, and others of the hellish crew rejoice at the prospect of devouring the rest."

[1] Bibl. nat., ms. lat. 17509, fol. 104-108.

And these metaphors become ever stronger:

" Those lords who do not work and live off the work of the poor are like those unclean parasites which imbed themselves in the skin, prey upon it, and live off the substance which serves them as a home."

The provosts were no less rapacious than their masters: they ground down and were ground down in turn. One might call them leeches: they sucked the blood of the miserable and were obliged to disgorge it for the profit of the seignior, more powerful than they.

What form did this exploitation of the poor by the lord and his agents not take? Means were found for everything; Jacques of Vitry, to renew the attention of his auditors and bring them to their senses, relates the following anecdote:

" One day, a bailiff, the officer of a certain count, wishing to please his master, said to him: ' Seignior, if you will listen to me, I will tell you a way to make a good sum of money each year.' ' With pleasure,' replied the count. ' Allow me then, seignior, to sell the sun on all your land.' ' How,' asked the count, ' can one sell God's sun?' ' Very simply: many of your men wash their clothes and dry them in the sun. If they give you no more than twelve deniers for each piece of cloth, you will make much money.' And this is how that bad officer led his seignior to sell the sun's rays."

Jacques of Vitry incessantly complained of the rapacity of the strong and the misery of the oppressed; he felt that this was the fundamental evil of feudal society, and he tried to make the guilty afraid. '' You have been ' ravening wolves,'' he told them, '' and that is why you shall go to howl in hell.'' But, for those whom the prospect of eternal pains would not sufficiently frighten, he had another argument, which was more human and more convincing:

" The great must make themselves loved by the small; they must be careful not to inspire hate. The humble must not be scorned: if they can aid us, they can also do us harm. You know that many serfs have killed their masters or have burnt their houses."

No preacher or moralist of this period of the middle ages has more clearly painted the sad effects of the avidity of the noble classes and has assailed feudal brigandage in more vigorous terms. After speaking of this thirst for money, which was the principal vice of the nobility, he might have gone further and have described the nobles with their passion for fighting and their bloody instincts, which the custom of pillage and the continuity of a state of war too well explain. This was the second salient characteristic, another general trait of feudalism. On this point, as on the other, history shows that the preachers could hardly exaggerate.

Here, for example, is Bernard of Cahuzac, a petty lord of Périgord, who is described by the historian, Peter of Vaux-de-Cernay. A veritable wild beast:

" He spends his life in looting and destroying churches, in attacking pilgrims, in oppressing the widow and the poor. It pleases him especially to mutilate the innocent. In a single monastery, that of the black monks of Sarlat, one hundred and fifty men and women were found, whose hands and feet had been cut off, or whose eyes had been put out by him. His wife, as cruel as he, aided in his deeds. She took pleasure in torturing these poor women herself. She had their breasts slit, or their nails torn out so that they would not be able to work."

Another example:

" Foucaud, a knight and a comrade of Simon de Montfort, angered even the warriors by his cruelties. Every prisoner who did not have the means of paying one hundred sous as ransom was condemned to death. He inclosed his prisoners in subterranean dungeons and let them die of starvation: sometimes he had them brought forth half dead and thrown into cesspools before his own eyes. It was said that on one of his last expeditions, he returned with two captives, a father and son, and that he forced the father to hang his own son."

To realize how far the love of war and of its butcheries could go—to what point pillaging, burning, and killing were a pleasure and a veritable need to the barons of this period— it is enough to study the life and the works of the troubadour, Bertran de Born. This poet was himself a noble and castellan; he spent his life fighting and in making others fight. He liked war for its own sake, because it was beautiful to see troops clash and blood flow; all the more because booty was thus won and princes were obliged to give largess to the

knights who fought for them. Bertran de Born's authorship
of the famous sirvente, "The·gay time of Easter that makes
flowers and leaves come forth is very pleasing to me," has
been contested. It is a martial song, in which this well-
known verse is found:

"I tell you that I never eat, sleep, or drink so well, as when I
hear the cry: 'Up and at them!' from both sides, and when I
hear the neighing of riderless horses in the thicket, and hear voices
shouting: 'Help! Help!' and see men fall on the green of the
moats, and see the dead pierced in the side by the shafts of spears
gay with pennons."

If this poetry was not of his writing,—which has never
been proved,—it is much like his style, as appears from the
following selection, the authenticity of which has never been
questioned:

"The joyous season approaches when our ships shall land, when
King Richard, wanton and valiant as he never was before, shall
come. Now shall we see gold and silver spent; newly built foundations shall break with envy, walls shall crumble, towers shall subside
and fall to pieces, and his enemies shall taste the prison and its
chains. I love the mêlée of shields with blue and vermillion tints,
flags and pennons of different colors, tents and rich pavilions spread
over the plain, the breaking of lances, the riddling of shields, the
splitting of gleaming helmets, and the giving and taking of blows."

This man could not understand why the barons should
make peace, and he covered those who did so with sarcasm.
"They are," he said, "like base metal, from which nothing
can be formed, however much one reshape and recast it; the
spur cannot make them stir." "I have broken on them,"
he says elsewhere, "more than a thousand goads without
being able to make a single one of them run or trot; there
is not one of them that one cannot clip, shear, or shoe."
"They are full of audacity at the beginning of winter," he
continues, "but they lose their courage in the spring, when
the time for action comes." To content Bertran de Born,
slaughter would have to be continuous; as soon as it ceased,
he wrote dejectedly:

"Bravery and valor are dead. There are kingdoms, but no more
kings; counties, but no more counts; there are strong castles, but

no more castellans. One can still see beautiful ladies, and beautiful clothes, and well-dressed people; but where are the doughty knights of the lays? Richard is a lion, but King Philip appears to me to be a lamb."

Richard the Lion-Hearted was the ideal of Bertran de Born; but to make a lamb out of Philip Augustus, because he only liked profitable wars, passes the bounds of poetic license. It must be noticed that the region in which our author lived, Limousin and the neighboring countries of Périgord and Angoumois, was perhaps the part of France where feudalism was most turbulent; where the nobles fought most bloodily among themselves or against their king. There, especially, war raged and was a permanent scourge. It was truly difficult to satisfy Bertran de Born.

However, his poems are not those in which the voluptuousness of carnage was voiced with the most expressive savagery. The authors of certain *chansons de geste,* contemporaries of Philip Augustus, in at least their later writings,—such as the poem *Lorrains* or *Girart de Roussillon,*—went further. Their heroes reached the limit of ferocity. In the song *Garin le Lorrain,* Duke Bégon, seizing in his hands the entrails of an enemy whom he had just killed, threw them in the face of William of Montclin, with these words, " Here, vassal, take the heart of your friend: you can salt it and roast it." Garin himself opened the body of William of Blancafort. " He drew the heart, the lungs, and the liver out of it. Hernaut, his companion, seized the heart, cut it into four pieces, and both strewed the road with these pieces of still palpitating flesh." After a battle, noble prisoners were kept, to be put to ransom; but as no profit could be made out of prisoners of an inferior class,—such as archers, arbalisters, and servants of the army,—they were massacred or mutilated, to make them incapable of service. The lay *Girart de Roussillon* leaves no doubt on this point. Here is a pertinent passage: " Girart and his men conducted the massacre; among the living they kept two hundred and eighty men, all owners of castles, and put them apart at one side." Later: " The Burgundians were barbarous and cruel; we had not a squire or a cross-bowman whom they did not give an empty sleeve or a wooden leg." Here the writer seems to condemn these practices; but, as a fact, no one gave them up, not even the king:

> "'By my head,' said Charles Martel, 'I do not worry over what you have said, Fulc; I laugh at your threats, as at a quince. Every knight that I take, I shall honor by cutting off his nose or his ears. If it be a squire or a foot soldier, he shall lose an arm or a leg.'"

In another passage thirty squires, all disfigured, arrive at the palace of the king:

> "Each had a foot or an arm cut off, or an eye put out. They came before the king in this state and said to him: 'Sire, it was in your service that we were mutilated in this way.'"

We know how much we can depend on the historical value of information furnished us by the *chansons de geste*. We know that even in his pictures of war, even in his recitals of battles, the poet could not help introducing features which were entirely fanciful or distorting the truth by stretching it beyond all measure. When, for example, we see the armies of kings or great lords meet in formidable clashes, general mêlées, or drawn battles,—in which enormous numbers of men, hundreds of thousands, appear in line and kill each other,—we say that the poet allowed his imagination to run riot. In actual history, as it appears in the wars of the Capetians and the Plantagenets, the armies were, on the contrary, very small, the battles extremely rare; there were skirmishes and ravages, but few engagements of great masses: decisive action was avoided, they did not venture to ruin the adversary in a single blow; they only aimed to ruin him by degrees: the nobles captured and ransomed much oftener than they killed each other. Besides, when one reflects that in the poems all knights are of herculean force; that with a single blow of the sword they strike off arms, legs, and heads; that they cut an enemy in two and cleave his helmet, his head, and his breast with a marvelous ease; when, too, one notes that, though wounded, they have an incredible power of resistance, so that, though transfixed, mutilated, or with brain laid bare, they resume the saddle and continue to fight as though they had felt nothing, one must say that here imagination had reached its utmost bounds.

Barring this kind of exaggeration, these tales of wars and battles contain a mass of material taken from real life. The poet needed not resort to imagination; he had only to look at what was going on about him. What he says of the ferocity of the warrior and of the massacre of useless prisoners is fully confirmed by historical documents. What he says of butcheries of peasants and of frightful devastation of an enemy's territory is also entirely true. War at that time consisted chiefly of destruction and pillage. The object was to do the greatest possible harm to the adversary, by setting his villages on fire and by massacring the peasants, who were his property and his source of income. Here the authors of the *chansons de geste* say no more than is found on every page of the chronicles. It was the citizen, the monk, and especially the peasant who bore the expense of feudal wars.

The lay *Girart de Roussillon* is very instructive in this respect. One of the heroes of this poem, speaking of an adversary, cries out:

"He may attack us, the cruel coward. He will chop down our vines and our trees, he will undermine our walls and our fish-ponds, he will open our water-mains."

And, farther on, the same definition of war:

"He sees a stronger come and attack him, cut off his vines, root up his trees, lay waste his land, and make it a desert; he sees his castles taken by storm, his walls broken, his moats filled up, all his men captured or killed."

Here is what victory meant to the leader of an expedition:

"He does not leave a good knight alive as far as Baiol, nor treasure, nor monastery, nor church, nor shrine, nor censer, nor cross, nor sacred vase; everything that he seizes he gives to his companions. He makes so cruel a war that he does not lay hands on a man without killing, hanging, or mutilating him."

But in *Lorrains* we find a more detailed and complete picture of the effects of the march of an army through an enemy's country. Here is a picture ready-made for us, in which nothing is lacking:

"They start to march. The scouts and the incendiaries lead; after them come the foragers who are to gather the spoils and carry them in the great baggage train. The tumult begins. The peasants, having just come out to the fields, turn back, uttering loud cries; the shepherds gather their flocks and drive them towards the neighboring woods in the hope of saving them. The incendiaries set the villages on fire, and the foragers visit and sack them; the distracted inhabitants are burnt or led apart with their hands tied to be held for ransom. Everywhere alarm bells ring, fear spreads from side to side and becomes general. On all sides one sees helmets shining, pennons floating, and horsemen covering the plain. Here hands are laid on money; there cattle, donkeys, and flocks are seized. The smoke spreads, the flames rise, the peasants and the shepherds in consternation flee in all directions."

Where the knights have passed, there is nothing left:

"In the cities, in the towns, and on the small farms, wind-mills no longer turn, chimneys no longer smoke, the cocks have ceased their crowing, and the dogs their barking. Grass grows in the houses and between the flag-stones of the churches, for the priests have abandoned the services of God, and the crucifixes lie broken on the ground. The pilgrim might go six days without finding any one to give him a loaf of bread or a drop of wine. Freemen have no more business with their neighbors; briars and thorns grow where villages stood of old."

*

*   *

The ideal of the noble who fought was to make the land of the enemy desert; and the noble was ever fighting. At this period war existed everywhere. War was the function, the profession of the noble; he was above all else a soldier, the leader of a band, and had corresponding tastes and habits; he not only loved war, but he lived from it. He passed his youth in preparing for it; when he became of age, he was knighted, and he waged war as long as his strength permitted him to do so, even in his old age. His home was a guard-room or fortress; his castle a means of attack and of defense. When by chance he was at peace,—which was not often,—he still kept up the appearance of war, by fighting in tournaments; for we shall see that tournaments were diminutive wars and the occasion of slaughter and booty. In spite of the (inconsiderable) advance of culture, in spite of the efforts of the clergy, of kings, and of several great lords who had become rulers, war was practically a permanent scourge, almost everywhere in France. In the society of that day war was the normal state.

We have some difficulty in admitting the truth of this para-doxical and monstrous fact. With our habits and peaceful customs, with the overscrupulous protection with which modern society surrounds us, our properties and our persons, we have great trouble in picturing to ourselves a country like the France of Philip Augustus—divided into provinces, whose inhabitants formed so many small nations, which hated each other; these provinces themselves subdivided into a multitude of seigniories or fiefs, whose owners were forever fighting; not only the barons, but the little castellans, living in an unsociable isolation and constantly fighting against their sovereigns, their equals, or their subjects; and, furthermore, those rivalries between city and city, village and village, valley and valley, those wars between neighbors, which then seemed to burst forth almost spontaneously from the diversity of the soil itself. How could laborers live in such chaos, in the midst of these hostile elements? How could the peasants, already so exhausted by the excesses of seigniorial exploitation and natural scourges, resist these daily disorders, of which they were always the first victims? That is what we wonderingly ask; and we can only answer that these men worked in the midst of devastation and pillage, as they lived in the midst of pestilences and famines; that the nobles always found enough men to murder and torture, and enough hovels to burn.

We must pass from province to province to convince ourselves of the reality of these innumerable wars, which put lay feudalism at outs with itself and with the other classes of society at one and the same moment throughout all France. Though information is precise and abundant for some regions, it is not for others: a complete and minute statement of these scenes of devastation would be impossible; in any case, it would be interminable. We can, however, choose certain striking events which left the strongest impression on contemporaries and which were, therefore, embodied in the records and the chronicles. Here and there we can point out the more general types of feudal wars, with an almost absolute certainty that what happened in one province also happened in others, and that the warlike and pillaging instincts of the caste of knights caused the same evils everywhere. Naturally, the commonplaces of political history—like those, for example, which concern the war of the Capetians with the Plantagenets and the great feudal lords—will not be discussed here. We remember that the wars and the conquests of Philip Augustus put a great part of France to fire and bloodshed for almost the whole of his reign; at least, until 1214, the date of his final victory at Bouvines. But, under this first substratum of historical wars, there were many others among the different classes of the feudal hierarchy—an infinity of small wars, devastation, and local conflicts, in which the inferior feudal barons were alone interested, but which were no less murderous and ruinous for the peasants.

War existed everywhere, and especially between seigniorial families. Questions of inheritance and of succession, which are now settled by civil justice, then usually ended in violent conflicts. When the eldest son of the lord, heir-presumptive to the fief, reached the age when he was made knight, he demanded a certain part of the domain and the seigniorial revenues, as he needed money for his pleasures, his friends, or for his appearance in tournaments. Sometimes he even demanded a formal partnership in the seigniorial power and the right to use the seal of the seigniory to legalize his acts: that is, his participation in the sovereignty as co-seignior and co-proprietor while awaiting the whole inheritance. There were fathers who consented to advance the inheritance, who benevolently gave the young cavalier domains, and even associated him with themselves in the government of the seigniory; others gave him money or land, but kept their seigniorial rights intact; still others objected to increasing their incomes at all and gave nothing. In that case the son, egged on by evil counselors, made open war on the father, and the whole fief was disturbed for several years. In this way is explained the long quarrel between the two lords of Beaujolais—Humbert III, the father, and Humbert IV, the son—at the end of the reign of Louis VII and at the beginning of that of Philip Augustus. We do not know the details of this family war; we only know from the arbitral act of the archbishop of Lyons, which terminated it in 1184, how great was the desolation in the country of Beaujolais and Lyonnais. Here are the expressions employed by the arbitrator:

" Among all the misfortunes which have struck our region, one must place first that tempest (*tempestas illa*), that pitiless war which Humbert of Beaujeu and his son waged against each other, and which men almost despaired of ever seeing ended."

In 1184, however, the belligerents decided to swear, by the relics at Lyons, to keep the peace. And then, says the charter:

" The father received his son like his natural heir, and as the legitimate seignior after him of his whole fief and domain of Beaujeu, and he swore to this before all the witnesses. The son, in his turn, did him homage. And it was in this way that, through our mediation, the young Humbert gave back to his father the greater part of the seigniory on which he had laid his hand."

The heir, then, had almost entirely despoiled the father of his fief.

In the chronicle of Lambert of Ardres, dedicated to the history of the petty seigniories of Guines and of Ardres, in Artois, we learn that Arnoul, son of Baldwin II, count of Guines, received the sword of knighthood in 1181. He was hardly in possession of his title before he began to claim the inheritance:

" Arnoul had a counselor, Philip of Montgardin, whom he kept in spite of the wishes of his father, the count of Guines. This counselor steadily urged the young man to claim the city of Ardres and the property which had come to him from his mother. There were long conferences and frequent interviews between the father and the son on this subject. The count of Guines was not satisfied with the attitude of his son; the intervention of Philip of Alsace, count of Flanders, was necessary to appease him; finally after long negotiations young Arnoul obtained Ardres and Colvide, but with only a part of their dependencies."

Here the difference between the father and the son, between the owner of the fief and the presumptive heir, does not seem to have resulted in war; at least, the chronicler does not say so; but evidently very little was lacking. Defiance of the heir by the holder of the seigniory was then a general rule in all stages of feudal society. It is well known how Henry II, the mighty master of the Plantagenet empire, acted toward his eldest son, Henry the Young, and also toward Richard the Lion-Hearted. It is also a matter of common knowledge that Philip Augustus was not even willing to give his son, Louis—the future Louis VIII, who was a model son—the sovereignty of Artois, which the heir-apparent held in his own right from his mother. Louis never bore the title of count or of seignior of Artois; he had no chancellery of his own; his charters were countersigned by his father's officers. Always jealous of his authority, Philip Augustus, to the end of his life, closely watched and restrained this son, who was more than thirty-five years old when he became king. "My son, you have never caused me any trouble," said Philip to him on his death-bed. Indeed, the old king had taken such precautions that it would have been very hard for his heir to cause him much worry. But we have just seen that such precautions were necessary, and that young knights, rapacious like their fathers, were anxious to speed the day of their inheritance.

Between the sons and their mothers other difficulties arose; for, after the death of the holder of a fief, the heir was obliged to leave his widowed mother in possession of a certain number of domains and castles, which were thus removed from his direct control. It was for this reason that war broke out, in 1220, between the widow of Arnoul II, the count of Guines, and her son, Baldwin III. It lasted two years; the mother and son finally made peace, *post multiplices discordias,* says the chronicle of Ardres, and these three words without doubt cover many depredations and murders.

Brothers did not agree any better, especially when misfortune decided that they should own a fief or a domain in common. This happened in districts where the right of the eldest son was not rigorously enforced; and then it was a source of interminable wars. Let us go into Limousin, at the beginning of the reign of Philip Augustus: two brothers were wrangling over the possession of the castle of Hautefort, the ruins of which are still to be seen above the village of Bellegarde, in the Dordogne, at the edge of a pond situated in the midst of the forest of Born. This château was a redoubtable fortress; but the seigniory of Born, of which it was the principal seat, was only of ordinary importance. Bertran de Born, the troubadour, and his brother, Constantine de Born, both residing at Hautefort, seemed to live there in harmony at first; then there was discord between them; they fought and each tried to expel the other from the paternal manor. According to Bertran de Born, the entire fault lay with his brother, who would not be contented with his part:

"If I have a brother or a cousin-germain, I divide the egg and the money with him, but if he wishes my own part also, then I drive him from the community."

Bertran finally got the upper hand, and Constantine, having been expelled, complained to his suzerains—the viscount of Limoges and Richard the Lion-Hearted, duke of Aquitaine. Then, said Bertran, the mêlée became general and the land of Hautefort was ravaged:

"Each day I fight, I exert myself, I ride, I defend myself, and I argue. My land is sacked and is burned. My trees are cut down, my grain is mixed with straw, and I have not an enemy, brave or cowardly, who does not profit by the occasion to attack me."

It is not certain that Bertran de Born defended himself as well as he says, for the castle of Hautefort, in spite of its very strong position, surrendered without striking a blow to Richard the Lion-Hearted, who besieged it in 1183. Constantine de Born entered it; but, a little while later, King Henry II made a present of it to the troubadour, who did not leave it again.

The law of primogeniture was a way of avoiding wars between brothers; and the barons made the surer of it by vowing their younger sons from infancy to an ecclesiastical career. But when the rights of inheritance were not entirely clear, when there remained only distant relatives or women to succeed to the fiefs, when different principles of heredity conflicted,—such as the principle of the succession of progenitors, of relatives, or that of representation,—then competition came into play and wars of succession broke out. These quarrels about inheritance occurred in many parts of feudal France at the time with which we are occupied; but the most celebrated, the longest, and the most disastrous of all involved the county of Champagne, which was claimed both by Erard of Brienne and by Blanche, countess of Champagne, for her minor son, Thibaud IV. It lasted fourteen years, from 1213 to 1227; the hostilities which resulted from it affected not only Champagne, but also a part of Burgundy, the Île de France, and Lorraine; the pope, the king of France, the emperor, and many French, Belgian, and German barons were involved in it. It gave rise not only to a number of skirmishes and local raids, but to two considerable battles. It resulted in diplomatic negotiations of extraordinary complication and interminable processes before all possible jurisdictions. Finally, it completely subverted feudal relationships; vassals changed from one party to another, as they found it to their interest, and changed their homage and their suzerain with a truly remarkable freedom. This typical letter sent by a baron to Blanche, countess of Champagne, is enough to illustrate:

" To Blanche, countess, and to Thibaud, her son, greetings. I, seignior of Sexfontaines, let you know by these letters that I was formerly your man and that of Thibaud, your son. But now there has just appeared an heir who has better founded rights and who asks my homage, and there is already a lien between us that will prevent me from ever leaving him. Know then, that I have joined the side of the legitimate heir and that I am no longer your vassal."

This was what the famous law of feudal vassalage was in practice—the keystone of the whole system of fiefs, of that monarchical edifice which seemed so regularly and so harmoniously ordered in the theories of the jurists of the thirteenth century. In fact, this bond of vassalage was deplorably fragile and inconstant; it vanished at the slightest excuse; the merest shadow of a claim, a gift of land, a hint of money was enough to cause a vassal to change his sovereign and to transfer his homage and his personal services to another seignior.

To wars between relatives, therefore, were added wars between sovereigns and vassals, which were no less disastrous and no less frequent. It would be impossible to enumerate them; they fill the history of France; for contentions over vassalage were the very basis of the wars of Philip Augustus with the Plantagenets and the counts of Flanders; and of the Plantagenets themselves with the barons of their continental domains. They also fill the provincial histories, for at that time there was not a single part of France that was not the scene of a war waged by a vassal, or by a league of vassals against the sovereign of the fief. These conflicts and these wars were, so to speak, the woof of all seigniorial existence. There are so many facts to relate, so many examples to give, that it is useless to collect evidence or to lay stress on what constituted the daily and normal life of our barons. We must not be deceived by appearances; at bottom, the sovereign was the enemy of his vassals: he was respected when he was strong; he was defied and attacked when he was not. On his side, the sovereign was not more respectful of the feudal bond. Here is a pertinent anecdote taken from the book of the Dominican, Stephen of Bourbon:

" There was in the diocese of Mâcon, about the year 1190, a certain viscount, who had several castles or donjons. Relying on his fortresses, he watched for opportunities to rob rich travelers and he lived on the plunder of his men. One day, however, perhaps through fear of the king of France, perhaps through personal conviction, he undertook a pilgrimage to the Holy Land, and confided his land and his castles to his overlord, Girard, count of Mâcon. The latter promised to marry the viscount's daughter to his own son William, already associated with the count of Mâcon. But, far from keeping his oath, he kept the land of his vassal for himself, and gave the daughter to one of his knights. In vain the heirs of the viscount appealed to the king: he refused to hear them."

As to the viscount himself, despoiled of everything, he died of misery and of hunger when he was about to embark at Genoa. Here the suzerain was no better than the vassal, and the disloyalty of the first was on a par with the immorality of the second.

We have not enumerated all the different kinds of wars in discussing this endemic malady of the feudal body. There were also the wars of lords against their own officers, the agents of the seigniory. The word agent brings up in our minds the idea of a more or less zealous but faithful and obedient person, attached by his own interests to the success of the state which employs him. It was otherwise in the middle ages. The seigniorial officer was himself a petty lord, as anxious for land and money as his seignior and striving in all ways for independence. We have noticed that Jacques of Vitry described the feudal agent as a leech, whom the master must from time to time compel to disgorge—a difficult operation and one that often required force. History shows that the preacher did not overstate the facts. Let us see what happened in 1203 in the county of Boulogne. The seneschal of Renaud, count of Dammartin, was a certain Eustache le Moine, an adventurer who had a most singular destiny. The count was informed that the seneschal was appropriating the taxes collected from the land which he administered. He summoned Eustache to render his accounts. Fearing that he would be thrown into prison, Eustache took refuge in the great forest of Boulogne. Renaud confiscated the possessions of his agent and burned his domains. On the day that the count was celebrating the marriage of one of his favorites, Eustache avenged himself by burning two of the count's mills, in honor of the event. The bloody war between the seneschal and his lord dragged on. Eustache stole his lord's horses and maimed his men. One day he was taken, and thrown into prison, but escaped and, crossing the channel, offered his services to John Lackland and to the English.

Finally,—for we must make an end, even though the material is inexhaustible,—war between nobles was not always caused by the hope of gain. With passionate and extremely susceptible temperaments, with men who had brutality in the blood and choler in their florid complexions, it needed only a trifle, a gesture, a word, a bit of mockery to provoke hostilities and an interminable vendetta. The assembly of barons in the army or in the court of the sovereign was a particularly fruitful source of disputes, which were often grave and were followed by bloody quarrels after the barons had returned to their fiefs. In the epic *Garin le Lorrain* there is a very vivid picture of the struggle which took place between the barons at the court of the king, in the presence of the king himself. The knights of the two parties of Lorraine and Bordeaux abused each other, in spite of the intervention of their sovereign, and, after having heaped each other with the most abominable insults, they came to blows.

" Garin struck Fromont on the head; so mighty was his fist that Fromont, stunned, measured his full length on the floor. Then the Bordelais left their seats and came to aid their seignior. The mêlée became general: men seized each other by the hair, they fought with their feet, their fists, and their teeth, all in the sight of the king, to whom no one would listen. But, in the midst of the severest fighting, Count Hardré went out, down the stairs, and ran to his inn. He took from the head of his bed a strong stick of oak, came back to the palace, closed all the exits, and reappeared before the Lorrains, who stood rigid with fear. Fourteen knights fell mortally wounded."

Hernaïs of Orléans, of the Lorrain party, came on the scene and, in turn, fell on the Bordelais.

" There was then a real butchery. The knights, vying with each other, set upon the Bordelais, who were soon mutilated and cut to pieces. The wounded hid under the tables, in the vain hope of escaping; they were found, drawn out of their hiding places, and killed."

And this fray at the court of the king was the beginning of the war between the Bordelais and the Lorrains, of which the epic tells us so many incidents.

Evidently, the imagination of the minstrel here had free play; but, on the whole, he only enlarged and blackened historic fact. In 1197, the court of Philip Augustus was held at Compiègne. A discussion arose between Renaud of Dammartin, count of Boulogne, and Hugh, count of Saint-Pol. Hot words were exchanged: Hugh of Saint-Pol struck Renaud full in the face, so hard that the blood flowed. Renaud drew his dagger and flung himself on his assailant. The king and

the bystanders interfered in time; but the count of Boulogne
bitterly reproached Philip Augustus for not allowing him to
avenge himself, and this was one of the grievances which led
him to ally himself for the first time with the enemies of the
king of France.

*

*   *

If the members of the feudal caste fought much among
themselves, they were not any more at peace with the other
elements of society. Internal wars were numerous; external
wars were not less frequent. In the middle ages social dis-
tinctions were more clean-cut, and class feeling was much
stronger and more persistent than in modern times. This
was, on the one hand, because passions were then more intense and customs more brutal; and, on the other hand, because the various social groups were separated by barriers
which were higher and more difficult to overcome.

The noble had an untamable antipathy and profound contempt for the villein: that is (using the word in its most
comprehensive meaning), for the serf, peasant, the laborer,
and the citizen or burgher. It would be easy to cite a
hundred passages of the *chansons de geste,* written at the
time of Philip Augustus, in which this contempt is very
clearly expressed. In these songs villeins who had succeeded
in emerging from their status, entering the military class,
and reaching knighthood are sometimes mentioned; but, in
such a case, the poet never fails to put strong protests into
the mouths of his noble characters. It is true that in real
life this transformation from villein to knight did several
times occur, especially in southern France, where the gulf
between the classes was narrower; but, on the whole, the
occurrence was rare. The noble considered the villein—
whether he was isolated, in a state of servitude, or part of a
community of more or less free citizens—as an inferior being, whom he could despoil and massacre without scruple.
In this light, certain incidents of the war against the Albigenses are very instructive. It was not only religious passion which animated the knights of the crusade against the
citizens infected with heresy: it was also the contemptuous
repulsion that these nobles of the north felt for the villein,

who in their eyes had no value. This, for example, explains
the horrors of the sack of Marmande in 1218. "The crusaders," says the historian of Philip Augustus, "killed all
the citizens with their wives and little children, and all the
inhabitants to the number of five thousand." But they
spared the count of Astarac, who had directed the defense
of the city, and all the nobles who had participated in it.
If the noble hated the peasant and crushed him without
mercy, the latter, when he could, repaid in kind. The same
year, 1218, William of Baux, prince of Orange, fell into the
hands of the inhabitants of Avignon, who were friendly to
the Albigenses: the citizens flayed him alive, then cut his
body into pieces.

One would think that relations between nobles and churchmen were less strained. Feudalism furnished a part of
the personnel of the church: many abbots, canons, and bishops belonged to seigniorial families; a number of prelates,
as we have seen, led a noble's life, the life of the castle, and
went to the chase and to war surrounded by knights and
armed men. The feudal classes and the clerics, as a whole,
constituted the privileged class, the proprietors of the soil.
Between the nobles and the clergy, or better between the
lay seigniors and the church seigniors, there was this in
common—that they exploited the lower classes, often by the
same tyrannical and odious processes. But not only did they
not agree, but they were continuously at war. The antagonism
between the nobles and the clergy at this period (and
one may say at all periods of the middle ages) is, indeed, one
of the most ordinary, most salient, and best proved facts of
social history. As a proprietor and as a sovereign, feudalism
was jealous of the cleric; it disputed his rights, his revenues,
his tithes, his patronage of parishes; it coveted the property
and the capital accumulated by him through the piety of
the faithful. Needy and wasteful, it disliked this spiritual
power which competed with it for property, for power, and
for money, and which enriched itself without limit; because
the church always amassed, and never or rarely surrendered
anything. Barons considered church property as an inexhaustible source of booty; they spent their lives in pillaging
the territory of monks, of canons, and of bishops, or at

least of those who did not defend themselves or who defended themselves poorly. The spiritual lord protected church goods as well as he could by appeal to pope, king, or duke; by excommunication, and by arms. There was not a corner of France where the nobles and clerics were not in disagreement. In brief, the clergy was always a tempting prey to the nobility; it was the competitor, it was the enemy.

In this last expression there is no exaggeration. This statement finds its proof in the general impression as well as in the details given by history; in the countless facts coming from every single province of France. And it is completely corroborated by a study of the works of Latin and vernacular literature, of the writings of preachers and religious moralists, as well as of the ballads written by the minstrels for the amusement of knights and ladies.

Let us first ask what the church thought and said about feudalism. She was hostile to it for two principal reasons: first, because she stood for peace and public order, and the nobles stood for just the opposite thing; and then especially because she was the continual victim of their aggressions and depredations. Out of a sense of duty, she supported the weak against them, but, out of self-interest, she defended herself, her rights, and her continually threatened properties and treasures. And this is enough to explain the bitterness and the violence of certain utterances of the clergy.

Archdeacon Peter of Blois, a wit of the time of Henry II and of Philip Augustus, uttered a stinging tirade against the feudalism and the military class of his day. It would seem that no priest ever spoke worse of a soldier. One of his letters was addressed to a friend, an archdeacon, whose nephews, who were knights, had expressed themselves insolently about the clergy. "I cannot," wrote Peter to his correspondent, "suffer the boastful self-esteem of your nephews."

"These young men dare to boast of the superiority of the military over the ecclesiastical state, libeling us, by comparing our manner of living and acting with theirs. Admitting that our profession is in decadence, theirs is not for that reason more elevated. They do not know what knights and chivalry mean; otherwise they would kiss the earth before the clergy, they would apply to their impertinent language the restraint which is proper for their age. The knighthood of to-day! Why, it consists of disorderly living! In these military circles, who is it that is reputed the strongest and the most worthy of esteem? It is he who says the most abominable things, who swears the most violently, who treats the ministers of God the worst, and who respects the church the least. . . . Since your nephews have adopted the profession of their companions in arms, they have also acquired their detestable habits. . . . What has become of military art, so well taught by Végèce and so many others? It no longer exists: it is the art of giving oneself up to all sorts of excesses and of leading a sottish life. Formerly the soldiers swore to defend the state, to stand firm in the field of battle, and to sacrifice their lives for the public interest; to-day our knights receive their swords from the hand of the priest, and thus declare that they are the sons of the church, that their arms serve to defend the priesthood, to protect the poor, to pursue malefactors, and to save their country. But in reality they do just the opposite: they have hardly donned the baldric before they rise against the anointed of the Lord, and throw themselves on the patrimony of the Crucified. They despoil and ransom the subjects of the church; they crush the miserable with unequaled cruelty; they seek the satisfaction of their illicit appetites and their extraordinary desires in the pain of others. Saint Luke tells us that the soldiers came to Saint John the Baptist and asked him this question: 'Master, and we, what shall we do?' The saint replied: 'Respect the goods of others, do not harm your neighbors, and be content with your pay.' Our soldiers, who ought to employ their strength against the enemies of the cross and of Christ, use it to vie with each other in debauchery and drunkenness; they waste their time in sloth; they starve in gross intemperance; by their degenerate and impure lives they dishonor their name and their profession."

We cannot quote all of this letter because, according to the custom of the time, Peter of Blois in every line drifts into quotations from the Bible and profane literature. With a great backing of texts, he recalls what the Roman soldier was—his sobriety, his endurance, his love of work; and the comparison with the knight of his period was not to the advantage of the latter. The satire grows ever more bitter and more stinging:

" To-day our warriors are reared in luxury. See them leave for the campaign; are their packs filled with iron, with lances and swords? No! but with leathern bottles of wine, with cheeses and spits for roasting. One would suppose that they were going to picnic, and not to fight. They carry splendid plated shields, which they greatly hope to bring back unused. On their armor and on their saddles are pictured scenes of battle; these are sufficient for them: they have no desire to see more."

To our archdeacon the knights were not even brave; they only had courage against defenseless men, and especially against clerics. That was especially why Peter of Blois was incensed at them.

" Oh, they are ever ready to take our tithes away from us, to despise the church and the clergy, to mock at excommunication, to defy God, to persecute priests, to despoil the church of what the liberality of their fathers has given her! They forget that God said to his priests: ' He that despiseth you despiseth Me, and he who toucheth you toucheth the apple of Mine eye.' "

This is the real feeling of churchmen toward feudalism. They did not spare the barons in their sermons. From the pulpit they told them some very plain truths. In a sermon addressed to the nobles, Jacques of Vitry strongly reproached them for their conduct toward clerics. First he condemned the indifference of the nobles to religious services:

" Formerly, they eagerly came and devoutly heard the word of God. To-day, there are few of them who deign to come to listen to the preacher, who care to sit at the feet of the spiritual doctors with the poor and the humble. They only have one idea, that is to hurry the curé and to urge him to finish his mass. When it is finished, they hasten to the material table, where they eat and drink. There they stay a long time without wearying. Oh! indeed, they do not sleep there, though they sleep or dream in the church at the spiritual table, which bores them."

Jacques of Vitry had a theory about the social classes and their respective functions. To him, the world was a vast body, all of whose members were subordinated to a common end. The clerics and the prelates were the eyes of this body, for it was they who taught men the way of safety, who pointed it out, and who served as guides. The barons and the knights were its hands and arms: God ordered them to defend the goods of the church, to protect the weak, to prevent the poor from being oppressed and despoiled; they should promote peace and justice and oppose violence. That is what they were for; and Providence gave them revenues so that they would not surrender their subjects to exaction and rapine. Finally, the common people (*minores*), the ordinary laymen, were the base of the social body, for they formed the lower parts of it; their function was to sustain and keep the eyes and the hands in good condition by their work. But the order of the knights did not at all fulfil its earthly function. These hands of the social body were, like the hands of a raving maniac, busy in plucking out the eyes and crushing the feet. Instead of defending the poor, the nobles despoiled and oppressed them; instead of protecting the church, they persecuted and attacked it.

Exasperated by the daily outrages of the nobles, the clerics were provoked to say audacious and even absurd things. In a manuscript of the Bibliothèque Nationale, Hauréau,[1] in 1886, found a treatise on canonical jurisprudence written by a cleric of the time of Philip Augustus. He thinks this cleric was an English canon, Robert of Courçon, who later became a cardinal and legate of Innocent III. Whoever he was, the author of this unpublished treatise was a very radical spirit, who condemned many abuses, notably the church's policy of receiving gifts from all hands without inquiring how the fortune given by the donors was acquired; he even opposed the acceptance of gifts from repentant sinners. He, too, had a social theory, or rather a socialistic theory, quite surprising for the middle ages. He wanted to rid society of all who did not work; not only of all the idle nobles who lived on their incomes or by brigandage, but even of all the citizens who were capitalists: that is, who practised usury, which in the middle ages meant financial or banking operations. There follows a literal translation of the passage in which he advances this curious theory.

" The evil from which we are suffering cannot disappear unless the following measures are taken: there should be convoked a general assembly of all bishops and all sovereigns under the presidency of the·pope; and then all the prelates and all the princes should ordain, under pain of excommunication and civil condemna-

---

[1] *Notices et extraits des manuscrits de la Bibl. nat.*, XXXI, part 2, p. 261.

tion, that each person be forced to work either spiritually or manually, so that no one may eat bread not gained by his labor, according to the words of the apostle: 'If any shall not work, neither shall he eat.' As a result, there would be no more idlers among us. Thus usurers and brigands would disappear."

Who would then remain in this Christian world? Only priests and workingmen, living on the wage of their spiritual or manual labors. " No one," says Hauréau, " in any place or in any book has ever written or uttered anything more extreme or more absurd." This is a waste of indignation. We have in the passage the bizarre revery of an ecclesiastic, of a man who desired more justice in the world, who disliked the bankers because the church at that time condemned banking and its profits, and who also detested lazy and malicious feudalism: that is, the nobles whom he characterized as brigands, *raptores*. This word well summarizes the attitude of the church, the principal victim of these excesses.

*

* *

It would be interesting to learn what feudalism, in its turn, thought and said of the clergy. But this is much more difficult. The nobles hardly ever wrote, and for a good reason. Not the feudal, but the ecclesiastical records, the chronicles of monks, have come down to us from that time. Therefore, we cannot ascertain at first hand anything but the opinion of clerics; which we find expressed in their correspondence, their sermons, and their literary works. The opinion of the feudal classes must be discovered indirectly.

In the first place, it may perhaps be deduced from their conduct towards the clergy. We have said, and we will show, that the barons spent their lives in pillaging ecclesiastical domains and waging ruthless wars against abbeys, chapters, and bishoprics, in which the person of the cleric was not much more respected than his property. They willingly confiscated religious treasures and did not hesitate to burn churches and cloisters, though they were ready to do penance afterwards. It is hard to believe that such men had any real consideration or sympathy for priests and monks. To be sure, religious sentiment was not wholly lacking among the soldiers; it manifested itself in the habits of the class, in superstition concerning relics, in the founding of abbeys, in pilgrimages to sanctuaries, and in the hatred of heretics. But, among the nobles, religious sentiment appeared especially at the time of sickness or at the approach of death: theirs was a religion of remorse and fear, an intermittent religion, quite compatible with their lack of respect for holy things and sacred persons in ordinary times.

In the absence of records left by the nobles themselves, it is only in the ballads that their real opinions can be found. Written as they were for the nobility, these epics pictured the life and expressed the feeling of the noble. The author of an epic saw all things with the eyes of the soldier, who profoundly despised everything that was not military, who comprehended and prized nothing but martial pursuits and the turbulent life of camps or castles. In a word, it is the feudal spirit more or less xaggerated that dominates and animates the ballads—a spirit of brutality and of violence, hostile to the peasant, insolent and rebellious to the king, contemptuous of the clergy.

For this incontestable fact must be noted that, in works like *Garin le Lorrain* or *Girart de Roussillon*, the church— that great power of the middle ages—played an inferior and incidental rôle. Clerics and monks were useful only as chaplains or secretaries to the barons, whose letters they read and wrote, or as reserves—to pick up the dead on the battlefield, to bandage the wounded, and to say masses for those who paid. The knights employed clerics, especially monks, but held them in low esteem. Odilon, one of the heroes of the lay *Girart,* haranguing his warriors, told them that, "if he found a coward among them, he would make him a monk in a monastery." In the lay *Hervis de Metz,* a knight cries out: " All these fat monks, all these canons, all these priests, and all these abbots ought to be soldiers. Oh, if the king would only give them to me! " It was not rare for the poet to represent the monk performing a disagreeable duty. In *Garin le Lorrain* and in *Girart,* the monk frequently acted as messenger, a trying and sometimes dangerous task.

One day, Girart of Roussillon, attempting to appease the wrath of King Charles Martel, his enemy, sent the prior of Saint-Sauveur as his ambassador. " Monk," said Girart to his messenger, " go find King Charles Martel, and humbly ask him to give me his confidence and friendship." The monk hastened to deliver the message. " Never until that moment was he so terrified." He came into the presence of the king, who asked him his name.

" ' Sire, I am Friar Bourmon. Girart, your vassal, sent me.'— ' How dared you come hither? '—' Sire, Girart sent me from afar. He will come to pay you full homage, according to the decision of your men and your barons, provided you will grant him a hearing.' ' His homage! What do I care about that? ' said Charles. ' I will not leave him a handful of earth, and as for you, Monk, who brought this message, I wonder what shameful treatment I can inflict on you.' The monk, when he heard these words, would fain have been far away. ' It was not by his strength,' continued the king, ' that Girart defeated me, for had I not been surprised, he would have been captured or killed; no place of refuge, however strong, whether town, citadel, or castle, would have saved him any more than a simple shepherd's hut. But it is you, Sir Monk, who shall pay for this. I will . . .' "

We do not know how to put the threat Charles Martel uttered. The poet adds, as a sort of refrain, " and the monk, when he heard these words, would fain have been far away." When he saw that Charles was wroth and when he heard the threats, he feared for his safety. Hardly would he have continued his mission had Charles been sorry for his words; therefore, as a sagacious man, he asked leave, in God's name, to retire: " I want," he said, " to go back to my master." " Monk," said the king, " I swear, by Jesus above, that, if I had Girart of Roussillon, I would hang him like a thief from the eaves of my house." And the messenger, hearing these words, did not say him nay, but would fain have been far away. " Monk, how dared you come hither? You would have done better to remain in your monastery saying mass, or in your cloister reading your book, praying for the dead or serving God, than to have brought me this message from Girart. If it were not for the fear of God and eternal death, I would have a mind to . . ." A new threat followed. The monk, hearing speech of this sort, knew not what to say, but took his servant by the hand and departed; and, having mounted his animal, he set out without once looking back.

He did not stop until he had reached Girart. The count asked him what he had accomplished. " Do not detain me ! " cried the monk. " I am overwrought. I am going at once to the monastery to ring the bell; then I shall say a Te Deum and a prayer to Saint Thomas for his mercy in saving me from the hands of Charles Martel. You can arrange matters as you please with him; but you shall never again have me as your messenger."

In *Garin,* one of the barons sent two monks to the court of the king: he had bribed them to swear falsely, and one of these unfortunate clerics was half-killed by a knight of the opposite party. In this instance the monk was not only ridiculous: he was odious.

The bards treated the archbishops and the bishops with more consideration, because they were great lords and formed a part of the feudal hierarchy. However, in the lay *Hervis de Metz,* the episcopacy is represented as egotistical, grasping, miserly, and unwilling to contribute to the expense of the defense of the kingdom. When the king asked the archbishop of Reims, the highest ecclesiastical personage in France, to contribute money for the war against the Saracens, the prelate declared that he would not give a denier. Then one of the barons cried out: " We want other words than these. In Gaul, there are twenty thousand knights whose fireplaces and mills are held by the clerics. Let them remember that, or, by the Lord God, things shall take a different turn." But the archbishop persisted in his refusal. " We are clerics," he said; " our duty is to serve God. We will pray to Him to give you victory and guard you from death. And, as for you, knights, God commanded you to aid the clerics and to aid Holy Church. Why so many words? I swear by the great Saint Denis that you shall not have an Angevin sou."

As to the head of the church, the pope, it was indeed not to be expected that an epic written by the contemporaries of Philip Augustus would leave out a personage who at that period dominated the entire world and commanded kings as well as the humblest of the faithful. Therefore, the pope has his place in the lays, but an unimportant one, very different from the position he really held in history. He did not even possess Rome; he was hardly a sovereign, but rather a person of secondary importance, who appeared in the suite of the emperor or of the king of France, whose chief chaplain he would seem to have been. Note these first verses of *Girart:* " It was Pentecost, in the gay springtime. Charles was holding his court at Reims. Many open-hearted persons were present. The pope was there and preached." Later the pope, as an ordinary bishop, went as one of the embassy that Charles Martel sent to Constantinople. To be sure, the poet ascribed to him a moral authority over bishops and barons; he made him the chief counselor of the king of France: " He was a churchman who knew much, and spoke wisely and to the point." In *Garin,* the pope stood for peace and tried, with small success to be sure, to calm feudal passions by reminding the barons that their first duty was to make peace among themselves and to march against the enemies of their faith. This all contains something of historical fact; but, on the whole, it is certain that the literature of chivalry lessens and at pleasure effaces the religious sovereign who dominated the middle ages.

On the whole, the feudal class despised the priest, as peaceful and lazy; it relegated him to the church, there to preach virtues contrary to those he practised. Besides, the noble envied the wealth of the church and considered himself robbed of all that was given to the church. The author of *Hervis de Metz* very naïvely and bluntly says as much at the beginning of his poem:

" To-day when a man falls ill, and lies down to die, he does not think of his sons, or of his nephews, or of his cousins; he summons the Black Monks of Saint Benedict, and gives them all his lands, his revenues, his ovens, and his mills. The men of this age are impoverished, and the clerics are daily becoming richer."

*

* *

But the nobles and the clerics did not stop with words. Wars between them were so frequent and so common that they hold a place of high importance in historical documents. If they occupied the attention of the chroniclers to such an extent, it is because they were so conspicuous a manifestation of the turbulence of medieval life, so evident a form of social disorder and of class antipathy.

There was war between the lay and the ecclesiastical seigniors in all provinces and in nearly all cantons. For there was not a city in France where the count did not find himself at variance with the bishop or the chapter. The step from disagreement to violence was not a long one in the middle ages; hence, every lord's donjon implied danger to the neighboring monastery. From the top to the bottom of the feudal system the same disposition appears: the men of the castle tried to deprive the men of the church of their lands, their revenues, their rights, and their serfs. At any rate, they made their living by pillaging ecclesiastical domains and appropriating treasures accumulated in the sanctuaries through the devotion of the faithful.

The hungry and needy noble from the inferior classes of feudalism found that the cleric and the monk were temptingly rich, and he attacked and despoiled them. The barons from the upper ranks complained that their political and judicial sovereignty was being appropriated by the tribunals of the church and by the temporal power of the clerics; and, accordingly, they attacked the ecclesiastical powers in order to prevent their expansion. One should not, however, look at these conflicts from so narrow or so mean a point of view as to exclude their larger significance. Undeniably, the sources show that the seigniors, both great and small, engaged very freely in pillaging the lands of the church; but in the conflict between the baron and the bishop, as in the struggles between the citizen and the cleric, the first manifestation of a lay spirit, the first revolt of the civil power against religious authority is to be found. In the lower levels of society we have the exploitation by the feudal lord, who forces the granary and the cellar of the monks, puts their serfs to ransom, steals their cattle, and returns to his castle when his raid is complete. In the upper levels, we have the great lords of France gathering about Philip Augustus, as they did in the year 1205, when they protested as a body against the exaggerated development of ecclesiastical jurisdiction, and opposed the political and financial encroachment of the papal

power. In each case it is war on the church; to the modern
world, the second is of greater interest.

The church knew how to defend herself against all kinds
of attacks. One need not believe, because of the complaints
of preachers like Jacques of Vitry, that the church was always an unresisting and resigned victim. She defended herself from feudal violence by her temporal power, by appealing to the king or the pope for aid, or by excommunication.
At the beginning of the thirteenth century this weapon of
excommunication was not as dulled as some have been wont
to say. To be sure, the seigniors of that time took excommunication and interdict more lightly than ever before; they
had become accustomed to them and could resist for a period
before yielding. But we know from many narratives that in
the end they were often compelled to make honorable reparation. In this epoch, when faith was still intense, a baron
could at a pinch endure a personal excommunication; it was
more difficult for him to force his subjects to submit to an
interdict.

If he became accustomed to these censures, the church was
in a measure responsible, for she had multiplied them beyond
all bounds. Not only did churchmen in their internal quarrels excommunicate each other without adequate reason, but,
on the pretext of defending themselves against laymen, they
most grievously abused this weapon. Taking the seigniors
of the time of Philip Augustus for any given date or any
one year, one would find surprisingly few of them who were
not, or had not been, censured with interdict or excommunication. To demonstrate this, it is sufficient to run through the
chronicles, the correspondence—especially that of the pope,—
and the cartularies of bishoprics and abbeys: the barons who
are mentioned are excommunicated or their lands are interdicted. The list of them would be interminable: it would
contain very nearly all the seigniors of France, not
excepting the king, the dukes, or the sovereign counts. This
proves, in the first place, that the misdeeds and aggressions
of feudalism were innumerable; it also proves that the church
punished too readily and too lightly. The popes themselves
were obliged to recognize this and to urge ecclesiastics to
exercise greater moderation.

We will illustrate this by a single example. There is no doubt that the counts of Champagne, at the end of the twelfth and beginning of the thirteenth century, were among the great barons who maintained the best order in their seigniory and showed the greatest respect for the church, its officers, and its goods. Blanche, countess of Navarre, and her son, Thibaud IV, who was for a long time held in tutelage, were neither persecutors nor pillagers. But we know of at least seven sentences of excommunication or interdict laid on them by the bishops of Champagne. If the seigniorial officers so much as seized the goods of a subject of an abbey or of a chapter, a censure was sure to fall on the countess. Things went so far that Innocent III had to ask several bishops of Champagne to be more restrained in pronouncing anathemas against the sovereigns of the fief and their subjects, and in laying interdicts on their cities and towns. Once Honorius III even cancelled a sentence of excommunication laid on Countess Blanche by the abbot of Saint-Denis.

It is clear that there were abuses, but these abuses are well explained by the irritation and the exasperation of the clerics at the incessant attacks of the nobility. When a count and a bishop—that is, two great barons—were involved, the contestants could be considered equals. But what could one do, and what other weapon besides excommunication could one employ, when the aggressor, in a coat of mail, surrounded by his band, and inaccessible in his tower, attacked an isolated monastery? And this was what occurred every day. It was the monk who was the ordinary victim of the small as well as of the great feudal captains. War on the monk was one of the principal occupations of feudal lords.

To obtain an inkling of the persistence with which a family of castellans, even of the lesser nobility, attacked a neighboring monastery, one has only to open a cartulary, such as that of the abbey of Saint-Avit, near Orléans. In it one finds that the seigniorial house of *Boelli*, or Boyau (the name is not aristocratic), is at variance for several generations with the monks of the abbey. In 1183, the monks complained that Joscelin Boyau imposed arbitrary taxes on their village of Séris and overwhelmed it with outrages. They appealed to the bishop of Orléans. The latter could not do much, and he sent them to the lord of the region, Thibaud V, count of Blois, who took the people of Séris under his protection—not, alas! for nothing, but in consideration of an annual rental of two *setiers* of hay for each house, payable at Blois. In the middle ages the miserable peasants had no choice: to escape destruction at the hands of the petty lords, they were compelled to suffer encroachment at the hands of the great. And even then the guarantee was very often illusory. One is led to believe that Thibaud's promise of protection did not have much effect, for, in 1198, the tenants of Séris once more complained that Foucher and Philip Boyau tried to compel them to turn and haul the hay on the seigniorial meadows. In 1217, the conflict became more bitter. Hamelin, the head of the Boyau family, was then a canon of Mans; despite that, he remained a proprietor and a seignior, and was as much as ever an enemy of the monks. He claimed that the men of Séris were bound to turn the hay on his fields, carry it to his granary of Beaugency, convey the trellis for his vines to the same place, bring him fuel at Christmas, send him annually a goose or three chickens, and pay the taille twice a year (an arbitrary procedure already enforced by his ancestor Joscelin). Finally, he claimed the right of high and low justice over the village. Unable to defend his men, the abbot of Saint-Avit again appealed to the bishop of Orléans, who made an agreement with Hamelin Boyau to end hostilities. Hamelin agreed to abandon all his claims, in consideration of the sum of twenty livres in cash. But all the members of this terrible family had not subscribed to the agreement. There was one, named Renaud, who had laid hands on certain properties of the men of Saint-Avit and of the abbey itself, and who refused to surrender them. In 1219, he was excommunicated. After five years it became necessary to aggravate the sentence; and we still have a letter to this effect, sent by the bishop of Orléans to the curés of all the parishes of his diocese. " Every Sunday and feast day," he wrote, " after having rung the bells and lighted the candles, you shall denounce the aforementioned Renaud as excommunicate and you shall consider as interdicted all those who have anything to do with him." Of this long strife between the monks of Saint-Avit and the Boyau family we have only given the incidents falling within the reign of Philip Augustus; but it had begun before, and it did not end until long after. In the middle ages, trials, conflicts, and wars lasted for centuries, and were transmitted, like an inheritance, from generation to generation; for, in spite of treaties and truces, every one reasserted his claims and no one renounced what he considered a right. What was happening in this little corner of Beauce in Orléans was taking place wherever a seignior and an abbot were rivals, and often the misdeeds were more serious.

In 1187, Raoul, seignior of Châteauroux, assembled a strong army, burned the villages of the abbey of Déols, massacred the inhabitants, and expelled the monks of Déols from several of their priories. Ten years later, Andrew of Chauvigny, his successor, was excommunicated for outrages against the same abbey. In Bourbonnais, Gui of Dampierre, the new lord of Bourbon, persecuted the priory of Saint-Pourçain, seized its fiefs and domains, ravaged its leased farms, and even went so far as to do violence to the persons of the prior and the monks. After him, Archambaud, his son, continued to treat the monks as enemies. The abbot of Tournus, superior of Saint-Pourçain, found it necessary to ask Philip Augustus to intervene. In the region of Reims and of Laon the abbeys, such as those of Saint-Martin of Laon and of Signy, were literally devoured by a host of barons—the seigniors of Coucy, Pierrepont, Rozoy, Rumigny, Château-Porcien, and Rethel. In a document of 1203, Roger of Rozoy confesses his mistakes and admits that he had often stolen the grain and the cattle of the monks. Sometimes the monks resisted, and one day there was a bloody battle in the woods between the men of the count of Château-Porcien and the lay brothers of the abbey of Signy. In Champagne, the seigniors of Joinville were at open war with the abbeys of Montier-en-Der and of Saint-Urbain; in Provence, the seigniors of Castellane, with the monks of Saint-Victor of Marseilles. It was the same in Vendôme, where the abbots of Trinité had, since the foundation of their abbey in the middle of the eleventh century, suffered the daily persecutions of the counts of Vendôme. Jean I, count of Vendôme, had forced the monks of Trinité to leave the abbey and to take refuge in one of their priories for fourteen months. He was excommunicated. Three years later, one fine day in 1180 he was seen entering the monastery barefooted, to beg pardon of the abbot. This was an exact repetion of a scene which had been enacted a little less than a hundred years before, when the grandfather of this very Jean, Geoffroi-Jourdain, who also had forced an abbot of Vendôme into exile, made his peace with the whole chapter. And Bouchard, the son and associate of Jean I, count of Vendôme, rivaled his father in violence, and burdened the subjects of the abbey with exactions and unlawful tithes to such a degree that Henry II, king of England, believed it necessary to compel him to release his victims. Covetousness of monastic goods was a strong passion among the feudal lords, an irrepressible tendency transmitted with the blood.

It is seldom that we possess the details of these conflicts or wars between the donjon and the abbey. However, one monk, Hugh of Poitiers, was thoughtful enough to relate the incidents of the interminable struggle which the celebrated abbey of Vézelay carried on against the counts of Nevers, its hereditary and indefatigable persecutors: a typical struggle, which lasted through the whole of the twelfth century, and caused the popes, the French bishops, and the kings of France to interfere almost every year, without ever completely succeeding in disarming the seignior and protecting the abbot. Unfortunately, this exceedingly instructive and often dramatic history of Hugh of Poitiers ends long before the death of Louis VII. For the period of Philip Augustus we have only the letters of Innocent III, which are, to be sure, detailed enough. One of them describes the relations between Hervé of Donzy, count of Nevers, and Gautier, abbot of Vézelay, in 1211 and 1212; and from it we can obtain a good idea of the persistence of feudal enmities and the vexations of all kinds to which clerics were exposed.

The underlying cause of this long conflict was that the abbot of Vézelay claimed to be a vassal of the pope, to belong solely to the domain of Saint Peter, and to owe no service, pecuniary or other, to the count of Nevers. The counts, on the other hand, claimed that they were the legal guardians and the natural patrons of the abbey, and that, therefore, the monks owed them many services, especially that of entertaining them and their knights when they appeared at the abbey—in other words, what the people of the middle ages called "food and lodging." As soon as Gautier was elected abbot in 1207, he had to endure the same exactions and indignities as his predecessors at the hand of Count Hervé of Donzy.

First, Hervé claimed that every newly installed abbot of Vézelay was in duty bound to pay him an accession fee; Gautier refused to recognize this claim but, to appease the enemy, like one appeases a dog by tossing him a bone, he gave the count a gift of five hundred livres. This did not satisfy the count, who found other means of extortion. He forced the abbot to pay nine hundred livres to a citizen of Bourges, although the monastery was in no wise indebted to this individual, under pretext that he, the count, was guarantor of the debt. A Jew, who had been converted and baptised, had given one hundred livres to the abbey; but later he returned to Judaism, as the pope said, "like a dog to his vomiting." Hervé of Donzy forced the abbot to turn the hundred livres of this renegade Jew into the count's treasury. He often sent his officers to seize the beasts of burden, the carts, or the subjects of the abbey, and used them to transport the supplies of his castles. Then, instead of returning them without delay, he kept them for three or four weeks. He let his agents cut down the forests of the abbot as they pleased; he received and protected malefactors who pilfered the goods of the monks; he summoned the abbot and the monks before his tribunal, although, according to their privileges, they were not liable to judgment before any lay court. Several times he blockaded the roads and paths which led to the abbey, so that the monks could not obtain the water and the wood which they needed. At harvest time, he prevented the servants of the abbey from gathering their grapes and selling their crops; and he laid violent hands on the carts which carried food, wine, and other necessities to the abbey. The abbot finally complained to Philip Augustus, who commanded Hervé to cease these persecutions. The baron was thereafter apparently quiet; but in fact hostilities continued: for, if the count himself did not attack them, he left the field free for all their other enemies.

Evidence of this is found in the fact that the land of the count was open to the coming and going of a band of robbers, who were one day surprised in one of his villas with booty taken from the monks. For some little time these malefactors established a sort of blockade around Vézelay, so effective that the monks and the servants of the monastery could not go out without peril. A vassal of Count Hervé, named Joscelin, overwhelmed the monks with outrages, and seized their horses and everything else that he found worth taking; he even went so far as to invade a priory of the abbey and appropriate its appurtenances. The abbot complained to the count; the latter, who with one word could have stopped the misdeeds of Joscelin and the other aggressors, did not see fit to restrain them. On the contrary, he himself seized the priory of Dornecy, took the revenues for six months, and prevented the monks from collecting the tithes. The monks of the priory, having no means of subsistence, would have abandoned the monastery in a body had not the count, yielding to better councils, restored their property. On the domain of Ascon, another property of the abbey, John, son of the provost, in spite of the opposition of the monks, succeeded in acquiring the provostship after his father, thus making the office hereditary. Instead of opposing this injustice, the count, in defiance of the prerogatives of the church, sanctioned it and commanded the abbot to appear before lay judges with the new provost.

These are the deeds of the count of Névers which provoked the abbot of Vézelay to clamor for justice and reparation. The count lent a deaf ear. One day, when the demands especially annoyed him, he threatened to throw the prior of the monastery and his colleagues into a fish-pond. It was finally necessary for half of the monks of the abbey to go to Nevers for a definitive interview with the count. They prostrated themselves before him and humbly proffered their request. He refused to grant it. Then they begged his councilors to urge him to come to some permanent understanding. After long negotiations, these replied that the abbey could obtain the good-will of the count only on the condition that the monks and the citizens of Vézelay pay him the sum of a thousand Provins livres (more than one hundred and fifty thousand francs). " It will ruin our community! " cried the monks. The citizens of Vézelay, overcome at having to pay so great a sum, declared to the abbot that, if he did not immediately go to Rome to beg the protection of the pope, they would all leave Vézelay and take refuge in the towns of the king of France. An urgent appeal was made to the bishops, to the archbishops, to the great barons of the realm, to the duke of Burgundy, and to Philip Augustus himself. All these persons, by prayer or by menace, insisted that the count of Nevers stop persecuting the abbey, make reparation for the damage inflicted upon it, and take the monks and citizens under his protection as he ought. Hervé of Donzy listened to none of this.

No longer able to endure it, the abbot decided to go to Rome to appeal to Innocent III. As soon as he was gone, the outrages multiplied. It was about vintage-time of 1211. The citizens and the monks of Vézelay thought that they could finish gathering their grapes in plenty of time. Suddenly the soldiers of the count rushed in, chased the pickers from the vineyards, overturned the grapes already picked, wounded the servants of the abbey, and took or killed their horses. The monastery lost five hundred livres; the citizens more than three thousand marks; besides which, the officers of Hervé wrecked the mill of the provost of the abbey and carried away the millstone and the ironwork.

Philip Augustus, notified anew, seriously threatened the count if he went on in this fashion. The count for some time thereafter heeded his warning. In passing, we should note that the king of France had a price for his intervention: all the profit the monks made from their wine went to the royal treasury. Finally, Innocent III, too, became active. In a letter of November 13, 1211, he commanded the bishop of Paris and Robert of Courçon, his legate, to excommunicate the count of Nevers and, if need be, lay his dominions under an interdict, if the king of France could not, within two months, compel the count to sign a treaty of peace with the abbey.

All these details sufficiently show the persistence of the

seigniors, their hatred for their victims, and the difficulty of inducing them to surrender their prize. Nobody could really do anything. The king of France himself only obtained an ephemeral satisfaction, obedience for a few days. The pope entered the lists with his thunders; would he have any better fortune? An excommunication coming from the head of the church had a particular gravity; however, it did not have any important effect; for Hervé of Donzy allowed himself to be excommunicated, and he remained excommunicated to the end of the year 1213. And then it was not the excommunication which obliged him to submit and to make peace with his enemy, the monastery. To subdue this recalcitrant, recourse to another weapon was necessary. The papacy had at its command a variety of resources.

Hervé of Donzy, seignior of Gien, had in 1190 become count of Nevers by his marriage to Mathilda, heiress of the ancient counts. This marriage had been arranged by Philip Augustus, who took the castle and city of Gien as his commission (the word is vulgar, but is very appropriate in this instance). Like all barons, Hervé had rivals and enemies. They discovered that the heiress whom he had married was his relative in the fourth degree, and at that time the church did not sanction such marriages, unless she had some particular reason for tolerating them. In 1205, in consequence of a formal protest by the duke of Burgundy, Innocent III ordered an inquiry into the relationship of Hervé and Mathilda: a pure formality, no doubt, which was without result, for, until 1212, no steps were taken toward the dissolution of the marriage. But in June, 1212, after the crisis of Vézelay and the excommunication of the count of Nevers, Innocent III, at just the right time, recollected that he had begun the inquiry and ordered it to be resumed. That touched the count in a sensitive spot, for, if the marriage was dissolved, the heiress would claim her inheritance, the county of Nevers, and Hervé of Donzy would fall back into the rank of petty seigniors. What the pope had foreseen happened: as soon as the count's agent in Rome learned that the order of inquiry had been despatched to France, he presented himself before Innocent, " troubled by a great grief," says the letter of the pope, " and humbly prayed us, giving us all possible assurances, that the business of the inquiry be countermanded; and promised, on the part of the count, that the abbey of Vézelay should suffer no more persecution.'' Innocent III commanded his agent to suspend the inquiry as soon as the count of Nevers made peace and gave reasonable satisfaction to the monks and to the church.

The terms of peace were dictated by the pope himself on April 12, 1213. He determined that the count of Nevers might appear in the monastery of Vézelay only twice a year, at Easter and at the feast of Mary Magdalene, and that the monks should at those times give him a hundred livres, his *procuration*. The abbot, on his part, was required to renounce all claims for damages, except for the tithes of Dornecy; for these the count was expected to give compensation. The sanction of the king of France was also necessary to this arrangement. On these conditions only was the count of Nevers to be absolved from excommunication.

Hervé of Donzy submitted. But there still remained the question which he had most at heart—the validity of his marriage. Innocent III kept this sword of Damocles suspended over Hervé's head for some time. The count wrote the pope an urgent letter, in which he protested that his marriage had lasted for thirteen years (*in conspectu ecclesiae*); that Mathilda had borne him a daughter; and that, finally, the pope ought to do him a favor, because he had taken a vow to go on a crusade. On December 20, 1213, he secured the papal dispensation which declared his marriage forever unassailable. All this was necessary to compel a feudal lord to respect an abbey. Yet one cannot positively assert that, once the peace was signed and the dispensation obtained, the count of Nevers did not again resume his former attitude toward the monks of Vézelay.

The temptation was too great and the prey too easy. On the whole, the feudal barons did not have much trouble in terrorizing and plundering monasteries located in the country or surrounded only by an ordinary market-town. It would appear more difficult to attack clerics in the cities, but in these the barons had the coöperation of the citizens, who were also hostile to monks and canons. The cathedral chapters, those rich and powerful communities of clerics which lived

in closed and fortified cloisters as well as the abbeys, excited
the cupidity of the laymen.   There was, then, a permanent
and often a lively conflict in cities, because the populace took
part in it.

In Chartres, for instance, the chapter of Notre-Dame and
the count of Chartres were in a perpetual conflict throughout
the middle ages.   The officers of the seignior, backed by the
citizens, incessantly harassed the canons, and grave incidents
often occurred.   In 1194, the countess of Chartres had one
of the servants of the chapter seized and imprisoned, and
all his goods confiscated.   In 1207, her agents wanted to take
a woman and two men from the chapter, and the excesses
which were committed in this connection were so extreme
that the quarrel was carried to the king's court.   In 1210, a
chorister of Notre-Dame was arrested and thrown into prison
by the officers of the count; in retaliation, the chapter laid
an interdict on the city.   A few months later a formidable
riot broke out; the cathedral was threatened, and the house
of the dean was much damaged with stones and axes.   Philip
Augustus was compelled to reëstablish order and to punish
the guilty, among whom were seigniorial officers.   In most
of the cities with chapters there were similar occurrences:
lawsuits and battles between barons and clerics, violations
of cloisters, plunder and destruction of canon's houses; fortunate, indeed, were those canons who suffered no bodily
injury!

In 1217, the chapter of Laon, victim of the persecutions
and the depredations of the count of Rethel, denounced him
at Rome.   The pope excommunicated him.   The count braved
the anathema for two years; finally, Honorius III decided
to take more vigorous measures against him: he ordered an
interdict laid on all his lands, and on all parts through which
he should travel, and absolved his vassals from the oath of
fealty as long as he remained under sentence of interdict.
"And, if the culprit still persists in his error," wrote the
pope, "let him take care that he is not condemned as a
heretic."   The same chapter had, the year before, been the
victim of a more serious attack—one that scandalized the
whole of France.   Enguerran of Coucy seized Adam of Cour-
landon, dean of the church of Laon, and kept him in prison

for more than a year. Excommunication, interdict, prayers, threats, the intervention of the archbishop of Reims and the king of France—all were tried to obtain the deliverance of the captive. It was not until 1218 that this Enguerran of Coucy decided to seek absolution and to give satisfaction to the chapter.

Attacks on the canons then complete the story. We do not mention aggressions against curés, because the sources of our epoch say nothing about them. But, perhaps, attacks on curés were less frequent, for the simple reason that the baron, being patron or even proprietor of the whole or a part of the parish church, could select a parson that suited him and could lay hands on the tithes without much hindrance. How could a plain curé have prevented this, even if he had not been nominated by the seignior? In any case, the curé was not in a position to resist, and the church condemned the exploitation of the inferior clergy only under compulsion. Monasteries, and chapters sometimes, succeeded in defending themselves; they were assisted by bishops, kings, and popes. We have already given examples of the intervention of the supreme head of the church, and must recognize the full importance of the rôle which Rome assumed in defending monks and canons against the excesses and depredations of feudalism. But the pope could not act everywhere at once or under all circumstances: he was far away, and usually he had only a moral authority to oppose to the assailants. The king of France also fulfilled his traditional duty of protector of churches; but he rarely did it gratuitously, and his police operations were very intermittent. The barons whom he warned to surrender some monastery might have objected that he himself did not always set the best example. "One day," relates Rigord, the historian of Philip Augustus, "the king, passing by Saint-Denis on affairs of the realm, installed himself in the abbey as though he were entering his own room (*sicut in propriam cameram suam*). The abbot of Saint-Denis, William of Gap, was overcome with fright (*nimio timore perculsus*), for the king required of him a thousand marks in silver. The abbot, having assembled the brethren of the chapter, tendered his resignation." That is how the king of France protected the monks of the most regal of his abbeys! In all stages of the feudal hierarchy, brigandage, violence, and extortion were employed in the systematic fleecing of monastic and capitular churches. For the few cases where seigniors were intimidated or repressed by royal soldiers and papal excommunications, how many murders, arsons, and robberies committed against the church remained unnoticed and unpunished?

On this subject there is a significant document which tells much about the acts of the feudal barons. It is a record of the statutes of the synod of Toul held May 8, 1192, by Eudes of Vaudémont, bishop of Toul. Here are a few of these statutes:

"It is forbidden under pain of anathema to celebrate religious services at any place, in which objects taken from churches or clerics are kept even for a single night.—The robbers and the receivers are excommunicated.—These interdicts and anathemas are applicable to princes and great barons who commit robberies.—The excommunication of the guilty shall be renewed every Sunday in the churches of the diocese.—Those who give them shelter are also excommunicate.—The anathema shall fall upon all men who abuse their rank and power by taking horses or wagons from monasteries. —If in spite of his excommunication a prince or baron has divine services performed the priest who officiates shall also be excommunicated and forever deprived of his prebend."

It is impossible to make a better statement showing the extent to which feudalism lived on pillage; or the power of excommunication to hold it in check.

*

* *

The bishops had to shift for themselves. Everywhere they were at war with the feudal barons: the count of Auxerre fought against the bishop of Auxerre; the duke of Normandy, against the archbishop of Rouen; the duke of Brittany, against the bishop of Nantes; the count of Auvergne, against the bishop of Clermont; the viscount of Béarn, against the bishop of Oloron; the count of Rodez against the bishop of Rodez; the count of Forez, against the archbishop of Lyons; the count of Armagnac, against the archbishop of Auch; the count of Foix, against the bishop of Urgel; the count of Soissons, against the bishop of Soissons; the viscount of Polignac, against the bishop of Puy; the nobility of Verdun, against the bishop of Verdun. All regions of France were victims of the same evil.

This enumeration, which could easily be lengthened, shows that conflicts between the two powers were part of the regular order of things. To be sure, they did not everywhere have the same causes and the same character: here they were simple acts of brigandage, there combats for sovereignty; here a listless and intermittent conflict, there a violent and merciless war. But everywhere the results were identical: depredation in the country, fights and brawls in the city, innumerable excommunications and interdicts on the part of the church, exasperation and vengeance on the part of the feudal lords, who did not halt even at assassination.

Let us glance into Béarn between 1212 and 1215, the time when Philip Augustus was engaged in the struggle against the great coalition which culminated at Bouvines. The viscount of Béarn, Gaston VI, was at war with the bishop of Oloron, Bernard of Morlaas. He was accused of sympathizing with the Albigenses. Bandits in his pay had entered the cathedral church of Sainte-Marie of Oloron and had committed all kinds of excesses—such as dashing the sacred utensils on the floor, amusing themselves by wearing the pontifical vestments, preaching, and even singing a mock mass. Gaston VI let this sacrilege go unpunished; he attacked the clergy; and was publicly considered a persecutor of the church. In 1213, the council of Vabres declared him excommunicated, and absolved his subjects from the oath of fealty. This excommunication lasted two years. Finally, Gaston submitted and made an apology to the bishop. There follows the proof of his defeat, written by himself.

"Know all ye, present and future, that I, Gaston, viscount of Béarn, at the suggestion of Satan have been guilty of many misdeeds against the church of Sainte-Marie of Oloron. I have caused much damage, both to this cathedral church and to the subjects of the bishop. For this reason and for many other excesses committed by me, I have been smitten by several excommunications. I have persevered for a long time in my obstinate resistance. Finally, the grace of God inspiring me, I decided to obey, and I earnestly prayed Bernard of Morlaas, bishop of the said church, to deliver me from the curse which bound me and to impose on me the penitence which I had merited. He has removed all the sentences of excommunication laid upon me. Although my crimes were without number and the objects taken by me from the church incalculable, still to indemnify the church for her losses, I have given her all the men and all the rights which I possessed in the town of Sainte-Marie of Oloron."

Here the bishop easily triumphed over the feudal power, because he was favored by exceptional circumstances. The Albigenses and their partizans had just been defeated in the battle of Muret. The south was in the hands of Simon de Montfort and the catholic bishops. The southern seigniors, who, like Gaston of Béarn, were at the same time the persecutors of the church and the supporters of heresy, had to yield to force and repent or have their lands confiscated by the leaders of the crusade.

In the north and in the middle part of France it was less dangerous to fight against the bishops. Let us glance into Auvergne, a savage country, where a pillaging feudalism had the habit not only of putting monasteries to ransom, but of fighting with the bishops of Clermont and of Puy. We shall later speak of the bloody drama which stained the bishopric of Puy. Clermont was the center of a long-standing war between the bishops and the counts of Auvergne, which had endured from the beginning of the twelfth century. The bishop, relentlessly despoiled and maltreated by his rival, escaped from prison and even worse dangers by calling the king of France to his aid. Louis VI and later Louis VII invaded Auvergne, forced the count to submit, and reëstablished the bishop in his see and in his domains; but the king had hardly turned his back, before the prelate and the baron were again at odds. The war was all the more bloody and furious because the bishop and the count often belonged to the same family. It happened that in this house of Auvergne the older brother inherited the county and the younger brother the bishopric. What feuds between brothers are, is well known. There was a similar case during the reign of Philip Augustus: Robert I, bishop of Clermont, and his brother, Gui II, count of Auvergne, were at open war for eighteen years, from 1197 to 1215, during which time the count was perpetually excommunicated and the bishop continually imprisoned.

It goes without saying that, if the count of Auvergne was a brigand, the bishop of Clermont was not exactly a sweet and angelic minister of peace. Intrenched in his strong castles of Lezoux and of Mauzun, he was a robber chieftain. Which of these brothers committed the first offense? According to the count of Auvergne, it was the bishop who began it; and, indeed, there is some question as to which of the two was the more irritating and belligerent. The count, in 1198, wrote to Pope Innocent III to implore his protection against the bishop (it was usually the reverse), and this protection he paid for in advance, by giving the Roman church the castle of Usson, which he had just constructed.

"I beg you to defend me against my brother Robert, bishop of Clermont. With his bands of free-booters and of Basques and in violation of all law, he devastates my land and subjects it to arson, murder, and brigandage. I cast myself at the feet of Your Holiness and beg you to stop these outrages and to annul the sentence of excommunication which he has pronounced against my land."

The count of Auvergne sought the support of the pope, because the bishop, as was usual in such cases, had appealed to the king of France. The question was still more complicated by the conflicting claims of England and of France to the sovereignty of Auvergne; the bishop was for the Capetians, and the count for the Plantagenets. This was what prolonged and embittered the hostilities.

Between the two brothers, periods of peace were not long. After a semblance of reconciliation in 1201, the war began afresh in 1206, more violent and more murderous than ever. The bishop was thrown into prison by the count for the third time; the latter was again excommunicated; but he revenged himself by stealing the goods of the church. He stormed the abbey of Mozac, which the abbot took pleasure in enriching; maltreated and dispersed the monks, demolished their buildings, appropriated their treasure, and, to cap the climax, carried away the famous relic of Saint Austremoine and placed it in one of his castles. An enormous scandal!

A bishop imprisoned; an abbey, under the protection of the king of France, violated and destroyed! From all the religious centers of Auvergne a loud cry of indignation rose to Philip Augustus, who finally decided to intervene effectively between the irreconcilable brothers. But he did not, as his father, Louis VII, and his grandfather, Louis VI, intervene as a distinterested arbitrator. He interfered to award himself the object of litigation—to appropriate the county of Auvergne, which he had coveted for a long time. The chief of his retainers, Cadoc, and his vassal, Gui of Dampierre, arrived, in 1210, with a great army. They besieged the castles of Riom and of Tournoël, took one after another the one hundred and twenty donjons of Count Gui, captured innumerable prisoners, among them the son of the count, and in three years finished the difficult conquest. When the French entered the famous fortress of Tournoël, perched on its volcanic rock and reputed inaccessible, they found in it a quantity of missals, of reliquaries, of sacerdotal vestments, and of other precious objects taken from Mozac and various other abbeys of the region.

The church had the last word: the bishop of Clermont succeeded, but to the detriment of his family and his political power. The county of Auvergne was dismembered forever: the king of France, installed at Riom, occupied the greater part of it; and Gui II, despoiled of his patrimony and obliged to take refuge in a neighboring province, could meditate at leisure on the inconvenience which results when civil power is out of harmony with religious power.

Other barons at the same time gave proof of this. War on the episcopacy had also broken out in Brittany with especial violence. There was the same difference between Gui II, count of Auvergne, and Peter of Dreux, count of Brittany, that there is between a needy and covetous mountain king and the suzerain and sovereign of a great province, independent by its traditions and its position. Peter of Dreux was a self-willed, determined man, with a definite political policy. He wanted to be master of Brittany, just as the king of France was of the Capetian domain, and to suppress all local powers, feudal as well as ecclesiastical. On account of this aim he deserved his surname of Mauclerc (*mauvais clerc*):

he passed his life in fighting the church, which was stronger
in Brittany than in any other place. In this country the
parish clergy collected, besides the tithe, the galling taxes of
tiercage (a tax levied on the inheritance of personal property) and of *past nuptial* (a tax on marriages). The
bishops enjoyed regal rights, and pretended not to recognize the sovereignty of the count. Therefore, after 1217,
Peter of Dreux made aggressive war on the bishop of Nantes.
He let his agents pillage and burn episcopal houses; take
their lands and their revenues; imprison, maim, and even
torture the clerics. The bishop and his chapter, forced to
leave Brittany, tried to find a refuge in the neighboring
dioceses.

Several times excommunicated by his victim, Peter of
Dreux even braved the pope. Honorius III, in 1218, reproached him for all his misdeeds and ordered him to abstain
" from these works of death, which would lead to eternal
damnation if he did not repent "; let him beware lest his
resistance to excommunication expose him to the suspicion
of heresy. In any case, if he persists in his conduct, the apostolic authority will punish him and will, if it is necessary,
absolve his subjects and his vassals from their oath of fealty.
" Open your eyes," said the pope in closing, " and take care
not to put your foot into such a dangerous net that you cannot withdraw it." The excommunication and the interdict
were not removed before the full submission of the count,
January 28, 1220. The conditions which were imposed on
him were severe: he had to restore all that he had taken,
disavow and punish his agents, indemnify all ecclesiastical
subjects who had suffered violence in the war, renounce their
homage, and finally promise to restore the bishop of Nantes
and his church to the condition in which they were at the
beginning of hostilities.

The men of the middle ages resigned themselves all the
more easily to the humiliation of defeat and of reparation,
because at that time no one was ashamed to yield to the
church; and, besides, they did not long observe the treaties
by which they abandoned their rights. A few years later,
Peter of Dreux renewed the war, this time much more skil-
fully, for he united all the lay seigniors of his duchy in a

persistent campaign against the privileges and the jurisdiction of the bishops.

But it was in another part of feudal France that the war between the count and the bishop reached its maximum of violence and of savagery. The count of Auxerre and of Tonnerre, Peter of Courtenay, a relative of Philip Augustus, was a passionate, brutal noble, absolutely lacking moderation and prudence. Opposed to him was the bishop of Auxerre, Hugh of Noyers, also a noble of rude disposition, very much attached to his temporal interests, and fully determined to bend neither before the feudal barons nor even before the king: in brief, an incorrigible and bellicose minister of God, a fighting bishop. These two men were destined to collide and to engage in continuous and bitter conflict.

Because of their quarrels, the city of Auxerre was under interdict for nearly fifteen years. One must imagine to what a convulsive and revolutionary condition a city under interdict was reduced, how consciences and social life were upset, to grasp the gravity of such a thing as the closing of the churches and the denial of the sacraments for so long a time. At most it was permitted to baptize children and give Extreme Unction to the dying. This critical situation, in the long run, became dangerous, for heresy appeared in the region, especially at Nevers and at La Charité, where certain miscreants had been burned, and the people could not be allowed to go without the sacraments and the mass. Hugh of Noyers and his chapter, knowing the obduracy of the count, finally adopted the following system: every time that the excommunicated count decided to enter the city, the bells of the great church of Auxerre were rung with all their force, to notify the inhabitants and the clerics. At that signal churches were closed, religious services were interrupted, and the city went into mourning. When the count left, the bells rang again, the sanctuaries reopened (except for the men and officers of Peter of Courtenay), and normal life was resumed. One can well understand how painful and irritating this procedure was for the count of Auxerre. "He could not," said the chronicler, "enter or leave the city without causing great confusion; and, above all, he did not dare stay long, because of the clamor of the people." The bishop had found an excellent means of dispossessing the count of his capital.

The anger of such an irascible man as Peter of Courtenay broke out from time to time in acts of vengeance. One day he entirely destroyed a church belonging to the bishop, the church of Saint-Adrien. Another time he had the eyes of one of the bishop's vassals plucked out. He plundered the domains of the church. In 1203, he was living in his city, which was, as a result, under interdict. The clergy had refused to give a little child ecclesiastical burial. The mother, weeping and wailing, sought Peter of Courtenay to lodge her complaint. With singular nicety, he ordered his officers to take the little body, to force the episcopal palace, and to inter the child in the sleeping-chamber of the bishop, before his bed. Hugh of Noyers hurled a new anathema against his enemy. Peter replied by expelling the bishop and his canons from Auxerre, saying that he did so at the command of Philip Augustus, who was also hostile to Hugh of Noyers. And in fact the king, who also had cause to complain of this troublesome prelate, sustained his relative, the count of Auxerre. The situation became grave, and the scandal intolerable. Innocent III wrote menacing letters to Peter of Courtenay and to Philip Augustus. The count laughed at them and continued his persecutions. One day he amused himself by pretending that he wanted to make peace with the church and end the affair honorably. He invited the bishop, the dean, the archdeacon, the cantor, and the other dignitaries of the chapter to come to Auxerre to receive his submission. The clerics, overjoyed, left their country homes, where they had taken refuge, to come back to the city; but they learned on the way that the count of Auxerre, far from thinking of a reconciliation, was sending his troops out after them. They immediately turned back, and, instead of stopping at a certain priory as they had intended, took another route. And it was well they did, for soon the soldiers of the count fell on this priory, broke down its gates with their axes, and searched all the cells like madmen, without finding those for whom they were looking.

The bishop realized that even the episcopal houses of the

country were no longer safe for him, and took refuge in the
monastery of Pontigny. Peter ordered the abbot of Pontigny
to expel his guest, and threatened to plunder the abbey in
case he was refused. Hugh of Noyers then decided to go
into exile. This time Innocent III lost patience: he wrote
to Philip Augustus that, if he did not force the count of
Auxerre to submit and allow the bishop to return to his city,
the king himself should be held responsible and should suffer
for the crime of his vassal. "Do not force me," said he,
"to lay the hand of correction on you, and take care that,
in persecuting a bishop noted as this one is for the rude
vigor with which he suppresses heretics, you do not gain the
reputation of being a fomentor of heresy."

Philip Augustus could not endure such a reproach. He
was then in the very midst of his wars with John Lackland
and his preparations for the conquest of Normandy: it was
no time for him to be embarrassed by a conflict with the
church. Peter of Courtenay, reduced to his own resources,
had to capitulate, and in 1204 he promised, seriously this
time, to humiliate himself before the bishop of Auxerre and
the archbishops of Bourges and of Sens. The demands of the
bishop surpass imagination. The chronicler of Auxerre tells
us that the ceremony of submission brought many clerics
into the city, and it is no wonder: the spectacle was certainly
novel. The count of Auxerre, barefooted, clad only in a shirt,
went into the bedroom of the bishop; with his own hands he
disinterred the body of the child buried there for some months,
"already putrid and emitting a sickening odor," and carried
the corpse on his own shoulders to the cemetery, where he
gave it final burial. "It was for his own safety," added
the chronicler, "that he humiliated himself thus before God;
God who knows how to bow the head and the neck of kings."

The vengeance of the bishop did not stop there. Peter
of Courtenay had as prime minister and executor a noble of
Auxerre, named Peter of Courçon, who was detested by the
clergy, because they knew it was he who had advised and
incited the count in the war he had waged against the church.
For a long time Hugh of Noyers could not injure this man,
because he was protected by the favor of his master. But
there came a day when Peter of Courçon fell into disgrace,

and the bishop of Auxerre hastened to profit by it. He had him arrested, put him on a cart with four wheels, and had him conveyed chained and bareheaded (he was absolutely bald) through all the streets and squares of Auxerre; he was followed by a hooting crowd.

To such a pass came the strife between the count and the bishop of Auxerre. Even after the death of Hugh of Noyers the strife continued. Peter of Courtenay was not on the best of terms with the bishop's successor, William of Seignelay, who also had a stubborn disposition, as was proved by his many conflicts with Philip Augustus. What would have happened one cannot tell, had not the count of Auxerre, one fine day, left the country to validate his rights to the Latin throne of Constantinople. Later, one finds in the *Chronique des évêques d'Auxerre* a very curious page, which shows to what degree the nobles of the region had been excited by their covetousness of ecclesiastical goods and their hatred of episcopal power. When, in 1220, Bishop William of Seignelay left Auxerre to take possession of the see of Paris, to which he had been transferred, his departure was a signal for an immense pillage by the great and petty barons of Auxerre. Barons and lords pounced upon the prey. Hervé of Donzy, count of Nevers, that persecutor of monks,—whose struggle with the abbey of Vézelay we already know,—entered Auxerre with an armed band, and most of the citizens, knowing of his cruelties and his exactions, fled. Seigniors of the lowest standing invaded the episcopal domains, sacked the villas of the bishop, ransomed and massacred his peasants. Even at Auxerre the chapter of the cathedral was not safe. The dean was seized by a noble and carried to a castle on the banks of the Saône, where he remained imprisoned a long time. One morning, as the monks were going to services, a troop of horsemen attacked them with naked swords, pursued them as far as the church, wounded one of them seriously, and crushed another under the hoofs of their horses.

Such incidents were happening almost everywhere; they gave a highly dramatic character to the war between the nobles and the clerics. But the fury of war and the exasperation of feelings could go still farther. The assassination of abbots and even of bishops by excommunicated nobles was fairly frequent. In 1181, and in 1207, two successive bishops of Verdun died violent deaths at the hands of seigniors with whom they were at war. In 1211, Geoffroi Belvant, abbot of Saint-Pierre of Couture, in Maine, was assassinated by Hamelin of Faigne, who contested with him the ownership of the fief of Semur. In reparation for this crime, Hamelin gave the monks an income of ten Mans sous, the fuel for one oven, and released the abbey from all homage. His sentence was light. In 1219, Gilles, lord of Saint-Michel in Laon, rid himself in the same way of the abbot of Saint-Michel, with whom he was at war. The murder was committed in the very cloister, and he who had planned it was barely fifteen years old. He promised, first, to go and fight the Albigenses; then to make a pilgrimage to Rome, where the pope would inflict penance upon him; every Friday, for fourteen years, he was to eat nothing but bread and water; he was to support three paupers, if he could not fast; three times a year, on a day of solemn procession, he was to discipline himself publicly; and he was to establish in perpetuity in the abbey of Saint-Michel a priest to pray for the soul of his victim. In 1222, the son of the viscount of Aubusson assassinated the prior of Felletin, a priory dependent on Saint-Martial of Limoges. But it was in 1220 that the great scandal of the epoch occurred. That would be a strange bit of history, an animated and tragic story, which would narrate the life and the strife of the bishops of Puy during the twelfth and thirteenth centuries against the unreasonable barons who surrounded them—the viscounts of Polignac, the seigniors of Montlaur, of Mercœur, of Rochbaron: a group of brigands who wanted a share of the proceeds of the pilgrimages to Notre-Dame of Puy; and who without truce quarreled with the prelate, intrenched in his cathedral church on the summit of Puy, about the sovereignty of Velay and the income from its taxes. In 1220, Bishop Robert of Meung, after having sustained a sanguinary war which poisoned his whole life, was assassinated by a knight whom he had excommunicated. Decidedly, it was a terrible epoch, and one in which it was not good to have enemies!

CHAPTER IX

THE NOBLE IN TIME OF PEACE

WHILE he was waging war on his own account or on that of the suzerain, in his own struggles or those of others, the noble was, as has been seen, by taste, habit, and necessity, a soldier whose service did not often cease. There were, however, in the interminable series of wars some intervals of peace and inactivity, especially during the winter season. When he had ceased pillaging, burning, and killing the enemy of the soil, how was he to employ his time?

In those days he had one favorite occupation, which was anything but peaceful. In order to keep his hand in training while resting, he battled in tournaments.[1]

In the historical ballad *Guillaume le Maréchal*, the recital of tournaments occupies almost three thousand of the twenty thousand verses. The author describes fifteen tournaments, which followed one another within a few years in the regions of Normandy, Chartres, and Perche. Moreover, he speaks only of the most celebrated and of those in which his hero took part. He says himself that he has not mentioned them all, and for this reason: " I cannot keep up with all the tournaments that take place; it would take great trouble to do that, for almost every fortnight there is a tournament in some place or other."

A tournament every fortnight! The frequence of this exercise is vouched for by other contemporary historians; by Lambert of Ardres, who shows us the counts of Guines and the lords of Ardres frequenting tournaments and spending money foolishly; by Gilbert of Mons, who informs so

---

[1] The tournament was called *torneamentum*, *gyrum*, or *hastiludium* in the Latin of contemporaries of Philip Augustus; *torneamentum* or *gyrum* because this military game, this practice at war, took place within fences or lists formed by palings placed in a circle or a square; *hastiludium* because the blows of the lance (*hasta*) play the important rôle, the lance being the noble's weapon *par excellence*.

well of the life of the lords of Lorraine and Belgium. According to him, every creation of new knights, every great marriage, had almost necessarily to be accompanied by a tournament, in which the young barons could exhibit their strength and bear their first arms. And this fact is fully confirmed by the ballad *Garin le Lorrain:* "Sire," said the messenger of Count Fromont to King Pepin, "the count has sent me to request a tournament for to-morrow morning. His son Fromondin is a new knight; the father wishes to see how he will bear his arms." The two tournaments which, in this lay, took place under the walls of Bordeaux were the immediate result of a gathering of knighthood.

But why this superabundance of tourneys? Because the tournament was a veritable military school; by these voluntary and regulated combats, one exercised and trained himself for that offensive and defensive strife which entirely filled the life of the noble. Thus it was, at least, that contemporaries justified the tournament. It will be sufficient to cite the well-known passage from the English chronicler, Roger of Hoveden:

"A knight cannot shine in war if he has not been prepared for it in the tournaments. He must have seen his own blood flow, have had his teeth crackle under the blow of his adversary, have been dashed to the earth with such force as to feel the weight of his foe, and, disarmed twenty times, he must twenty times have retrieved his failures, more set than ever upon the combat. Thus, will he be able to confront actual war with the hope of being victorious."

But was this a common institution throughout the whole of feudal Europe? No. It was thought, and indeed stated, in the time of Philip Augustus that the tournament was essentially a French custom, a fashion of our own, which spread quickly, it is true, into the neighboring provinces. With this opinion the English chroniclers agree; they call tournaments, French struggles (*conflictus gallici*); and the poem *Guillaume le Maréchal*, indeed, shows us Englishmen and Flemings constantly coming to France to frequent tournaments. It is for this, without doubt, that William Marshal, although a combatant of the first rank, proclaims the superiority of the French: "I speak of the French first. There is good reason why they ought to stand first: because of their pride, their valor, and the glory of their country." This confession from an English mouth is to be noted. According to several authors of the time, Richard the Lion-Hearted was the first to introduce into England the custom of tournaments, his object being to take away from the French just that incontestable superiority which their training had given them. The English took it up with such passion that Richard, a very practical financier in spite of his knightly tastes, saw a way of getting revenue by imposing a tax upon the knights who entered the lists.

Of French origin or not, be that as it may, the institution of the tournament was more flourishing in France than anywhere else; and, to get a clear impression of this fact, one should read the descriptions of scenes upon which the biographer of William Marshal dwells with an evident delight.

First of all, one notices that the tournament did not differ much from war properly so-called; that they were practically alike, except for the systematic pillage of fields and the massacres of peasants. The nobles armed themselves for the tournament exactly as for real battle; if they usually strove to capture each other for the sake of taking profit from ransoming their prisoners, it still happened that they wounded and killed each other. In 1208, when Philip Augustus decided to knight his son, Louis—that is, to emancipate him,—for the sake of precaution he caused him to subscribe to certain promises, among others never to take part in a tournament. Prince Louis, the future Louis VIII, had to content himself with attending the tournaments, which took place near his residence, as a simple spectator, wearing a helmet only: that is, in undress uniform, so that he might not be impelled to descend into the lists and use his lance. Why this precaution? Because Prince Louis was the only male heir to the crown, and the life of an heir-presumptive must not be subjected to any risk.

One of the reasons for the church's prohibition of the tournaments was simply that they were dangerous and even fatal to the nobility. But not the whole of the tournament depended on the battle. There were districts and circum-

stances in which the tournament was no more than a
parade, a military procession in the lists where the nobles
rode, richly clad and followed by servants, who bore their
arms. Such was the tournament of 1184, which was given at
Mainz in connection with the knighting of the son of Frederick Barbarossa. Gilbert of Mons states that this tournament was a peaceful one (*gyrum sine armis*). The knights,
he adds, were pleased with these festivities, at which they
carried their shields, lances, and banners with great pomp,
and coursed their horses, but without delivering any blows.
It may be that this was the German custom; it was certainly
not the French custom; indeed, all the tourneys described in
the poem *Guillaume le Maréchal* were serious combats, in
which they fought in earnest, even to the shedding of blood.

In these encounters it was not, indeed, a question of individual tilts between picked knights. The knighthood of several provinces appointed a rendezvous, and entire armies
entered the lists, to charge with eagerness upon one another.
In the tournament at Lagny-sur-Marne more than three thousand knights were engaged, and the biographer of William
Marshal relates in detail the composition of the force:
Frenchmen, Englishmen, Flemings, Normans, Angevins, and
Burgundians came to blows. It was on these occasions, especially, that rivalries, or rather those provincial hatreds which
played such a great part in the wars of the times, were given
free rein. Considering the number of combatants, a tourney
like that of Lagny, which was fought in the open field, exactly resembled a decisive action of real war. On the other
hand, let one compare the account of this historical tournament with the imaginary tourney described by the author
of *Garin le Lorrain,* and he will admit that, in this instance,
poetry has only borrowed its facts from history.

" The plain seemed to be nothing less than a forest of glittering
helmets, above which floated brilliant pennons. . . . The two armies
having come face to face, slowly approached each other until they
were not further separated than the range of a bow. Who would
make the first attack, who would be the first to make a sortie from
the lines? It was the young Fromondin. His shield hard against
his breast, he encountered a knight and unhorsed him, hurled himself on another whom he likewise overthrew. His lance was shat-

tered, but with a fragment he still thrust and threatened. . . .
Already order in the two armies was gone; the mêlée became general.
Each lance crossed another, and the earth was covered with their
débris; the vassals were thrown and their terrified horses fled; the
wounded uttered horrible cries; and it was not in one place, but
in twenty or forty different places that they thrust at each other
to give or take death. Led by William of Montclin, Fromont, and
Bernard of Naisil, the men of Bordeaux steadily advanced and at
length reached the battle of Garin.[1] The hero resisted their efforts
for a long while; five times he fell and remounted another horse;
woe to the man who did not escape the edge of his sword! With
one blow he cut down the Fleming, Baldwin; with a second, Bernard of Naisil; finally covered with sweat, he went to a place apart
where no one dared to follow him. There he was able to unfasten
his helmet and refresh himself for an instant. The French, overwhelmed by numbers, were about to abandon the field to the
Bordelais when the Angevins, Normans, and Bretons came to their
aid; all that they could do was to collect them again under the
standard."

The only difference between this tournament and that of
Lagny is that the latter was less bloody. In any case, according to the biographer of William Marshal, the knights
who were taken prisoners mattered more than those who
were killed or grievously wounded.

"Banners were unfurled; the field was so full of them that the
sun was concealed. There was great noise and din. All strove to
strike well. Then, you would have heard such a crash of lances
that the earth was strewn with fragments and that the horses could
not advance further. Great was the tumult upon the field. Each
corps of the army cheered its ensign. The knights seized each
other's bridles and went to each other's aid."

Soon the young king of England, the eldest son of Henry
II, gave the signal for the grand mêlée. Then began a desperate strife in the vineyards, the ditches, across the thick
forests of vine-stocks. One could see the horses falling, and
men sinking, trampled under foot, wounded and beaten to
death. As always, William Marshal distinguished himself;
everything he struck with his sword was cloven and cut to
pieces; he pierced bucklers and dented helmets.

In the epic of the *Lorrains*, the tournament finished, the

---

[1] That is, the body of the army of Garin.

heroes are seen returning to camp with their spoils: that is to say, with the prisoners for whom they will take ransom. This was the gain of the day, the utilitarian and practical side of the tournament. This is particularly brought out in the biography of William Marshal. The knights went to tournaments for the sake of getting money; William Marshal engaged in tourneys in order to get a supply of horses and harness, and prisoners to ransom. In a certain joust, " he won at least twelve horses." He was associated with a daring companion, named Roger of Gaugi, and the two made innumerable captures, of which their clerks kept track. " The clerks proved positively, in writing, that, between Pentecost and Lent, they took three hundred knights prisoners, without counting horses and harness."

And what curious incidents are further related in the poem *Guillaume le Maréchal!*—the exchange of visits by knights on the eve of the tournament, at the inns, where they chatted gayly over two jugs of wine; Marshal running through the crowded streets of a little village at night in pursuit of a thief who had taken his horse. This same Marshal had had his helmet so dented in the tournament that he could not take it off after the battle, and was obliged to seek a blacksmith and put his head on the anvil so as to free himself from this unlucky casque by hammer-blows. In these bloody jousts, in which the nobility delighted, everybody found profit: the " joy women " who rushed to them, the common people who loved these exhibitions, and the merchants who held a market in the neighborhood of the lists.

Only the church did not approve of tournaments, and used all her power to prevent them. She condemned them as she did war, and for the same reasons. At the end of the twelfth century, especially, she had a very powerful motive in opposing this useless nonsense, in which the nobility spent money and blood, instead of devoting both of them to religion, in expeditions to the Holy Land. The tourneys harmed the crusade, and that was enough to make the church seek to suppress them. From the beginning of the twelfth century religious prohibitions were multiplied. At the Lateran council, in 1179, Pope Alexander III had renewed the prohibitions of his predecessors and threatened the organizers and com-

batants with anathema. A decree of this council calls tournaments " those detestable festivals or fairs at which knights
have the habit of meeting in order to show their valor and
come to blows, those fêtes from which issues death to the
body and damnation to the soul." The council decided that
those who should be killed in them should be deprived of
ecclesiastical burial. Innocent III renewed the same prohibitions at the Lateran council in 1215; ecclesiastical writers
were urged to wage a campaign against this deplorable institution. A contemporary of Philip Augustus, the historian
and monk, Cæsar of Heisterbach, says in his *Dialogues:*
" Will those who perish in the tournaments by that same
blow go to hell? That is a question which need not be asked,
unless, indeed, they be saved by contrition." And he tells
the story of a Spanish priest, to whom appeared certain
knights killed in tournaments, begging that some one pray
for them to deliver them from the eternal flames. Another
legend, of a later time it is true, shows us demons in the
form of crows and vultures fluttering over lists where about
sixty jousters lay dead, most of them asphyxiated by dust.
Ever since St. Bernard, churchmen had only words of repro-
bation with which to designate tourneys, " those execrable
and accursed festivals."

In their turn, preachers thundered from the pulpit.
Jacques of Vitry expressed himself at length on this
subject:

" I remember that on one tournament day I chatted with a knight
who frequented them a great deal and invited many heralds-at-arms
and players. In other respects he was religious enough and did
not believe he was doing wrong in giving himself up to this sort
of sport. I attempted to demonstrate to him, how in the tourneys
one committed the seven capital sins: the sin of pride which comes
from self, since these reprobate soldiers come to joust in order to
dazzle the spectators, to vaunt their exploits and to carry off the
prize of vain-glory; the sin of envy, for each one is jealous of his
companions to see that they are reputed braver under arms, and
exhausts himself in trying to surpass them; hate and passion have
there also a splendid field for exercise, since striking one another
is a feature, and generally men come away wounded unto death."

As for the sin of sloth or melancholy, as Jacques of Vitry
calls it, one can see that the preacher is a trifle embar-

rassed, but he extricates himself from the difficulty by this phrase:

" The lovers of the tourney are so absorbed in their vain pleasures that they no longer show any activity in acquiring the spiritual goods necessary for their salvation; and as for the melancholy, it often comes to them from the fact that, not having been able to triumph over their adversaries, and even having been obliged to flee ignominiously, they return home in a very melancholy state."

Quite a subtile explanation; but the preacher takes his revenge with the sin of avarice or plunder. First the jousters, he says, were brigands, since they seize the person of an adversary or at least take his horse away from him; but, further, tournaments always give place to detestable pillage: nobles despoil their subjects without mercy; wherever they ride they injure the crops and cause incalculable harm to the poor peasants. Then comes the sixth mortal sin, gluttony; one could not deny that it appeared in tourneys, since on this occasion the knights invited each other to banquets and spent their substance and even that of the poor in useless drinking. Ah! certainly, " they are exceedingly generous with another's goods." *Quidquid delirant reges plectuntur Achivi!* Finally comes lust. Do not the jousters first of all seek to please immodest women, to parade before them their strength and their exploits? They even go so far as to wear their colors, or objects which these women have given them. It is, then, because of the disorders and cruelty committed in tournaments, because of the homicides and spilling of blood, that the church has determined to refuse Christian burial to those finding death in that manner.

Neither sermons of this sort, nor terrifying legends, nor thundering anathemas by clerics influenced the nobility or succeeded in abolishing tournaments. Habit, the passion for fighting, the fashion, against which all legislation is powerless, continued stronger than the papacy and councils. The church was herself obliged to recognize that she had not succeeded in imposing her will, and had constantly to relax her rigors, to temporize, and come to terms with the evil which she wished to destroy. Of this we have very clear proof in one of the letters of Innocent III. Here is what happened, in 1207, in the diocese of Soissons.

Nivelon of Chérizy, bishop of Soissons, one of the heroes of the fourth crusade, and an energetic man, under pressure from the papacy sought to organize a new expedition for a crusade or at least for the Latin Empire. He found that the tourneys, as always, did his project harm, so, with the pope's consent, he excommunicated all the jousters in a body. Murmurs, protests, and revolt from a majority of the knights who had taken part in the tournament of Laon resulted. They declared that, as the measure was directed against them, they would refuse to take the cross and would not give a sou towards the needs of the Holy Land. Nivelon, perplexed, asked permission of Pope Innocent III to soften the rigor of his own anathema for a time. Innocent III accorded it to him and felt himself obliged to explain his conduct to the archbishops and bishops of the province of Tours, and probably also to the prelates of the other provinces. He managed it by means of a circular:

" It is not our intention to authorize tourneys, which are forbidden by our holy canons. But since the measures we have taken have seemed to us momentarily to offer grave inconvenience we have permitted the bishop to relax the sentence of excommunication, both of those whom he himself has sentenced, or of any others."

This was *opportunism* in the highest degree; but in the middle ages the popes reputed to be the most inflexible, as Gregory VII himself, knew infinitely better than the local clergy how to accommodate principles to the necessities of the practical and present. When the nobles who were banned by the bishop of Soissons learned that they had been absolved, they manifested joy and determined that each one of them should send a certain sum of money to the Holy Land. But to promise and to fulfil are two different things. Innocent III commissioned the archbishop of Tours to see to it that the knights, having once returned to their province, should pay, according to their promises. If they should fail in their pledges and refuse to pay, then they should be made to understand, by a new excommunication, that the decree of the Lateran council relating to tournaments had lost none of its validity.

Feudalism might conclude from this incident that, though tournaments were theoretically forbidden, it was easy in fact to make ecclesiastical authority shut its eyes. As with very many of the things of this world, it was a matter of money. One must not forget that the participation of the French nobility in the fourth crusade in 1200 was decided in a tournament at Écry-sur-Aisne. The church could only approach the nobles with ease when they happened to be assembled in great numbers; in order, then, for the tournament to be sanctified and legitimate, it was sufficient for the knights present to take the cross.

*

* *

The hunt in the great forests filled with deer was also a battle, a school of war. The idea of peace in the minds of men of the middle ages associated itself naturally with that of the chase. For proof of this we want nothing but this passage from *Girart de Roussillon:* '' Now the knights enter upon a long rest; this will be a propitious time for dogs, vultures, falcons, falconers, and huntsmen.'' On another page of the same poem we have King Charles Martel, when he had ceased making war on his vassals or on the Saracens, saying to his barons: '' Let us hunt by the river and in the woods; that is much better than staying at home.'' Along with the tournament, the chase was the pastime *par excellence.* And all the inhabitants of the château were hunters; the noble lady accompanied her husband and rode with a sparrow-hawk on her wrist. She was very well skilled in flinging the bird and in recalling it, and the success of the chase was often her work. As to the son of the castellan or baron, he hunted with his father and mother from the age of seven years; this was an important part of the physical education which was given him.

The chase was not merely a way for knights and barons to escape inactivity; it was a passion, an immoderate passion, often even such a mania that the church was obliged to condemn it, and for many reasons: first, because the noble, preoccupied with roving the forest, forgot even religious services; and then, because the harshness of the law, which regulated the exercise of the chase and made seigniorial forests and game things sacred and inviolable, had in many respects become an intolerable scourge. The peasant did not have the right to defend himself or to protect his crops against the deer. In 1199, the inhabitants of the *Île de Ré* resolved to abandon their island, because of the tribulations which the rapidly multiplying deer caused them. Matters had come about to the point where they could neither reap their harvests nor gather their grapes. The lord of the island was Raoul of Mauléon. The abbot of the monastery of Notre-Dame of Ré, accompanied by the imploring inhabitants, went to him and begged him to renounce his right of the chase. Raoul consented not to leave any other game in the island, save hares and rabbits. But feudalism did not give something for nothing; the peasants were forced to pay the lord ten sous for each plot of vineyard and for each *setier* of land.

For one noble who relaxed his hunting-law, how many others maintained it with fierce greediness? It cannot be said that, in this respect, the legislation of Philip Augustus was as hard as that of his contemporary, Henry II, the king of England; the latter, by his assize of 1184, had restored the forest ordinances of his predecessors, which provided that any man found guilty of hunting in the royal forests should have his eyes put out and his limbs mutilated. This made William of Newburgh, an English chronicler, say that Henry II punished the killing of a deer as severely as the murder of a man. Still, the French baron no longer considered the matter lightly, when, several years after the death of Philip Augustus, Enguerran of Coucy hanged three unfortunate young nobles from Flanders, who had hunted upon his domains. Angered at this, the king committed the high baron to prison and did not release him until he had promised to pay a fine of ten thousand livres and make a pilgrimage to the Holy Land.

It must be said, to be just to feudalism, that the chase was not merely a pleasure, a school of horsemanship, and of training for war; it was also an indispensable source of food supplies. These soldiers, hereditary hunters and great eaters, despised meat from the market. Generally they ate venison, served in quarters or in pies of plentiful width. If we are to believe our old poems (for the chronicles relate but little on this score), the favorite repasts of our feudal ancestors were those in which morsels of wild boar and bear alternated with roasts of swan and peacock, and with fish from the seigniorial fish-ponds, the whole basted with large bumpers of wine flavored with honey and spices.

The *chansons de geste* of the period contain passages which show in a concrete manner what the chase was at that time and how strong was the passion with which the nobles devoted themselves to it. The entire beginning of the poem *Guillaume de Dole* is filled with a description of a hunting party which lasted several days and of the meals on the grass, which were a necessary feature. But it is in *Garin le Lorrain* that the chase is described with the greatest wealth of detail. First of all, a seigniorial interior in time of peace:

"Duke Bégon was in the château of Belin with his wife, the beautiful Béatrix, daughter of Duke Milon of Blaye. He kissed her lips and face; the lady smiled at him sweetly. In the room before them played their two children; the older was named Garin and was twelve years old, while the second, Ernaudin, was only ten. Six noble pages were playing games, running, skipping, laughing, and playing in competition with one another. The duke looked at them. He heaved a sigh. The beautiful Béatrix noticed it. 'What are you troubled about, my Lord Bégon,' said she, 'you so high, noble, and brave a knight? Are you not a rich man in the world? Gold and silver fill your coffers, the vair and the gray your wardrobes; you have goshawks and falcons on their perches; in your stables are coursers, palfreys, mules, and prize horses. You have prevailed over your enemies. Within a six days' journey from Belin, there is not a knight who would fail to come at your request. For what can you sigh?'"

What ailed Duke Bégon? He was not fighting any more; therefore, he was bored. There being no war to wage, he went hunting afar, under the pretext of paying a visit to his brother Garin:

"'I have received news of the forest of Pevèle and Vicogne in the freeholdings of Saint-Bertin. In that forest there is a wild boar, the strongest of which any one has ever heard tell; I shall hunt him, and if it please God and I live, I shall carry his head to Duke Garin in order to give him a surprise.'"

No sooner said than done.

" Bégon loaded ten beasts with gold and silver, in order to be
assured of good service and lodging everywhere. With him he took
thirty-six knights, some good, skilled huntsmen, ten pairs of dogs,
and fifteen servants to arrange the relay."

We pass over the incidents of the journey. Bégon was
entertained at the château of Valentin by Bérenger the Gray,
" the richest commoner of the country." To him he disclosed
his intention:

" ' I have been told of the forest of Pevèle and of the great
wild boar that hides there. I have resolved to go and hunt him and
bring back his head to my dear brother, Duke Garin.' ' Sire,'
answered his host, ' I know where the animal stays, and the covert
where it takes shelter. To-morrow I can guide you to its home.'
Transported with joy at these words, Bégon took off the newly
furred sable mantle which had come to him from Slavonia, saying,
' Take it, my noble host, you shall come with me.' Bérenger took
the gift with a bow, and returning to his wife said to her: ' See
this beautiful present; there is a great advantage in serving a
noble man.'
" When the day broke, the chamberlains came to serve the duke,
presenting him with a hunting-coat and tight boots. His gold spurs
were fastened on; he mounted his racing steed, hung his horn about
his neck, seized his strong boar-spear in his hand, and set out with
Rigaud and the thirty-six knights who were followed by the hunters,
and ten trace of dogs. Thus, they crossed the Schelt and entered
the forest of Vicogne, led by Bérenger the Gray. Soon they
approached the spot where dwelt the boar.
" At once began the baying and yelping of the dogs. They were
unleashed; they bounded through the thicket and found the tracks
where the boar had dug and rooted for worms. One of the dog-
keepers unloosed Blanchart, the good blood-hound, and led him to
the duke, who stroked him on his flanks, gently patted his head
and ears, and then set him on the track. Blanchart disappeared
and rapidly approached the animal's lair. It was a narrow place
between the trunks of two uprooted oaks, sheltered by a rock and
moistened by a thread of water running from a nearby spring.
When the boar heard the baying of the blood-hound, he stood erect,
spread his enormous feet, and, disdaining flight, wheeled around
until, judging himself within reaching distance of the good hound,
he seized it and felled it dead by his side. Bégon would not have
given Blanchart for one hundred marks of deniers. Not hearing his
barking any longer, he ran up with sword in hand; but he was too
late, the boar had gone. The knights dismounted from their horses

and measured his hoof-prints, which were a good hand's breadth in length and width. 'What an infernal demon!' said they. 'There is no danger of our taking another for him.' They remounted and began the chase; soon the great forest re-echoed with the sound of their horns and the baying of the dogs.

"The boar foresaw that he could not strive against so many enemies. He then sought refuge toward Gaudemont—this was the corner of the forest which served him as covert. Pressed here by the pack, he did what, perchance, no other boar would have dared attempt; he abandoned the covert, came into the open fields, crossed the country of Pevèle, sprinkled with forests and isolated farms, and made thus a good fifteen leagues straight ahead, without making an instant's stop, and without a single detour."

A boar making fifteen leagues in plain view is an exaggeration of the minstrel, one of those fanciful stories which find a place in even the truest of narratives.

"The horses did not have strength enough to follow him; the wearier ones were stopped by ponds, marshes, and water-courses; the good horse of Rigaut himself fell with weariness into the midst of a bog. Then, as the day began to wane, and the rain to fall, they begged the party to return to Valentin with their host. Food awaited them there. They sat down to the table, all deeply regretting the absence of Bégon, whom they had left in the forest.

"We have said that the duke rode an Arab steed presented by the king. There was not a more indefatigable courser in the world; when all the dogs refused to advance, Baucent seemed as fresh as in the morning when he left the château. So he followed the boar in his rapid flight. Perceiving that his three grayhounds were wearied, Bégon lifted them up before him and took them in his arms until he saw them gather new strength, and, therefore, new ardor. Little by little, the other dogs overtook him, so that presently he could collect them at the entrance of a clearing which showed them the boar's tracks. In an instant the forest resounded with their loud incessant baying.

"Chased thus from Vicogne to Pevèle, and from Pevèle to Gohière, the boar had finally come to bay in front of a thicket to await his enemies there. He began by refreshing himself in a pool; then raising his brows, rolling his eyes, and snorting, he bared his tusks, dashed upon the dogs, and ripped them open or ground them to pieces one after the other, with the exception of the three grayhounds that Bégon had carried, which, more active than the others, could guard themselves against his terrible teeth. Bégon arrived, and first of all saw his dogs stretched out dead, one near the other. 'Oh, son of a sow,' he cried, 'it is you who have disemboweled my dogs, have separated me from my men, and have brought me I know not where. You shall die by my hand.' He dismounted

from his steed. At the outcry which he made, the boar, in spite
of bushes and ditches, leaped upon him with the rapidity of a barbed
arrow. Bégon let him come on without stirring, and struck at his
breast with the boar-spear which he was holding straight before him.
The point pierced the heart and went out at the shoulder-joint.
Mortally wounded, the boar swerved to one side, weakened and fell,
never to rise again. Bégon at once withdrew the spear from the
wound whence issued rivers of black blood which the dogs lapped
up before lying down side by side about the boar."

This is a complete picture of a seigniorial chase in the
time of Philip Augustus. The adventure, alas! turned out
badly for the hunter. Isolated and lost in the woods, he was
killed by the foresters in the service of one of his enemies.
This kind of occurrence was not rare, in fact. The chase,
as it was then practised, always held its dangers, though they
were less, perhaps, than those one faced in tournaments.

*

*   *

But one cannot always hunt. Tired out, the noble has
returned to the donjon. To-morrow, if peace still lasts, what
are to be his diversions? There are at least two which again
are violent exercises and are, as always, preparations for war.
These are the " quintain " and the " behourd."

The quintain is a manikin covered with a hauberk and a
shield and fastened to the top of a post. The play consists
in the knight's dashing on the post, his horse at a gallop
and his lance couched, and piercing the hauberk and buckler
with a single lance-thrust. Sometimes, to increase the difficulty of the play, several armed manikins are arranged in a
row, and the point is to run them through and overturn them
all. This is the test which is ordinarily imposed upon new
cavaliers and which takes place before the witnesses of dubbing, the ladies.

As to the behourd, it is simply a form of training for tournaments and is a sort of fencing or tilt on horseback. The
knights arrange themselves two by two, and one of them turns
upon his partner, trying to pierce his shield with a lance.
This sometimes becomes dangerous play, for one grows excited in it, and in the heat of the strife forgets that it is an
amusement. This very thing happened more than once, as
the first verses of *Girart de Roussillon* prove:

" It was Pentecost, in the gay springtime. There was many a
man with a brave heart. The pope came and preached. When
the mass had been said the king repaired to his hall which was
strewed with flowers. Below Girart and his fellows tilted at
quintain and indulged in many an exercise. The king learned of
it and forbade them to do it. He feared that from such games
disputes might arise."

A more complete description of quintains is that borrowed
from the same poem, in the recital of the marriage of Fulc.

" On that day he dubbed a hundred knights, giving horses and
arms to each one. Then in the meadow which bordered on Arsen
he arranged for them a quintain equipped with a new shield and
a strong and glittering hauberk. The young men ran their courses
and other people came to watch them. . . . Girart saw that they
were beginning to quarrel with each other, and in his heart he was
much troubled. The crowd pushed toward the quintain. The hundred young men had made their trial; some had succeeded, others had
failed, but no one had more than indented the mail of the hauberk.
The count called for his boar-spear. I oon brought it to him. It
was the spear which Arthur of Cornwall had carried when
formerly fighting in a battle in Burgundy. The count spurred his
horse into the lists; he struck the target and made a hole of such a
size that a quail could have flown through it. Then he broke and
cut the shield under the ventail. There was no knight who equaled
him or who could ever have sustained a struggle against him.
" The count struck out with such force that, with a blow, he split
one of the straps and tore off the other, all the while holding his
weapon so firmly in hand that he again drew it out. And his men
said, ' What strength. When he makes war, it is not to take sheep
or cattle; he is intent against his enemies; he has drawn much blood
from their bodies.' "

Still, the nobles of this time knew more peaceful pastimes.
In the inclosures and pits they had animals, especially boars
and bears, with which they amused themselves by making
them fight. If it was warm, they sought the orchard—to
drink, to play dice, chess, or even a sort of game of back-
gammon. Or, perchance, they received strolling players, to
whose songs and music they listened. Sometimes they had
veritable orchestras, and the musical instruments of this
period were not so rudimentary as one might believe. They
had violins or hurdy-gurdies, harps, double-basses or mono-
chords, horns, trumpets, blowpipes, a kind of clarionet, tam-

bourines, and kettledrums. In the bad weather of winter, the castellan warmed himself under the hood of the immense fire-place or profited by his enforced inaction by having himself cupped and bled near the fire. For these rough temperaments were in need of frequent bleedings. Almost every month, the women as well as the men proceeded to the *minutio*—that is, the bleeding. When the unfortunate Queen Ingeborg of Denmark had been imprisoned in the château of Étampes by the order of Philip Augustus, one of the grievances against her husband, to which she referred with the most bitterness in her letters to Pope Innocent III, was that she was not any longer allowed to have a physician to bleed her regularly.

As to the playthings of the children of nobility, they reflected the bellicose spirit of the times: such as bows and crossbows, with which they amused themselves at killing birds. A manuscript, written at the end of the thirteenth century, has preserved for us a picture of one of their favorite toys. It strangely resembles one which still serves the children of to-day—the jumping-jack, which is operated by means of two crossed cords. But these feudal jumping-jacks are naturally soldiers, which are armed from top to toe and fight each other with the great swords and shields in their hands.

Finally, the noble had one other diversion; a very costly one, it is true. This was to entertain guests at the château, such as pilgrims and wandering knights, and to give feasts in their honor. He was hospitable not only to the point of virtue, but even to the point of self-denial. Here we could again invoke the testimony of the *chansons de geste;* but we have too many of them. A historical document by Lambert, the curé of Ardres, outlines the life of Baldwin II, count of Guines and lord of Ardres. This count of Guines reigned from 1165 to 1205. He possessed to a great degree the most important of feudal qualities, that of liberality. He took pleasure in giving magnificent entertainment to all noted personages who crossed his territory—such as counts, knights, townsmen, archbishops, bishops, archdeacons, abbots, priors, provosts, archpriests, priests, canons, and clerics of every sort; and every entertainment was accompanied by sumptu-

ous banquets. The curé of Ardres, who, in his desire to laud
his master, makes the above enumeration, describes at length
the solemn reception he tendered William of Champagne,
archbishop of Reims and uncle of Philip Augustus, when that
worthy in 1178 passed through Ardres on his way to England, to visit the tomb of Saint Thomas à Becket. The feast
was especially striking: there were innumerable dishes; wines
from Cypress and Greece, flowing in floods, and flavored,
as usual, with spices. With a shade of disdain, the chronicler
adds that the French requested pure water, with which to
weaken the drinks served them. But the count of Guines,
ever faithful to his habits of good living, had secretly given
an order to refill the jugs with an excellent white wine of
Auxerre, which the clerics of the archbishop's suite took to
be water and drank without distrust. But the deception was
discovered. The archbishop was dangerously near being of-
fended; he summoned the count and demanded a ewerful
of water. Baldwin went out smiling, as if he would make
reparation; but he amused himself before the servants by
upsetting and trampling under foot all the water receptacles
he could find. He then returned to the banquet-hall, to do
honor to the archbishop, and, says the chronicler, appeared
with a foolish sportiveness, pretending drunkenness before
the young men and guests, who themselves had drunk more
than was within reason. Disarmed by this good-humor, William of Champagne promised the count to conform to all his
wishes.

We can take this merry personage as the comparatively
peaceful type of lord with a domestic temperament. His bellicose tastes appeared to be limited to the construction of
châteaux. It does not seem that he fought too much, or
that he ever quitted his fief to make a pilgrimage to the Holy
Land. He was content to remain in the midst of his vassals
and serfs, to whom he rendered fair justice. Ordinarily, he
possessed a more sensible spirit than did his peers. When his
wife, Christiana of Ardres, died in childbirth, he was so filled
with grief that he was on the verge of going insane. For
several days, says the curé of Ardres, he recognized no one
and scarcely knew what he was doing. His doctors would
not permit any one to approach him. Nevertheless, he recov-

ered his reason, and consoled himself quickly enough; for his historian affirms that he became the father of several children in the year following his mourning.

The curé of Ardres, indeed, presents him to us as he was, with his good qualities and his faults. For example, he reproaches him for his immoderate passion for the chase: "This lord," he says, "heard the hunter's horn more readily than the bell of the chaplain, and took more pleasure in throwing the falcon and applauding the exploits of his bird than in listening to a priest's sermon." Moreover, he did not hide the fact that his master was the greatest woman-hunter that he had seen "since David and Solomon," and that "Jupiter himself could not be compared to him in this respect." After having given the names of several of his natural children, he adds: "Since I do not know the exact number, and since their father himself does not know them all by name, I will refrain from saying more about them. By trying to enumerate them, I fear I should weary the reader." The chronicle of a neighboring country, that of the abbey of Ardres, is more instructive. It tells us that thirty-three children of Baldwin II, legitimate or natural, were present at his funeral.

CHAPTER X

FEUDAL FINANCE AND CHIVALRY

WAR, tournaments, hunting, and receptions, open to all-comers, cost very dearly. In order to keep up this style of life, it was necessary to oppress subjects cruelly and take much booty from the enemy. Even so, one could not make both ends meet. And it is one of the striking and characteristic traits of feudal life that the noble, great and small, appears to be constantly in need of money, poor, on the watch for financial expedients, always indebted, and a prey of usurers of all kinds. This explains his rapacity and brigandage, as the fruit of the instincts which impelled him. It was a deplorable reasoning in a circle: the barons robbed, pillaged, and killed because they needed money to pay for military expeditions, which cost a great deal and did not bring in enough. Unless one were a Philip Augustus or a Henry Plantagenet, able to operate on a large scale and to make vast conquests, one got nothing out of it. A seigniorial budget of this time is ordinarily a budget with a deficit.

Nearly all important acts of the internal politics of Hugh III of Burgundy explain themselves by this penury, by the need of making money. He gives the county of Langres to the bishop of Langres, to the detriment of the ducal power, because he owed the latter an enormous sum. For five hundred francs he gave up the right of military service from the inhabitants of Dijon; his liberalities toward the Burgundian villages had the same cause. And his son, Eudes III, followed his example: he sold and pledged the rights and domains of the duchy to monasteries and burghers to secure money. One sees him, for example, in 1203 borrowing sixty livres from the canons of Beaune for a quarter of a year only; it was in December, and he promised to repay the sum on the first day of Shrove-tide.

The lesser lords of Burgundy, the viscounts and castellans,

were involved like their dukes. Money was necessary, especially when they left for the crusades, and they placed their
revenues and even their fiefs as security with the monks or
the Jews. For, if the Christian would not or could not lend,
the Jew was always ready to do so. In 1189, at the close
of the third crusade, Andrew of Molesme pledged his fief
for sixty livres to the abbey of Molesme; Robert of Ricey
pledged his land of Gigny for ten livres; Girard, lord of
Asnières, ceded his land to the abbey of Jully for ten livres
and a cow. In 1203, at the time of the fourth crusade, the
lord of Nully was obliged to mortgage his land: he died, and
his widow and his son were compelled to sell their patrimony
to pay what he owed to the Jews. The viscount of Dijon,
William of Champlitte, borrowed three hundred livres from
an Italian banker,—a Lombard, as they then called them,—
Peter Capituli, on the revenues of his land of Champlitte.
But he could no more pay the interest than he could repay
the principal. The creditors demanded that the countess of
Champagne seize his domains. The duke of Burgundy, Eudes
III, had to intervene and redeem the lands of his vassal, by
himself borrowing the amount of the debt from the Jews.

All the great lords of France were in the same condition;
even the counts of Champagne, for whom the fairs of Champagne were a veritable gold mine. When Count Henry II
left for Palestine, he borrowed money from ten bankers: they
were not paid until after his death, by Thibaud III, his successor. Yet, after his arrival in the Holy Land, Henry II
found himself in such straits " that it often happened," says
his historian, Arbois de Jubainville, " that he got up in the
morning not knowing how the people in his household and
himself would be fed that day." Several times he was
obliged to pledge his personal belongings to the tradesmen,
who even in Champagne had refused to give him anything
on credit. The Countess Blanche of Champagne, and even
more her son, Thibaud IV, the writer of lays, were also in
the hands of Christian or Jewish usurers. The Christians
lent for two months, and the Jews for a week. The latter,
after having demanded three deniers per week, were forced
to content themselves with two, by virtue of an ordinance of
1206, published jointly by the countess of Champagne and

Philip Augustus. It was then decided that the Jews could lend at no higher rate than forty-three per cent. a year, not counting compound interest. With transactions of this nature it is intelligible how the financial difficulties of the counts of Champagne had merely become aggravated, and how in the month of May, 1223, Count Thibaud IV was reduced to taking the gold table and the gold cross of Saint Stephen's church at Troyes to pledge them to the abbey of Saint-Denis. The monks of Saint-Denis lent him two thousand Parisan livres, nearly two hundred and fifty thousand francs in our money. Twenty-seven years after, in 1252, they were not yet paid.

These are not isolated facts. In the other French regions the situation of the nobles was the same. Always without money, the legal means which they employed to acquire it only augmented their needs. A count of Saint-Pol, Hugh Candavène, leaving for the fourth crusade, wrote to one of his friends, in 1204, to tell him of the taking of Constantinople; but first he told him of his personal affairs, which he had confided to his friend's care.

" I am greatly obliged to you for having been so careful about my land. I tell you that since my departure I have received nothing from any one whatever, and I have only been able to live by what I myself can get, so that up to the day of the fall of Constantinople, we were all reduced to the most extreme want. I was obliged to sell my mantle for bread, but for all that I kept my horses and my arms. Since the conquest, I am enjoying good health, and am honored of every one. However, I am not without worry over the products of my land, for if God permits me to return home, I shall find myself much involved, and it will be necessary for me to pay my debts from the resources of my seigniory."

Here is one lord who is careful about paying his creditors. But it is an error to think that all of his fellows took the same care. Most of them transmitted the task of paying their debts to their heirs and successors. Others merely refused to pay, or even essayed to get rid of their creditors conformably to aristocratic tradition—by violence, blows, or the prison. But this method did not always succeed.

It is interesting to note that the church, which filled all the divers missions of medieval society, was still charged with

securing the execution of contracts of loans. She launched
her thunder against the disloyal or reluctant debtor. Excommunication then had the effect of arrest or imprisonment
for debt. We will mention only two examples. The count
of Champagne, Thibaud IV, having refused to pay three
bankers, one of whom was a Jew, was excommunicated, and
Champagne put under the interdict. The same baron, in a
pressing need of money, borrowed an important sum from
three Roman bankers, the Ilperni family. He was obstinate
and would not pay, in spite of the repeated demands of the
creditors and in spite of the repeated exhortations of the
pope, who often came to the rescue of the Italian bankers.
Thibaud found their insistence annoying. Not only did he
not pay, but, profiting by the sojourn of one of the three
Ilperni brothers in Champagne, he caused him to be seized,
thrown into prison, put in irons, and threatened him with
the gallows. The unfortunate man was obliged to give his
debtor twelve hundred livres, which the count divided with
his councilors, taking one thousand livres himself and giving
them the balance. Upon complaint of the Roman bankers,
the pope ordered Thibaud to·restore the twelve hundred livres
and to pay the previous debt; and declared that, in case of
resistance, he would cause an excommunication, with lighted
candles and sounding bells, to be published every Sunday and
feast-day in all the churches of the county. Thibaud pretended to submit, acknowledged his debt by letters patent,
and asked a delay. The time expired and he still refused
to pay. The pope announced that, if the debt was not paid
in full, he would put two of the most important cities of the
county, Provins and Bar-sur-Aube, under interdict. We do
not know how the affair ended. The count of Champagne had
the bright idea of taking the cross, and a crusader became
doubly holy. The pope relented and, instead of dealing
rigorously with Thibaud, wrote him again, making an appeal
to his good faith, a poor guarantee for the creditors.

It did not always happen that pope or bishops intervened
in their favor. When the creditor was a Jew, things went
very simply. A great baron did not trouble himself about
the Jews. When their complaints became embarrassing, he
issued a decree of expulsion against them, according them

permission to return upon making a payment of money. Or, if his ill-humor was more enduring, he decreed, with a stroke of the pen, that no interest should be paid them. The lesser lords understood this proceeding very well. Did the Jewish creditor press them too strongly?—they addressed themselves to the suzerain of the province, to the count or the duke, with a present, and obtained a letter of the kind which the duke of Normandy, king of England, in 1199 gave to the wife of the lord of Conches, Roger IV of Tosny. Here is the letter, the conciseness of which is admirable:

" The king of England, duke of Normandy, to Henry of Grayen. We command you, that you cause Constance, Lady of Conches, to be quit of the debt of twenty-one silver marks, which she owes Benoit the Jew of Verneuil, upon the payment of the principal; this is why we desire that she do not pay interest on the debt. I, myself, witness, at Laigle, June the twentieth."

It was difficult to deal in this fashion with Christians, especially when the Christians were monks of great abbeys or the citizens of a powerful commune, and especially when they belonged to the order of knights. At the time of Philip Augustus' death, in 1223, Amauri, son and successor of Simon de Montfort, the hero of the Albigensian war, found himself reduced to a very critical situation by his poverty. In order to keep up the struggle against the count of Toulouse, he had promised a wage to the knights of northern France. But this he had no means of paying, and the knights in question had no other way of securing the money owing them than locking up their debtor, their military chief, in a safe place and extorting five sous per day, more than the promised wage, from him. This same Amauri was so involved that he was forced to mortgage his own relatives: his uncle, Guy of Montfort, and several other nobles, were detained as prisoners at Amiens as security for a sum of four thousand livres, which the conquerors of Languedoc owed the merchants of that city. Here are the details, which explain why the house of Montfort, on the verge of bankruptcy, decided to transfer its rights over the conquered country to the king of France.

It is not necessary to go to the lesser nobility for the type of prodigal noble who is indebted and reduced to the worst expedients. One finds them even in royal families. The chronicler Geoffroi of Limousin, prior of Vigeois, says that the eldest son of the powerful Plantagenet King Henry II, whom contemporaries call Henry the Young or the " young king of England," daily received a sum of fifteen hundred sous (fifteen thousand francs in our money) from his father as spending-money; and his wife Margaret drew a daily income of five hundred sous (five thousand francs) from the treasury of England. A good revenue, *egregius reditus,* says the chronicler; but it was not sufficient for the young king, whose prodigality knew no bounds. His creditors were legion, and when in 1183, jealous of his brother, Richard the Lion-Hearted, he fell to quarreling with his father and fighting against him with the aid of highwaymen, this son of a king was by his wants obliged to become a chief of brigands. To pay his soldiers, he first levied a forced loan of twenty thousand sous on the burghers of Limoges; then he presented himself at the abbey of Saint-Martial and demanded the loan of the treasure of the monks. He forced his way into the cloister, drove out the majority of the monks, and opened the sanctuary. There he found a gold table from the altar of the Holy Sepulchre, and five statues of gold; the gold table of the high altar with its dozen golden statues of the apostles, a chalice of gold, and a silver vase of the most marvelous workmanship; some crosses and relics, etc., having altogether a value of fifty-two marks in gold and a hundred and three marks in silver. All these precious objects were valued, says the indignant prior of Vigeois who was an eyewitness, at twenty-two thousand sous, which was far below their value; for they did not take into account either the workmanship or the gold used in gilding the silver objects. Henry the Young carried the treasure away, after having given the monks a document, sealed with his seal, recognizing the debt. It is needless to say that he never paid it. Some months after, mortally wounded at the château of Martel, he died in the most abject poverty. The abbot of Uzerches was obliged to pay his funeral expenses. The people of his household died of hunger; they mortgaged even their master's horse to get food. Those who carried the body fainted from hunger, so that the monks of Uzerches had to revive them. One of the familiars of the young king said that he had even sold his hose for bread.

The debts and the embarrassing condition of this heir-presumptive of the Plantagenet empire are recorded in *Guillaume le Maréchal,* which gives some curious details on this point:

> "In the châteaux, in the city, everywhere that he went, Henry the Young had such heavy expenses that when he began to think of leaving he did not know what to do. He had distributed horses, clothing, and food so freely that his creditors wept: three hundred livres to this person, one hundred to another, and two hundred to a third. 'That comes to six hundred,' said the scribes; 'who will become surety?' 'My lords, here no one has money,' answered the men of the prince; 'but you will be paid within a month.' 'By our faith,' said the burghers, 'if Marshal takes the debt in hand just as it is, we will not worry, and we will consider ourselves paid.'"

This was perhaps too much confidence, for the earl of Pembroke, William Marshal, the intimate friend and devoted councilor of the young king, was himself not very rich. We know that he was obliged to take booty in tournaments; he even occasionally robbed travelers on the highways. In one of the previous chapters we read how he fell in with a monk, who was eloping with a woman, and appropriated all the money which the fugitives had about them, an act of brigandage which his biographer considers as a legitimate windfall and a proper pleasantry.

Marshal then set out to take the body of the unhappy prince to his father, King Henry II. One of the creditors of the young king, Sancho, probably a Basque or Navarrese, was the chief of his retainers. He was creditor for a considerable sum.

> "He knew that he would not be paid unless he used some artifice. He knew that the young king loved William Marshal well, and placed more faith in him than in all others. He spurred his horse before Marshal, and seized his horse by the bridle. 'I have seized you and I lead you away; come with me, Marshal.' Marshal asked why. 'Why? You know very well. I want you to pay me the money which your lord owes me.' Marshal then understood that he was not being forced, and he did not try to resist. Sancho said to him: 'I do not want to lose what is due me; that is why

I do not let you go. But I intend to give you the advantage. You shall be free for a hundred marks.' 'Seignior,' answered Marshal, 'what are you saying? This game would be too bitter for me. I am only a poor squire, who scarcely possesses a furrow of earth; truly I do not know where to find so much money. But do you know what I will do? I give you my word of honor that I will return to you as a prisoner, and will come to your prison on the day you assign.' And Sancho said: 'Certainly, that is your right; and I willingly grant it to you, for you are a loyal knight.' "

After having signed the agreement, Marshal continued his journey and finally came to the presence of the king of England, Henry II, to whom he delivered the body of his son. Here the scene has a certain grandeur:

" The sad truth was bitter to the old king, for this was the son he had loved most. But he was of so courageous a heart that he sought to appear unmoved by the most troublesome news. Marshal, angry at this affected indifference, began to recount how his son had fallen ill, how he had suffered martyrdom, how he was truly repentant, how he had borne his great sorrow and great misfortunes with admirable patience. 'O, that God had saved him,' said his father very simply, for his sorrow oppressed his heart more than he wished to show, but his great grief kept him silent. 'What shall I do, Sire?' asked Marshal. 'Marshal, I have only one thing to say. You will go with your lord and take his body to Rouen, as you had intended.' 'Sire,' said Marshal, 'that is impossible. I have given my word to become a prisoner in Sancho's prison. You know him well, he to whom your son owed so much money. It is the truth, but for one hundred marks he will release me.'

" The king then called one of his familiars, Joubert of Pressigny. 'Go find Sancho for me. Tell him to grant Marshal time for the payment of the hundred marks.' Joubert went with Marshal; the latter rode pensively. 'Marshal,' said Joubert, 'what makes you so downcast?' Marshal answered: 'Truly, I have enough to think of, if thinking of one's troubles is of any use in relieving them. The death of my lord, then this debt with which I am charged, trouble me, for I have not the means to pay it. I have indeed the right to be troubled.' 'Marshal,' returned Joubert, 'would you be thankful to the person who managed things so as to relieve you of this worry? Well, I assure you that you will be rid of your debt.' 'Dear Sire,' said Marshal, 'I would be very grateful to whoever would render me this service, if such good luck could come to me.' 'Then let me arrange the matter. You have never had the money; it is not just that you should pay it. Do not worry, I will undertake this affair and try to bring it to a good end.'

" Our two companions arrived at the home of Sancho, and greeted

him in behalf of the king. Joubert told him at once that the king
had assumed the payment of the debt resting on Marshal. 'You
promise it?' said the retainer. 'Yes, truly.' 'Then it is done.'
The two knights took leave without delay. Presently Sancho went
to the king and demanded his hundred marks. The king thought
that the retainer had made a mistake. 'What hundred marks, my
good friend?' said he. 'The debt, Sire, which you took upon yourself to liberate Marshal.' 'Some one has misinformed you,' said the
king. 'I never undertook anything of the kind, and I am bound
in no way. I only asked a delay of you.' Sancho, greatly worried,
took an oath upon the glory of God: 'Joubert, speaking for you,
told me that you would assume the debt.' They at once sent for
Joubert. 'How is it,' said the king to him, 'that this man claims
this money from me?' 'Sire, I will willingly tell you. In short,
I told him on your behalf, that you would assume the debt. You
said as much here; even here I heard it. I have proof of what I
say.' Then the king said: 'O, well, so be it! Let the debt be
charged to me. My son has cost much more than that and would
to God that I could still pay for him.' His eyes closed with grief
and the tears flowed from them; but it was not for long."

The young king of England, in short, with his foolish
prodigality realized the ideal of the knights of his time. In
the class of barons and castellans a deficit and debts were not
a disgrace. On the contrary, it was the sign of nobility; and
the prodigality, which in the eighteenth century brought
down *lettres de cachet* and imprisonment on the sons of a
family, and to-day subjects them to a guardian, was in the
time of Philip Augustus more than an elegance: it was a
virtue. It was the current conception of feudalism, and
especially of the poets and minstrels, who lived at its cost.
This virtue was called " largess." It is celebrated in a thousand passages of the minstrels' lays. " Be generous to all;
for the more you give the greater honor you shall obtain,
and the richer you shall be. He is not a true knight who
is too covetous," says the author of *Doon de Mayence*.
" An avaricious king is not worth a farthing," we read in
Ogier le Danois. There is the same sentiment in the
chanson of *Garin*, " No avaricious prince can keep his land;
there is injury and grief while he lives." It is a kind of
commonplace among the troubadours and trouvères to complain that the lords of their time were no longer so liberal
as in former centuries. The author of the *Chanson de la*

croisade des Albigeois, William of Tudela, says of himself at the beginning of his work:

" Master William composed this song at Montauban, where he was. Truly, if he had good luck, if he were rewarded as are so many of the common players, so many of the cheap fellows, surely no talented man of courtesy would fail to give him a horse or a Breton palfrey, to carry him easily over the sand, or raiment of silk or velvet; but we see the world going so decidedly to the bad that rich men—a worthless lot,—who should be gracious will not give the value of a button. As for me, I do not ask them for the value of a coal, or for the sorriest cinder they have in the hearth. May God and the Holy Mother Mary Who made the sky and air, confound them! "

We need not accept everything the poets of the middle ages say: they all say the same thing at all times. Their theme was that feudal lords were never generous enough; they were insatiable. In fact, all the nobles of this time were lavish. Public opinion did not permit them to live meanly, and they practised the virtue of largess with the utmost non-chalance. To them war was the occasion of immense expense, and we have seen that war never ceased. But peace was no less costly, for it involved receptions, religious and military fêtes, marriages, and knightings. But there were no fêtes in the middle ages without prolonged feasting, without the distribution of clothing, furs, money, and horses. The higher his rank, the more a man gave to friends, vassals, players, and all-comers: so that money slipped from the hands of our knights and never remained in them.

To get a good idea of what war then cost a baron, one should read the minute biography of Baldwin V, count of Hainault, father-in-law of Philip Augustus, written by Gilbert of Mons. There was not a year when this lord did not make several military expeditions, usually at his own expense, whether on his own account, as a feudal duty, or to fulfil the obligation of vassalage. In this chronicle, so important for its accuracy of detail, each page contains such phrases as these: " The count of Hainault, in order to go to war, to remain there, and to return, was under arms five weeks; his expenses were one thousand eight hundred and fifty silver marks, full weight.'' The allusion is to the campaign which took place in December of the year 1181, but the war burst out anew after Epiphany of 1182. There had been only a short truce for Christmas, the first of the year, and Twelfth Day. The new campaign lasted almost until Lent. It took six weeks, says Gilbert of Mons, and, when the count of Hainault returned home, he had a new debt of one thousand six hundred marks of silver. The summer of 1182 passed without war, an extraordinary thing for Baldwin V. But in the autumn he went to a tournament, and there he had bad luck. While he was engaged in the joust, some men of Louvain, subjects of the duke of Brabant, stole all his baggage, clothes, wagons, beasts of burden, and saddle-horses. Baldwin in his rage declared war on the duke of Brabant. A campaign ensued in October and November of 1182. It was interrupted by a peace, valid until Epiphany, 1183. During the peace the count of Hainault attended another tournament held between Braine and Soissons. He did not participate, but contented himself with recruiting knights and mercenaries. In March, 1183, he made war in France against Philip Augustus on behalf of Philip of Alsace, count of Flanders, his brother-in-law. In the spring of 1184, he was obliged to appear at the grand court at Mainz, where Frederick Barbarossa assembled all the princes of the empire and nearly seventy thousand knights. As usual, the barons vied with each other in splendor and prodigality: who could collect the largest number of knights under his banner, pitch the most and richest tents in the plain, and throw the greatest amount of money and gifts to the common soldiers and the minstrels? After this ruinous fête in July and August of 1184, the count of Hainault again found himself at war. He carried on a bloody struggle against the count of Flanders and the duke of Brabant, who had joined to crush him. And so it continued to the year 1195, in which he died. Baldwin ceased warring, attacking, and being attacked only because death took his weapons out of his hands.

One wonders how these men could endure the perpetual traveling, the enormous fatigue, and the interminable struggles; and wonders, especially, how they could support themselves in pecuniary matters. Their endurance seems to have had no limits, but their treasure was not inexhaustible. The military resources of their own fiefs were not sufficient for

them to lead armies into campaigns so often as they did.
They had recourse to mercenaries, whom they recruited from
all sides. There is a curious page in the chronicle of Gilbert
of Mons which tells us what the Count Baldwin paid certain
of his auxiliaries; to one, six hundred livres, assigned on a
village near Valenciennes; to another, four hundred livres,
on a village of Brabant; to another, land in fief and twenty
livres. The latter became lord of Belaing near Valenciennes,
with a revenue of seven hundred livres; the others had fiefs
of less importance yielding thirty and twenty livres. Still
the count of Hainault did not satisfy them with this assign-
ment of fiefs. He had from time to time to make presents
of horses, clothing, and cash in order to preserve the zeal
and devotion of this paid soldiery.

Compare with this page of history certain passages from
Girart de Roussillon, and we will see that it deals with the
same time, the same customs, and the same men. In the
following passage the poet seems to be merely a commentator
on the historian:

> " Girart seated himself under a laurel, and having sent for his
> councilor, Fulc, had gold and deniers brought to him, likewise
> mules, palfreys, and coursers with which to pay the soldiers. He
> wrote a hundred letters, sealed them, and summoned the knights
> throughout the land. To those who desired money Girart gave it.
> There were shortly four thousand of them who directed their way
> toward Dijon. He sent his messengers for the Burgundians as far
> as the mountains, for the Bavarians and Germans, even to Saxony.
> Wherever he knew of a good warrior he sent for him, making him
> promises of rich gifts."

Further on we find the theory of obligatory prodigality,
especially toward poor knights, set forth. The seignior must
maintain them in peace as well as in war.

> " The young warriors said: ' The war is over; there will be no
> more skirmishes, no more wounded knights, no more broken shields.'
> ' That none be discouraged at it,' said Fulc [one of the heroes
> of the poem], ' I shall willingly give them a living and clothing if
> I cannot give them more.' Fulc spoke to Girart and to King
> Charles Martel. ' Now,' said he, ' see to it that each of you counts
> and rich barons gives the poor knights enough to assure their sub-
> sistence. Summon them to be enrolled for the defense of the land,

as has become the custom. And if there is an avaricious rich man, a felon at heart whom the maintenance and gifts cost too much he shall be deprived of his fief, and it shall be given to the valiant. For hoarded treasure is not worth a coal.' "

Count Baldwin (to return to history) was not one of the stingy rich, for reading Gilbert of Mons we see what happened:

" At Easter, 1186, he assembled the council of his secretaries and his familiars in his château at Mons. There the condition of his finances was made known; it was disquieting enough. His personal expenses, the cost of maintenance, and the pay of the soldiers amounted to a considerable sum. The deficit was forty thousand Valenciennes livres. The count of Hainault then, in spite of himself and with regret, decided to resort to an extreme measure: he burdened the inhabitants of his county with extraordinary taxes. In seven month he collected enough to pay almost all his debts."

What a time this was when the rulers could employ such a convenient method of almost instantly balancing their budgets! It was enough to squeeze the sponge: that is, the exploitable subject, the peasant, and the burgher. But all feudal barons, especially the lesser ones, did not have this resource. They remained in debt and accumulated deficits until finally they had to sell their fiefs. Thereafter they vanished by going on the crusade: it was a method of liquidation then in common use.

*

*   *

We would, however, like more precise and accurate information about the financial situation of the noble class. We lack contemporary accounts and budgets: it would be especially interesting to have the book of receipts and expenditures of one of these barons who maintained their splendor and threw their money out of the window. Unfortunately, for the time which we are studying, this kind of document scarcely exists. We have the accounts of the household of Philip Augustus for the year 1202 and 1203, and they are far from being prodigal; and, of seigniorial budgets, we possess only a fragment of the accounts of Blanche of Navarre, countess of Champagne, covering the years 1217, 1218, and 1219. However, the study of these accounts, incomplete and mutilated as they are, is instructive and one can draw certain general conclusions from them, for, except in proportion, the life of a king or a high baron of this time was not different from that of an ordinary seignior. In all the grades of the hierarchy the nobles had the same instincts, the same passions, the same needs to satisfy. They drew their money from practically the same sources, and spent it in about the same fashion. But the accounts of Blanche of Champagne, in the first place, reveal that this noble dame, frequently short of money, contracted many debts, for they contain abundant reference to the payment of interest. The bankers lent to her for a rather short time, generally for two months, at most for six, and at a rate of twenty-five per cent. interest, the relatively moderate rate of Christian bankers. We have seen that the Jews ordinarily lent at forty-three per cent. But as usury was officially interdicted and prohibited, especially to members of the church, the keeper of accounts was careful to represent the payment of the enormous interest as a reimbursement for expenses which the lender had had.

The county of Champagne was, like all fiefs, in a state of war, because the countess, in the name of her minor son, young Thibaud IV, had to defend herself against the dangerous and implacable rival, Érard of Brienne. The expenses of war, therefore, have a very important place in the accounts: putting the fortifications of Champagne and Brie into a state of defense; cleaning the moats, repairing of walls of villages; money to distribute among the paid soldiers; food to send to the troops at Vassy; sums to transport prisoners into a safe place, for lost arms, for spies, for horses, for the oxen which were sent to the army at Clermont and were led astray, etc. It was not only war which cost money; it was necessary to negotiate, to maintain solicitors and ambassadors, to sustain numerous processes at Rome or at Paris. And then there were the expenses of traveling allowed to agents and lawyers and to ordinary messengers who were sent to Italy, to Spain, to Philip Augustus, there to represent the countess and her son and to defend their interests. And then there is the chapter of presents, of gifts, of alms, and all the expenses of " largess." Political presents: first, two hundred cheeses of Brie sent to Philip Augustus, a quantity of armor sent to the Emperor Frederick II, bales of materials and clothing sent to Rome to wheedle the pope or his cardinals; in Champagne itself, eternal gifts of money, furs, and robes to clerics, women, and nobles; alms for widows and sick servants, and, finally, clothing for newly created knights.

The more detailed accounts of Philip Augustus are still more deservedly a mine of interesting information. The expenses of war naturally predominate: it is the budget of a conqueror. Every line deals with the payment of knights, retainers, mounted and afoot, of crossbowmen, with buying and transportation of munitions and of rations for armies and garrisons; with the construction or repairing of towers, of châteaux, and of walls. Then come the expenses relating to hunting, to falconry, and to the equipment of the chase; alms given to religious establishments and the emoluments granted to royal officers; gifts of clothing and of furs to the queen, the prince royal, and the children of the latter; the maintenance of the wardrobe of the king himself; pensions given to noble lords and ladies; and innumerable presents of money and horses to persons of all classes. It was especially at the great fêtes of the year—Christmas, Easter, and Pentecost—that clothing, " robes " as they then called them, were distributed to the royal family and the members of the entourage. After this partial account, which touches only two years, it is difficult to determine whether the budget of Philip Augustus was better balanced than that of the majority of greater and lesser lords. We may, probably, safely answer in the negative as far as the period before the great conquests—that is, before 1204, the year in which Normandy was taken—is concerned; for it was exactly during this first half of the reign that the historians mentioned the violent exactions practised by Philip Augustus to the detriment of a certain number of bishops and abbots. They all, like the monk Rigord, considered his acts a series of religious persecutions. It was simply the effect of a deficient budget. The king met it as he could by forced loans from the treasure of churchmen, who showed themselves more or less refractory. During all the *ancien régime* this remained an essential of monarchical tradition: when the king had no more money, he seized it with consent or by force wherever he found it in the pocket of the cleric; which never prevented him from being considered the eldest son of the church, and never diverted the church from being the best supporter of monarchy. So far as he could, the baron followed the king's example.

*

* *

As in the budget of the countess of Champagne, some articles of the royal accounts for 1202 and 1203 relate to the gifts which were bestowed on new knights. This is a feature of the times, a consecrated usage to which we must now give our attention. The fêtes of chivalry were, perhaps, the occasion of the greatest expense of French nobility. They voluntarily ruined themselves to make a display of generosity and luxury, and here poetry and history again agree perfectly in the information they give us.

Let us consider history first. The curé Lambert, chronicler of the county of Guines and the seigniory of Ardres, describes the solemnities connected with the knighting of the young Arnoul, son of Count Baldwin II, in 1181. The ceremony was to take place on Pentecost. Baldwin had convoked his sons, his natural children, and all his friends to his court. He himself dubbed his eldest son knight by dealing him the light blow, or rather striking him with his fist on the nape of the neck, which was the principal sign of knighting. There was no participation by the church in this important ceremony. If she had had a part, the curé Lambert would have spoken of it. Here we have the purely feudal chivalry, military and secular, of ancient tradition. The solemnity was joyously celebrated by a feast, at which the most delicate foods and the choicest wines were served. And the curé of Ardres, in recollection of the sumptuous love-feast, at which he no doubt had done his whole duty, naïvely exclaims that the guests endeavored to give themselves a foretaste of the eternal joys of paradise. He describes the knight, newly clothed in his armor, advancing into the midst of the assemblage and distributing handfuls of gold and precious objects to the crowd of domestics, clowns, players, buffoons, minstrels, men, and women, who were not lacking at this feast.

" He gave to all who asked in such a way that the memory of his generosity must remain forever engraved upon their memories. He gave all that he possessed and could acquire. He gave even to the point of folly, making gifts, great and small; he gave not only what he possessed, but also what he did not own, what he had borrowed from others. He kept scarcely anything for himself."

The next day the procession threaded the streets of Ardres to the sound of bells. Monks and clerics chanted hymns to the Trinity, sang the praises of the newly invested knight, and, in the presence of the people who shouted and leaped for joy, the knight made his way into the principal church. "For two years from that day," adds the chronicler, "Arnoul traveled about the country and frequented all tournaments, not without the aid of his father," which, without a doubt, means that the treasure of the count of Guines experienced a considerable drain.

The consequence of this chivalrous extravagance was that the young Arnoul, a little later, reached the end of his resources. He then no longer felt any scruples on the choice of financial expedients. Some years after his knighting the kings of France and England decided to take decisive steps to succor the Holy Land. All of the nobles took the cross, and the general tax, known as the Saladin Tithe, was imposed on all persons who did not. Arnoul, like all the other lords, took the cross and made a vow of pilgrimage; but he carefully avoided setting out for Jerusalem. He was a practical man: he preferred to remain in his fief and lead a life of ease. He collected the tithe, but, instead of devoting it to the purpose of the crusade, instead of even employing it to aid the poor, he used it for his own satisfaction. He was the pauper: the money for the crusades enabled him to figure brilliantly at all tournaments, at banquets, and to buy expensive clothing. And what remained of it, says the chronicler indignantly, he gave to any one who happened along. He renewed his prodigality: to one he gave a present of a hundred marks, to another a hundred livres; to one he gave the silver chalice of his chapel, to another the silver pyxes, and to yet another the silver plate. He gave everything away—clothing, hangings, tapestries: he gave even the horses provided for the expedition to the Holy Land.

To give largess at the expense of the crusade was overstepping all bounds, and the good curé of Ardres, in spite of his respect for his masters, dared to qualify the proceeding as "irreverent" and "impudent."

In the chronicle of Gilbert of Mons chivalry also appears as an occasion of boundless expense. In 1184, the grand court held at Mainz by the Emperor Frederick Barbarossa was the scene of many military investitures. The new knights, their friends, and all the lords of high rank rivaled each other in prodigality. "It was not only," says Gilbert of Mons, "to do honor to the emperor and his sons that the princes and the other nobles ruined themselves in largess: it was also for the glory of their own names." Five years later, Count Baldwin V of Hainault celebrated the knighting of his own son at Speyer. The knights, clerics, and domestics of his court received a goodly number of saddle-horses, palfreys, and coursers from him. Minstrels of both sexes were impartially showered with gifts. At the court of France, under similar circumstances, money flowed in streams. In 1209, Prince Louis, the eldest son of Philip Augustus, was invested with knighthood in the great assembly of Compiègne. "On the holy day of Pentecost," says the chronicler, William of Armorica, "Louis received the baldric of knighthood from the hand of his father with such solemnity, in the presence of such a concourse of grandees and royalty, before such a multitude of men, and with such an abundance of provisions and gifts, that to this day nothing to equal it has been seen." On the same day one hundred other young men were knighted, says an English chronicler. It is to be regretted that the middle ages have not transmitted to us an account of the expenses of the knighting of the son of Philip Augustus, as they have left us an account of the expenses of the dubbing of a brother of Saint Louis and a son of Philip the Hardy in 1237 and 1267, respectively: in them one would already have seen the evidence of royal prodigality, money given to the minstrels, horses, armor, and robes lined with ermine and sable lavished on new knights;

gilded girdles, silver cups, and jewels offered to the ladies; the heavy expenses which the pitching of tents and the sumptuous preparations for the banquet entailed.

If historical texts of this period do not give us all desirable details about the ceremony of investiture and the fêtes of chivalry, we may look for them in contemporary *chansons de geste.* These often speak of the ceremonies of knighting and of the largess which accompanied them. The material which we find in them agrees perfectly with that found in the chronicles. Without doubt, the feudal poets in this instance simply described the facts which they had before their eyes.

In the ballad *Garin le Lorrain* there is a brief but expressive notice on the knighting of Bégon. Bégon presented himself to King Pepin:

"'Sire,' said he, 'we are of an age to carry arms: make four knights of my brother Garin, Fromont, William, and me. We greatly desire it.' 'I consent,' responded the king. And immediately requesting arms and rich clothing he commenced by dubbing Garin, then Bégon, then Fromont and William. Rich was the distribution of the vair and gray, and grand was the feast. After the banquet they emerged from the palace. The new knights mounted their coursers, took their shields, and tilted for a long time. Bégon, whose shield was ornamented with fine gold, rode his course with the rapid certainty of a winged falcon."

Further on the description becomes more detailed, and at the same time more complete. The story concerns the knighting of Fromondin, son of Fromont, at the very height of the war, fought under the walls of Bordeaux, between the two great factions of the song, the men of Bordeaux and Lorraine. The uncles of the young man, Bernard of Naisil and Baldwin of Flanders, admired his deportment.

"'Just see,' said they, 'what a bold nephew we have! Why do we not ask the mighty Fromont to knight him.' 'We could not do better,' replied the Fleming. On rising from the table they went to find Count Fromont. 'Your son,' said Bernard to him, 'has become large, strong of arm, and deep of chest; is it not time to make him a knight? It is certain that he will know how to cross a lance and fight our mortal enemies better than any one else; and if you wait until judgment-day, you will never see him more fit to be knighted.' 'These are strange words,' answered Fromont; 'Fromondin is still too young to support the weight of arms.' 'O, do not say that,' said Bernard; 'reflect that you are getting old, that your hair is becoming white, that the time for your ease is coming; rest you then, and leave to your son the burden of war.' Fromont could not hear these words without reddening with anger. 'You provoke me, Sire Bernard,' said he. 'To hear you talk, I am an old man in my dotage. I can still mount my horse well enough, however, and I have no need of any one to defend my rights. To-morrow we shall have a pitched battle, and I will meet you; and these are my conditions: that he of us who shall be worsted shall have his spur cut off next the heel with a sharp sword.' 'Good nephew,' said Bernard, 'many thanks; I had rather not. And, please God, I did not intend to provoke you. I spoke to you thus with good intention, and because your friends asked me to do so.' 'You wish it?' said Fromont. 'Ah, well! So be it; I give my consent.'"

This first scene, in which the resistance of the father is so vividly pictured, is not pure fancy. There is something decidedly human in this reluctance of the knight who does not wish to abdicate and retards the knighting of his son as much as he can, because to him it is the sign of advancing age and of the physical decadence which threatens him. And, furthermore, it must not be forgotten that for the young lord knighting meant his majority, emancipation, and partnership in the paternal sovereignty; his entry into a partial possession of the future heritage. It is not surprising that the father hesitated and put off this maturity as long as he could. Historical fact here confirms what poetry relates. It will be enough to mention the case of Philip Augustus, a very suspicious father, who for the longest time possible deferred the admission of his heir, Prince Louis, to knighthood. Louis of France was not knighted until he was over twenty-two years of age, and yet the king, before consenting to the knighting, took all sorts of precautions and exacted rigorous promises from his son, in the form of a treaty, which has come down to us in the registers of the chancellery: to employ in his service only knights and retainers sworn to the king, never to borrow money from the communes and burghers without paternal consent, and even to hold certain seigniories, from which he was to have the revenues as feudal vassal and under a perpetually revocable lien.

The Fromont of the poem did not resist so long, and he did not impose heavy conditions on his son. We return to the poem. The knighting of Fromondin is decided upon. The young man has returned to his lodgings. Fifty vessels are filled with water; it is the knightly bath, an ordinary hygienic measure which the church later converted into a symbolic purification.

" The first is for the young noble, the others for the young varlets who are to be armed with him. The chamberlains bring in robes and garments of velvet. The squires lead the mules, coursers, palfreys, and prize horses. Fromont had sent his son Baucent his own steed, the one he loved best, with a saddle which came from Toulouse. Fromondin in mounting leaped from solid earth (that is to say, without stirrups) with such energy that he went too far and jostled Bernard of Naisil. ' Oh, Sire,' he said laughingly to his uncle, ' You shall live with me; I pray you.' ' Gladly,' answered Bernard, ' but on condition that you do what I wish: you shall delight in spurring the horse, in distributing your honors to noble knights, and in giving the vair and gray to the poor. I cannot repeat it too often: a true prince exalts himself by giving largess; and if he is avaricious every day of his life is detrimental to others!' ' I will do your pleasure,' answered Fromondin."

It was also decided that he was to bear his first arms in a tournament: that is, in a real battle, more bloody in *Garin* than in reality.

The day of the tournament arrived. Although the poet does not expressly say so, Fromondin doubtless passed the night in the church, in the vigil of arms, for he is described as returning to his lodgings after having heard the morning mass, taking light refreshment, and then going to bed to sleep.

" The day dawned beautifully and the sun beamed. Count Fromont was the first to leave his bed. He opened his window, and the fresh brilliance struck him full in the face. In a moment he was dressed and shod. He went completely armed from his room, ordered his horse, and rode through all the quarters of the town waking the knights. He came to his son's lodgings and found the young man asleep in his bed. Fromont called Bernard: ' Come,' said he, ' see my son. He should have been given a chance to get bigger and stronger, but he must be clothed in the white hauberk!' And then in a loud voice, ' Come, Fromondin, get up. You must not sleep too long, good sire. The great tournament ought already to be forming.' The young man leaped from his bed on hearing the voice, and the squires entered to serve him. They quickly booted and clothed him. In the presence of all, Count William of Montclin girded the sword on him with a golden belt. 'Dear nephew,' he said, 'I enjoin thee not to trust false and dissolute men; given a long life thou shalt be a mighty prince. Always be strong, victorious, and redoubtable to all thy enemies. Give the vair and gray to many deserving men. It is the way to attain honor.' 'Everything is in God's hands,' answered Fromondin. Then they led to him a costly horse. He mounted him with an easy bound, and they handed him a shield emblazoned with a lion."

This is the ceremony of knighting and the words of the patron which comprise almost the whole of knightly ethics.

Farther on another knighting is described. But this one is of a comic character. It is the knighting of the son of a villein, Rigaut, son of Hervis, and in the eyes of our feudal bard a villein could not be anything but ridiculous. This Rigaut was, however, very brave and strong, and he was descended from high nobility: this was why, as an exception to the rule, he was to be knighted. But he was an ill-bred rustic and did not know the forms.

"Bégon said to him, 'You shall be a knight; only go and bathe a little, and then some one will give you the vair and gray.' 'To the devil with your vair and gray, if I must take a bath for it,' he answered; 'I have not fallen into a moor or a marsh; I have nothing to do with vair and gray. At the home of my father, Hervis, there is enough fustian for my use.' 'I have charged myself with clothing you,' said Bégon. They gave Rigaut the rich mantle and piece of ermine which covered him and trailed on the earth more than a foot. Rigaut found this very inconvenient. A squire carrying a knife to serve the knights passed by. Rigaut asked for the knife, and cut off a foot and a half of the pelisse. 'What are you doing, my good son,' said his father. 'It is the custom for new knights to wear the trailing robe of vair and gray.' 'It is a foolish custom,' said Rigaut; 'how could I run and jump with this pelisse trailing?' 'By my head,' said the king, 'he is not far wrong.' Then Bégon asked for the sword, Froberge, seized the gold hilt, and himself attached it to Rigaut's belt, who allowed him to do it. Then he raised the palm of his hand and let it descend so sharply on his cousin's neck that he well-nigh stretched him upon the ground. Angrily Rigaut drew his new sword a foot and a half as if to strike the good knight Bégon. Hervis, his father, stopped him: 'What are you doing, madman?

It is the custom; it is thus that one makes knights.' 'It is a bad custom,' said Rigaut; 'bad luck to him who first established it.' The bystanders began to laugh, but his father went on: 'Listen to me; if you are not a brave and hardy knight I pray God Who died on the cross, not to let you live a day longer.' 'If he is not a brave man,' said Bégon, 'I hope to lose the château of Belin.'"

Here ends the description of a grotesque knighting, but instructive, because it contains all the details of the ceremony in use, including the dubbing with a stroke of the fist.

The last case of this kind which our poem presents is the knighting of Gerbert, son of Garin. It is the most complete, if not the most poetic, of all. The investor of Gerbert must have been Pepin the emperor himself.

"The king said to the Burgundian, Aubri: 'You will give the young man his bath; then we will give him the vair and gray.' They heated the bath. Gerbert, having returned to his lodgings, got into his bath and remained a little while. The other vessels accommodated eighty pages. The emperor for love of Garin made them all knights. They all shared in the vair and gray, a present of the radiant queen. As for Gerbert he received a precious velvet robe, enriched with flowers of gold and richly bordered and seamed with ermine. The embroidery alone had cost four gold marks. The emperor took a hauberk from the treasure of Saint-Denis which he himself had formerly taken from a king he had killed. The links were small, strong, light, and white as the hawthorn-flower. A burnished helmet was placed on the young man's head, and it was the king himself who belted the sword which contained a tooth of Saint Firmin in its hilt to his side. When he raised the palm of his hand to strike the nape of the neck the king said: 'Knight, be brave and hardy; shun all bad deeds!' 'I pledge myself,' answered Gerbert. A valuable horse had been led in; the bridle and the saddle, enriched with gold, were valued at a thousand Paris livres. Gerbert mounted him easily. They gave him a curved shield, blazoned with a golden lioncel. He seized the lance with its gilt banner, spurred his horse with both heels, stopped short, and returned to the emperor. How he was then admired and applauded by matrons and maidens, burghers and servants! 'He knows how to ride a horse,' said one, 'how to lead an army, and defy his enemies.' After that they knighted twenty other knights. Gerbert gave them burnished helmets, white hauberks, and mighty steeds. You may imagine that there was plenty of gold for the jongleurs and minstrels assembled to make the feast more beautiful.

"Thus clothed and mounted, Gerbert and his knights returned to the palace. The king took him in his arms and kissed his cheeks and lips. Water was sent for. All sat down at the table, and when they had eaten and drunk at leisure, they went with the queen to hear vespers in the royal chapel. Then they returned to Notre-Dame, where the new knights were to keep vigil. Gerbert remained there all night, and when day came he heard mass and presented a rich offering. And then the new knight hastened to his inn."

The fête ended with a sumptuous banquet at the palace.

"The king took Gerbert by the hand and seated him at the table near himself. As one might suppose, there was not lacking goose, gosling, and roast peacock. On rising from the table the horses were ordered and they left Paris for the tilt. The queen, of beautiful and noble figure, proposed to follow them accompanied by ten maidens. Gerbert on a large, fiery courser, lance in hand, his arm covered by a rich shield, was regarded by all. It was said that his horse, his arms, and he were all a single being. The tilt was accomplished without difficulty or quarrel."

Thus historians and bards agree in picturing the chivalry of the end of the twelfth century. It was an imposing, sumptuous display, in which the foolish extravagance of the nobles knew no bounds. It was the triumph of "largess." The knightly investiture, given by a father or a suzerain, had a wholly military and secular character; the sign of investiture was made as simple as possible, and the moral contained in the sermon of investiture quite rudimentary, indeed: the young man is simply required to be brave, terrible to his enemies, and generous to his friends. The religious element was limited to the vigil of arms in the church and the mass heard in the morning, but there is no investiture by the priest, or the bishop, nor even the benediction of the sword placed on the altar; this came later, during and primarily at the end of the thirteenth century.

Could one, then, say that the religious or sacerdotal investiture did not exist at the time of Philip Augustus as well as the pure lay investiture, and in certain cases even predominate? Such a statement would be imprudent; for here is a famous example of ecclesiastical knighting recorded by a historian.

In 1213, the conqueror of Languedoc—the devout Catholic, Simon de Montfort—wished to knight his son Amauri. He was at Castelnaudary, at the time of the feast of Saint John, with the two bishops of Orléans and Auxerre. He asked the bishop of Orléans to consent to confer knighthood upon his son by putting the baldric on him. The bishop for a long time refused, says the chronicler Peter of Vaux-de-Cernay: he knew that it was contrary to custom, and that ordinarily only a knight could create a knight. However, at the insistence of the count and his friends, he finally decided to do it. It was in summertime. Simon de Montfort pitched large tents in the plain outside the city, which was much too small to contain the multitude of onlookers. On the day fixed the bishop of Orléans celebrated mass in a tent. The young Amauri, his father on one hand and his mother on the other, approached the altar. His parents offered him to the Lord and asked the bishop to consecrate him knight in the service of Christ. Immediately the two prelates knelt before the altar, belted the sword on him, and sang the *Veni Creator* with profound devotion. And the chronicler adds these significant words: '' What a new and unusual way of conferring knighthood. Who could restrain his tears? '' This mode of knighting was, perhaps, not so extraordinary as Peter of Vaux-de-Cernay thought, for in a ritual of the Roman church, drawn up at the beginning of the eleventh century, there already is the formula of prayer to be used by bishops in conferring knighthood. However, the very words of the chronicler prove that in France knighting by bishops was not common. Simon de Montfort introduced it: he inaugurated the ecclesiastical tradition; he invited the church to take chivalry and make a kind of sacrament of it, and it is very possible that such an example set by the hero of the crusade against the Albigenses induced a large number of devout Catholic families to proceed in the same manner.

CHAPTER XI

THE NOBLE DAME

WHEN the French noble was in possession of knighthood—
that is to say, when he was a full warrior and qualified to
govern his fief—he married. The woman whom he married
brought him lands, castles, and at the very least revenues.
It was the only way for him to meet the demands on his
budget and to rank among the proprietors and sovereigns,
unless he was associated with his father while awaiting his
inheritance. This brings us to the interesting question of
marriages and the more general question of the noblewoman
and of the lady of the manor in the middle ages.

At the end of the twelfth century the feudal régime fully
and definitely recognized the woman's right to succeed to the
fief and to possess the seigniory. She inherited the land and
the power, thus emerging from the semi-domestic state to
which French society had so long confined her. Christianity
struggled laboriously against the customs of the time, in
order to secure her emancipation, and feudalism decidedly
advanced her. On the other hand, as head of a religious
house, as abbess, or dignitary of an abbey, the noblewoman
was considered ever more capable of curing souls. There
was, then, an evident progress in feminine destiny—progress
closely interwoven with that of general civilization. It will
be seen, when we speak of the literary nobility and of the
development of courtesy in the time of Philip Augustus,
that that culture tended to raise woman to a superior condition in certain parts of seigniorial France. But it must
be admitted that the life led by the nobles did not usually
have the important consequences that certain historians have
been pleased to point out. When, for example, one reads
in a lecture of Guizot on the History of French Civilization
that the life of the château created the family spirit, encouraged domestic virtues, brought out the noble sentiments

of gallantry, and refined the mind, he must not accept the statement without reserve. What, after all, was the château? A military post, a barracks; and it has never appeared that barracks were a very suitable place for the creation and development of delicate morals, and of sentiments of courtesy founded on the respect for woman.

In the majority of cases the lady of the manor, in the time of Philip Augustus, was still what she had been in the centuries preceding feudalism: a virago of violent temperament, of strong passions, trained from infancy in all physical exercises, sharing the dangers and pleasures of the knights of her circle. The feudal life, full of surprises and dangers, demanded of her a healthy mind and body, a masculine carriage, and habits all but masculine. She accompanied her father in the chase; in time of war, if she were a widow or if her husband were on the crusade, she conducted the defense of the seigniory; and, in time of peace, she did not recoil before the longest and most dangerous pilgrimages. She even went on the crusade on her own account. It was in this way that Margaret of France, the sister of Philip Augustus,—twice a widow, first of the young King Henry of England, the eldest of the sons of Henry II; then of King Béla III of Hungary,—sought to aid the crusaders who were fighting in the Holy Land in 1197. She sold her dowry, and took the money thus realized to the Orient. She disembarked at Tyre, where her brother-in-law, Count Henry of Champagne, met her; and she died eight days after her arrival. In 1218, in France, one sees an interesting spectacle in the county of Champagne: a war between the countess of Champagne, Blanche of Navarre, guardian of her minor son, Thibaud IV, and their rival Érard of Brienne, was fought to the death. And Blanche conducted this war in person, as leader of her troops. She invaded Lorraine, burned Nancy in passing, and joined the camp of the Emperor Frederick II. Later, in the neighborhood of Joinville or of the Château-Villain, she led her knights in person, waging a real pitched battle against her principal enemies; and she won the victory.

How were these young noblewomen, destined to become so energetic, brought up? Strictly historical documents do not inform us. The chronicles only mention the women of the military aristocracy in connection with marriages, divorces, or genealogy; in informing us of their children and their lineage. Women did not have a place in general or local history, except when they held or transmitted fiefs, thus actively aiding in the circulation of lands and seigniories by entering or dissolving marriages. On the other hand, they were rarely mentioned in letters: at most, one finds in the works of certain ecclesiastical authors letters like those which the theologian Adam of Perseigne wrote to a noblewoman, Mathilda of Blois, countess of Perche. She had asked him for a rule of conduct by which to live as a Christian in the world. The abbot of Perseigne gave her excellent precepts of religion and morals. He counseled her, above all, to abstain from games of chance, from wasting her time at chess, and from taking pleasure at the indecent farces of the players. He also advised her to be moderate in matters of dress, and he ridiculed the gown with the long train, comparing the women who wore them to foxes, with whom the tail was the most beautiful ornament. One conclusion appears from the letter—that the ladies of the manor were gamesters. We know this from the *chansons de geste*, which often present them as engaged in interminable games of dice and chess.

If we may believe the preachers and monks who wrote the more or less satirical treatises on morals, women must also have had other faults. The least of these were being coquettes, spendthrifts, ruining their husbands, wearing false hair, rouging, and proudly displaying their gowns with trains. The authors of the sermons incessantly stormed against the extreme length of the gowns; a diabolical invention, they said. But all this is commonplace and not at all characteristic: there is nothing in it that is entirely peculiar to the middle ages. As to the more serious reproaches, there is a question of how far one can rely on the allegations of the preachers. By profession they saw the dark side of everything, unduly exaggerated human infirmities, and struck hard rather than justly. Can one rely any more on the satires of the monks? The monks were often pessimists, disposed to slander everything of their age, and accustomed especially to consider woman as a perverse and infernal being, who had ruined and always would ruin the human race.

In every case we find only vague generalities in ecclesiastical literature. In it woman, as a whole, without distinction as to social condition is attacked, and it would be very difficult to obtain precise information from it relating to the life of women who were born and bred in the château.

In the poems of a martial nature, where the soldier occupies the whole stage and plays the principal rôle, the feminine side is sacrificed. The young girl does not appear, except to perform the duties of hospitality, and hospitality understood in the broadest sense, toward the knight who is the guest of her father. It was she who was charged with greeting him, with disarming him, with making ready his chamber and his bed, with preparing his bath, and even (we have on this point many unquestionable texts, especially in *Girart de Roussillon*) with massaging him in order to help him go to sleep. We must accept the middle ages as they were, with all the simplicity of their customs. That society was much freer than ours in words and in action: *honi soit qui mal y pense.*

One gathers from the *chansons de geste* that it was the young women who made all the advances in love to knights entertained at the paternal mansion. The latter resembled Hippolytus of Greek legend: they dreamed only of war and the chase. Maidens thought them handsome, and they told them so without the least embarrassment: it was they who made the declaration of love. And, more remarkable still, their advances were sometimes very coldly received. To be sure, the authors of these martial poems, the minstrels who sang to amuse the barons after drinking, had a clumsy hand for treating such delicate matters. Their observations on the position and customs of the woman of high rank could not be very profound or drawn from the better sources. Have not writers at all times been inclined to give as the expression of general truth the various scandalous deeds or the pathological cases which they from preference study? What idea of the French bourgeoisie would a foreigner obtain to-day if he knew it only from the books of our modern novelists?

One cannot, then, judge the woman of the epoch in general from the *chansons de geste*. What can be most clearly

inferred from these recitals is that their authors had a very
limited and very inadequate respect for woman, and this was
simply because she was still considered by feudal society as an
inferior being, whom one could slander and treat rudely. To
tell the truth, married women in the *chansons* appear in a
more favorable light than young women, which is singular.
In the poem *Garin le Lorrain,* in *Girart de Roussillon,* the
noble lady, the lawful wife of the baron, was usually a virtuous person, who loved her husband and was devoted and
faithful to him. We are, for example, told of Beatrice, wife
of Duke Bégon, who, carried away by a traitor, desperately
resisted and said to the ravisher, " I will allow myself to be
broiled and roasted before I will permit you to approach me."
The wife of Girart of Roussillon, the Countess Bertha, is a
model of conjugal devotion. But, on the other hand, the
minstrels have no scruples in presenting women of the highest nobility, even queens, as exposed to the insults and brutality of knights.

In the lay *Garin* the wife of King Pepin, Blanchefleur,
was one day obliged to snatch from the hands of a Bordeaux
chief, Bernard of Naisil, an unfortunate messenger sent to
the king by the opposite side, whom Bernard was about to
murder in the open court before the eyes of his sovereign.
" Your place should be in the forests," she cried indignantly, " robbing pilgrims and infesting the highways."—
" Silence, foolish and immodest woman," responded the furious Bernard. " The king must have been out of his senses
when he burdened himself with you. A violent death to
him who brought about your marriage! Only reproach and
dishonor can come of it."—" You lie! " responded the queen;
" thief, murderer, traitor, perjurer! The king of France
should not have permitted you to appear in his court."
Then, after that avalanche of insults, she fled in tears to her
chamber. Instead of interposing and defending his wife, the
king remained silent. The poet evidently intended to make
him play an unimportant, even a ridiculous, rôle. It was
the hero of the lay, the Duke Garin, who avenged the honor
of the queen. He arrived at the palace just at the moment
when the queen came out of her room. Lorrain looked at her
and saw her beautiful eyes bathed with tears. " Beautiful

queen," he said, " who could give you any cause for annoy-
ance? By the living God, there is no one under heaven—I
except my lord, the king—who, if he dared as much as to
contradict you, would not become my mortal enemy. Who
has insulted you?"—"Sire," said Blanchefleur, "that
traitor, that brigand, Bernard of Naisil, has disgraced me
before the king." Garin immediately went to Bernard, violently pushing aside the ranks before him, seized him by the
hair, threw him to the ground under his feet, broke four
of his teeth, and, after ripping up his chest with his spurs,
left him.

If the minstrels, the authors or composers of poems, can
always be believed, the husbands themselves did not refrain
from ill-treating their wives. A word or a request which
displeased them was enough. In *Garin,* the Queen Blanchefleur asked the king to declare himself in favor of the party
of Lorrain. " The king heard it and anger showed in his
face: he raised his fist and struck her on the nose, so hard
that he drew four drops of blood." And the lady said,
" Many thanks; when it pleases you, you may do it again."
One could cite other scenes of the same sort in which there
is always a blow on the nose with the fist: it almost became
a habit. Feudal poets also energetically reproved the knight
who took counsel with his wife, and they were pleased to
attribute speeches such as these to their heroes: " Woman,
go within and eat and drink with your attendants in your
gilded and painted rooms; busy yourself with dyeing silks:
that is your business. Mine is to strike with the sword of
steel."

It must be remembered that this way of treating women as
though they were beings of a secondary order, of abusing
them, and of roughly sending them to the women's quarters,
was the result of a fancy which at the least singularly exaggerated actual fact. Without speaking of the romances of
the courteous type which belonged to the cycle of the Round
Table, and of which we will speak later, there were other
lays almost contemporaneous with Philip Augustus, as that
of *Guillaume de Dole,* in which the woman, even the young
girl, played a rôle which was all to her credit. In this last
poem the action consists almost entirely in bringing to view

the courage and ability of the young lady, Liénor, the sister of William of Dole, who victoriously struggled against a calumny of which she was the victim, and found a reward for her virtue in a marriage with the emperor. It is true that the lay *Guillaume de Dole*, though it is foreign to the British cycle and celebrates chivalrous bravery and the tournament, is not precisely inspired by the feudal and martial spirit which animates the epics. It represents an intermediate type between the purely military type and the romances of adventure—a romance of love according to the customs in certain seigniorial courts, which were more polished and more courteous than others.

One can conclude that, even in the time of Philip Augustus, the courteous spirit favorable to women was very rare in feudal society; and that, in a great majority of the feudal seigniories and manors, there persisted the old tendency, the disrespectful and brutal attitude toward women, described and, if you please, exaggerated in the greater part of the *chansons de geste*. The amorous fancies of the troubadours of the south and of some trouvères of Flanders and Champagne should not delude us. The sentiments which they expressed were simply, we must believe, those of a select few, of a very small minority of knights and barons, who were in advance of their century. The greater part of feudal society understood the statements concerning women otherwise: woman was considered to be of an inferior substance, and treated accordingly by fathers and husbands. History proves this. It shows us the sovereign and smaller lords acting with the same violence, the same absolute lack of deference and courtesy. Henry of Anjou, king of England and ruler of the Plantagenet empire, was troubled by his wife, the famous Eleanor of Aquitaine, in his pleasures as also in his policies regarding his sons: he kept her imprisoned for many years. We know, on the other hand, with what brutality Philip Augustus conducted himself toward the unfortunate Ingeborg of Denmark, whom he abandoned the day after the marriage. We know how he kept her prisoner, first in a certain convent; then shut up in the tower of Étampes, where she remained for a very long time. If the complaints of the victim herself can be believed, her husband, not content with submitting her to a régime of rigorous seclusion, would not even give her enough to eat or to wear. Must it be assumed, in order to explain this contemptible harshness, that Philip Augustus and Henry II were men of a particularly inhuman temperament and rulers without mercy? Ordinary barons acted in the same way. In 1191, we see a seignior of the county of Burgundy, Gautier of Salins, maltreating his wife, Mathilda of Bourbon, and throwing her into prison. She, fortunately for her, succeeded in escaping and sought refuge with her parents. Such instances were, without doubt, not exceptional: they simply prove that, in spite of all the theoretical gallantries of the poets, the middle ages, even at the end of the twelfth century, were still in practice very hard for the woman, noble though she was, and that the precepts of chivalry, which enjoined deference to the weaker sex, were far from being realized.

*

* *

This will appear still more clearly if we consider feudal marriages. On this subject poetical and historical sources are in remarkable accord. Long ago it was said: In the manners and customs of that epoch marriage was, before all else, a union of two seigniories. The seignior married in order to extend his fief, as well as to raise sons capable of defending it; in his eyes a wife represented, above all, an estate and a castle.

The first consequence of this peculiar conception was that the husband was chosen by the father or suzerain, and the feeling of the young girl to be married was not consulted in any way. The feudal heiress passively received the knight or baron who was destined for her. She was, in a sense, absorbed in the estate or the castle: she formed a part of the real estate; she passed with the land to the one who was to possess it, and her consent mattered little. As a young girl, orphan, or widow she could not resist her father, who held the seigniory, or the suzerain, who in certain cases had acquired the disposal of it. On this point, as always, feudal usage appears in the *chansons de geste* in striking relief. The kings are to be seen distributing fiefs, and the women who represent them, to their faithful vassals as if it were purely a question of material interests. It will do here to recall a few very curious pages from the poem, *Lorrains*.

King Thierri of Maurienne said to Duke Garin:

" ' Free and noble page, I cannot love you too much, for you have defended this fief for me. Before dying I wish to repay you: here is my little girl, Blanchefleur, fair of face; I give her to you.' The maiden was only eight and a half years old; she was already the most beautiful person to be found in a hundred countries. ' Take her, Seignior Garin, and with her you shall have my fief.'— ' Sire,' responded Garin, ' I take her on the condition that the Emperor Pepin will not oppose it.' "

Garin then went to find the Emperor Pepin:

" ' Before leaving the world,' he said to him, ' King Thierri sent for me and gave me his daughter, and with her the fief of Maurienne; I have received the gift, Sire Emperor, on the condition that it would be agreeable to you.' ' I willingly grant it,' responded Pepin."

But then Fromont, another vassal, rose up and cried out, with anger in his eyes:

" ' I, I oppose the gift. Sire, you hunted one day near Senlis, in the forest of Montmélian. It then pleased you to give to the brother of Garin the duchy of Gascony. At the same time you promised to give me the first vacant estate which I should demand. There were more than a hundred witnesses to it. Maurienne is to my liking and I lay claim to it.'—' You are mistaken,' said the king. ' What a father at the hour of his death gives his child with the consent of his vassals no one has the right to take away. When another fief reverts to me, however large it be, I shall invest you with it.'—' No,' said Fromont, ' the fief of Maurienne has reverted to you; I demand it and I will have it.' "

There was a dispute between the two barons: they began by heaping each other with abuses, then they came to blows, and Garin dealt Fromont a heavy blow with his fist, " which stunned him and stretched him out on the floor." This rivalry and the blow with the fist were the cause of a savage war which fills the whole poem, the war between the Lorrains and the Bordelais.

In the preceding passage the question at issue was the fief

of Maurienne, and not at all the young girl whose destiny was attached to it. She had no importance; she fell to the grantee of the fief—that was all. But to return to Fromont. King Pepin refused him the heiress and the fief of Maurienne. But he wished to marry: he sought his cousin, the Count Dreux, and related to him what had happened at the court of the king; how Garin had " given him his fist on the teeth ":

" ' You are wrong,' said the Count Dreux, ' to insist on having Blanchefleur. Were you then afraid of getting no wife? Whenever you wish, instead of one, you may have ten. I have just returned from seeking a noble and advantageous marriage for you: it is with the lady of Ponthieu, Hélissent, a sister of the Count Baldwin of Flanders. Her husband recently died; she has only one small child: once in the heritage you will no more have to fear a single enemy.' "

Fromont accepted the expected heritage. Dreux proceeded to Baldwin and requested the hand of his sister for Fromont:

" ' I gladly grant it,' responded Baldwin. ' To be sure, my sister is a beautiful and rich woman: from the ocean to the border of the Rhine, there is none who can compare with her; but Count Fromont is rich in possessions and friends.'—' Now,' added Dreux, ' we must not lose time; long delays are rarely profitable; for if the emperor knew that the land of Ponthieu were vacant, he would give your sister to the first fellow from his kitchen, who would roast a peacock for him.'—' You speak the truth,' responded Baldwin."

Here, with the natural exaggeration of poetry, we have indeed an historical fact: the omnipotence of the suzerain, especially of the king, who could give the heiress of a vacant fief to whom he chose. See how the marriage in question was announced to the interested person.

Dreux and Fromont arrived at the palace of the count of Flanders:

" Baldwin called his sister. On seeing her appear, all arose, and each admired the noble grace of her figure and the beauty of her face. The Fleming took her by the hand: ' My beautiful and dear sister, let us speak a little apart. How are you? '—' Very well, God

be thanked.'—'Well, then, to-morrow you shall have a husband.'—
'What did you say, my brother? I have just lost my lord: it is only
a month since he was laid in the grave. I have by him a beautiful
little child, which by the grace of God shall some day be a rich man; I
should think of protecting him, of adding wealth to his inheritance.
And what would the world say if I should so quickly take another
baron?'—'You will do it, however, my sister. He whom I give
you is richer than was your first husband; he is young and handsome: he is the son of Hardré, the Count Palatine; he is the valiant
Fromont. Hardré dying, the estate of Amiens and many others
will revert to him.' When the lady heard the name Fromont, her
feelings suddenly changed: 'Sire Brother,' she said, 'I will do so
since you desire it.'"

We admit that there was on her part a timid attempt at
resistance, and that probably she was not indifferent toward
the proposed husband. But, even if she had been, she would
have had to submit; the wish of the head of the family or
of the suzerain could not be opposed. And just as curious
as the brutality with which the marriage was imposed, was
the rapidity with which it was concluded:

"Immediately the Fleming called Fromont: 'Come, come free
and noble knight; come also Dreux and all our other friends'; and
seizing the right hand of the lady he placed it in that of Fromont
before them all. They did not wait a day, they did not wait an
hour: on the spot they proceeded to the church. Clerics and priests
were notified. There they were blessed and married. The nuptials
were celebrated in the palace with magnificence; they jested, they
laughed, they were entertained in a hundred ways; then if any one
had a desire to complain it was not Count Fromont."

The poem continues with an account of a battle; and it
would seem that the author had entirely forgotten the young
Blanchefleur and her fiancé, Duke Garin. It is true that
she was only eight and a half years old and could wait. It
returns to her, however, and relates how the archbishop of
Reims advised the Emperor Pepin not to keep the promise
which he had made to give Blanchefleur to Garin, because,
if Garin married her, Fromont, enraged, would cease to be
the king's man and great peril would ensue:

"'What would you have me do?' said the king.—'Keep the
maiden for yourself. You are both young; she has no less land

than you yourself: you could not wish a more honorable union.'—
'Ah, indeed,' responded the king, 'marvelous words! What, Sire
Archbishop, do you wish me to perjure my honor, to deceive those
who have served me best?'—'No,' said the archbishop, 'I was
not thinking of that. But everything could be arranged with honor:
I know two monks ready to swear to-morrow that Blanchefleur is
a relative of Garin; act on their testimony, and by noon they will
be separated.'—'If it is thus,' said the king, 'I shall go to see the
maiden, and if she suits me I shall become her husband.' "

We must assume that Blanchefleur had grown in the interval, for the king found her to his liking. The plan was
carried out as the archbishop had arranged it: the two monks
swore that the fiancés were relatives within the prohibited
degrees; Garin and Blanchefleur were separated. The king
then bluntly announced to the young girl that he wished to
marry her:

" 'I intend to marry you myself.'—'Good Sire,' she responded,
'I thank you: you do me great honor; but I call God, Who never
lies, to witness, that I would not give Garin the Lorrain for the
honor of being queen. Garin is the one man in the world whom I
could love most. However, since my desires and those of my father
cannot be followed, I am ready to obey you.' "

Garin was then tempted to express his displeasure by in-
juring the king, but his brother threw himself before him:

" What! Senseless Lorrain, what would you say? Relinquish
Blanchefleur; if you wish a wife you can find ten for one, all of a
lineage equal to hers. Take her, Sire, may it be for your happiness."

It was thus that Pepin married Blanchefleur. The nuptials
were " grand and rich." At the formal feast Garin served
as cupbearer:

" He was beautiful of form and face: one could not find a better
built man in the world, or one of more courteous appearance. And
the new queen took great pleasure in looking at him; her eyes went
constantly from him to Pepin, and the king seemed ever smaller
and more insignificant. Ah, why did she have to come to the court!
Why had she not sent for Garin in Maurienne? He would have
become her husband. . . . Alas! it was too late, and after all she
could only accuse herself! "

In the preceding passages we find all the elements of feudal marriage, and all the customs which attach to it: the identification of the heiress, the noblewoman, with the fief; a betrothal while one of the parties was still in infancy; the absolute right of the father over his daughter, and of the suzerain, especially of the king, over his vassal; the unsentimental character of the marriage, which is considered solely as the union of two rich and powerful feudal landholders; the practically complete effacement and passive submission on the part of the woman, who was consulted neither as to her wishes nor as to her heart: these are the things which clearly appear in the narrative of the poet. One dare not say that these elements were invariable and that one may not find certain passages in the epic in which, when marriage was the question, women revolted against the power which held them down and refused suitors who were imposed on them; but these are the exceptions which confirm the rule. And this rule, these customs and manners, actually existed in the society of that time; allowing for the exaggerations of detail inherent in poetic works, they are true historical facts, elements of real life.

It is not necessary to have thoroughly studied the chronicles contemporaneous with Philip Augustus to ascertain that betrothals between infants who were still in the nursery, and that marriages actually contracted between girls of twelve and boys of fourteen (for example, the marriage of Baldwin VI of Hainault and of Marie of Champagne in 1185), were very common facts in the history of the seigniory. It is also proved by innumerable examples that the seigniorial marriages were usually the result of agreements made long before between the possessors of the fief, when the children were still under age, and that these matrimonial agreements were made and unmade to fit the changes and necessities in the general policy of the heads of the seigniories. For girls and boys were then only the figures on a chessboard, so that individual tastes or the particular wishes of the children of the noble family were unknown or were constantly sacrificed to the political and material interests of the house. History, as well as poetry, shows us that fathers and suzerains were autocrats, who imposed decisions.

It is sufficient in this regard to allude to the numerous cases in which Philip Augustus made use of his absolute right in marrying his vassals, or in preventing them from marrying against his will.   In history, as in the epics, the girls were all married young, willingly or unwillingly, and widows were not left time to weep for their husbands, inasmuch as it was imperative that the fief should be managed by a man; so that in those feudal amours sentiment had no part.   Why be astonished, then, at the extreme easiness of divorces and at the strange vicissitudes in the careers of many of the noble dames?

From the natural trend of things they themselves acquired the habit of changing masters.   To have three or four husbands was a minimum.   The slightest motive, the least physical defect, a simple illness, might cause a man to repudiate a woman; but the documents justify the assertion that many of the separations were divorces by mutual consent. The church vainly attempted to impose its veto; it was overruled, obliged to close its eyes.   And yet the principle of the indissolubility of marriage is said to have had the force of law in that catholic society!   Plain deception!   Another very rigorous ecclesiastical rule, that which forbade the marriage of blood relations even in the most distant degree of blood relationship, gave all the facilities that these changeable temperaments required.   And, thanks to the complicity of the clerics, marriages were broken as easily as they were entered.

The great circulation of the women and fiefs through noble society and, because France was then fecund, the many children of these marriages had as their result the inextricable entangling of rights or claims to seigniorial domains.   Each husband bore the feudal titles of his wife, and kept them after a divorce.   On the other hand, the joint heirs of the paternal power were named like their father.   The complication turned to chaos, even for contemporaries.

One of the heroes of the fourth crusade, William of Champlitte, had in 1196 married Alix, lady of Marche.   She died, and before the year passed William was married to Elizabeth of Mont-Saint-Jean, widow of Aimon of Marigny, by whom she had four sons.   In 1200. William and Elizabeth were divorced, and each married for the third time—William, an Eustachia of Courtenay, another widow, and Elizabeth, Bertrand of Saudon. The latter was also a widower and brought to his wife six sons, not counting the daughters, negligible quantities. William of Champlitte died in 1210, and his widow Eustachia, in her third marriage, became the wife of William, Count of Sancerre. She lost her third husband. Did she marry a fourth? The documents do not say; but such a case was common enough. From what took place in a single family during a period of fifteen years, one can imagine the infinite confusion which entire France presented.

*   *

The condition of woman and of marriage may best be seen from the details of certain episodes in which the fiction of reality sometimes surpasses the imagination of romance.

The count of Boulogne, Matthew of Alsace, married three times; and died in 1172, leaving only two daughters, Ida and Mathilda. Ida, the elder, was only twelve years old, and until her marriage her uncle, Philip of Alsace, count of Flanders, was legally vested with the administration of her fief. A noble heiress was not only under the power of her guardian; she was dependent on the high sovereign of the seigniory, whose consent was necessary to her marriage. But the county of Boulogne depended on three suzerainties— Flanders, England, and France. Louis VII and Henry Plantagenet demanded that Philip of Alsace consult them regarding the choice of a husband. It was a difficult situation. To please one of the kings was the surest way of displeasing the other. The guardian escaped the dilemma by keeping the fief and the heiress. At twenty, Ida was not yet married, which was an unusual situation. But this system of delay could not last very long: the vassals and subjects of the county of Boulogne would not consent to remain without a chief. Philip of Alsace gave his niece to Gérard III, count of Gueldre, a well-chosen personage, because he was neither the vassal of France nor of England; he did not owe homage to either of the two kings (1181). But he did not possess the heiress or her dowry long, as he died within a year. His widow immediately left Gueldre and returned to Boulogne, being obliged to employ main force in carrying away the jewels and other objects of value which Gérard had given her.

Everything had to begin over. Ida, with her inheritance, was much wooed. In 1183, when she was twenty-two, Philip of Alsace married her to a German, Berthold VI, duke of Zähringen, who was sixty. She followed him to his estates in Suabia, leaving Boulogne under the administration of the count of Flanders. For three years her subjects did not hear of her. In 1186, she returned to them, a widow for a second time; but, contrary to the rule, she retained her freedom for four years. The historian, Lambert of Ardres, maintains that she used it indiscreetly.[1] The curé perhaps had an evil tongue, but, as he is the only one who tells us of the matrimonial adventures of the countess of Boulogne, we are forced to follow his account, which is not lacking in interest.

The county of Boulogne bordered on the county of Guines; and the son of the count of Guines, Arnoul,—a noble of good appearance, a great frequenter of the tournaments, a friend of minstrels and scholars, whom he showered with gold,— made an impression on the young widow. He was, too, the preferred candidate of Philip of Alsace, who held the county of Guines in strict dependence on the Flemish seigniory. For the same reason he was unsuitable to the king of France, who was an enemy of the count of Flanders: Philip Augustus brought forward Renaud of Dammartin, a brilliant knight, as rival. It is true that Renaud was married, but in that epoch that sort of obstacle did not hinder any one. He hastened to renounce his wife, Marie of Châtillon; and, becoming free, he entered the lists a little late, without doubt, for Ida had already conferred with Arnoul, who pleased her, and was almost engaged. Nevertheless, she yielded to the entreaties of her cousin-german, Isabella of Hainault, queen of France, and consented to enter into a conference with Renaud of Dammartin. She presently agreed that she would marry him, if he obtained the consent of her guardian.

But Philip of Alsace absolutely refused to give his niece to one connected with the king of France. In consequence of this opposition, Ida returned to the side of Arnoul of

[1] " Giving herself over to all the delights of the secular world."

Guines. She had many secret interviews with him, and even went with him to Ardres to attend the funeral services of a messenger whom she had sent to him. Arnoul wished, by all means, to keep her and to marry her at once. She convinced him that this was impossible, and formally promised to return to him. But Renaud, who had renounced his wife for a better, would not resign himself to losing everything. He kept a close watch on the countess of Boulogne and his rival, and saw that he must take fortune by the forelock. With a few confederates he carried Ida away from the castle where she was staying; carried her in one dash to Lorraine and shut her up in the castle of Rista. How vigorously did the victim of the abduction resist? The curé of Ardres does not satisfy our curiosity. In any case, Ida sent Arnoul a secret message from her place of captivity, complaining of the violence which she had suffered and promising to be his wife, if he would come and free her. Arnoul did not hesitate. He set out with two knights. His preparations, however, had taken some time. In the interval Renaud succeeded in winning back the heart of the prisoner and obtaining her pardon, so that she revealed the whole plot to him. When Arnoul and his friends arrived at Verdun, the bishop of the town, whom Renaud and Philip Augustus had attached to their cause, had them seized, chained, and thrown into prison. Renaud married the heiress without further trouble, and returned to France with her to take possession of the county of Boulogne. The protection of Philip Augustus was never gratuitous. In 1192, the new husband had to sign an agreement by which he declared himself the liegeman of the king for the people of Boulogne, agreed to surrender Lens and its surroundings, and to pay a relief of seven thousand livres.

Thus the noblewoman was a prize over whom suitors disputed; whom they carried away from father, guardian, even from husband! A contemporary of Ida of Boulogne, Stephen, count of Sancerre, carried away an heiress, whom the lord of Traînel had married only a few days before, and made her his first wife. This was the application to marriage of the law that might makes right, which, with all respect to jurists, was the fundamental principle of feudalism.

Need one say that in southern France the matrimonial

bond was no stronger and no more respected? The marriage of Montpellier is a parallel to the marriage of Boulogne.

The king of Aragon, Alfonso II, sought the hand of Eudoxia, daughter of the Greek emperor, Manuel Comnenus. His suit was granted, and the princess set out for Spain. But the Aragonese found that his fiancée was very tardy and he had little faith in the Byzantine promises. Eudoxia and the Greeks of her suite arrived at Montpellier, and there, to their surprise, learned that the king of Aragon, losing patience, had married Sancia, a daughter of the king of Castile! During this time the Emperor Manuel died. What was going to become of his daughter, stranded at the other end of the Mediterranean? William VIII, lord of Montpellier, proposed marriage to her: an alliance with the imperial family, eventual rights to the throne of Constantinople, was a beautiful dream for a petty baron! Eudoxia, little flattered, hesitated at first; then, at the entreaties of the kings of Aragon and Castile, she yielded. The marriage was solemnized in 1181, on the express condition that the first child, whether boy or girl, should inherit the seigniory of Montpellier.

Five years later William VIII and Eudoxia had had enough of each other. It appeared that the Grecian princess was disagreeable, haughty, capricious, and extravagant; she had only one daughter; and her brother, Alexis II, was dethroned, which defeated the ambitions of the seignior of Montpellier. The latter then thought of repudiating his wife, and all the more, as on a visit to Alfonso II, at Barcelona, he had fallen in love with a relative of the queen of Aragon, Agnes of Castile. In 1187, William VIII left Eudoxia and married Agnes, '' in order to have sons,'' he declared in the preamble to his marriage contract.

The church held the proceeding improper and the reason insufficient. The bishop of Maguelonne, John of Montlaur, addressed a complaint to the pope, who ordered the seignior of Montpellier to take back Eudoxia, under pain of excommunication. William, however, brought Agnes to Montpellier, and Eudoxia resignedly shut herself up in the monastery of Aniane. In spite of the pontifical prohibition, seven years passed and Agnes continued to reign, while William, having become the father of several sons, persistently sought,

with the dissolution of the first marriage, the approbation
of the second from Rome. In 1194, Pope Celestine III finally
issued the canonical sentence which annulled the marriage of
Agnes. It was labor lost! Celestine III passed away; and
his successor, Innocent III, better disposed toward the lord
of Montpellier, who was an enemy of the Albigenses and of
heresy, took him under his protection. In making a show
of orthodoxy, William VIII without doubt hoped to induce
the pope to close his eyes to the irregularity of his marriage
with Agnes, and to legitimatize his son. Innocent III de-
layed until 1202 in condemning what the church could not
tolerate. William died a short time afterwards, leaving the
seigniory to the eldest of the six sons of Agnes, William IX,
and making monks or canons of the others: Marie, the daughter of Eudoxia, found herself disinherited in favor of the
male children of the second marriage, even though she was,
by virtue of the agreement, the legal heir to the fief.

Sad destiny, that of Marie! Her father and stepmother,
Agnes, in order to get rid of her, married her at twelve years
of age (1194) to the viscount of Marseilles, Barral of Baux.
Shortly afterward the viscount died, leaving his wife an inheritance, of which William and Agnes shamelessly appropriated a large share. In 1197, they again married the widow,
now fifteen years of age, to the count of Commignes, Bernard
IV, a notorious debauchee, who had already gotten rid of two
legal wives. He was not long in repudiating her, as the
preceding wives, and marrying a fourth, despite the opposition of Innocent III. And, sadder still, the deserted Marie
found herself robbed of her inheritance by the son of the
very Agnes who had supplanted her mother!

Touched by this succession of misfortunes, the citizens of
Montpellier, who were good Catholics and unwilling to remain
under the domination of a bastard condemned by the pope,
decided to recognize the right of the daughter of Eudoxia.
They also hoped to obtain from a new master the full and
complete recognition of their commune. They aimed, then,
to give Marie a third husband, capable of defending her,
and they proposed her to the king of Aragon, Peter II, whose
wife had died. Marie was, it appears, decidedly unattract-
ive; but the king eagerly accepted the unique opportunity of

adding to Catalonia a neighboring fief which brought in a large revenue. He married the heiress of Montpellier on the fifteenth of June, 1204, without first taking the precaution of annulling her marriage with the count of Comminges, and he swore '' on the Holy Gospel of God that he would never separate from Marie, that he would never have another wife as long as she lived, and that he would always be faithful to her.'' The immediate consequence was the downfall of the son of Agnes—the bastard William IX, whom Peter of Aragon succeeded, agreeable to the general wish of the inhabitants of Montpellier.

When he was in possession of the seigniory his attitude changed. Never was an oath of matrimonial fidelity more outrageously violated. Soon he thought of nothing but a divorce, and treated the poor Marie as Philip Augustus had treated Ingeborg. The correspondence of Innocent III shows how persistently the king of Aragon sought the dissolution of his marriage. Persecutions and humiliations of every sort obliged Marie to leave Montpellier and seek refuge at Rome with her one protector. There she died in 1213, venerated as a saint. Rumor said that her husband poisoned her. It is certain that the news of her death left him very indifferent.

*
*   *

Whether the barons of France lived at home or in the distant colonies, which the crusades created in the Orient, their habits did not change; the feudal régime, which they transplanted by conquest, produced the same results everywhere.

In 1190, during the siege of Acre, Sibyl, the queen of Jerusalem, and her two daughters, died. Guy of Lusignan, her husband, thereby legally lost the royalty which he had held from her, and the eighteen-year-old sister of Sibyl, Isabella, became the rightful heiress. But she was married to a noble of ordinary lineage, Onfroi of Toron. Could this petty seignior, who had neither men nor money, be allowed to wear the crown of Jerusalem? The great vassals of the kingdom and the dowager queen, Marie Comnenus, simply decided that Isabella must be parted from her husband and marry one of the heroes of the crusade, Conrad, marquis of Montferrat. This was the reverse of the usual situation: here it was not the wife, but the husband, who was to be sacrificed to political interests.

Marie Comnenus ordered Albert, archbishop of Pisa, legate of the Holy See in the Orient, to nullify the marriage, giving as the reason the fact that Isabella was only eight years old when she married Onfroi. Called before the tribunal of the legate, the latter declared that in reality Isabella had been betrothed to him at eight years of age, but that on her majority she had ratified the engagement and that the marriage had become effective three years since. How could this reply be met? In canon law the argument was unassailable. One of the barons who was present at the investigation rose up: " The truth is," he cried, " that Queen Isabella never gave her consent to this marriage." This contradiction, according to feudal custom, should have resulted in a judicial duel, but Onfroi alienated the sympathies of everybody by refusing to fight with his contradictor: he must be in the wrong, since he did not dare to face the judgment of God.

If, however, the church was to annul the marriage, it was imperative for Isabella to declare that she had never consented to it. But the young woman, who loved her husband, at first refused to make the declaration. During the siege of Acre she occupied a tent near that of Onfroi. Many barons, among others the count of Champagne, visited her, to persuade her to make the necessary sacrifice; in case of resistance they would have to use force. Hearing the noise which was going on in the tent of his wife, Onfroi said to his companion, a noble of Champagne, Hugh of Saint-Maurice, " Sire Hugh, I fear that those who are with the queen will compel her to say something diabolical." At that moment a knight entered and cried, " They are carrying away your wife." Onfroi instantly rushed out and ran after her: " Madame," he said, " you are not on the road which leads home; return with me." Isabella did not reply, and with bowed head continued on her way. This was the separation in fact, in anticipation of the legal separation.

By force of entreaty Isabella came to accept the idea of a new union. Before the legate of the pope she deposed that she had never willingly lived with Onfroi since reaching her majority. Immediately the nullification of the marriage was pronounced. When the barons of the kingdom of Jerusalem came to swear the oath of fidelity, she said to them: " You have separated me from my husband by force; but I do not wish him to lose the property he possessed before marrying me. I will give him Toron, Châteauneuf, and the other properties of his ancestors." Indeed, that was little enough.

The marriage of Conrad of Montferrat and Isabella was performed by a relative of Philip Augustus—the martial bishop of Beauvais, Philip of Dreux. But Onfroi was not resigned: he complained to all-comers, demanding that they give him back his wife. He had many adherents in the lower ranks of the Christian army. " It is a crime," they said, " thus to separate a couple by force." And certain prelates of an independent mind, like the archbishop of Canterbury, shared this point of view. The barons were obliged to justify themselves, so one of them said to Onfroi: " Seignior, do you wish us all to die of hunger for your sake? It is much better to give the queen a courageous husband, who knows how to direct the army and enables us to live cheaply." History does not tell us whether the " divorcée " submitted to this argument.

Two years later, April 28, 1192, Conrad of Montferrat fell under the blow of an assassin, and Isabella found herself the widow of a second husband, during the life of the first. The barons of Jerusalem did not for a moment think of asking whether she would take back Onfroi. Their choice had fallen on the count of Champagne, Henry I; and, after eight days of widowhood (three days, according to certain reports), Isabella was married to the new suitor. The chroniclers, accordingly as they upheld the cause of Philip Augustus or that of Richard the Lion-Hearted, relate the story in different ways, but they agree on the point that it was necessary to impose the third marriage on Isabella by force.

In September, 1197, Henry of Champagne, king of Jerusalem, was in his turn the victim of a tragic destiny. One evening he fell, how is not known, from a window of the castle of Acre and was killed. It appears that Isabella had grown fond of him, for, when she learned of the accident, "she left the castle in distraction, uttering cries, lacerating her face and her nails, tearing her hair and her clothing, which fell about her in shreds to her waist. A few steps and she met the men who were carrying the corpse: she threw herself on the remains of her husband and covered them with kisses."

In the name of church and of morals, Innocent III attributed the death of Henry of Champagne to the just anger of God. " In the Orient," he wrote, " a woman has been twice in succession delivered from an impure union; and those illicit marriages have obtained the assent and even public approbation of the clergy of Syria. But God, in order to frighten those who might seek to imitate such a detestable example, has promptly and in a glorious manner avenged his violated laws!" What power had the anathemas of bishops and of popes against the habits and covetousness of the mighty? Never did they exempt woman from being a victim of the brutal whims of a master or of the cool calculations of political or personal interest, which prevented her from being independent.

If, then, love was excluded from marriage, it was obliged to seek compensation elsewhere. Was it found in conjugal unfaithfulness? The *chansons de geste* generally present the married woman as virtuous, very attached, and devoted to her husband: from which it must be concluded that adultery was uncommon in the feudal world. But we must not make too much of the statements of writers. Do we believe them to-day when they assert that there is adultery everywhere? The authors of our old epics who did not give it any place were perhaps no nearer the truth. Let us only say that, in regard to the virtue of the ladies of the manors, the information furnished by chroniclers, moralists, and satirists does not absolutely agree with that of poets, entertainers, and the flatterers of the barons upon whom they depended. And, as if to make up for the absence of love in the legal associations of the two sexes, the middle ages worked out a very fine solution: outside of marriage knights and ladies contracted mystical unions, where the heart and spirit were, in theory, alone concerned. History proves, it is true, that in many cases they did not hold to the ideal and that practice violated the theory.

A passionate admirer of the middle ages, Léon Gautier, himself had to admit that feudalism had " a deplorable influence " on marriage and domestic ties. One may judge the soundness of his conclusions from the preceding pages.

CHAPTER XII

COURTESY AND THE LETTERED NOBILITY

If it is true that, in the time of Philip Augustus, the largest part of the French nobility presents itself to us in the same guise as in the epoch of the first crusade, an élite class does appear imbued with new ideals and sentiments. "Courtesy" appeared. Courtesy is taste for the things of the spirit, respect for woman and for love.

Courtesy was born in southern France. The troubadours of this country taught to a nobility occupied with wars and pillage the refinements of chivalrous love and the worship of woman. The epic of northern France knew only three powerful motives for human actions: religious sentiment, with a hate of everything not Christian; feudal loyalty, or devotion to a suzerain or the chief of a band; and, finally, love for battle and booty. The lyric poetry of the first troubadours sang entirely of war, with those savage accents which one still finds in Bertran de Born. In the decline of the twelfth century there appeared in the poems of the south the chivalrous lord, whose first desire was to please the lady whom he chose to be the sole inspiration of his thought and his action. He tried to merit her love by rendering himself illustrious at war or in a crusade, and by showing all the qualities and virtues of nobility. This "courteous" love was incompatible with the feudal marriage, which was an affair of personal interests and of politics. The chosen lady was the suzerain of the knight who, on bended knees with his hands joined in hers, swore to devote himself to her, to protect her, and to serve her faithfully till death. As a symbol of investiture she gave him a ring and a kiss. It seems that this idealistic marriage was sometimes blessed by a priest. History shows that in the seigniorial courts of the south, at least in the most polished and lettered ones, the courteous marriage was practised in fact and public opinion encouraged it.

The epoch of Louis VII and Philip Augustus was justly marked by a magnificent efflorescence of this lyric poetry of the troubadours, so interesting in the variety of its forms, its rather limited but very live inspiration, and its delicate and subtle analysis of moral sentiments. There is a great contrast between the brutal heroism of the son of *Garin* and the wholly psychological poetry of a Bernard of Ventadour. To quote from this latter:

"To sing is worth hardly anything if the song does not come from the heart, and the song cannot come from the heart if there is no delicate profound love there. It is not in the least marvelous that I sing more than all other singers, for my heart turns more toward love; body and soul, knowledge and sense, force and power, I have put them all into love. In good faith and without deceit I love the best and most beautiful; the heart sighs, the eye weeps, for I love too much; and I have done myself harm by it. What can I do since love holds me? Love has placed me in a prison which no other key than mercy can open. And I have found no mercy. When I see her I tremble with fear as fire in the wind; I have no more reason than a child, so much am I troubled by love. And may a woman have pity on a man who is thus conquered."

This poetry enchanted the court of Raymond V, count of Toulouse; of William VIII, lord of Montpellier, of the Countess Ermengarde and the Viscount Aimeri at Narbonne, of the counts of Rodez, the lords of Baux in Provence. Not all the poets were sons of serfs, like Bernard of Ventadour, or simple professional players, like Peyre Vidal. There were also noble castellans like Bertran de Born, high barons like Raimbaud of Orange, sons of kings like Alfonso of Aragon and Richard of Aquitaine. Of five hundred troubadours whose names we know half at least, it seems, belonged to the noble class.

Courteous customs spread quickly in northern Spain and northern Italy—countries which practised the same ethics as Languedoc, Aquitaine, and Provence. Little by little they gained the French regions to the north of the Loire, France properly so-called, the residence of the Capetians, Normandy and the British Isles, the domain of the Plantagenets, and finally Champagne and Flanders.

The epic itself gains from the sweetness of the new sentiments. At the beginning of a martial song, like *Girart de Roussillon*, a mystic marriage is celebrated between Girart and the young princess, destined for King Charles Martel. The poem *Guillaume de Dole* replaces the recitals of battles for the descriptions of chases, tournaments, and pleasures of the court, and puts in the first place the love of an emperor of Germany for a beautiful Frenchwoman. The romances of adventure of the " Arthurian " cycle, or the cycle of the Round Table, supplanted in the favor of the Plantagenets, the Capetians, and the courts of Flanders and Champagne, the war-song of the type of *Garin*. Christian of Troyes of the reign of Louis VII and Raoul of Houdenc under Philip Augustus employed the fashionable love epic where chosen knights realized the ideal of prowess and gallantry. In *Tristan et Iseult, Érec, Cligès, Lancelot, Ivain, Perceval*, and *Méraugis* the hero sought the hand of a young girl with that exalted constancy which triumphs over all obstacles. The analysis of sentiment was sometimes as refined as in the poems of less subtile troubadours. The noble auditors of these romances (quite as long as the *chansons de geste*) had indeed a much keener spirit and a more delicate sentiment than their fathers. They understood ideal love and became interested in the intimate conflicts of the heart.

Imitation of the troubadours then brought about a French poetic enthusiasm; the minstrels of the north adopted most of the forms of southern poetry: the *chansons*, properly so-called, the *tençons* or argumentative dialogues, and the *jeu parti*, another form of poetic contest. This borrowed literature, in which so many of the contemporaries of Philip Augustus distinguished themselves,—as the castellan of Coucy, Audefroi of Arras, Conon of Béthune, Gâce-Brûlé, Hugh of Berzé, Hugh of Oisy, and John of Brienne,—displaced a more original and more savory lyric style which sprang from the soil of northern France: the motets, rondeaux, lays, and pastoral poems of the twelfth century. Many of these imitators of poetry belonged to the nobility. In this seigniorial society, which now began to polish and define itself, history uncovers new elements.

First, the educated woman, herself a patron of letters, was no longer an exception in the châteaux. The great ladies of the north seemed ambitious to rival the famous countess of Dié (Beatrice of Valentinois), the hardy, passionate poetess of Provence. Queen Eleanor of Aquitaine; her daughter, Marie of France, countess of Champagne and the inspiration of Christian of Troyes; Blanche of Navarre, mother of Thibaud le Chansonnier; and Iolande of Flanders, to whom was dedicated the romance *Guillaume de Palerne*, attracted and pensioned poets. At Troyes, at Provins, and at Bar brilliant gatherings of knights and ladies were held, where questions of gallantry and the casuistry of love were discussed. Toward 1220, there came out a code of courteous love, turned into Latin by André le Chapelain. The judgments of the " courts of love " which he cites to the number of about twenty, although not resting upon actual fact, were yet not purely imaginary. They exhibit a singular state of mind, judging from the medley one finds in them of immoral theories and right precepts for the softening of customs and social intercourse.

In the high places of feudalism men themselves showed taste for intellectual pleasures, appreciated books and those who made them, and set themselves to write in prose and verse. The counts of Flanders—Philip of Alsace, Baldwin VIII, and Baldwin IX, the first Latin emperor—formed a dynasty of well-lettered men. Philip of Alsace imparted to Christian of Troyes an Anglo-Norman poem, from which the latter drew his famous tale *Perceval*. Baldwin VIII had Nicolas of Senlis translate into French a beautiful Latin manuscript which he possessed, the *Chronique de Turpin*. Baldwin IX exhibited a particular taste for history and historians. He had collected summaries of all the Latin chronicles relative to the Occident, a sort of historical *corpus*, and had them put into French. Surrounded by players, both male and female, whom he paid generously, he himself cultivated poetry, even Provencal poetry. In Auvergne the dauphin, Robert I, collected books which constituted a library entirely composed of writings relating to the heretical sects, which caused doubt about his orthodoxy.

The petty lords imitated the great. One of the first trouvères who introduced southern lyric poetry into the north was a noble of Cambrai, Hugh of Oisy. Conon of Béthune, in the lay which he dedicated to the third crusade, curiously jumbled the lover's regrets with the religious sentiments which impelled him to the Holy Land. Indeed, the crusader sang less to God than to his lady:

"Alas, Love! What a cruel leave I must take from the best one who was ever loved and served! May the good God restore me to her, as surely as I leave her with sorrow. Alas, what have I said? I am not leaving her. If the body goes to serve our Lord the heart remains entirely in her power. On to Syria, sighing for her."

It is, indeed, a long cry from the *chanson de Roland* to this; the wild enthusiasm of the barons of the first crusade is well calmed.

The noble warriors of the eleventh and twelfth centuries left to their chaplains or the monks who followed the army the task of relating the exploits of Christian chivalry, and this is how the crusaders of the time of Philip Augustus wrote in good prose and in brief, picturesque language the description of the great events in which they had taken part. A baron of Champagne, Lord Geoffrey of Villehardouin; a petty knight of Picardy, Robert of Clary; and a prince of Flanders, Henry of Valenciennes, who became emperor of Constantinople, described the fourth crusade for us.

The type of this noble, civilized and softened by the beginning of a literary culture, is Baldwin II, count of Guines, of whom Lambert of Ardres has left us in his chronicle the curious portrait which we have before had occasion to mention.[1] This baron was not only occupied with his dogs, his falcons, and his concubines, but, like his suzerains, the counts of Flanders, he had intellectual tastes. He lived surrounded by clerks, savants, and theologians, of whom he was very fond and with whom he was ever in argument:

"The clerics had taught him more things than were necessary, and he passed his time questioning them, in making them talk, and in puzzling them with his objections. He coped with masters of arts, as well as with doctors of theology; so well, indeed, that his interlocutors listened with enthusiasm, crying: 'What a man! We

[1] Chapter IX.

cannot but overwhelm him with praises, for he says wonderful things. But how can he, being neither a cleric, nor an educated man, understand literature in this way ?" "

He attracted to his court one of the great scholars of the land, Landri of Waben; had him translate the Canticles into the vernacular, and often made him read passages from it, " in order to comprehend its mystic virtue." Another scholar, Onfroi, translated for him fragments of the Gospels and the life of Saint Anthony; these texts were explained to him and he grasped them. Master Godfrey put into French for him a Latin work treating of physics. The Latin grammarian, Solin, author of the *Polyhistor*, a sort of potpourri of science, history, and geography, was translated and read in his presence by one of the celebrities of Flanders, the cleric Simon of Boulogne, one of the authors of the romance *Alexandre*.

The biographer of Baldwin of Guines was astonished at the number of manuscripts which the count had collected in his library:

" He had so many and he knew them so well, that he would have been able to compete with Augustine in theology, with Denis the Areopagite in philosophy, with Thales of Milet [1] in the art of telling droll stories. He could have demonstrated to the most celebrated players his knowledge of *chansons de geste* and tales. For his librarian he had a layman, Hasard of Audrehem, whom he himself trained."

Finally, a work, the nature of which the chronicler forgot to explain, was composed at the château of Ardres, at the instigation and under the eyes of the count, by a cleric, Master Walter Silens:

" After his name, the book was called the *Livre du silence,* and it gained for its author the recognition of the master, who overwhelmed him with horses and vestments."

Though hyperbolic, this praise is not immaterial to history. Feudalism here appears in a new aspect. We shall not conclude that all the nobles of this time became protectors of

[1] Thales for Aristides; an error of the good curé of Ardres.

art, literature, and science. While the elite, partly through conviction, partly through snobbishness, protected literature, became educated and showed to woman—at least, in literature—a respect to which she had not been accustomed, the majority of lords loved only war and pillage. The cultured noble class and the brutal violent herd were to live side by side for a long time to come, but it is already a curious sight to see a part of the feudal world trying to break away from its traditions of barbarism and making an effort to transform itself.

CHAPTER XIII

PEASANTS AND BURGHERS

At the time of Philip Augustus and during the greater part of the middle ages properly so-called—that is, to the end of the thirteenth century—the social question did not exist, in the sense that it was not raised by any one and that it did not affect public opinion. How could it be otherwise? The opinion of the laboring classes, of those who would gain by a change, could not make itself felt; they had no spokesman. Besides that, it must be remembered that the middle ages were essentially conservative, and that, as a matter of principle, they did not seek to progress. Its most general and persistent belief was that all innovation was dangerous, bad in itself, and that one must hold to old things, to that which had always existed. The middle age had the cult of tradition: it distrusted everything derogatory to customs and established rights; it was altogether hostile to changes. To be sure, we see some serfs and some burghers working for their emancipation and especially for the improvement of their lot by pacific or forceful means; but this change, this evolution, or this revolution, was unconscious or instinctive on the part of the inferior classes, and was produced by necessity, not by virtue of a principle, a rational conception of the needs of society and the rights of the disinherited. They were not working to realize a theory, a social ideal, but to give satisfaction to their personal desires, whether those of one man or those of a group. Each worked for himself and cared little for his neighbor: this it is which, among other things, explains why the French villages which established the communal régime were not united in vast urban confederations as were the villages of Germany and Italy at certain times.

The single theory recognized by all, the single social conception in force in the France of the middle ages, was not a theory of progress or of movement, but quite the contrary: it was the *status quo*. Men approved the state of things which had existed for a time, which every one believed to be immemorial, and they firmly adhered to it. This social theory, consecrated by tradition, which had been set forth by the publicists of the church from Bishop Adalberon of Laon, contemporary of Hugh Capet, to the preacher Jacques of Vitry, a contemporary of Philip Augustus, could be summarized as follows: Society is divided by Divine Will into three classes or castes, each of which has its proper function and which is necessary to the existence and life of the social bodies: the priests, who are charged with prayer and conducting mankind to salvation; the nobles, on whom devolves the mission of defending the nation by arms against its enemies and causing justice and order to reign; the people, the peasants and burghers, who by their labor nourish the two upper classes and satisfy all their desires for luxuries as well as necessities. It was extremely simple. Sometimes, however, the clergy varied the formula and gave it a metamorphical turn—such, for example, as that we find in John of Salisbury and Jacques of Vitry. Society was like the human body: the priests were the head and eyes, because they were the spiritual guides of humanity; the nobles were the hands and arms, charged with protecting the others; the people of the country and the towns formed the legs and feet— that is to say, the base upon which all the rest stood.

This is the order of things instituted by Providence, consequently necessary and immutable. There is nothing to change. It is entirely exceptional that from time to time some hardy spirit dares to conceive of other things. Recall the preacher of the beginning of the thirteenth century, whom we mentioned above (Chapter VIII). He wished that the nobles and wealthy burghers could be eliminated from society,—the nobles in so far as they were brigands, the bourgeoisie in so far as they were usurers,—since both did nothing and were detrimental to the rest; so that only priests and laborers, those who worked spiritually and manually, remained. This is an individual fancy, and these fancies were very rare. General sentiment knew only the theory of the three castes: those who prayed, those who fought, and those who nourished and clothed the other two. All was thus harmoniously ordained, and the middle age condemned those who would derange this harmony. It did not comprehend them and considered them enemies of society. Only a few preachers and satirists from time to time took the liberty of saying that practice did not correspond very closely to the theory; that the three bodies did not accommodate themselves to their tasks as they should: that the priests left the domain of prayer too freely, neglected the services, and preached too little by their example; that the nobles, the soldiers, instead of confining themselves to repelling the enemy and policing the land, thought only of fighting amongst themselves and of trampling the feeble under foot; that, finally, the people of the country paid too many tithes to the clergy, and that the people of the towns were too much inclined to seek emancipation from the seigniorial yoke and to encroach on the rights and properties of churchmen. Evidently, all the wheels of this social mechanism did not revolve as they should and as the theory intended, and all was not perfect in this world of feudalism and the church. But the middle ages had no thought that these fundamentals could be changed, that this hierarchy could be injured, or that the lower classes for instance had not been made exclusively to work for the benefit of the other two. Everything was well regulated, because it was ruled by God. The vices and disorders in the operation of society came solely from the feebleness or the pride of men: all would be well if each one conscientiously fulfilled his duty, confined himself to his task, and did not seek to leave his class.

Here is the first reason, a general reason, why the true middle age—the period which preceded the fourteenth century—did not know of the social question: it was not on principle occupied with improving the moral and material conditions of the common people. It held to the universally accepted dogma of the necessary and divine immutability of society.

Another reason, which we have already tacitly indicated above, was that the only opinions which were declared and known were those of the privileged classes. But these classes did not only not comprehend the utility of a change, but were even indifferent to the miserable lot of the wretched third class. They were more than indifferent: they despised the peasants and burghers while they exploited them, and their contempt often turned into hostility. Disdain, even disgust, on the part of the proprietor and seignior for the cultivator and artisan whose work supported him is one of the most characteristic features of the middle age.

To the knight or baron the peasant, serf or free, was only a source of revenue, of income: in time of peace they oppressed him at home as much as they could with imposts and corvées; in time of war in foreign territories they pillaged, murdered, burnt, trampled upon him, in order to inflict the greatest possible destruction upon the adversary. It was of this that war consisted. The peasant was a creature to exploit at home, and to destroy abroad, and nothing more.

The burgher was also regarded as a source of revenue. He was spared a little more because he stood together with many others behind walls. He was less of a prize and succeeded better in defending himself. On their side, the nobles had need of the products of his industry and trade. They commenced also to understand that there was a profit for the seignior in facilitating the development of towns. When the burgher was rich, and they could not extract money from him by imposts or brutal force, they borrowed from him; they used him as a banker, whom they repaid partially or not at all. All of which did not prevent the noble from despising the burgher and from pillaging and burning the towns, if war furnished an occasion for it.

This is how feudalism looked upon and treated the villein; this is the bald truth. It is reflected very accurately in literature. If one opens no matter what *chanson de geste* of the time of Philip Augustus, more than anything else one observes the peasant and burgher playing the rôle of victim. Descriptions of pillaging and burning of country and town abound. And there is not a word of pity for the peasants whose houses and crops are burned and who are massacred by hundreds or carried away with feet and wrists in bonds; for the women tortured by the soldiers, for burning cities, for despoiled merchants, or for the common people of the feudal armies, the worthless prisoners who were mutilated or murdered in cold blood after the battle: all this is normal, is right; it is the natural course of things.

The inferior classes are not only victimized; they are disgraced. It is clear that in the eyes of the noble the villein is a kind of inferior being, wholly despicable, whose life does not count. In our oldest feudal epics, in the *Chanson de Roland*, men and things of the lower order do not find a place. This submerged humanity is not worth the trouble of being described: it does not exist. Beginning with the middle of the twelfth century, when the lords willingly or by force granted the people the first franchises and when the first communes were founded, feudal poets were forced to note that the villein existed and lived, but they made an insignificant place for him and mentioned him only to ridicule him. But this was hardly true at the time of Philip Augustus; even at the beginning of the thirteenth century, when franchises multiplied and the burghers became more important, their manner of writing and speaking tended to change. In the great majority of minstrels' lays which date from this period contempt for the " villein " is the prevailing sentiment: it expresses itself by means of commonplaces and stereotyped phrases, which are found in abundance.

It would be easy to cite some hundreds of passages in all kinds of literature in which the spirit of feudalism exhibits itself in the most brutal form. It was the tradition that the villein could not, even in physique, be anything else than disagreeable to the eyes and different from others. One cannot conceive of him otherwise. He is ugly, repugnant, and grotesque. See how the *chanson, Garin le Lorrain,* the typical war poem, represents the villein Rigaut:

" He had enormous arms and massive limbs, his eyes were separated from each other a hand's breadth, his shoulders were large, his chest deep, his hair bristling, and his face black as coal. He went for six months without bathing; none but rain water ever touched his face."

This villein is, however, a rugged warrior; it is apparent to all the nobles, and for this reason the poet condescends to allow him to play a certain rôle in battles. He even performed so many feats that, as an exception to the rule, it was decided to dub him knight. But he is not a knight like others, and we have previously noted the violent and ridiculous scene which took place at his knighting and which evoked the laughter of all the nobility.

Another description of a villein uses almost the same language: this is the charming idyl of *Aucassin et Nicollete*. Aucassin, lost in the midst of a forest, all at once finds himself in the presence of a peasant:

"He was large and marvelously ugly and hideous. He had a huge head, blacker than coal, the space of a palm between his eyes, large cheeks, a great flat nose, large lips redder than live coals, long, hideous, and yellow teeth. His clothing and shoes were of cow-hide, and a large cape enveloped him. He leaned on a great club."

The morals of the villein corresponded to his physique. He was both stupid and vicious. He uttered the most enormous follies. The author of *Miracles de Notre-Dame*, Gautier of Coincy, a contemporary of Philip Augustus and a holy man, said of the villeins, "They have such hard heads and stupid brains that nothing can penetrate them." "How could the villein be gentle and free?" we read in *Escoufle*, a romance of adventure composed before 1214. In the chanson *Girart de Roussillon* the traitor who delivers the château of Roussillon to King Charles Martel is necessarily a villein by birth, and on this occasion the author does not spare a remark to the effect that it is always dangerous to rely on this breed. This, too, is a commonplace in the *chanson de geste*. In the poem *Girart de Viane*, as in most others, villein is synonymous with coward: "Cursed be he who was the first archer; he was a coward and did not dare to come to close range." This contempt of the nobles for the foot-soldiers who were used in the van of all feudal armies shows itself on all occasions. For example, in the poem *Gaufrey:* "There were sixty thousand knights, not counting the foot-soldiers, of whom no count was taken." These foot-soldiers, these archers, these common soldiers, of whom the poets so willingly make fun, formed the base and valueless element of the army; they were relegated to the out-

skirts of the camp on the waste lands; and in action, if they
were in the way, the knights unhesitatingly rode over their
bodies.   Throughout the middle ages the nobles had this
habit.   They did not wait for the great battles of the Hundred Years' War to disgrace and abuse the unhappy foot-
soldiers.

It would seem that in the romances of adventure of the
Breton cycle, in which the nobility appears less ferocious
and less gross and talks the language of courtesy, the sentiment of scornful hostility toward the villein would be milder
and more reserved.   But here the tone is not sensibly different, and, in the poems of Christian of Troyes and of his
imitators at the beginning of the thirteenth century, masses
of villeins are seen giving way before knights like flocks
of frightened beasts.   We read in *Érec:* '' The count came
to the place.   He came to the villeins and threatened them.
He held a rod in his hand, and the villeins fell back.''   And
in *Cligès* a noble says to his man: '' You are my serf, I am
your lord, and I can give and sell you and your body and
take your belongings like things which are mine.''   In romances of the courteous class, the conception of the social
order is almost as hard on the peasant as in the martial poems.

The burghers or townsmen were no better treated than
countrymen.   In the eyes of the lords a burgher could only
be a drunkard, a thief, and a usurer.   So it is that in the
lay, *Aiol,* they represent the butcher Hagenel and his wife
Hersent as malicious slanderers.   They were feared and
detested.

" Dame Hersent, wife of a butcher of Orléans, a woman with a
large paunch, was a slanderer. Both were natives of Burgundy.
When they came to the great city of Orléans they did not have
five sous. They were wretched, begging, weeping, dying of hunger;
but by their thrift, they profited so much through usury that in
five years they had amassed a fortune. They had two-thirds of the
town under mortgage; everywhere they purchased ovens and mills,
and displaced honest men."

But Dame Hersent, seeing Knight Aiol pass, insulted him
on a crowded street, and the knight angrily answered her

in the same language, " You are hideous and ugly and impudent," a whole litany of insults.

This is how the feudal bard, who wished to please the nobles, describes the rich burgher, the man who advanced himself by his thrift and who was to constitute a great power in the third estate. If, in place of a villein by birth, he describes a degenerate noble, degraded and transformed into a villein by contact with the lower class, the portrait is no more flattering. Everything that touches this infamous class is contaminated. One of the comic elements of the song *Garin* is the courier or messenger Maumel, surnamed Galopin or Tranchebise—the type of the degenerate, naturally a very bad character, though coming from a good family. This frequenter of taverns loved only gaming and drinking and he lived among the ribalds. Some one went to rouse him in his hovel, to tell him that Duke Begon, his first cousin, needed him and had sent for him. " He my cousin! " answered the young truant. " I disown him. I do not need so rich a relative. I like the tavern, the joy of wine, and the license which surrounds me better than all the duchies on earth." By paying his expenses at the tavern, however, they persuaded him to come away. Duke Bégon, his cousin, said to him, " Where are you from, good friend? " " From Clermont, seignior. I am called Galopin. My brother is Count Joscelin; I am his senior, and one would scarcely doubt it upon seeing me." " I am on bad terms with him," answered Bégon. " I, however, recognize that you are my cousin and, if you are willing to stop your follies, I will make you a knight and give you your part of Auvergne." Galopin at these words burst into laughter and said: " I would infinitely rather drink and listen to courtesans than have a county; but say what you want of me or I will return to wine." They charged him with a message for the king of France at Orléans. As soon as the mission was fulfilled he went straight to the tavern, where he spent the whole night. Dame Héloïse sent for him and said, " Where do you come from, my friend? " " From the tavern, dame." " God, what a sight! But I have five hundred casks of wine, of which you shall have all you want." " By the Heart of Saint-Denis," answered Manuel, " I love wine, but I also love good company." The lady heard him and laughed " indulgently."

*

*   *

We are now informed on the sentiments and actions of the nobles. It remains to learn the feelings of the other privileged class, the churchmen. Two currents must be distinguished here: the ecclesiastical and the feudal.

The Christian current is that collection of ideas on the family, the state, and humanity which flowed from the same source as Christianity and which the clergy of the middle ages still professed and could not disavow, in spite of the change which primitive religion had undergone in the ten centuries which followed the fall of the Roman Empire. There always was an ecclesiastical theory on the original equality of men, on their fraternal duties, on the evil of wealth and of power, on the necessity of succoring the poor and the unfortunate, and of protecting the weak against the strong. Clerics of the time of Philip Augustus could not altogether forget that the Founder of their religion had preached the respect of the weak and humble, had exalted poverty, and given the church an essentially democratic basis. Whatever was the depth of the gulf, well-nigh an abyss, which separated the church of the twelfth from that of the first three centuries of our era, the evangelical spirit had not completely disappeared from the mass of Catholic priesthood. In short, however aristocratic certain of its parts had become, the clergy of the middle ages was still recruited from all levels of society; it was not closed to the lower classes. By alms and hospitality it continued to fulfil one of its highest missions, that of relieving human misery: for it bore the whole burden of public charity. The evangelical spirit also found a way of making itself felt in an important part of the monastic clergy: it inspired religious reform. Did it not at the very time of Philip Augustus raise up Francis of Assisi, the apostle of poverty and renunciation, the man who wished to found a new church on charity, on love, on human coöperation, in short on a kind of Christian communism directly inspired by the Gospels and Christ?

On the other hand, it must be remembered that the

church often identified her cause with that of the exploited classes; for it was especially her peasants and her lands which were victims of the brutality and covetousness of the nobles. In defending them, in excommunicating the nobles, in creating institutions of peace, it is true that she was defending herself and that she was moved by her own interests; still, by the fact that she fought to diminish oppression and violence, she rendered a service to the unfortunates. Out of this came the indignant Philippics of the preachers against the nobles who lived by brigandage, and their eloquent appeals in favor of the peasants and the artisans.

But one must also consider another side of the ecclesiastical life and feeling, for there are other things and other facts which prove that in reality the clerics of the middle ages showed almost as much cruelty to the peasants and burghers as did the men of the sword. In fact, the feudal conception prevailed in the church, which consisted of the priesthood. The sentiments and the acts of the privileged religious aristocracy dominated. This aristocracy, proprietor of considerable lands and enormous numbers of serfs, both male and female, was an integral part of the feudal system. It sought to preserve its rights and revenues; it defended them with jealous harshness, and succeeded all the better because the lands were inalienable. It also harshly exploited the inferior classes: no one has as yet been able to demonstrate that the serfs of the church were better off than those of the lay lords, and it is absolutely certain that the bondage of the church endured for a much longer time than that of the nobles and the king. There were even found some clerics who upheld serfdom, not only as a necessary and legitimate, but as a divine institution. Finally, the famous theory of the three classes had been drawn up by churchmen, repeated century after century in their writings, and maintained by them as though it were the expression of the will of God and of the social law.

It is enough to give a page from one of the most intelligent and educated prelates France had known up to the end of the twelfth century—the historian, bishop, and philosopher, John of Salisbury. In it we find this metaphor on the social body and its members:

" I call the feet of the state those who, exercising the humble professions, contribute to the terrestrial progress of the state and its members. These are the laborers, constantly attached to the soil, the artisans who work in wool or wood, iron or brass, those who are charged with the care of maintaining us, those who make the thousands of objects necessary to life. It is the duty of the inferiors to respect their superiors, but these in their turn must come to the aid of those who are below them and devise means of caring for their needs. Plutarch rightly gives the advice to be thoughtful of the humble, that is to say, of that part of the nation which is most numerous, the smaller number always yielding to the greater. Out of this has come the institution of magistrates whose duty it is to protect the lowest of subjects against injustice so that the work of the artisans may procure good shoes for the state. The commonwealth is in some sort unshod when the laborers and artisans are a prey to injustice. There is nothing more shameful for those who conduct the magistracy. When the mass of people are afflicted it is as if the prince suffered from the gout."

These are the terms in which clerics speak of social problems when they speak of them at all. This is all that a bishop finds to say in teaching the privileged classes their duty and in advising them not to trample too ruthlessly on the people.

Finally, it is well established that, in theory as in fact, the church continued to be hostile to the emancipation of burghers; church lords who freed their burghers were even less numerous than lay lords. They were equally opposed to the liberation of industry and to the erection of bodies of independent handicrafts: observe, for example, what a prolonged resistance an ecclesiastical seigniory like the abbey of Saint-Maixent was compelled to make to secure the suppression of the fiscal rights which ground down the artisans of their domain.

In fact, churchmen did not have a political economy which was higher or more generous than that of the laity: not only did the bishops and abbots always hinder the communal movement—which need not surprise us, since it was almost always directed against the property and the jurisdiction of the church,—but the most authoritative organs of the church, in speaking of the burghers and the communes, used the same insulting and spiteful terms as the feudal poets. To Jacques of Vitry they are all usurers, robbers, and, worse still, heretics.

" This detestable race of men go directly to their ruin; none among them, or at least very few, will be saved: they all march with great strides toward hell. How, indeed, could they ever expiate the iniquities and villainies of which they are guilty? We see them all, already singed by hell-fire, seeking the destruction of their neighbors, destroying the cities and other communes which they persecute, and rejoicing at the death of others. Most of the communes make desperate war: all of them, men and women, are happy over the ruin of their enemies. . . . The commune is like the lion of which the Scriptures speak, which brutally devours, and also like the dragon which hides itself in the sea and seeks to devour you. It is an animal whose tail ends in a point capable of hurting its neighbor and the stranger, but the multiple heads rear themselves against each other: for in the same commune they envy, slander, supplant, deceive, harass, and destroy each other. Without they have war; within, terror. But what is detestable above everything else in these modern Babylons is that there is not a commune where heresy does not find her adherents, her followers, her defenders, her believers."

We abridge this passage: it is a mixture of the true and the false; but it gives us the spirit of the church and her feeling toward the most evident progress which the popular masses had realized. It is, then, entirely true that the privileged classes were hostile to social changes and that the lower classes could count only on their own labor and energies for an improvement of their condition.

*   *

The peasants led the hardest and most miserable existence. We see them defenseless against the calamities of nature, the victims of brigandage and feudal wars, succumbing under the exploitation of the nobles and the lords of the church: a threefold or fourfold exploitation, because they had at the same time to pay and serve their direct lord, the high suzerain of the province, the curé of the parish and his superiors, and in addition suffered the unreasonable demands of the seigniorial officials, the provost and forester, more annoying and rapacious than the master of the fief. Finally, if the peasant was a serf—and he usually was in most of the French provinces at the beginning of the thirteenth century,—to all this there must be added the shame of servitude, which is an hereditary blemish; the odious and humiliating exactions, the legal disability of marrying, of moving about and of making wills; and even then we have an inadequate idea of the complexity of the misfortunes and the miseries in which the peasants struggled.

This lamentable situation historians and chroniclers convey to us indirectly and unconsciously, by implication in the ordinary narration of episodes of brigandage or deeds of war. In reading them one soon divines that they did not clearly see the evil and the sufferings caused by the quarrels and conquests of lords and kings. Clerics who wrote history did not stop at these details, and they have not a word of pity for the victims. It is exceptional for the trouvère, Benedict of Sainte-More, writing the history of the dukes of Normandy in French verse, to state the sad condition of the class of men who labored and suffered to minister to the needs of the clergy and nobility.

"It is certain that the preachers and knights have greater abundance to eat, and to clothe and shoe themselves, that they live more tranquilly and more securely than the laborers who have so much misfortune and sorrow. It is the latter who enable the others to live, who nourish and sustain them; and yet, they endure the severest tempests, snows, rains, tornadoes; they till the earth with their hands, with great pain and hunger. They lead a thoroughly wretched life, poor, suffering, and beggarly. Without this race of men I truly do not know how the others could exist."

The preachers in their sermons give us more of the facts. They often forcefully denounced all cruelty, not so much out of compassion and charity, out of pity for the social misery of their auditors, as out of the satisfaction it gave them to condemn the nobility, the military class, the enemies of the church and ravishers of her lands. The clerics, themselves victims of the brigandage of the knights, defended their property and their cause by speaking boldly of the sufferings of the country people. It is difficult to go further than the preacher Jacques of Vitry, for instance, in a sermon addressed to the mighty and the nobles, in which he

says: " You are ravening wolves, and that is why you shall
howl in hell. . . . Everything the peasant has in a year
gained by hard labor, the lord wastes in an hour." He did
not spare the pilferers of the peasant, " those men who,
by their iniquitous exactions and rapaciousness, despoil and
oppress their subjects, who live on the blood and the sweat of
the poor." He flayed the masters who took mortmain, those
" robbers of the goods of the dead," with particular vehemence. Taking mortmain is nothing less than taking the
livelihood of the widow and the orphan! It is homicide;
nay, more than that, it is sacrilege. These men outrage the
souls of the dead. " Like vultures they feed upon corpses."
According to the preacher, the lords did not content themselves with fleecing the peasant: they jested and practised
harsh pleasantries at his expense.

" Many say to us when we reproach them with taking the poor
laborer's cow: ' What is he complaining of, seeing that I left him
his calf, and his life has been spared. I have not done him the
evil I could have done had I wished. I have taken the bird and have
left him the feathers.' Take care, my brethren, that you mock not
the Lord God. These peasants have indeed to be your men; you
must not oppress them nor cruelly abuse their servitude. The great
must be friendly to the small and not make themselves hated. They
must not despise the humble, for if these can render service they
can also be dangerous."

Sage words these, but they moved no one. These invectives of the preacher at least prove how profound was the
evil. " Everywhere," says he, " one sees the strong oppressing the weak, and the great devouring the small." This,
briefly, is a description of medieval society.

The peasant was the scapegoat of that society. It was
chiefly on him that the iniquities and violence, the disorder
and general anarchy fell. It seems, then, that the priest
when addressing himself to this unfortunate class should,
above everything else, have brought them words of sympathy, of encouragement, and of consolation. With this in
mind, it is illuminating to read an unpublished sermon which
Jacques of Vitry wrote for the peasants and laborers, *ad
agricolas et operarios*.[1] One is thoroughly undeceived on

[1] Bibl. nat., ms. latin 17509, fol. 124.

reading it. There is no evidence of compassionate sympathy in it; not the slightest allusion to the sufferings of country-folk. The preacher begins by telling them that manual labor is a good thing, because it is recommended by Holy Writ, and because, without it, the state could not exist. He reminds them that, as a consequence of Adam's sin, labor was imposed on his descendants as an expiation, and that the Lord said, '' Thou shalt eat thy bread in the sweat of thy brow.'' He no doubt thinks that he is paying them a great compliment when he adds: '' When the peasant works the soil with the intention of performing this penitence enjoined on man by the Lord, he deserves as much merit as the cleric who chants all day in church or who keeps the matins at night.'' And he closes his preface with the declaration: '' I have seen many poor laborers who by their work supported their wives and children; they took greater pains than the monks in their cloisters or the clerics in their churches.'' After all, this comparison of the wretches who tilled the soil with churchmen was a bold step, for which we have Jacques of Vitry to thank. He thus raised the peasant in his own eyes.

Only, one will notice that he does not pity them, that he does not encourage them in enduring their misery. This guide of souls especially sought the correction of their faults; his sermon is a satire and in it he puts his finger directly on the evil. The principal vice of the peasants is cupidity and avarice: this is what makes them commit so many acts of injustice. He pictures them as losing their souls in order to gain a patch of land. This one encroaches on the field of his neighbor, with the object of taking a few feet from him; another moves the boundaries to his own advantage; a third allows his animals to graze on a pasture which does not belong to him. He blames them all for not having charitable hearts. Why not permit the beggar to glean after the harvest in the fields and vineyards? Why not give the poor a small part of their harvests, God's portion? In place of giving their old clothes to the needy they would rather let them rot. And when they hire workmen they treat them badly, pay them poorly or not at all. As for the day laborers, they likewise have no conscience: when the farmer

is there they make haste and take care, but when he turns
his back they do nothing at all, *segnes sunt et otiosi.*

These reproaches are not those which in reality come clos-
est to the heart of churchmen. They had two other much
more serious grievances against the peasant: the first was
that he was loth to pay his tithe, and that he did not acquit
himself as he should of his religious duties. For example,
he had not enough respect for the law of Sunday observance. Jacques of Vitry was compelled to speak of it.

"Take care that avarice does not lead you into working on
Sundays and holidays. You must do no menial work on these
days: you must work only for your soul's salvation. You shall
neither buy nor sell unless it be necessary for your subsistence on
that day; even then you will do better by conducting your business
the eve before. There should be no marketing, no business, no
sessions of the court on holidays. Even animals should rest. Cart-
ing on Sundays is forbidden."

But the preacher adds a reservation, which is typical of the
time.

"Unless you are obliged to labor or harvest, unless the enemy
captures and kills the laborers of the fields on week-days and
leaves you only Sundays to work in safety; for necessity makes
law."

But how could any one tell what were holidays? There
were so many of them! The means, answers Jacques of Vitry,
is to go regularly to church on Sundays: the priest will tell
you of the holidays and which of them are to be celebrated.
Unfortunately, there are those among you who are so negligent, so barbarous that they rarely set foot inside of a church.
These do not know what days are holidays. At most, they
discover it when they no longer see the carts in the field or
hear the sound of wood-chopping. There are some peasants
who not only work on holidays, but, seeing others go to mass,
profit by their absence to steal: as there is no one in the
fields and vineyards, these marauders plunder the vines and
orchards at the expense of their neighbors.

These are interesting sidelights on the ethics of the peasants of the beginning of the thirteenth century. But why

be astonished that these beings, degraded by servitude, daily oppression, and by perpetual terror, had low morals? One very liberal cleric, who composed the famous Latin poem *Hélène et Ganymède*, about this time said that peasants were only a species of cattle (*rustici, qui pecudes possunt appellari*). He confesses that, in certain cases, the manner of living and the habits of these wretches were not of a quality to raise them in the estimation of the dominant classes. There is an interesting passage in the treatise of the abbot of Aumône, Philip of Harvengt, on the continence of clerics, in which he states the following fact:

" Last year several of our brothers were sent to certain parts of Flanders to attend to some of the business of our church. It was in summer. They saw most of the peasants walking about in the streets and on the squares of villages without a bit of clothing, not even trousers, in order to keep cool; thus naked they attended to their business not in the least disturbed at the glances of passers-by nor by the prohibitions of their mayors. When our brothers indignantly asked them why they went thus naked like animals they answered: 'What business is it of yours? You do not make laws for us.' "

And the abbot adds by way of moral: " What astonishes me is not the bestial impudence of these peasants; it is the absolutely reprehensible tolerance of those who see them and do not prevent their going about in this way."

But the masters of the soil and the seigniory little cared about the fashion in which this human herd lived. The only things which interested them were the services and the money they drew from them. The population, liable to forced labor and taxation, could live just as bestially as it pleased: it sufficed if it fulfilled its obligations. No more was demanded.

* * *

The class of literature which is comic and often indecent, but always full of fact, is, next to sermons, the only historical source which informs us with any precision on the material and moral conditions of the peasant. All that one can say is that it is not favorable to him, because it is especially a bourgeois literature, and the burgher of the time

had the same contempt for the rustic as had the feudal lord.
Besides, the narrators generally emphasized only the physical
and moral deformities of country-folk. They pictured them
as ridiculous and badly formed. See how the author of *Aloul*
treats them: "They have one squint eye and the other is
blind. They have a shifty look. They have one good foot
and the other twisted." Their filth was repulsive. A villein,
leading some donkeys in Montpellier through the street of
the Épiciers, passed before a shop where some varlets were
pounding odoriferous herbs and spices in a mortar; he immediately fainted, suffocated by the odors to which he was
unaccustomed. To bring him back to consciousness nothing
more was necessary than to put a shovelful of manure under
his nose: at once he recovered, thinking himself in his element. The moral of the story is that "no one should leave
his place." Later, Rutebeuf says, in one of his fables, that
the devil did not want the villeins in hell because they smelled
too badly.

The railleries concerning him are often malicious. They
do not even admit that he ate good food. "They were
obliged to eat thistles, briars, thorns, and ordinary straw; on
Sundays they had hay. One should see them grazing on the
fields with the horned cattle, on all fours and wholly naked."
They are disagreeable, always discontented and critical.
"Everything displeases them, everything tires them. They
cry for good times, but hate the rain. They hate God if
He does not do everything they want just as they want it."
Their stupidity passes all bounds: for example, that of the
villein of Bailleul, whose wife made him believe that he was
dead. They were gross and brutal, treating their wives like
beasts of burden. One of them, without being angry,
dragged his wife by her hair and showered her with blows,
on the principle: she must have some occupation while I
work in the field; unoccupied she would think of evil things.
If I beat her, she will weep the whole day long, which will
make the time pass; and, on my return in the evening, she
will be the more tender. This agrees perfectly with the theory
about women of the authors of fables; she was considered
an inferior creature, whom one could beat without giving
food. One story literally says: "God took woman from

Adam's side; but one bone does not feel blows and has no need of food.''

However, these savage natures are sometimes interesting. The peasant of literature is not always stupid; he is sometimes represented as a jovial, good fellow; clever, insolent even to the mighty, and knowing how to get his revenge. One of the stories tells of a lord who held a full court and free table which caused his avaricious and grumbling seneschal, furious at such liberality, to receive those who presented themselves in a very ill-humor. He addressed an ugly, filthy peasant, who did not know where to seat himself, with gross invective and concluded his remarks by giving him a '' buffet ''—that is, a slap on the face—and said to him, '' Seat yourself at that buffet yonder,'' the word buffet having two meanings. Now, the lord had agreed to give a scarlet robe to the person adjudged to be the author of the best farce. Minstrels and storytellers all took their turn. Finally, the peasant, who had succeeded in getting his meal, came up and administered a resounding slap to the seneschal's cheek. There was great excitement; the lord questioned the assailant. '' My lord,'' said he, '' listen to me. Just now, when I entered the house, your steward met me. He gave me a hard buffet and spitefully told me to seat myself at the buffet, adding that he would give it to me. Now that I have eaten and drunk, Sire Count, what would you have me do if not return him his buffet? And here I am ready to give him still another if he is not content with the first.'' The lord laughed and bestowed the prize on him.

Another villein, to whom Saint Peter refused to open Paradise, under the pretext that it was not made for men of his sort, shows that he had a glib tongue. He earnestly apostrophized the apostle, reproached him with being harder than stone and with having thrice denied his Master. Saint Paul, who was sent to bring the intruder to reason, was no better received: the peasant called him a horrible tyrant and reminded him that he had stoned Saint Stephen. Finally, God the Father Himself intervened, and the rustic, without being disturbed, pleaded his cause: '' As long as my body lived in the world it led a clean and pure life. I gave of my bread to the poor; I warmed them at my fire; I let them want neither trousers nor shirts I confessed according to the rule and received your body properly. To him who died under these conditions, they told us from the pulpit, God pardons his sins. You will not lie to me.'' '' Villein,'' said God, '' I submit; your pleading has gained you Paradise. You have been to a good school; you know how to talk well.''

Here the peasant has a fine rôle. He is also the hero of another story, entitled *Constant du Hamel*, where he set his head at once against all the authorities of the village and triumphed over those who wished to scoff at him. Our story-tellers have presented no facts more vividly than the two- and three-fold tyranny from which the population of the country everywhere suffered. A villager, Constant du Hamel, had a wife, as beautiful as wise, who was desired by the three petty tyrants of the locality—the curé, the provost, and the forester. One day the three suitors met at a tavern and, while drinking, plotted the downfall of the woman who resisted them; they combined to destroy her husband. This ingenious plan was the invention of the curé. He commenced the persecution by accusing Constant, in a sermon before the whole congregation, of having married his '' commère,'' who had been his godmother. He excommunicated him, drove him from the church, and only removed the anathema upon the payment of a sum of seven livres.[1]

The provost, in his turn, made the unfortunate villager appear before his tribunal, and there a scene was enacted which must often have occurred in actual fact. He commenced by putting him in chains, and threatened him with something still worse. '' You shall be put on the gallows.'' Then he said to Clugnart, his servant, '' Go quickly and say to my seignior that I have my hands on the traitor who stole his wheat.''—'' Ah! sire provost,'' cried Constant, '' may God help me: I am not guilty.'' The provost replied: '' That is the stuffing with which you wish to fill me; the tracks of

---

[1] More than eight hundred francs in our money. One might remark by way of historical comment, that an article of the council of Rouen of 1189 accused the curés of scandalously abusing the right which they had of excluding parishioners who displeased them, or from whom they wished to make some profit, from the church and the sacraments. The methods employed by the curé of the fable were, then, in accordance with well established tradition.

the grain-thief were traced to your garden." " Seignior," said the villager, " it is my enemies who have charged this crime to me; but, while the truth is being discovered, take my property in order that I may have peace." " And what will you give to my seignior if I set you free? " " Sire, I will give twenty livres."[1] " Very well; you may return to your home." In the stories all the provosts are alike: they taxed their subordinates with the same impudence. They are represented as snobbish, avaricious, greedy, harsh towards poor people: one of them, invited to the table of his seignior, secretly made provision for his luncheon on the following day; another replied to a poor woman from whom he had taken two cows: " By my faith, old woman, I will return them to you when you have paid me your share of the many pence hidden in your pot." They were simply brigands.

Finally came the forester, " the one who guards the woods of the lord," " very handsome and of a fine carriage and well armed with bow and sword." The forester accused Constant du Hamel of having that night cut three oaks and a beech tree in the forest of the seignior. The innocent man was indignant, but the forester menaced him with his naked sword, seized his oxen, and Constant was obliged to pay a hundred sous for the pretended offense. Many historical texts of this period show that the forester was one of the most formidable of seigniorial agents and the most abhorred by the rural people, whom he oppressed with fines. In a letter addressed to one of his friends, Peter of Blois strongly censured him for permitting himself to be associated as clerk of the accounts, as secretary to the royal foresters, and for being proud of that position: " You are, then, going to labor at putting into writing the tyrannical exactions of which the poor people are the victims. Know that you will cause the unfortunates, who shall be entered on the list of fines in the circuit of the foresters, to be inscribed on the book of the dead by our Lord."

Provosts and foresters, all the agents, functionaries, or tenants of the seignior who oppressed the villagers, were perhaps the most direct cause of their suffering, their most intolerable scourge. The preacher, Jacques of Vitry, in his

[1] About twenty-four hundred francs in our money.

sermon " to the nobles," compared them sometimes to leeches, whom the seignior in his turn pressed to make them disgorge; sometimes to crows, which circle croaking around a cadaver which the master has plundered, to feed on the remains. And yet that was historical fact.

We do not, for a good reason, relate how the wife of Constant du Hamel and her servant managed to bring the three persons who had wished to ruin her together in the home of the villager; how they all three found themselves, in a rather light costume, in a cask filled with feathers; and how the peasant, after being completely revenged on his enemies, let them out and set all the dogs in the village on them. What interests us here is not entirely the rare victory of a villein over his persecutors, but the details of the method of oppression and the portrayal of seigniorial exactions.

Let us look at another very much more detailed account, which very probably dates from the beginning of the thirteenth century: a document entitled *Le conte des vilains de Verson*. To tell the truth, the tale, if it is not one of them, has some resemblance to the *fabliaux*, being like very many of them written in lines of eight syllables. It is a poem of two hundred and thirty-five lines, which was found in a register of quit-rents in the Archives of Calvados. It tells us of an insurrection in the village of Verson, which strove to free itself from the corvées and rents by which it was subjected to the abbey of Mont-Saint-Michel. The author, hostile to the popular cause, gives only obscure and insignificant details of the revolt, but he gives an interminable list of obligations with which the villeins were burdened. There is no tirade on the sufferings of the rural population which speaks so eloquently as this simple enumeration.

At Saint-Jean the villeins of Verson had to reap the meadows of the seignior and carry the hay to the manor. Then they had to clean the trenches. In the month of August there was the great corvée, the grain harvest, which had to be carried to the barn. Their own fields were subjected to field-rent: they had to summon the bailiff, who carried their sheaves away in his cart. In September came the swine-tax: if there were eight hogs, they carried the two finest to the lord, who did not choose the poorer, and for each of the seven others they paid a denier. At Saint-Denis they paid quit-rent; then the *pourpréture*—that is, the right of inclos- ing their fields. If they sold a piece of land, the seignior had a right to a thirteenth. At the beginning of winter came a new corvée: they had to prepare the seigniorial land, bring the seed from the barns, and each sow and harrow a piece of land. At Saint-André, three weeks before Christmas, they paid the *oublée*, a kind of cake, " for the private room." At Christmas they carried hens to their lord, and, if they did not bring " good and fine ones," the provost would seize their deposit—for each peasant deposited with the provost a se- curity, which could be seized in case he attempted to evade his obligations. Then the villeins owed the *brésage*, a tax of two setiers of barley and of nine quarters of wheat.

The enumeration continues mercilessly. If the villein of Verson married his daughter outside of the seigniory, he paid three sous; and the author of the list remarks that formerly the villein " took his daughter by the hand and gave her over to his lord." But here, as in most texts, the famous " right of the seignior " is mentioned only as belonging to the customs of a former time. On Palm Sunday they owed the sheep-tithe, and, if the peasants were not able to pay it on that very day, they were at the mercy of the seignior. At Easter they owed a new grain corvée: the seed had to be secured, sown, and harrowed. Then the peasants were obliged to go to the smithy to shoe their horses, for it was the time to go into the woods and cut trees; but in this instance they received pay, a " rich wage," says the writer: two deniers a day. Finally, they owed the corvée of cartage, the *sommage*.

The last page of the selection is devoted to reminding the peasants that they are subject to the *banalité* of the mill and of the oven. The miller may take from them a bushel of grain and a palette of flour, plus a full handful, plus the right of *valetage* " for the service of portage." Finally, we see the wife of the villein carrying her bread and pies to the common oven. But the baker's wife, often in a bad humor, " is haughty and proud," and the baker himself, sullen. He says that he is not paid a proper amount; swears by the teeth of God that the furnace will be badly heated, that it will not make good bread, and that the bread will be poorly baked and "sour."

It would seem that this enumeration of imposts, of corvees, and the suffering which they brought, should have moved him who described them. On the contrary, he is bitter and hostile. "Go and make them pay," he says. "They ought to pay well. Go, take their horses; take both cows and calves, for the villeins are felons." And his last word is this, "Sire, know that under heaven I do not know of a meaner people than the villeins of Verson." Feudalism was not content with oppressing the peasant: it boasted of its own excesses, and did not realize that its victims would attempt to throw off the yoke.

*

*   *

The peasant, however, was everywhere obliged to resign himself to his miserable condition, like the beast which lives and dies where it is fastened. He often attempted to escape, to change his lot, and he went at it in three different ways: he fled from the seigniory and took refuge in a neighboring fief; he resisted the impost, rebelled, and by force won his partial or total emancipation; or, finally, he bought exemptions and privileges from his seignior, he peacefully obtained a charter of rights. Let us follow him in the three different ways and see what comes of him.

First, the abandonment of the seigniory by flight, the exodus of individuals and even of whole populations in a body, was a more frequent fact in France of the middle ages than one is disposed to believe. It is supposed that the peasant of that time did not move, that he was riveted to the soil. But, on the contrary, a close study of the documents reveals a very real and intense movement of rural people. They were much less settled then, far more nomadic, than they are to-day. Not only was there, beside the class of farmers fixed to the soil, a class of wandering pioneers, the "woodmen," who made a business of going from forest to forest; but it is certain that this class of woodmen was always reënforced by fugitive villeins escaping from serfdom. These desertions, these individual or collective emigrations, these movements from one seigniory to another, were such frequent facts that in the twelfth century certain local laws, especially in Burgundy and in Franche-Comté, went so far as to allow the peasant to leave the fief to which he belonged on two conditions: that he renounce all his movable and immovable property—he was supposed to be destitute on leaving the seigniory; and, second, that, by an act called the disavowal, he informed his lord of his intention of becoming the subject of another. But we must consider that this custom was not general and that the legal sanction accorded to emigration was distasteful to the majority of feudal proprietors.

In general, then, there was not any other way of escaping, except deserting the fief—that is, flight. But the condition of the fugitive serf, over whom the master and his agent could always exercise their right of pursuit and claim, was still unhappy enough. The lords, in fact, combined to prevent their serfs from escaping: they concluded agreements by which they gave each other the right of pursuing deserting peasants in one another's territories, and pledged themselves not to harbor a neighbor's serf. Thus it was that Philip Augustus signed an agreement with the seignior of Sully-sur-Loire in 1187, and with the countess of Champagne in 1205, by which the contracting parties swore not to keep each other's serfs, but to mutually surrender them. In 1220, the royal officers residing at Chartres and in the adjoining region received a circular from the king, running thus:

"Philip, by the grace of God, King of France to all bailiffs and provosts to whom these presents shall come, greeting. We command you by this decree to proceed to the arrest of the serfs of Abonville, Boisville, and of Germignonville who refuse to obey our dear and faithful abbot of Saint-Père of Chartres. You may seize them wherever you find them outside of the cemetery, the church, or other sacred place. You shall keep them closely imprisoned, and shall not give them their liberty until the abbot of Saint-Père demands it of you."

In spite of the leagues of proprietors, desertions and emigrations constantly multiplied; it was so difficult to prevent the peasant from leaving the fief that the lords, instead of preventing the flight of the serf and imprisoning him, came to accept his departure and even his settlement upon the land of another. But, among themselves, they signed conventions of *parcours* or *entrecours* (*percursus* or *intercursus*); it was more liberal and certain: the contracting parties mutually granted the right of retaining each other's serfs. They were indemnified by the exchange. Treaties of " intercourse " were numerous in the epoch of Philip Augustus. Let it suffice here to mention the one concluded in 1204 between the duke of Burgundy and the countess of Champagne, and the one concluded between the countess of Champagne and the count of Nevers, Peter of Courtenay, in 1205. But it was sometimes a dupes' agreement, especially when the king of France was one of the signers: as they were more peaceful and less exposed to brigandage on royal territory—the serfs of lay and ecclesiastical lords flocked thither; a void was created in the fiefs bordering upon the Capetian domains, to the profit of the king.

In reality, despite treaties and oaths, the lords did all they could to steal serfs, to attract and retain the peasants of others, and to prevent their own from going away. And King Philip Augustus distinguished himself more than any one in this dishonest game. What he did in this line in the royal domain, every baron did in his own: it was a game at getting the most and losing the least possible. When Philip, in 1205, signed a treaty of " intercourse " with the countess of Champagne, the latter complained that the serfs of Champagne had left in great numbers and taken refuge in the king's free city, Dixmont (Yonne): the king, however, declared that he should keep all the serfs who had gone there before the present contract. In 1212, when the bishop of Nevers also complained to him of seeing his land deserted by the serfs for those of the king, Philip did accept this clause: " If an episcopal serf settles in our domain, we will have him seized and, if after an investigation of his condition it is proved that he belonged to the bishopric, we will return him to the bishop." But he left the serf the right of buying himself off and thus to remain free on the royal land, and stipulated that the bishop should have only half of the ransom money; the other half should go to the king. Thus, Philip Augustus not only benefited by the presence in his town of a man who did not belong to him, but he found the means of getting money, in addition to having another subject. And this curious convention of 1212 contains still another clause most favorable to royalty. Many of the serfs of the bishop of Nevers had formerly sought refuge in the royal towns of Bourges and Aubigny-sur-Cher. The bishop had given up reclaiming them, but he maintained that they should at least be compelled to ransom themselves and that, by the terms of the treaty, he should receive one-half of the sum paid by them. Not in the least, replied Philip; the convention does not apply to them; they are covered by prescription. This was how the king of France understood business.

Again it was often the lords who favored the emigration of the country people, in order to enrich themselves at the expense of a neighbor. And it was not necessary for the peasant to go far to escape from his proprietor; it was enough for him to go to a neighboring locality, into a city of the commune or into one of the new cities, one of those places of refuge where residence brought freedom immediately or at the expiration of a year and a day.

It was possible, to be sure, to prevent individual desertions to a slight degree and to bring back the deserter; but, when the whole population of a canton wished to emigrate *en masse*, it was not easy to detain it. In 1199, the inhabitants of Île de Ré, exasperated by the severity with which the lord of Mauléon exercised his hunting right, and troubled by deer in their crops and vineyards, prepared to emigrate in a body. To keep them, Ralph of Mauléon, in return for a payment of ten sous for each quarter of vineyard and setier of land, " graciously " promised thereafter not to allow any other game in the island than hares and rabbits.

When the lord remained inflexible his land was deserted: it meant the exodus of a whole village, or even of a whole canton. In 1204, the serfs of the bishopric of Laon moved in great numbers to the domain of a neighboring lord, Enguerran of Coucy. The refugees were well received. But the bishop protested. He proved before the royal justice that he had never signed a treaty of " intercourse " with the seignior of Coucy, and that consequently the latter had not the right to retain his serfs. The peasants of Laon had to return to the episcopal domain.

He did not always flee who wished to; but, in spite of everything, desertions were numerous, continuous, so that many of the lords of the time came to realize that the only effective means of preventing them was to soften the severity of the exploitation of their subjects.

* *

When they were not of a mind to leave the country, and when the lord refused to yield, country-people resorted to a refusal of the impost and to open revolt. The documents of the time of Philip Augustus prove that the peasant showed himself ever more averse to the payment of feudal dues. The collection of tithes, especially, was accomplished with difficulty, because the church which collected them was not so well armed as the lay seignior and had not the same effective means of overcoming the taxpayers. The council of Rouen, in 1189, recalled the faithful to their duty:

"Since many people refuse to pay the tithe, three notices will be given to warn them to pay fully the tithe collected on wheat, wine, fruits, animals, hay, flax, hemp, and cheese; in a word, on all the products which are annual. If the third summons is futile they will be excommunicated."

" People must pay the tithes," said the council of Avignon (1209), and " should pay it before any other impost," added the council of the Lateran (1215). A letter of Pope Celestine III to the bishop of Béziers denounced the procedure of certain peasants who, obliged to carry the products constituting the tithe to the dwelling of the curé, took it into their heads to subtract the cost of transportation. The pope ordered the bishop to excommunicate them if they persisted. In 1217, Honorius III allowed the canons of Maguelonne to censure those under their jurisdiction who did not pay the whole of their customary tithes or retained a portion of it under the pretense of covering the expenses of planting, of cultivation, or of harvesting.

These are significant facts. It is not without reason that the preacher thundered from the pulpit against the peasants who did not pay their tithes. Witness Jacques of Vitry in a sermon addressed to the peasants and laborers:

"There are some among you who, at the peril of their souls, through avarice retain the tithe due to the church. But they are guilty not only of theft, but of sacrilege: the tithe is the property of God and His ministers; the duty to pay it is inscribed in the New Testament as in the Old; the tithe is the tax which you owe God, the sign of His universal dominion. Those who pay it are indeed the enemies of the devil and the friends of God; those who withhold it not only compromise their eternal salvation, but they are liable to lose all they have in this world: God sends them drouth and famine, though years of abundance are never lacking to those who pay."

Feudal collectors, like those of the church, complained that receipts were diminishing, and in order to facilitate their task the bishop of Paris, Maurice of Sully, in one of his sermons, urged his diocesans to be more exact:

"Good people, render unto your earthly lord what you owe him. It must be remembered and accepted that you owe your earthly lord the cense, the tallage, forfeit, services, cartage, and purveyance. Pay it all in full at the time and place required."

But it was often in vain that the church urged the peasants to submit. When the lord refused all concessions, when he acted cruelly toward the poor payers, their exasperation often terminated in acts of vengeance and in riots. Jacques of Vitry attempted to put feudalism on its guard against the possible consequences of its violence and oppression. "It is a dangerous thing, that despair," he said to them: "one sees the serfs kill their lords and set fire to their castles." Benedict of Sainte-More, the historian of the dukes of Normandy, writing at the end of the twelfth century, thought as much of the present as of the past when he recalled the riot of the Norman peasants in the eleventh century, letting them utter this angry cry:

"We have been weak and insane to have bent our necks for so long a time. For we are strong and hard men, more used to war and soldier, and stouter-limbed and larger than they are or ever were. For every one of them there are a hundred of us."

It was by the same reasoning, without doubt, that at the beginning of the thirteenth century the Norman peasants of the village of Verson, whose miserable condition we have clearly seen, attempted to revolt against their lord, the abbot of Mont-Saint-Michel. We do not know whether they succeeded, but attempts of the same sort occurred everywhere.

Between 1207 and 1221, the peasants in an archdeaconry of Orléans refused to pay the tithe on wool. The bishop of Orléans, Manasses of Seignelay, tried to compel them by means of excommunication. The furious peasants formed a plot against the bishop, arose one night as one man,— *quasi vir unus,* says the historian of the bishops of Auxerre,— and besieged him in the castle where he lay. They would have killed him, but he succeeded in escaping, and he forced them to atone for their rebellion.

In 1216, the villagers of Nieuport, near Dunkerque, were in dispute with the canons of Sainte-Walburge of Furnes over the fish tithe. The deputies of the chapter appeared to receive it, and the peasants fell upon them, killing two priests and grievously wounding a cleric. Excommunicated by the church authorities, they finally regained the grace of the church, but at what price shall be seen:

" The chief offenders, to the number of twenty-five, whether sheriffs of the village or simple residents, had within a year to make a pilgrimage beyond the seas, and could not return before a year had elapsed, and they had taken part in processions in twenty-six different churches at their own expense, without other clothing than their trousers, going barefoot, and carrying the rods with which they were disciplined. One hundred other persons among the notables were also obliged to take part in these processions. The community of Nieuport had to build three chapels, give fifty livres to a convent of nuns, indemnify the parents of the dead priests who had belonged to the nobility, indemnify the wounded priests, construct a fortress costing one thousand livres for the count of Flanders in order to prevent new troubles; finally give the count of Flanders forty livres a year on the day commemorating the assassination."

In certain regions of France these insurrections of villagers had a particular object. They attempted to imitate the inhabitants of larger towns and cities and organize themselves into communes. That was why Pope Celestine III, in 1195, forbade the serfs of the church of Notre-Dame of Paris to form a " commune " or conspire against the chapter.

At the end of the reign of Philip Augustus the village of Maisnières, situated near Gamaches and dependent on the abbey of Corbie, assumed a communal constitution without having asked the authorization of the abbot, who probably would have refused it. The abbot, informed thereof, proceeded to the new commune, which refused to receive him; the citizens even violently expelled him. The freed peasants annexed a neighboring hamlet to their commune, subjected it to the taille, then seized a priest who was found on their territory, and maltreated him. The abbot of Corbie summoned them before an arbitral tribunal composed of churchmen, who decided against the villagers; the dissolution of the commune was ordered and the rebels were sentenced to a fine of one hundred marks (1219).

In the same year the inhabitants in Chablis, subjects of the chapter of Saint-Martin of Tours, also attempted to found a commune. They had organized under oath and had levied taxes. The canon of Tours caused the bailiffs of Philip Augustus and those of the count of Champagne to intervene promptly, and the commune of Chablis disappeared.

Neither the insurrection of Verson, that of Maisnières, nor that of Chablis is known to us through chronicles, Chance preserved knowledge of them to us in a few charters which escaped the destruction that befell thousands of others, and these in a few lines relate the futile efforts of the peasants. If it were not for this accident, history would know absolutely nothing of them. We cannot help believing that many other revolts of the same sort completely failed, and that those which to-day attest success belong to the exceptions.

There was one, however, of which the chroniclers have spoken with some care; it was the insurrection of the serfs of the bishopric of Laon, composing seventeen villages, the center of which was Anizy-le-Château, and which embraced a territory twenty-four kilometers square. This insurrection lasted eighty years: it began during the reign of Louis VII and did not end until the middle of the reign of Saint Louis; furthermore, these villagers struggled vigorously, and at times successfully, against the combined forces of feudalism and of the church, and from time to time they had the kings of France as allies. It is from this circumstance that we should consider their attempt. Their history is the most instructive instance of the persistent and energetic efforts of the country people to gain their liberty.

In 1174, Louis VII had given the serfs of Laon a communal charter, very like that which governed the burghers of Laon. Three years later the bishop of Laon, Roger of Rozoy, assisted by the seigniors of the region, took his revenge: he surrounded the serfs in the neighborhood of Comporté and executed a frightful butchery. When, in 1180, Philip Augustus became king the wretches had again fallen under the yoke of their bishop. In 1185, the oppression and exactions had advanced to such an intolerable point that they decided to carry their protests to the king. Philip Augustus, who had a grudge against the bishop of Laon, made himself mediator; he fixed the amount of taxes which the bishop was authorized to collect from his subjects, and the service assessments which the serfs owed the two officers of the bishop, the vidame and the provost. Further, he created twelve sheriffs taken from their midst, charged with allotting the taxes and settling differences which might arise between them and the bishop. No appeal, except to royal justice, was allowed from the decisions of these magistrates appointed by the king.

The villagers of Laon demanded more: they desired to have a commune. Between 1185 and 1190, under circumstances of which we know practically nothing, Philip Augustus gave them this privilege. He revoked it in 1190, when he was leaving for the crusade, and desired to please the clergy. But the tenacity of the peasant who wished to free himself was at least equal to that of the clergy which intended to remain master. At the beginning of the thirteenth century the seventeen villages, still cruelly oppressed, made an attempt to emigrate *en masse* to the land of a neighboring seignior, Enguerran of Coucy. This did not succeed. Two years later, in 1206, the serfs of Laon took advantage of a disagreement between the bishop and the chapter of Laon. They succeeded in getting the canons on their side. The latter, becoming the advocates of the popular cause against the bishop, accused Roger of Rozoy in the courts of justice of mistreating his subjects and of crushing them with illegal taxes. The case was argued before the metropolitan chapter of Reims, acting as a court of arbitration. The judges gave a decision adverse to the bishop. They sided with the villagers and restored things to the status in which they had been in 1185. They revived the decree of Philip Augustus, fixing a maximum of taxes to be collected by the bishop and determined that, in case of a misunderstanding between the bishop and his peasants, the settlement of the difference should belong to the chapter of Laon. This was subjecting the bishop to the guardianship of his canons. Roger of Rozoy was so deeply humiliated by it that he fell ill and died shortly afterwards.

But insurrectionary movements of rural peoples rarely had a successful issue, and on the whole the peasants suffered more than the seigniors. The residents of cities, protected by their numbers and by their walls, could gain freedom by force; the villagers, who had no means of resistance, simply drew upon themselves judicial condemnation or massacres, without any gain to themselves. The great mass of serfs, the free farmers and tenants, preferred to obtain the liberties which they desired by peaceful means, especially by purchase. The epoch of Philip Augustus witnessed an extraordinary increase of charters of liberties granted by the seigniors, not only to cities and burghers, but also to villages and ordinary hamlets—that is, to peasants.

Undoubtedly, the motive of the seignior who gave the franchise, thus limiting his own power, was in a majority of cases personal gain: the peasants gave him a rent or a cash payment. It also happened that a seignior recognized the urgent necessity of repeopling his fief, which had become deserted in consequence of his own exactions, or that he feared his serfs might abandon his land and go to that of a neighbor, where free cities abounded. In that case he himself freed his villagers. It was rarely that he acted solely under the sway of humanitarian or religious principles, to make sure of his spiritual salvation, *pro salute animae, pietatis intuitu*. He was usually liberal out of personal motives.

In certain regions feudalism, desirous of avoiding a struggle with the peasantry, tolerated the federation of villages, such as that of the serfs of Laon, and permitted them to erect communes. Philip Augustus had favored the rural confederation of Cerny-en-Laonnais (1184), and the abbot of Saint-Jean of Laon, following his example, sanctioned that of Crandelain (1196). At the end of the twelfth century the counts of Ponthieu permitted the erection, or voluntarily established those of Crécy, of Crotoy, and of Marquenterre. This curious application of the principle of association had already been put into practice in the time of Louis the Fat, but it was the epoch of Philip Augustus which witnessed its full development. The residents of the village formed an association; and many rustic communities, taking a similar oath, formed a permanent body, which had its mayor, its jurisdiction, its militia, its treasury, and its seal. The members of these confederations varied in quality as well as in numbers. Certain rural communes consisted of villages, all unimportant; others were composed of a fairly well populated city, or even of a country town with a certain number of hamlets under its headship. In one case, the association consisted of three or four members; in the other, it included about fifteen localities. The constitutions of these rural groups were modeled on those of the large urban communes of the neighborhood, whose protectors without doubt knew of their creation.

Still, this kind of emancipation of rural peoples was exceptional and prevailed only in a few provinces. The greater number of villages bought or obtained individual franchises from their seigniors, who, without entirely freeing them, softened their domination by freeing them from the heaviest and most odious duties.

At the end of the twelfth century and the beginning of the thirteenth the charter of Lorris reached the maximum of its dispersion. While Louis VII and Philip Augustus liberally distributed it in the royal domain and as far as Nivernais and Auvergne, the lords of Courtenay and Sancerre spread it in their estates (Montargis, Mailly, Selle in Berry, Chapelle-Dam-Gilon, Marchenoir, etc.), and the counts of Champagne themselves introduced it into Chaumont-en-

Bassigny and into Ervy. Its influence, especially toward the reduction of the scale of judicial fines, made itself felt in the majority of the contracts which were then being made in ever greater numbers between the seigniors and peasants.

In 1182, the archbishop of Reims, William of Champagne, granted the little district of Beaumont in Argonne a charter, which served as the model for the majority of charters of enfranchisement granted to the rural districts of the counties of Luxembourg, Chiny, Bar, Rethel, and of the duchy of Lorraine. In Champagne it was in competition with the charter of Soissons and the fundamental law of Verviers. It gave the villagers not only considerable liberties, but also practical autonomy—the privilege of freely electing representatives, sheriffs, mayors, and the free use of the forests and rivers. But the seigniors who adopted and spread the law of Beaumont did not prove themselves as generous as the founder: sometimes they reserved the right of naming the mayor, sometimes they sought to exercise that right in opposition to the inhabitants; everywhere, if the villagers had not agreed in choosing their magistrates on the day fixed for the election, the seignior named them.

Other constitutions, less dispersed than those of Lorris and Beaumont, little by little transformed the civil and economic conditions of rural districts. " Rural sheriffdoms " were created in the domains of the countess of Champagne and of the churches of Reims. The village did not form a unity, but it was represented by a mayor. The sheriffs, who exercised all the local functions of the administration of justice (for example, at Attigny, the charter of which dates from 1208), were not elected. The peasants remained in subjection; but in the matter of imposts and corvées they were guaranteed against the caprice of their masters.

*

*   *

If the chroniclers contemporary with Philip Augustus infrequently speak of the peasants, and mention only a few of the revolts which shook society, they could not conceal the considerable rôle which citizens and cities began to play. The work of William of Armorica abounds in descriptions of cities. In Flanders it was Ghent, " proud of its houses ornamented with towers, of its treasures, and of its large population; Ypres, famous for its wool dyeing; Arras, an ancient city filled with riches and eager for prosperity; Lille, which boasts of its excellent merchants and displays the cloth which she has dyed, and the fortune which is hers, in foreign lands.'' In Normandy it was Rouen, or it was Caen, the opulent city, '' so .full of churches, houses, and inhabitants that she found herself scarcely inferior to Paris ''; in the valley of the Loire it was Tours, '' situated between two rivers, pleasant because of the waters which surround it, rich in fruit-trees and in grain, proud of its citizens, powerful through its clergy, and adorned by the presence of the most holy body of the illustrious Saint Martin; Angers, a rich city, around which lie fields of vineyards which furnish drink for Normans and Bretons; Nantes, enriched by the fish-filled Loire and carrying on a trade in salmon and lamprey with distant countries.''

The monk of Marmoutier, who about 1209 wrote a brief account of the ecclesiastical history of Touraine, complacently depicted the city of Tours overflowing with riches. He went into ecstasies over the beautiful fur-trimmed clothing of the inhabitants, over their battlemented and turreted houses, over the sumptuousness of their tables, the luxury of their gold and silver dishes. Generous to saints and churches, charitable to the poor, they had all the virtues: modesty, loyalty, education, martial courage. As to the women of Tours, '' they are all so beautiful and charming that the truth here passes all belief and the women of other countries are ugly in comparison. The elegance and richness of their dress enhances their beauty, which is perilous for all who see them; but their firm virtue protects them, and these roses are as pure as the lilies.''

Rigord and the Armorican often mention Paris—its streets, bridges, churches, walks, and halls. They speak of its walls, of the tower of the Louvre, and its two châtelets. And one remembers the enthusiastic description of Paris written by Guy of Bazoches between 1175 and 1190:

"I am in Paris, in that royal city where the abundance of natural gifts not only captivates those who dwell therein, but invites and attracts those who are afar. Just as the moon surpasses the stars in brightness, so this city, the seat of royalty, raises its proud head above all others. It is situated in the midst of a delightful valley surrounded by a crown of hills which adorn it in emulation of Ceres and Bacchus. The Seine, that superb river which comes from the east, here flows level with its banks and with its two branches forms an island which is the head, the heart, and the marrow of the entire city. Two suburbs extend to the right and left, the smaller of which would be the envy of many cities. Each of the faubourgs is joined with the island by a bridge: the *Grand pont* facing the north in the direction of the English Channel, and the *Petit pont* which looks toward the Loire. The former, large, rich, and bustling with trade is the scene of busy activity; innumerable boats filled with merchandise and riches surround it. The *Petit pont* belongs to the dialecticians, who walk there while debating. On the island, on the side of the king's palace, which dominates the whole city, there is seen the hall of philosophy, a citadel of light and immortality where study alone reigns supreme."

Even in the *chansons de geste,* though feudal in character, the cities began to be the object of detailed and accurate descriptions. In *Aubri le Bourgnignon* the rich Flemish cities of Arras, Courtrai, and Lille appeared; in *Aiol,* Poitiers and Orléans with their jeering inhabitants; in *les Narbonnais,* Narbonne with its port full of vessels, and Paris, " that admirable city where stands many a church with its bell, and which is traversed by the Seine in two deep channels, which teem with vessels full of wine, salt, and great riches."

The romances of the Round Table or the Arthurian Cycle, inspired by the spirit of courtesy, are not to the same degree as the *chansons de geste* the expression of military passion. As a typical work of this character one can mention the *Graal,* of Christian of Troyes. The hero of this romance, Gauvain, came to a thickly populated city, which was very rich and very prosperous. The poet gives us a detailed description of it; in a long passage he mentions most of the trades which flourish there. This practice of describing a city almost became a compulsory commonplace for his imitators, notably Ralph of Houdenc, who at the time of Philip Augustus wrote the *Vengeance de Raguidel.* Not only does Christian of Troyes take considerable pains to describe the city and its artisans, but he seems to desire the citizens to take part in the plot. An enemy of Gauvain incited the commune against him; the citizens besieged him, and they were led by the mayor and their sheriffs. Even municipal magistrates came to play a rôle in feudal literature. And we meet the same thing in other poems. The lay *Parise la duchesse,* which comes from the beginning of the thirteenth century, portrays the citizens of an imaginary city called Vauvenice. They revolt against their seignior, Raymond, because he substituted a bad woman for the real and lawful duchess, Parise. Under the leadership of their mayor they enter the city, find the false duchess, cut off her hair, cut off the bottom of her dress, and expel her thus disgraced from the city.

The residents of the new cities, which feudalism and the church founded merely to people their seigniories, also began to appear in the poems of the time of Philip Augustus. The lay *Renaud de Montauban,* which has as its heroes the four sons of Aimon, contains in legendary form a true historical fact: the erection of the new city of Montauban, in 1144, by Alphonse-Jourdain, count of Toulouse. By this creation he aimed to oppose to the consular republics of the south—the old cities which had escaped from his power—a new type of modern bourgeoisie, privileged but directly subject to the seignior and exploited by his agents. This event caused a sensation in the bourgeois world of the middle of the twelfth century. The fancy of the minstrels enveloped it with romantic details. They fancied that the four sons of Aimon one day perceived a high hill at the confluence of the Garonne and the Dordogne: there, with the permission of King Yon, they erected a fortress, which received the name of Montalban; about its walls eight hundred families came to live, recognizing the four heroes as their lords, and pledging themselves to pay an annual tax. And, according to the poet, these families divided themselves according to their trades:

"One hundred of the citizens became tavern keepers, another hundred bakers, another hundred tradesmen, and another hundred fishermen; there were a hundred who carried on commerce, going even as far as India; finally, the three hundred who remained shared the balance of the work among themselves. Gardens and vineyards began to be put under good cultivation."

This is imaginary, but interesting.

Scenes from city-life, especially market scenes, began to be introduced into feudal epics. They are found in *Aiol*, and especially in *Moniage Guillaume,* which have depicted this life in a very lively manner. William, for example, goes to the market to buy a fish:

" The mariners press around him. One takes him by the cope, others pull him, others push him. Each cries loudly in his own language. ' Here! ' cry some; ' Here! ' cry others; ' good fish, at your own figure! ' ' Seigniors,' says William, ' for God's sake don't jostle me so, you will hurt me.' "

The poem *Hervis de Metz* belongs to the terrible *Lorrains* group. It is the story of a noble of Metz who sent his son to make a fortune at the Champagne fairs. But the young knight understood fancying horses, dogs, and falcons better than dealing in furs, cloths, or precious metals; he contented himself with spending the money which his father had given him in merry company. The bard seizes this occasion to give a lively description of the activity in the markets of Troyes, of Provins, and of Laigny. It is a singular mixture of heroic episodes and scenes from urban life.

It is evident, then, that even feudal circles began to notice what people did in cities. The minstrel spoke of the shop-keepers and the merchants in other rôles than as victims of the pillage and the cruelties of nobles. Cities and citizens became subjects of description.

It is unfortunate that, in forming an idea of what the material conditions of cities at the time of Philip Augustus were, we have no other documents than the narratives of historians, letters, and the works of fiction. What authentic monuments do as a matter of fact remain? A few fragments of some wall, like those we see in Paris, and of churches: all the rest have disappeared. There are no longer any burghers' homes of that epoch. The greater number of them were wooden: it goes without saying that they have long since been destroyed. As to the stone houses, they were then very rare, and the only positive fact about them is that they date from the end of the twelfth or the first twenty years of the thirteenth century. Certainly the oldest do not go back beyond the time of Saint Louis. There is not even a town hall, an

assembly hall of the citizens, a city hall, which can positively be attributed to an earlier time, save perhaps the city
hall of Saint-Antonin, in Tarn-et-Garonne.

*

*   *

At the same time that the historical and literary documents
of the reign of Philip Augustus for the first time in the
middle ages give us adequate and specific details about cities,
about their external appearance, and about the material conditions of urban life, they also (and this is likewise new)
inform us of the social importance of the bourgeoisie who
inhabited them. Previous to this epoch history scarcely spoke
of the bourgeoisie, except as anonymous groups, which obtained charters of privilege or communal liberties from their
seignior with his consent or by compulsion. From the end
of the twelfth century they are described in a more specific
and concrete form : in each important center the great burgher
families began to be known by their names, their affiliations,
and their pedigrees; frequently they deal with the seigniorial
power; they hold the city magistracies, possess lands, and
even noble fiefs; they exercise high functions in the courts
of feudal lords. This participation of the urban class in
political life dates from the reign of Philip Augustus.

Let us first imagine ourselves at the center of the Capetian
dominions, in Paris. In 1190, an absolutely unprecedented
thing occurred there. The king of France was about to leave
on the crusade, and before this great journey he made a
political will, in which he arranged for the regency and
regulated the exercise of public powers. Personages of the
blood-royal, officially charged with this regency, were designated in it: they were the queen-mother, Adèle of Champagne, and William of Champagne, the uncle of Philip
Augustus and archbishop of Reims. But it appears, from
the very terms of the act of 1190, that the king had very
little confidence in these regents, for he designated a council
of associates, one might even call them overseers, consisting
of officials of the palace, monks, and six Paris burghers. The
part played by the burghers was considerable : the guardianship of the treasure and even of the royal seal was confided
to them during the king's absence; each of them was to have

a key to the coffers located in the Temple. In case the king died during his pilgrimage, a certain sum was to be set aside for the use of the heir, Prince Louis, and the guarding of that sum was confided not only to the six burghers, but also " to all the people of Paris." Thus Philip Augustus gave the representatives of the Parisian bourgeoisie a high hand in the finances and general administration of the realm.

We know the names of these burghers, the first in the history of France, who took a part in government. The names were indeed plebeian: Thiboud the Rich, Othon of the Grève, Ébrouin the Money-changer, Robert of Chartres, Baldwin Bruneau, Nicolas Boisseau. During the eighteen months that Philip Augustus remained in the Orient, a certain number of royal diplomas were despatched in the name of the council of regency; they were sealed with a special seal, having forms of this kind: " In the presence of our bourgeois "; " under the witness of our bourgeois." And these bourgeois were then designated: there were, besides the six preceding, other notables, or members of their families—such as John, son of Ébrouin; Matthew the Small; Ébrouin, son of Raimbaud. It is, then, a fact that the wish of Philip Augustus in this matter was carried out and that the Parisian bourgeoisie actually took a part in the regency, a thing which had never before occurred. And, yet more remarkable, Philip Augustus desired that during his absence representatives of the bourgeoisie should be associated with the agents who exercised his functions, not only in Paris, but in all villages of the dominion: for another clause in the testament of 1190 decrees that in all cities the royal provost should carry on the affairs of his city, the seat of his jurisdiction, with the assistance of four burghers, of whom two at least should be chosen by him from the locality itself.

However, the participation of the bourgeoisie in the central government and the local administration was only temporary; when Philip Augustus returned he took back his full and complete authority. But such a mark of confidence shown the inhabitants of the cities left a grateful memory with them, and not all traces of their experience at government disappeared: new relations and habits were created; the alliance established between royalty and the cities out-

lived the particular circumstance which brought it to life.
After 1190, the bourgeoisie still appeared among the associates of the sovereign, and one of the leaders of the Parisian
bourgeoisie, Eude Arrode, held the position of pantler in
his court. His name figures many times in royal diplomas:
in 1211, Philip gave him two houses in Paris; and, 1217, he
gave him several fishing-places in the Seine near the *Grand*
and *Petit pont*. He was evidently a man in the king's confidence. In 1219, a member of his family, Nicolas Arrode, and
another burgher, Philip Hamelin, enjoyed the provostship of
Paris.

The same condition was found in all seigniories. The
counts of Champagne, at the end of the twelfth century,
used the bourgeoisie of their fiefs as sergeants, provosts, and
bailiffs, and admitted them to the council and to court—that
is, to the administration of the central power. It is enough
to mention Lambert Bouchut of Bar-sur-Aube. This Lambert Bouchut, from 1220 to 1225, occupied one of the high
offices of the county of Champagne: he was treasurer of the
county. He was already in the court of Champagne in 1195,
employed in many capacities—such as judge, arbiter, expert,
and agent on many diplomatic missions; and, in 1224, when
the count of Champagne joined King Louis VIII on the expedition to Saintogne, this burgher of Bar-sur-Aube appears
to have exercised the functions of administrative chief in
Champagne during the sovereign's absence, under the title of
" bailiff of the court."

If the aristocratic bourgeoisie began to hold a considerable
place in the councils of the realm and of the high suzerains,
it exercised a much greater power in its own society, in the
cities. There it possessed municipal powers, and in the north
as in the south we see magistracies handed down as an
inheritance within single families. We begin to become acquainted with dynasties of burghers.

At Rouen it was the family of Fergaut which, in 1177,
occupied the mayoralty, the chief position of the commune.
The mayor was already a great personage. In many charters of the Plantagenet kings his name figures with that of
the chancellor and the royal judge, and with the names of his
equals, the municipal counselors numbering one hundred:

Nicolas Groignet, William Cavalier, Luce of Donjon, William Petit, Nicolas of Dieppe, etc. Several of the bourgeoisie of Rouen succeeded Fergaut as mayor in the first twenty years of the thirteenth century, and in the list of mayors other plebeian names appeared—such as John Fessart (1186), Matthew the Fat (1195-1200), Sylvester the Money-changer (1208-09), Nicolas Pigache (1219-1220).

At La Rochelle the rich bourgeois families, Auffrei and Foucher, stood in the front rank. Alexander Auffrei, in 1203, founded the celebrated almonry of La Rochelle, and Peter Foucher, in his will drawn up before 1215, like a great seignior bequeathed considerable property to the abbey of Fontevrault. He was a friend of Queen Eleanor of Aquitaine; in 1209, she gave this Peter Foucher, her burgher whom she called *" dilectum et fidelem hominem nostrum,"* to the monks of Fontevrault: that is, she transferred the revenues which she drew from Foucher to the abbey.

At Bordeaux the great families of Colomb, Calhau, Monedeir, and Beguer contended for the high offices of the commune throughout the thirteenth century. Already, in 1220, Guilhem Aramon Colomb was mayor; the documents, indeed, tell of still earlier ones: Peter Audron in 1218 and Peter Lambert in 1208. This Peter Lambert is known to us through a single interesting charter. In 1208, the king of Castile, the enemy of John Lackland and an ally of Philip Augustus, besieged Bordeaux. The Bordelais, in order to defend themselves, had to destroy a few churches and hospitals belonging to the priory of Saint-Jacques of Bordeaux. To indemnify the monks the mayor, Peter Lambert, granted them a charter, drawn up in his name and in that of the commune, by which he permitted them to build as many houses as they wished on a certain part of the moat, provided they did not entail, sell, or rent them to any one. The charter began thus: " Peter Lambert, mayor of Bordeaux; the jurors, and the whole commune of Bordeaux; to all those who shall see this present charter, greeting."

At the same time the great shipowners of Bayonne, the Dardir, and those of Marseilles, the Manduel, whose name appeared in so many acts relating to commerce or public works of the region of Provence, were, because of their wealth, men of power, who treated with high barons and prelates almost as equals. When these families of rich burghers were at the head of a free town, of a commune, or of a wholly independent consular city, their pride passed all bounds. In their collectivity they formed a veritable seigniory; they entered the feudal hierarchy and considered themselves upon the same level as the sovereign barons. And, in fact, having become masters of the municipal soil, they possessed all the prerogatives attached to sovereignty. They had legislative power, the right of proclamation or ordinance, judicial power, both civil and criminal, and the right of levying taxes upon the town. Like the lords, they possessed a shield, a watch-tower which was their donjon, ramparts which protected them, a gibbet, and a pillory in token of high justice. A republic like Avignon, in its treaty concluded with Saint-Giles in 1208, proudly declared that "it obeyed no one but God." It claimed complete autonomy, the right of peace and war, and it was not wise to provoke the wrath of its bourgeoisie; having surprised their enemy, Baron William of Baux, in an ambuscade, the inhabitants of Avignon burned him alive and cut his body to pieces.

For it was not only in the administrative and judicial organisms and in political sovereignty that the bourgeoisie of this time came to take its place. It also began to appear as a military force, as an element in the royal and seigniorial armies. For the first time, historians tell us of bourgeois militia with some detail, and to a certain degree even praise it, which is indeed a novelty. William of Armorica relates how King Henry II of England, invading Vexin in 1188, tried to take the town of Mantes. To the great astonishment of the English, the bourgeoisie came out from their walls completely armed and advanced in good order against the enemy; so well that he, thinking it was a trap, retreated. And the historian makes Henry II say:

"What is this French foolishness and whence comes this presumption? The common people of Mantes, which numbers hardly five thousand souls, dares to think of measuring itself against the innumerable army of my knights! These folk who ought rather to burrow into their caves and barricade themselves behind their gates, march upon our naked swords!"

The feudal world was so little accustomed to this boldness on the part of the villein that William of Armorica felt himself obliged to devote a passage of fifteen verses to celebrate the exploits of the men of the commune of Mantes in lyric fashion:

"O Commune, who can worthily praise thee? What a triumph for thee to have forced the King of England to retire even a pace, not daring to look thee in the face! If my poetic genius were equal to the subject, thy valor should become known throughout the entire world. For however little credit my verses may obtain, thy name shall always be in the mouths of our descendants and thy glory shall be sung by remotest posterity."

The same historian shows that the communes served not only as fortresses, capable of arresting the march of an invading army, but also sent their militia afar and united with the knights of Philip Augustus: for example, at the battle of Bouvines. For a long time we have been in doubt about the meaning of this passage from William of Armorica, though it seems quite clear. One opinion, which it is very difficult to root out, is that the militia of Corbie, Amiens, Beauvais, Compiègne, and Arras aided in deciding the victory, whereas in reality the men of the commune appeared in the battle only to be repulsed and overthrown by the German knights. The communal militia never rendered great service in the army, even to kings or lords who employed it. Chivalry, as we have said before, did not take account of this foot-soldiery and rode over it, to come to blows with the enemy the more quickly. It was the communes themselves, considered as places of safety and as a means of defense, which were truly useful to the sovereigns on whom they depended.

*

*   *

The advancement of the villein into public functions, his entry into politics and affairs, and even into the military world, brought upon him imprecations and cries of anger from the feudal poets. They did not pardon him for coming out of his caste: all these parvenus could do nothing but deceive; bad luck to those employing them! "Ah, God! how badly has he rewarded the good warrior," one reads in *Girart de Roussillon,* "who out of the son of a villein made first a knight, then his seneschal and councilor, as did Count Girart of that Richier to whom he gave a wife and vast lands; that fellow then sold Roussillon to Charles the Bold." Count Richard, hero of the lay *Escoufle* (a romance of adventure, written before 1204), received the confidences of the emperor, relative to the villeins. He avowed that he was no longer master of his empire and that he could not go fear-free from one town to another. He had made a mistake in trusting himself to his serfs and in letting them rise in dignity; now they possessed his châteaux, his cities, and his forests. Finally, he begged Richard to take the office of constable and to come to his aid. The count searched France for the bravest knights, and at the end of a year and a half he had rid the imperial lands of all the villeins who occupied châteaux. Moral: "Never let a serf come to your court as your bailiff. For the nobleman is ashamed and abashed to have a villein for a master. How could it be possible for the villein to be either gentle or free?"

Such was the opinion of feudalism with regard to the newly arisen bourgeoisie. This feeling was neatly expressed in another poem composed at the beginning of the thirteenth century, *Roman de la Rose* or *Guillaume de Dole.* The great personage of the poem was an emperor of Germany named Conrad. Now this emperor was greatly loved by all his nobility, "because he was not one of those kings or barons who were these days giving their servants (that is, to their villeins) rents and provostships," at the risk of see-ing their lands "destroyed," all the world "depreciated," and themselves shamed. This Emperor Conrad, this wise man, chose his bailiffs from among the vavasors: that is, from the nobles of inferior class, who fear God and despise shame. As to the villeins and bourgeoisie, instead of placing them in office, he let them amass wealth, well knowing that their money would be his and that when he wished he could levy upon their treasure. And this was an excellent system. There was never a fair where the merchants did not buy a horse for the emperor. Their presents were worth more than a tax. So perfect was the policing of his realm "that merchants could travel with as much security as monks."

This is the society of which the feudal poets dreamed: the nobles remaining in possession of all the offices, and the bourgeoisie confined in their towns, where they were permitted to make a fortune for their lord's profit. Otherwise, what do those two curious pages, chosen from many others of the same nature, prove? In the epoch of which they deal, the rise of the bourgeoisie, the utilization of burghers in all social functions began to seriously disquiet the nobles and soldiers, who were obliged to bow before these villeins when they were invested with public power. But the lords had a difficult problem; they opposed the rising tide in vain. They were outflanked, and the minstrels, willy-nilly, introduced into their lays the bourgeois element, which they so detested and despised.

Let one, for example, read that part of the lay of the *Lorrains* which has Anseis, the son of Gerbert, as its hero. The author of the selection pictures a certain Count Hernaut, who, finding himself at the point of death and wishing to avenge himself upon his sons for betraying him, caused the mayor of Bordeaux to come before him.

"He caused Oudin, the mayor, to come before him and the judges of the village to be assembled. 'Oudin, dear Sire,' he said to him, 'you have jurisdiction over all the crimes of Bordeaux upon the sea. You are charged with punishing malefactors. Those who do evil must be killed. But for love's sake I pray you to cause me to be avenged upon my sons.' Oudin replied: 'Leave us in peace, Sire. From you we have nothing to fear, and you cannot command any one.'"

And he explained this proud reply by reminding the count that he was the king's man and not his. The tone which this burgher mayor of Bordeaux employed in speaking to a great lord is significant; and it is noteworthy that the author of the poem, who probably wrote in the first half of the thirteenth century, states that the commune of Bordeaux was dependent upon royal and not upon seigniorial authority.

In these feudal lays even the bourgeois militia appeared and held a certain place. It is true that it was often introduced to be scoffed at; it was represented as consisting of poltroons. At the beginning of the *chanson, Girart de Roussillon,* the poet introduces the bourgeoisie of Roussillon charged by Count Girart with protecting the ramparts of the town which King Charles was besieging. When night arrived, each of the members of this civil guard found it pleasanter to go to bed and abandon his post. And immediately a traitor profited by this baseness of the villeins to deliver the place to the besiegers. At the end of the poem the citizens are presented in a more favorable light: They merit much praise for their devotion to their lord; they weep with joy on learning that Girart has returned from exile, and they valiantly join in the struggle which he is obliged to undertake to reconquer his heritage.

In spite of himself, the feudal bard has been induced to present to us a type of villein not altogether repugnant or ridiculous. There were some of these villeins who became knights, like Rigaud of Garin, one of the heroes of that epic, who fought like a lion and could cope even with the king of France. Yet, as has been seen, in certain respects Rigaud remains grotesque. In the case of others—for instance, Simon in *Berthe aux grands pieds* or David in *Enfances Charlemagne*—the comic disappears. Finally, it occurred to poets to give a good rôle to folk of the lowest rank. The lay *Daurel et Béton* glorified a simple player, and in that of *Amis et Amiles* two serfs gave proof of admirable devotion to their master.

The bourgeoisie advanced, and daily made a larger place for itself in society.

INDEX